PUBLISHING

EXCITING EXTRA ONLINE RESOURCES INCLUDED

NOW THIS EXAM KIT COMES WITH
FREE ONLINE ACCESS
TO EXTRA RESOURCES AIMED AT HELPING YOU PASS YOUR EXAMS

IN ADDITION TO THE OFFICIAL QUESTIONS AND ANSWERS IN THIS BOOK, GO ONLINE AND EN-gage WITH:

- Fixed Tests
- Interim Assessments
- Exam paper Guides
- Latest Official ACCA exam questions
- Answers updated to include legislation relevant to next exam
- Frequent and varied new additions to these resources – watch this space!

And you can access all of these extra resources anytime, anywhere using your EN-gage account.

How to access your online resources

If you are a Kaplan Financial tuition, full-time or distance learning student

You will already have an EN-gage account and these extra resources will be available to you online. You do not need to register again, as this process was completed when you enrolled. If having problems accessing online materials, please ask your course administrator.

If you purchased through Kaplan Flexible Learning or via the Kaplan Publishing website

You will automatically receive an e-mail invitation to EN-gage online. Please register your details using this e-mail to gain access to your content. If you do not receive the e-mail or book content, please contact Kaplan Flexible Learning.

If you are already a registered EN-gage user

Go to www.EN-gage.co.uk and log in. Select the 'add a book' feature and enter the ISBN number of this book and the unique pass key at the bottom of this card. Then click 'finished' or 'add another book'. You may add as many books as you have purchased from this screen.

If you are a new EN-gage user

Register at www.EN-gage.co.uk and click on the link contained in the e-mail we sent you to activate your account. Then select the 'add a book' feature, enter the ISBN number of this book and the unique pass key at the bottom of this card. Then click 'finished' or 'add another book'.

Your Code and Information

This code can only be used once for the registration of one book online. This registration will expire when the final sittings for the examinations covered by this book have taken place. Please allow one hour from the time you submitted your book details for us to process your request.

elIM-3ONG-l1wy-K36s

For technical support, please visit www.EN-gage.co.uk

Professional Examinations

Paper P7 (INT)

ADVANCED AUDIT AND ASSURANCE

EXAM KIT

PUBLISHING

British Library Cataloguing-in-Publication Data

A catalogue record for this book is available from the British Library.

Published by:

Kaplan Publishing UK

Unit 2 The Business Centre

Molly Millar's Lane

Wokingham

Berkshire

RG41 2QZ

ISBN: 978-1-84710-785-5

© Kaplan Financial Limited, 2009.

Printed and bound in Great Britain.

Acknowledgements

The past ACCA examination questions are the copyright of the Association of Chartered Certified Accountants. The original answers to the questions from June 1994 onwards were produced by the examiners themselves and have been adapted by Kaplan Publishing.

We are grateful to the Chartered Institute of Management Accountants and the Institute of Chartered Accountants in England and Wales for permission to reproduce past examination questions. The answers have been prepared by Kaplan Publishing.

CONTENTS

Section

New features in this edition

In addition to providing a wide ranging bank of real past exam questions, we have also included in this edition:

- An analysis of all of the recent new syllabus examination papers.

- Paper specific information and advice on exam technique.

- Our recommended approach to make your revision for this particular subject as effective as possible.

   This includes step by step guidance on how best to use our Kaplan material (Complete text, pocket notes and exam kit) at this stage in your studies.

- Enhanced tutorial answers packed with specific key answer tips, technical tutorial notes and exam technique tips from our experienced tutors.

- Complementary online resources including full tutor debriefs and question assistance to point you in the right direction when you get stuck.

December 2009 – Real examination questions with enhanced tutorial answers

The real December 2009 exam questions with enhanced "walk through answers" and full "tutor debriefs", updated in line with legislation relevant to your exam sitting, is available on Kaplan EN-gage at:

www.EN-gage.co.uk

You will find a wealth of other resources to help you with your studies on the following sites:

www.EN-gage.co.uk

www.accaglobal.com/students/

INDEX TO QUESTIONS AND ANSWERS

INTRODUCTION

The style of current Paper P7 exam questions is different to old syllabus Paper 3.1 questions and significant changes have had to be made to questions in light of the recent amendments to International Standards of Auditing.

Accordingly, many of the old ACCA questions within this kit have been adapted to reflect the new style of paper and the new guidance. If changed in any way from the original version, this is indicated in the end column of the index below with the mark *(A)*.

Note that the majority of the questions within the kit are past ACCA exam questions, the more recent questions are labelled as such in the index.

The pilot paper is included at the end of the kit.

KEY TO THE INDEX

PAPER ENHANCEMENTS

We have added the following enhancements to the answers in this exam kit:

Key answer tips

All answers include key answer tips to help your understanding of each question.

Tutorial note

All answers include more tutorial notes to explain some of the technical points in more detail.

Top tutor tips

For selected questions, we "walk through the answer" giving guidance on how to approach the questions with helpful 'tips from a top tutor', together with technical tutor notes.

These answers are indicated with the "footsteps" icon in the index.

ONLINE ENHANCEMENTS

 Timed question with Online tutor debrief

For selected questions, we recommend that they are to be completed in full exam conditions (i.e. properly timed in a closed book environment).

In addition to the examiner's technical answer, enhanced with key answer tips and tutorial notes in this exam kit, you can find an answer debrief online by a top tutor that:

- works through the question in full

- points out how to approach the question

- discusses how to ensure that the easy marks are obtained as quickly as possible, and

- emphasises how to tackle exam questions and exam technique.

These questions are indicated with the "clock" icon in the index.

 Online question assistance

Have you ever looked at a question and not know where to start, or got stuck part way through?

For selected questions, we have produced "Online question assistance" offering different levels of guidance, such as:

- ensuring that you understand the question requirements fully, highlighting key terms and the meaning of the verbs used

- how to read the question proactively, with knowledge of the requirements, to identify the topic areas covered

- assessing the detailed content of the question body, pointing out key information and explaining why it is important

- help in devising a plan of attack

With this assistance, you should then be able to attempt your answer confident that you know what is expected of you.

These questions are indicated with the "signpost" icon in the index.

Online question enhancements and answer debriefs will be available from Spring 2010 on Kaplan EN-gage at:

www.EN-gage.co.uk

Section A-Type Questions

Section B-Type Questions

Professional/ethical considerations and practice management

Assignments

Completion and Reporting

ANALYSIS OF PAST PAPERS

The table below summarises the key topics that have been tested in the new syllabus examinations to date.

	Pilot 07	Dec 07	Jun 08	Dec 08	Jun 09
Regulatory Environment					
International regulatory framework					
Money laundering	✓	✓			
Laws and regulations					
Professional & Ethical Issues					
Code of ethics	✓	✓	✓	✓	✓
Fraud an error					✓
Professional liability			✓		
Practice Management					
Quality control	✓	✓	✓		
Obtaining professional work					
Tendering					✓
Professional appointments			✓		✓
Assignments					
Audit planning:					
Materiality					
Audit risk		✓			
Business risk	✓		✓		✓
Financial statements risk			✓	✓	
Understanding client environment					✓
Audit evidence:					
Sufficient/appropriate					
Specify audit procedures	✓	✓	✓	✓	✓
Analytical procedures					✓
Related parties			✓		
Written representations					
Work of experts				✓	
Work of internal audit					
Group audit	✓		✓		
Audit evaluation/review					
Review procedures					
Evaluation of findings					✓
Initial engagements					
Comparatives					

	Pilot 07	Dec 07	Jun 08	Dec 08	Jun 09
Inconsistency with other info.					
Subsequent events					
Going concern				✓	
Audit related services					
Comparison with audit		✓	✓		
Interim review					✓
Due diligence			✓		
Assurance services					
Levels of assurance					
Risk assessment					
Operational performance measures		✓		✓	
Value for money					
E-commerce					
Prospective financial information					
Forensic audit	✓	✓		✓	
Internal audit					
Outsourcing		✓			
Reporting					
Audit reports					
Critically appraise form and content	✓	✓	✓	✓	✓
True and fair					
Special purpose audit reports					
Reports to management					
Draft a report					
Assess/advise on content				✓	
Other reports					
Assurance vs. audit reports					
Report on PFI					
'Negative assurance'		✓			
Current Issues					
Ethics and corporate governance					
Information technology					
Transnational audit					✓
Social/environmental audit				✓	
Other issues		✓	✓		

EXAM TECHNIQUE

- Use the allocated **15 minutes reading and planning time** at the beginning of the exam:
  - read the questions and examination requirements carefully, and
  - begin planning your answers.

  See the Paper Specific Information for advice on how to use this time for this paper.

- **Divide the time** you spend on questions in proportion to the marks on offer:
  - there are 1.8 minutes available per mark in the examination
  - within that, try to allow time at the end of each question to review your answer and address any obvious issues

  Whatever happens, always keep your eye on the clock and **do not over run on any part of any question!**

- Spend the last **five minutes** of the examination:
  - reading through your answers, and
  - **making any additions or corrections**.

- If you **get completely stuck** with a question:
  - leave space in your answer book, and
  - **return to it later.**

- Stick to the question and **tailor your answer** to what you are asked.
  - pay particular attention to the verbs in the question.

- If you do not understand what a question is asking, **state your assumptions**.

  Even if you do not answer in precisely the way the examiner hoped, you should be given some credit, if your assumptions are reasonable.

- You should do everything you can to make things easy for the marker.

  The marker will find it easier to identify the points you have made if your **answers are legible**.

- **Written questions**:

  Your answer should:
  - Have a clear structure
  - Be concise: get to the point!
  - Address a broad range of points: it is usually better to write a little about a lot of different points than a great deal about one or two points.

- **Reports, memos and other documents**:

  Some questions ask you to present your answer in the form of a report, a memo, a letter or other document.

  Make sure that you use the correct format – there could be easy marks to gain here.

PAPER SPECIFIC INFORMATION

THE EXAM

FORMAT OF THE P7 EXAM

		Number of marks
Section A:	2 compulsory questions	50-70
Section B:	2 questions from 3	30-50
		100

Total time allowed: 3 hours plus 15 minutes reading and planning time.

Note that:

- Questions 1 and 2 normally focus on reasonably large scenarios. The first question usually requires some form of risk assessment. The second question normally considers another form of engagement or a specialised area of audit, such as group auditing.

- Most of the marks available for question 1 are for applying your knowledge of audit procedures to the scenario, rather than simple 'knowledge dumping.'

- Question 3 typically requires you to perform a review of evidence gathered on an assurance assignment. You are normally asked to discuss what 'matters you would now consider' and what 'further procedures you would recommend.'

- Question 4 normally asks you to discuss the ethical and professional issues relevant to a few short scenarios.

- Question 5 focuses on reporting, typically audit reports, although reports to those charged with governance are also possible. You normally have to discuss the impact of certain issues on the wording of the report and the assurance opinion offered.

- All requirements will be broken into numerous sub-requirements that test a range topics.

- The majority of marks available on P7 are for applying your knowledge to specific case studies. There is little scope for 'knowledge dumping,' so only do this if the question specifically asks for it, e.g. when a definition is requested.

PASS MARK

The pass mark for all ACCA Qualification examination papers is 50%.

READING AND PLANNING TIME

Remember that all three hour paper based examinations have an additional 15 minutes reading and planning time.

ACCA GUIDANCE

ACCA guidance on the use of this time is as follows:

This additional time is allowed at the beginning of the examination to allow candidates to read the questions and to begin planning their answers before they start to write in their answer books.

This time should be used to ensure that all the information and, in particular, the exam requirements are properly read and understood.

During this time, candidates may only annotate their question paper. They may not write anything in their answer booklets until told to do so by the invigilator.

KAPLAN GUIDANCE

In relation to P7, we recommend that you take the following approach with your reading and planning time:

- **Skim through the whole paper**, assessing the level of difficulty of each question and identifying which **two** of the section B questions you wish to attempt.

- **Write down** on the question paper next to the mark allocation **the amount of time you should spend on each part.** Do this for each part of every question.

- **Decide the order** in which you think you will attempt each question:

  This is a personal choice and you have time on the revision phase to try out different approaches, for example, if you sit mock exams.

  A common approach is to tackle the question you think is the easiest and you are most comfortable with first.

  Others may prefer to tackle the longest questions first, or conversely leave them to the last.

  Psychologists believe that you usually perform at your best on the second and third question you attempt, once you have settled into the exam, so not tackling the longer question first may be advisable.

  It is usual, however, that students tackle their least favourite topic and/or the most difficult question last.

  Whatever your approach, you must make sure that you leave enough time to attempt all questions fully and be very strict with yourself in timing each question.

- Read the requirements and then the detail of the questions **1 and 2** carefully.

  Always read the requirement first as this enables you to **focus on the detail of the question with the specific task in mind**.

  For written questions:

  Take notice of the format required (e.g. letter, memo, notes) and identify the recipient of the answer . You need to do this to judge the level of sophistication required in your answer and whether the use of a formal reply is appropriate.

  P7 marks are normally awarded for depth of explanation and discussion. For this reason lists and bullet points should be avoided unless specifically requested. Always plan the structure of your answer and use sub-headings, as this always improves the quality and clarity of your response. You may also be asked to write a report or a memo. Professional marks are awarded for these questions so do not ignore their format.

  For all questions:

  Spot the easy marks to be gained in a question.

  Make sure that you do these parts first when you tackle the question.

  By covering all questions you can often help yourself as you may find that facts in one question may remind you of things you should put into your answer relating to a different question.

- With your plan of attack in mind, **start answering your chosen question** with your plan to hand, as soon as you are allowed to start.

 Always keep your eye on the clock and do not over run on any part of any question!

DETAILED SYLLABUS

The detailed syllabus and study guide written by the ACCA can be found at:

www.accaglobal.com/students/

KAPLAN'S RECOMMENDED REVISION APPROACH

QUESTION PRACTICE IS THE KEY TO SUCCESS

Success in professional examinations relies upon you acquiring a firm grasp of the required knowledge at the tuition phase. In order to be able to do the questions, knowledge is essential.

However, the difference between success and failure often hinges on your exam technique on the day and making the most of the revision phase of your studies.

The **Kaplan complete text** is the starting point, designed to provide the underpinning knowledge to tackle all questions. However, in the revision phase, pouring over text books is not the answer.

Kaplan Online fixed tests help you consolidate your knowledge and understanding and are a useful tool to check whether you can remember key topic areas.

Kaplan pocket notes are designed to help you quickly revise a topic area, however you then need to practice questions. There is a need to progress to full exam standard questions as soon as possible, and to tie your exam technique and technical knowledge together.

The importance of question practice cannot be over-emphasised.

The recommended approach below is designed by expert tutors in the field, in conjunction with their knowledge of the examiner and their recent real exams.

The approach taken for the fundamental papers is to revise by topic area. However, with the professional stage papers, a multi topic approach is required to answer the scenario based questions.

You need to practice as many questions as possible in the time you have left.

OUR AIM

Our aim is to get you to the stage where you can attempt exam standard questions confidently, to time, in a closed book environment, with no supplementary help (i.e. to simulate the real examination experience).

Practising your exam technique on real past examination questions, in timed conditions, is also vitally important for you to assess your progress and identify areas of weakness that may need more attention in the final run up to the examination.

In order to achieve this we recognise that initially you may feel the need to practice some questions with open book help and exceed the required time.

The approach below shows you which questions you should use to build up to coping with exam standard question practice, and references to the sources of information available should you need to revisit a topic area in more detail.

Remember that in the real examination, all you have to do is:

- attempt all questions required by the exam

- only spend the allotted time on each question, and

- get them at least 50% of the marks allocated!

Try and practice this approach on every question you attempt from now to the real exam.

EXAMINER COMMENTS

We have included the examiners comments to the specific new syllabus examination questions in this kit for you to see the main pitfalls that students fall into with regard to technical content.

However, too many times in the general section of the report, the examiner comments that students had failed due to:

- "misallocation of time"

- "running out of time" and

- showing signs of "spending too much time on an earlier questions and clearly rushing the answer to a subsequent question".

Good exam technique is vital.

THE KAPLAN PAPER P7 REVISION PLAN

Stage 1: Assess areas of strengths and weaknesses

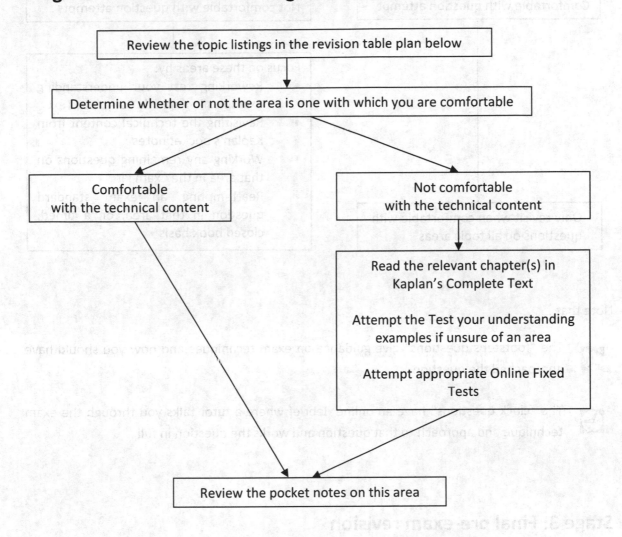

Review the topic listings in the revision table plan below

↓

Determine whether or not the area is one with which you are comfortable

Comfortable with the technical content

Not comfortable with the technical content

Read the relevant chapter(s) in Kaplan's Complete Text

Attempt the Test your understanding examples if unsure of an area

Attempt appropriate Online Fixed Tests

Review the pocket notes on this area

Stage 2: Practice questions

Follow the order of revision of topics as recommended in the revision table plan below and attempt the questions in the order suggested.

Try to avoid referring to text books and notes and the model answer until you have completed your attempt.

Try to answer the question in the allotted time.

Review your attempt with the model answer and assess how much of the answer you achieved in the allocated exam time.

Fill in the self-assessment box below and decide on your best course of action.

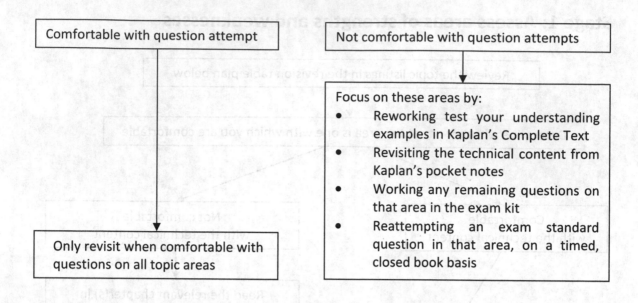

Note that :

The "footsteps questions" give guidance on exam techniques and how you should have approached the question.

The "clock questions" have an online debrief where a tutor talks you through the exam technique and approach to that question and works the question in full.

Stage 3: Final pre-exam revision

We recommend that you **attempt at least one three hour mock examination** containing a set of previously unseen exam standard questions.

It is important that you get a feel for the breadth of coverage of a real exam without advanced knowledge of the topic areas covered – just as you will expect to see on the real exam day.

Ideally this mock should be sat in timed, closed book, real exam conditions and could be:

- a mock examination offered by your tuition provider, and/or

- the pilot paper in the back of this exam kit, and/or

- the last real examination paper (available shortly afterwards on Kaplan EN-gage with "enhanced walk through answers" and a full "tutor debrief").

THE DETAILED REVISION PLAN

Topics	Complete Text (and Pocket Note) Chapter	Questions to attempt	Tutor guidance	Date attempted	Self assessment
1. Audit planning, risk assessment and materiality	9, 10 & 11	5 & 7	Audit risk (and the sub-components of business and financial statements risk) is fundamental to P7. However, rather than discussing what audit risk is you need to be able to perform a risk assessment for specific information given in a scenario.		
2. Audit procedures	12	7 & 8	Throughout the P7 exam you will be required to provide examples of principle audit procedures. The assertions you are testing will usually be very narrowly defined and this represents a significant step up from F8. You therefore need to know the sorts of procedures available to an auditor and then rehearse applying them to specific scenarios.		
3. Non-audit engagements	16 - 20	4, 27 & 29	There are many non-audit engagements that you could be asked to discuss. Therefore ensure that you know: the typical sorts of engagement; how they are planned; how they are performed; and how they are reviewed. You also need to consider the ethical/professional impact of an auditor accepting these engagements.		

4.	Evaluation and review procedures	13	25 & 28	At the review stage of an audit you need to consider a number of issues: whether there is sufficient appropriate evidence on file; if the audit plan has been followed; whether there are any material errors in the information under review; and the impact of these issues on the reports you will have to issue.
5.	Ethics and professional issues	2 - 8	18 & 19	You need to be able to discuss and apply the code of ethics to given scenarios. In addition you also need to consider a wide range of practice management issues, such as: internal quality control; legal requirements; commercial strategy; and professional liability.
6.	Engagement reporting	14 & 15	37 & 36	One of the fundamental weaknesses identified by the examiner is a lack of understanding regarding the nature of audit report modifications. It is therefore important that you are able to assess a scenario and identify how it might impact upon your audit opinion. You also need to be able to discuss the content and purpose of reports to those charged with governance.

Note that not all of the questions are referred to in the programme above. We have recommended an approach to build up from the basic to exam standard questions.

The remaining questions are available in the kit for extra practice for those who require more question on some areas.

TECHNICAL UPDATE – CLARITY PROJECT

OVERVIEW

In 2004 the International Audit and Assurance Standards Board began a comprehensive overhaul of all the International Standards of Auditing (ISAs). The aim of the project was to issue a set of updated ISAs, which were easier to understand and encouraged more consistent standards of auditing across the world.

The new "Clarified" ISAs became effective for audits beginning on, or after, 15 December 2009. In response, ACCA has incorporated the new ISAs into the syllabus for the June 2010 exam session onwards.

The purpose of the supplement is to ensure that candidates studying for the June 2010 audit exams and beyond are fully aware of the changes that will affect the exam. To fully illustrate these changes the supplement includes the following:

- A summary of the objectives of the 'Clarity Project;'

- A detailed guide of the changes to the Complete and Essential Texts

- Illustrative examples of changes to past paper questions published in the Exam Kit; and

- A summary of key revisions to ISAs;

THE OBJECTIVES OF THE CLARITY PROJECT

The overall aim of the project was to enhance the understandability of the ISAs. Not only should this encourage consistent application of auditing standards, there should also be an improvement in audit quality. It is hoped that this initiative will contribute significantly to the convergence of auditing standards worldwide.

In order to achieve this aim the ISAs have been redrafted to make their objectives and the responsibilities of the auditor clearer. As a result all standards now adopt the following structure:

- Introduction;
- Objective;
- Definitions;
- Requirements; and
- Application and other explanatory information.

The language used in the standards is also less ambiguous, making it clear exactly what is expected of an auditor applying ISAs.

In addition to redrafting the existing standards, a number of them have also been revised with the aim of improving audit practice. This means that the guidance provided has been updated to reflect current issues and developments.

The clarified ISAs appear much more prescriptive than their predecessors. It is hoped that this will reduce ambiguity and improve the consistency of audit. However, many commentators have raised concerns about the lack of flexibility in the clarified ISAs may lead to problems when considering factors such as risk and cost. It also reduces the scope for auditor judgement, something that many academics would argue is vital to the health of successful and efficient auditing.

Practically, firms will be compelled to update their audit approaches and manuals and staff training will undoubtedly be required. Thorough engagement planning and monitoring will also be necessary in the transition period to ensure that the new ISAs are being faithfully applied. Of course, this could lead to modest costs, which will undoubtedly be passed onto clients.

UPDATES REQUIRED TO THE COMPLETE AND ESSENTIAL TEXTS

Chapter 3	Section 1 "Engagement Acceptance" (pg 54[1]) should now, in addition to the points noted, reflect the auditor's responsibility to consider the acceptability of the financial reporting framework applied in the financial statements to be audited, as per the detailed ISA guidance below. In section 3 (pg 57 of Complete) the title of ISA 210 requires updating to *"Agreeing the Terms if Audit Engagements"*
Chapter 9	In section 2 "The Impact of ISAs" (pg 193) the quote from ISA 200 needs to be updated to reflect the redrafted wording of the standard, as follows: "Reasonable assurance is a high level of assurance. It is obtained when the auditor has obtained sufficient appropriate audit evidence to reduce audit risk to an acceptably low level." (paragraph 5)
Chapter 10	In order to reflect the revision of ISA 320, section 3 "Materiality" (pg 211) should emphasise the significance of auditor judgement and consideration of the unique circumstances of the entity. The concept of 'performance materiality' must now also be considered along with materiality for the financial statements as a whole (see full standard review below).
Chapter 11	In addition to the principles discussed in the chapter the revised ISA 600 now specifies a number of procedures that auditors of consolidated group accounts must perform. These procedures are relevant to sections 1-5 (inclusive) of the text (pg 247-251). A comprehensive list can be found in the analysis of ISA 600 below.
Chapter 12	The suggested methods of obtaining audit evidence listed in section 2 (pg 280) require updating to match those listed in ISA 500, namely: inspection, observation, external confirmation, recalculation, reperformance, analytical procedures and enquiry. Section 4 "Management Representations" (pg 284) needs to emphasise the stricter guidance with regard to the use of written representations as audit evidence and the requirement to obtain representations regarding management's responsibilities, as described in the review of ISA 580 below.

---

[1] All page references refer to the Complete Text, unless specified otherwise

	Section 5 "Relying on the Work of an Expert" (pg 285) should be updated to read "ISA 620 *Using the Work of an Auditor's Expert."* In addition, the distinction between an auditor's expert and a manager's expert should now be made clear.
	The same section should also be altered to read "ISA 610 *Using the Work of Internal Auditors"* (pg 286) and in section 7 "ISA 230 *Documentation"* should be changed to "ISA 230 *Audit Documentation"* (pg 290).
	Section 9 "Related Parties" (pg 291) should be updated to reflect the revision of ISA 550 *Related Parties,* as discussed in detail below. The text should reflect the requirements to assess the risk of fraud due to related party transactions and the additional procedures required when previously unidentified related parties are identified.
Chapter 13	The following standards have been renamed as follows: • ISA 510 *Initial Audit Engagements – Opening Balances* (pg 308); • ISA 710 *Comparative Information – Corresponding Figures and Comparative Financial Statements* (pg 309); and • ISA 720 *the Auditor's Responsibility Relating to Other Information in Documents Containing Audited Financial Statements* (pg 311); The answer to TYU 2 "Aspersion" part (a) (pg 338) should be altered as follows: Where is reads: "If suitable disclosure is not made, the audit opinion would be qualified 'except for' disagreement," change to "If suitable disclosure is not made the audit report would be modified on an 'except for' basis due to a material misstatement in the financial statements."
Chapter 14	The chapter needs to be adjusted to reflect the fact that guidance relating to the nature and wording of the audit report has been split amongst three ISAs, namely: 700, 705 and 706, as discussed in the standards review below. In addition, all references to 'disagreements' and 'limitations of scope' need to be replaced with 'material misstatements in the financial statements' and 'the auditor is unable to obtain sufficient appropriate evidence.' This mainly affects page 358. However, all test your understandings and answers should also adopt the revised terminology. Section 6 "Special Purpose Audit Reports" (pg 364) should be updated to refer to the new guidelines of ISAs 800, 805 and 810, as discussed in the standards review below.
Chapter 15	The chapter needs to be updated to reflect the fact that the topic is now covered by two standards, ISAs 260 and 265. In addition, references to 'material weaknesses' in internal control (e.g. on pg 385 and 386) need to be redefined as 'significant deficiencies' in internal control
Chapter 21	In section 3 "Impact of Outsourcing on Audit Practice" (pg 477) the expandable text "ISA 402 – Audit Considerations Relating to Entities Using Service........" needs to be updated. Namely the title needs to be amended to ISA 402 *Audit Considerations Relating to an Entity Using a Service Organisation* and the additional requirements for assessing the service organisation's controls (discussed in the standards review below) need to be incorporated.

ILLUSTRATIVE CHANGES TO THE EXAM KIT

The project has not had a significant impact on the usefulness of past paper questions as a revision tool. All of the questions in the exam kit have been reviewed and, where answers do not reflect the requirements of the revised and redrafted standards, have been updated.

It should, however, be expected that the content of the new standards, particularly those subject to significant revision, will be examined in the coming sittings. For that reason candidates should take note of the key updates discussed below.

Examples of the key amendments to the P7 exam kit include:

Qn 1 "Champers Co:"	The answer has been amended to reflect the changes to ISA 315. Under the redrafted standard the requirement to obtain an understanding of "the nature of the entity, including its selection and application of accounting policies" has been split into two separate requirements; "the nature of the entity" and "the selection and application of accounting policies"
Qn 7 "Island Co:"	The answer has been amended to reflect the merger of ISAs 540 & 545. No amendment to recommended procedures was deemed necessary.
Qn 24 "Poppy Co"	The answer has been amended to reflect the merger of ISAs 540 & 545. No amendment to recommended procedures was deemed necessary.
Qns 34 to 43:	All answers have been updated to reflect the changes to ISA 705. The main amendment has been the removal of the terms 'disagreement' and 'limitation of scope' to be replaced with 'the accounts contain material misstatement' and 'the auditor was unable to obtain sufficient appropriate evidence.'

KEY REVISIONS TO ISAs

Standard	Summary of Changes[2]
ISQC 1	*Quality Controls for Firms that Perform Audits and Reviews of Financial Statements, and Other Assurance and Related Services Engagements* Redrafted.[3]
ISA 200	*Overall Objectives of the Independent Auditor and the Conduct of an Audit in Accordance with International Standards of Auditing* Revised and redrafted. This standard sets out the overall objective of the independent auditor. The new ISA 200 makes clear the purpose of the objectives in each of the other ISAs and explains that the auditor should use these objectives when planning and performing audits. It also includes material explaining some of the fundamental concepts related to an audit, such as: ethical requirements relating to an audit; professional scepticism; professional judgement; limitations of an audit; sufficient appropriate evidence and audit risk; and responsibilities of management.
ISA 210	*Agreeing the Terms of Audit Engagements* Redrafted. Now includes specific reference to determining whether the financial reporting framework to be applied is acceptable. Without a suitable accounting framework management do not have an acceptable basis for preparation of the financial statements and the auditor will not have a suitable basis for auditing the financial statements.
ISA 220	*Quality Control for an Audit of Financial Statements* Redrafted.
ISA 230	*Audit Documentation* Redrafted.
ISA 240	*The Auditor's Responsibilities Relating to Fraud in an Audit of Financial Statements* Redrafted.
ISA 250	*Consideration of Laws and Regulations in an Audit of Financial Statements* Redrafted.

---

[2] To understand the full impact of the 'Clarity Project' please refer the full text of the IAASB's International Standards of Auditing

[3] Please see "Objectives of the Clarity Project" for summary of key changes to redrafted ISAs

Standard	Summary of Changes[2]
ISA 260	*Communication with Those Charged with Governance* Revised and redrafted. Additional requirements include: • Explaining why significant accounting practices, that are acceptable according to financial reporting requirements, are not appropriate to the circumstances of the entity; • Documenting matters communicated orally; • Communication of difficulties encountered during the audit; • Requirement to report material weaknesses in internal control removed to ISA 265.
ISA 265	*Communicating Deficiencies in Internal Control to Those Charged with Governance and Management* This is a new standard. 'Material weaknesses' reclassified as 'significant deficiencies.' The aim was to define a threshold of significance for when deficiencies in internal control should be communicated. The threshold was identified as follows: • When a control is designed, implemented or operated in such as way that it is unable to prevent or detect misstatements on a timely basis; or • Such as control, as necessary to prevent and detect misstatement is missing. The auditor has to determine whether individually or in combination the identified deficiencies constitute a 'significant deficiency.' All such 'significant deficiencies' have to be communicated to those charged with governance in writing. Other deficiencies, which are of insufficient significance to communicate to those charged with governance in writing, should be communicated to management.
ISA 300	*Planning an Audit of Financial Statements* Redrafted
ISA 315	*Identifying and Assessing the Risks of Material Misstatement Through Understanding the Entity and its Environment* Redrafted
ISA 320	*Materiality in Planning and Performing an Audit* Revised and redrafted. The focus of the revision to ISA 320 is the consideration of not only the size of an item but its nature and the circumstances of the entity. The standard explains that: • Misstatements, including omissions, are considered to be material if they, individually or in aggregate, could reasonably be expected to influence the economic decisions of users; • Judgements about materiality are made in light of surrounding circumstances, and are affected by the size and nature of a misstatement, or a combination of both, and • Judgements about matters that are material to users of the financial statements are based on a consideration of the common financial information needs of users as a group.

Standard	Summary of Changes[2]
	The new standard includes the definition of a new concept, 'performance materiality.' This states that the auditor should set materiality for the financial statements as a whole (as per the old standard). However, in addition the auditor should establish an amount set at less than materiality when designing the nature, timing and extent of further audit procedures. The aim of which is to reduce the risk that misstatements in aggregate exceed the total for materiality for the financial statements as a whole. Performance materiality also refers to the amounts set a less than materiality for the financial statements as a whole when considering particular classes of transaction, account balances or disclosures. The new standard clarifies that the determination of materiality requires the exercise of professional judgement. However, it does recognise that a simple percentage may be used as starting point when determining materiality to the financial statements as a whole (benchmarking). Such benchmarks include: total revenue; profit before tax; gross profits; total expenses; total equity; and net assets. However, if using such benchmarks the auditor should consider the following: • The elements of the financial statements; • Whether there are items upon which the attention of the users tends to be focussed; • The nature of the entity, its life cycle, and it's industry/economic environment; • The entity's ownership structure and the way it is financed; and • The relative volatility of the benchmark.
ISA 330	*The Auditor's Response to Assessed Risks* Redrafted
ISA 402	*Audit Considerations Relating to an Entity Using a Service Organisation* Revised and redrafted. The revision increases the focus on when the auditor intends to use a service auditor's report as audit evidence. When performing risk assessment the auditor should perform the following procedures to ensure that the service organisation's controls are operating effectively: • Obtaining a Type 2 report, if available. This is a report on the description, design and operating effectiveness of controls at the service organisations. It contains a report prepared by management of the service organisation and a reasonable assurance report by the service auditor; • Performing tests of control at the service organisation; • Using another auditor to perform tests of control at the service organisation on their behalf. If the auditor intends to use a report from a service auditor they should perform procedures to ensure they are satisfied with the competence and independence of the service auditor and that the service auditor's report provides sufficient appropriate evidence about the effectiveness of controls.

Standard	Summary of Changes[2]
ISA 450	*Evaluation of Misstatements Identified During the Audit* Revised and redrafted. All misstatements must be communicated to management on a timely basis, unless they are clearly trivial. Management should be asked to correct all misstatements identified during the audit. The auditor shall obtain an understanding of management's reasons for refusing to adjust any of the misstatements. Prior to evaluating the significance of uncorrected misstatements the auditor should reassess materiality to confirm whether it remains appropriate to the financial statements. Then the auditor must assess whether uncorrected misstatements are, individually or in aggregate, material. To do this they should consider the size and nature of the misstatements, both in relation to the financial statements as a whole and to particular classes of transaction, account balances and disclosures. The auditor shall obtain a written representation from management and those charged with governance that they believe the effect of the uncorrected misstatements is immaterial, individually and in aggregate.
ISA 500	*Audit Evidence* Redrafted
ISA 501	*Audit Evidence – Specific Considerations for Selected Items* Redrafted
ISA 505	*External Confirmations* Revised and redrafted. When using external confirmations the auditor shall maintain control over external confirmation requests. If management refuses to allow the auditor to send a confirmation request the auditor shall: enquire as to management's reason; evaluate the implications; and, where possible, perform alternative procedures. The auditor must evaluate the reliability of confirmations received and when a response is not received the auditor shall perform alternative procedures. Negative confirmations provide less persuasive evidence. Therefore they should not be performed as the sole substantive procedure unless: the risk of material misstatement is low; the population being assessed comprises a large number of small balances; a very low exception rate is expected; and the auditor is not aware of any circumstances that would cause recipients to disregard requests.
ISA 510	*Initial Audit Engagements – Opening Balances* Redrafted
ISA 520	*Analytical Procedures* Redrafted
ISA 530	*Audit Sampling* Redrafted

Standard	Summary of Changes[2]
ISA 540	*Auditing Accounting Estimates, Including Fair Value Accounting Estimates, and Related Disclosures* Revised and redrafted. Merged the old ISA 540 *Audit of Accounting Estimates* and ISA 545 *Audit of Fair Value Measurements,* because the principles and techniques apply to both. The new standard introduces the requirement for greater scepticism when auditing such balances, including an assessment of management bias. It also places a greater emphasis on obtaining an understanding of the client's estimation process – and related controls – when performing risk assessment procedures in accordance with ISA 315. The revised standard clarifies the procedures that an auditor shall perform in response to the assessment of material misstatement. These include: • Determining whether events occurring up to the date of the auditor's report provide evidence regarding the estimate; • Testing management's method of measuring the estimate and the assumptions used; • Testing the effectiveness of controls over management estimates; • Developing a point estimate or a range to evaluate management's point estimate
ISA 550	*Related Parties* Revised and redrafted. The new standard requires the auditor to consider the susceptibility of the financial statements to material misstatement, whether due to fraud or error, that could result from the entity's related party transactions. To assist with this objective the auditor shall obtain an understanding of the controls that management has established to identify, authorise and account for related party relationships and transactions. If the auditor identifies related parties that were not previously indentified or disclosed they shall: • Communicate that information to the rest of the engagements team; • Request that management identifies all transactions with the related party and enquire why they failed to identify them; • Perform appropriate substantive procedures relating to transactions with these entities; • Reconsider the risk that other, unidentified, related parties may exist; and • Evaluate the implications if the non-disclosure by management appears intentional. If the auditor identifies related party transactions outside the entity's normal course of business they should also: • Inspect the underlying contracts or agreements to establish: the business rationale; the terms of the transaction; and whether appropriate disclosures have been made; • Obtain evidence that the transactions were appropriately authorised.

Standard	Summary of Changes[2]
ISA 560	*Subsequent Events* Redrafted
ISA 570	*Going Concern* Redrafted
ISA 580	*Written Representations* Revised and redrafted. **NB**: This standard was revised due – mainly – to concerns that auditors may be over-reliant on written representations. The main emphasis of the standard is that, whilst written representations provide necessary audit evidence, they support other forms of evidence and do not on their own provide sufficient appropriate audit evidence. In addition to this clarification the new standard also requires the auditor to obtain the following written representations about management's responsibilities: • That they have fulfilled their responsibility for the preparation of the financial statements; • That they have provided the auditor with all relevant information and access to records, as agreed in the engagement terms; and • That all transactions have been recorded and reflected in the financial statements. The new standard clearly states that if the auditor concludes that there is sufficient doubt about the integrity of management, thus rendering the written representations unreliable, or if management does not provide the written representations requested then the auditor shall disclaim an opinion on the financial statements in accordance with the revised ISA 705.
ISA 600	*Special Considerations – Audits of Group Financial Statements (Including the Work of Component Auditors)* Revised and redrafted. The revised standard introduces a number of new requirements that the group auditor needs to undertake to achieve greater consistency in group audit practices, particularly when other/component auditors are involved. These include: • During acceptance procedures the engagement partner shall consider whether sufficient appropriate evidence can reasonably be expected to be obtained in relation to the consolidation process and the financial information of the components of the group. If component auditors are to be involved the partner will consider whether the group engagement team will be able to be involved in the work of component auditors; • The engagement team will establish an overall group audit strategy, which will be subject to review by the engagement partner; • The team shall obtain an understanding of the group, its components and their environments, group-wide controls and the consolidation process; • The engagement partner shall assess the professional competence of the component auditor's, their regulatory environment and whether they will comply with required ethical standards;

Standard	Summary of Changes[2]

	• The engagement team shall set materiality for the group as a whole when establishing the overall group strategy but will also consider specific classes of transactions, accounts balances and disclosures for which misstatements of lesser amounts could reasonably be expected to effect the decisions of users. They will also establish materiality for the components of the group where component auditors will perform the audit.
	
	• The engagement team should define the threshold above which misstatements cannot be regarded as clearly trivial.
	
	• The engagement team shall determine the type of work to be performed by the group engagement team, or the component auditor, on the financial information of the components.
	
	• For a component that is of individual financial significance to the group the audit shall be performed using component materiality;
	
	• For a component that is significant because it is likely to include significant risks of material misstatement of the group financial statements due to its nature or circumstances, one or more of the following shall be used:
	  – An audit of the financial information using component materiality;
	  – An audit of one or more classes of transaction, account balances or disclosures relating to the risk of material misstatement of the group financial statements; and
	  – Specified audit procedures relating to the risk of material misstatement of the group financial statements.
	
	• For components that are not significant to the group the group engagement team shall perform analytical procedures at group level. If this is not sufficient further procedures are recommended by the standard.
	
	• If the component auditor performs the audit of a significant component the group engagement team shall be involved in the risk assessment to identify significant risks of material misstatement of the group financial statements.
	
	• The group auditor shall communicate its requirements to the component auditor on a timely basis. This includes:
	  – The work to be performed and the use made of that work;
	  – The form and content of the component auditor's communications to the group team;
	  – A request that the component auditor will cooperate with the group team;
	  – The ethical requirements relevant to the group audit;
	  – Component materiality and the threshold for triviality;
	  – Identified significant risks of material misstatement of the group financial statements;
	  – A list of identified related parties.
	
	• The group engagement team shall request the component auditor communicates matters relevant to the group audit, such as: compliance with ethical standards; compliance with audit instructions; identification of the financial information upon which the component auditor is reporting; instances on non-compliance with laws and regulations; uncorrected misstatements; indicators of management bias; significant deficiencies in internal control; other significant matters communicated to those charged with governance of the component; other matters relevant to the group audit; and the component auditor's overall conclusion.

Standard	Summary of Changes[2]
ISA 610	*Using the Work of Internal Auditors* Redrafted
ISA 620	*Using the Work of an Auditor's Expert* Revised and redrafted. The revised standard focuses on the use of an auditor's expert. The consideration of the use of management's experts is referred to in ISA 500. Before using an expert the audit shall agree, in writing: • The nature, scope and objectives of the expert's work; • The roles and responsibilities of the auditor and the expert; • The nature, timing and extent of communication between the two parties; and • The need for the expert to observe confidentiality. The procedures for evaluating the experts work have also been clarified. Namely the auditor must consider: the consistency of the findings with other evidence; the significant assumptions made; and the use and accuracy of source data. The auditor should not make reference to the use of an expert in their audit report unless it is required to aid the understanding of a modification to the audit opinion. In such circumstances the auditor shall indicate that the reference to the expert does not diminish the auditor's responsibility for the opinion.
ISA 700	*Forming an Opinion and Reporting on Financial Statements* Redrafted
ISA 705	*Modifications to the Opinion in the Independent Auditor's Report* Revised and redrafted. The revision discusses the form and content of the audit report when a modification is considered necessary. The main revision is that all references to the terms 'disagreement' and 'limitation of scope' have been removed. Instead the auditor should express an appropriately modified opinion when: • They conclude that, on the basis of evidence obtained, the financial statements as a whole are not free from material misstatement; and • They are unable to obtain sufficient appropriate evidence to conclude that the financial statements as a whole are free from material misstatement. When the auditor expects to modify their opinion they should communicate to those charged with governance, explain the circumstances behind the decision and the proposed wording of the modification.
ISA 706	*Emphasis of Matter Paragraphs and Other Matter Paragraphs in the Independent Auditor's Report* Revised and redrafted. This standard deals with those additional communications in the auditor's reports that do not affect the wording of the audit opinion, namely the 'Emphasis of Matter' and 'Other Matter' paragraphs.

Standard	Summary of Changes[2]
	The new standard clarifies the purpose of these paragraphs: • 'Emphasis of Matter' paragraph: this is required to refer to a matter appropriately presented or disclosed in the financial statements that, in the auditor's judgement, is fundamental to the users' understanding of the financial statements; and • 'Other Matter' paragraph: this is required to refer to a matter not presented or disclosed in the financial statements that, in the auditor's judgement, is relevant to the users' understanding of the audit, the auditor's responsibilities or the audit report. Once again, if the auditor expects to include such additional matters in their audit report they must communicate the fact, and an example wording, to those charged with governance.
ISA 710	*Comparative Information – Corresponding Figures and Comparative Financial Statements* Redrafted
ISA 720	*The Auditor's Responsibilities Relating to Other Information in Documents Containing Audited Financial Statements* Redrafted
ISA 800	*Special Considerations – Audits of Financial Statements Prepared in Accordance with Special Purpose Frameworks* Revise and redrafted. The key revision is that 'other comprehensive bases of accounting' have been renamed as 'special purpose frameworks.' In the case of an auditor's report on special purpose financial statements: • The auditor's report shall describe the purpose for which the financial statements are prepared and, if necessary, the intended users, or refer to a note in the special purpose financial statements that contains the information; and • If management has a choice of financial reporting frameworks in the preparation of such financial statements, the explanation of management's responsibility for the financial statements shall make reference to its responsibility for determining that the applicable financial reporting framework is acceptable in the circumstances.
ISA 805	*Special Considerations – Audits of Single Financial Statements and Specific Elements, Accounts or Items of a Financial Statement* Revised and redrafted. The standard refers to the fact that ISAs are written in the context of an audit of financial statement and that, where necessary, they are to be adapted to the audits of other historical financial information. Therefore in planning and performing the audit of a single financial statement or of a specific element of a financial statement, the auditor shall adapt all ISAs relevant to the audit as necessary in the circumstances of the engagement.

Standard	Summary of Changes[2]
ISA 810	*Engagements to Report on Summary Financial Statements* Revised and redrafted. The objectives of the auditor are: • To determine whether it is appropriate to accept the engagement to report on summary financial statements; • To form an opinion on the summary financial statements based on an evaluation of the conclusions drawn from the evidence obtained; and • To express clearly that opinion through a written report that also describes the basis for that opinion. The auditor has to form an opinion on whether the financial statements are consistent, in all material respects, with the audited financial statements or that the summary financial statements are a fair summary of the audited financial statements.

Section 1

PRACTICE QUESTIONS – SECTION A

1   CHAMPERS CO (A) *Walk in the footsteps of a top tutor*

> *Timed question with Online tutor debrief*

Champers Co operates a large number of restaurants throughout the country, which are operated under four well-known brand names. The company's strategy is to offer a variety of different dining experiences in restaurants situated in city centres and residential areas, with the objective of maximising market share in a competitive business environment. You are a senior audit manager in Carter & Co, a firm of Chartered Certified Accountants, and you are planning the audit of the financial statements of Champers Co for the year ended 31 May 2009. Extracts from the draft operating and financial review are shown below:

Key financial information

	31 May 2009 Draft $ million	31 May 2008 Actual $ million
Company revenue	1,500	1,350
Revenue is derived from four restaurant chains, each		
Happy Monkeys family bistros	800	660
Quick-bite outlets	375	400
City Sizzler grills	300	290
Green George cafés	25	-
Company profit before tax	135	155
Company total assets	4,200	3,350
Company cash at bank	116	350

Business segments

The Happy Monkeys chain of restaurants provides family-friendly dining in an informal setting. Most of the restaurants are located in residential areas. Each restaurant has a large children's play area containing climbing frames and slides, and offers a crèche facility, where parents may leave their children for up to two hours. Recently there has been some media criticism of the quality of the child care offered in one crèche, because a child had fallen from a climbing frame and was slightly injured. One of the Happy Monkeys restaurants was closed in December 2008 for three weeks following a health and safety inspection which revealed some significant breaches in hygiene standards in the kitchen.

The Quick-bite chain offers fast-food. The restaurants are located next to busy roads, in shopping centres, and at railway stations and airports. Champers Co has launched a significant marketing campaign to support the Quick-bite brand name. The draft statement of comprehensive income for the year ended 31 May 2009 includes an expense of $150 million in relation to the advertising and marketing of this brand. In January 2009 the company started to provide nutritional information on its menus in the Quick-bite restaurants, following pressure from the government for all restaurants to disclose more about the ingredients of their food. 50% of the revenue for this business segment is derived from the sale of 'chuckle boxes' – self-contained children's meals which contain a small toy.

The City Sizzler grills offer a more sophisticated dining experience. The emphasis is on high quality food served in luxurious surroundings. There are currently 250 City Sizzler grills, and Champers Co is planning to expand this to 500 by May 2010. The grills are all situated in prime city centre locations and are completely refurbished every two years.

The Green George café chain is a recent addition to the range of restaurants. There are only 30 restaurants in the chain, mostly located in affluent residential areas. The restaurants offer eco-friendly food, guaranteed to be free from artificial flavourings and colourings, and to have been produced in an environmentally sustainable manner. All of the 30 restaurants have been newly constructed by Champers Co, and are capitalised at $210 million. This includes all directly attributable costs, and borrowing costs capitalised relating to loans taken out to finance the acquisition of the sites and construction of the restaurants. Champers Co is planning to double the number of Green George cafés operating within the next twelve months.

Laws and regulations

Two new regulations were issued by the government recently which will impact on Champers Co. The regulations come into effect from September 2009.

(i)   Minimum wage regulation has increased the minimum wage by 15%. One third of Champers Co's employees earn the minimum wage.

(ii)   Advertising regulations now forbid the advertising of food in a manner specifically aimed at children.

Three audit juniors are joining your team for the forthcoming audit of Champers Co, and you have asked them to read through the permanent file to familiarise themselves with the client. One of the juniors has told you that he appreciates that auditors need to have a thorough understanding of the business of their client, but he does not know what aspects of the client's business this relates to, or how the understanding is developed.

Required:

(a)   **Prepare briefing notes to be used at a planning meeting with your audit team, in which you:**

(i)   **i.identify and explain the aspects of a client's business which should be considered in order to gain an understanding of the company and its operating environment; and** **(6 marks)**

(ii)   **ii.recommend the procedures an auditor should perform in order to gain business understanding.** **(4 marks)**

Professional marks will be awarded in part (a) for the clarity, format and presentation of the briefing notes. **(2 marks)**

(b)   **Using the information provided, evaluate the business risks facing Champers Co** **(13 marks)**

(c)   Describe the principal audit procedures to be performed in respect of:

(i)   the amount capitalised in relation to the construction of the new Green George cafés; and   **(5 marks)**

(ii)   the amount recognised as an expense for the advertising of the Quick-bite brand.   **(4 marks)**

(Total: 34 marks)

 Calculate your allowed time, allocate the time to the separate parts...............

2   DRAGON GROUP *Walk in the footsteps of a top tutor*

 Timed question with Online tutor debrief

(a)   Explain FOUR reasons why a firm of auditors may decide NOT to seek re-election as auditor.   **(6 marks)**

The Dragon Group is a large group of companies operating in the furniture retail trade. The group has expanded rapidly in the last three years, by acquiring several subsidiaries each year. The management of the parent company, Dragon Co, a listed company, has decided to put the audit of the group and all subsidiaries out to tender, as the current audit firm is not seeking re-election. The financial year end of the Dragon Group is 30 September 2009.

You are a senior manager in Unicorn & Co, a global firm of Chartered Certified Accountants, with offices in over 150 countries across the world. Unicorn & Co has been invited to tender for the Dragon Group audit (including the audit of all subsidiaries). You manage a department within the firm which specialises in the audit of retail companies, and you have been assigned the task of drafting the tender document. You recently held a meeting with Edmund Jalousie, the group finance director, in which you discussed the current group structure, recent acquisitions, and the group's plans for future expansion.

Meeting notes – Dragon Group

Group structure

The parent company owns 20 subsidiaries, all of which are wholly owned. Half of the subsidiaries are located in the same country as the parent, and half overseas. Most of the foreign subsidiaries report under the same financial reporting framework as Dragon Co, but several prepare financial statements using local accounting rules.

Acquisitions during the year

Two companies were purchased in March 2009, both located in this country:

(i)   Mermaid Co, a company which operates 20 furniture retail outlets. The audit opinion expressed by the incumbent auditors on the financial statements for the year ended 30 September 2008 was qualified by a disagreement over the non-disclosure of a contingent liability. The contingent liability relates to a court case which is still on-going.

(ii) Minotaur Co, a large company, whose operations are distribution and warehousing. This represents a diversification away from retail, and it is hoped that the Dragon Group will benefit from significant economies of scale as a result of the acquisition.

Other matters

The acquisitive strategy of the group over the last few years has led to significant growth. Group revenue has increased by 25% in the last three years, and is predicted to increase by a further 35% in the next four years as the acquisition of more subsidiaries is planned. The Dragon Group has raised finance for the acquisitions in the past by becoming listed on the stock exchanges of three different countries. A new listing on a foreign stock exchange is planned for January 2010. For this reason, management would like the group audit completed by 31 December 2009.

Required:

(b) Recommend and describe the principal matters to be included in your firm's tender document to provide the audit service to the Dragon Group. **(10 marks)**

(c) Using the specific information provided, evaluate the matters that should be considered before accepting the audit engagement, in the event of your firm being successful in the tender. **(7 marks)**

Professional marks will be awarded in part (c) for the clarity and presentation of the evaluation. **(2 marks)**

(d) (i) Define 'transnational audit', and explain the relevance of the term to the audit of the Dragon Group; **(3 marks)**

(ii) Discuss TWO features of a transnational audit that may contribute to a high level of audit risk in such an engagement **(4 marks)**

(Total: 32 marks)

 Calculate your allowed time, allocate the time to the separate parts...............

3 **BLUEBELL CO** *Walk in the footsteps of a top tutor*

Bluebell Co operates a chain of 95 luxury hotels. This year's results show a return to profitability for the company, following several years of losses. Hotel trade journals show that on average, revenue in the industry has increased by around 20% this year. Despite improved profitability, Bluebell Co has poor liquidity, and is currently trying to secure further long-term finance.

You have been the manager responsible for the audit of Bluebell Co for the last four years. Extracts from the draft financial statements for the year ended 30 November 2008 are shown below:

Extracts from the Statement of Comprehensive Income		
	2008 $m	2007 $m
Revenue (note 1)	890	713
Operating expenses (note 2)	(835)	(690)
Other operating income (note 3)	135	10
Operating profit	190	33
Finance charges	(45)	(43)
Profit/(loss) before tax	145	(10)

Note 1: Revenue recognition

Revenue comprises sales of hotel rooms, conference and meeting rooms. Revenue is recognised when a room is occupied. A 20% deposit is taken when the room is booked.

Note 2: Significant items included in operating expenses:		
	2008 $m	2007 $m
Share-based payment expense (i)	138	–
Damaged property repair expenses (ii)	100	–

(i) In June 2008 Bluebell Co granted 50 million share options to executives and employees of the company. The cost of the share option scheme is being recognised over the three year vesting period of the scheme. It is currently assumed that all of the options will vest and the expense is calculated on that basis. Bluebell Co operates in a tax jurisdiction in which no deferred tax consequences arise from share-based payment schemes.

(ii) In September 2008, three hotels situated near a major river were severely damaged by a flood. All of the hotels, which were constructed by Bluebell Co only two years ago, need extensive repairs and refurbishment at an estimated cost of $100 million, which has been provided in full. All of the buildings are insured for damage caused by flooding.

Note 3: Other operating income includes:		
	2008 $m	2007 $m
Profit on property disposal (iii)	125	10

(iii) Eight properties were sold in March 2008 to Daffodil Fund Enterprises (DFE). Bluebell Co entered into a management contract with DFE and is continuing to operate the eight hotels under a 15 year agreement. Under the terms of the management contract, Bluebell Co receives an annual financial return based on the profit made by the eight hotels. At the end of the contract, Bluebell Co has the option to repurchase the hotels, and it is likely that the option will be exercised.

Extracts from the Statement of Financial Position	2008 $m	2007 $m
Property, plant and equipment (note 4)	1,265	1,135
Deferred tax asset (note 5)	285	335
Deferred tax liability (note 6)	(735)	(638)
Total assets	2,870	2,230

Note 4: Property, Plant and Equipment (extract)

On 31 October 2008 all of Bluebell Co's owned hotels were revalued. A revaluation gain of $250 million has been recognised in the statement of changes in equity and in the statement of financial position.

Note 5: Deferred Tax Asset (extract)

The deferred tax asset represents unutilised tax losses which accumulated in the loss making periods 2004–2007 inclusive. Bluebell Co is confident that future taxable trading profits will be generated in order for the tax losses to be utlilised.

Note 6: Deferred Tax Liability (extract)	Temporary differences relating to Property, plant and equipment $m
1 December 2007	638
Charged to equity	88
Charged to tax expense	9
30 November 2008	735

Required:

(a) Using the specific information provided, identify and explain the financial statement risks to be addressed when planning the final audit of Bluebell Co for the year ended 30 November 2008. **(14 marks)**

(b) Describe the principal audit procedures to be carried out in respect of the following:

(i) The measurement of the share-based payment expense; **(6 marks)**

(ii) The recoverability of the deferred tax asset. **(4 marks)**

A new internal auditor, Daisy Rosepetal, has recently joined Bluebell Co. She has been asked by management to establish and to monitor a variety of social and environmental Key Performance Indicators (KPIs). Daisy has no experience in this area, and has asked you for some advice. It has been agreed with Bluebell Co's audit committee that you are to provide guidance to Daisy to help her in this part of her role, and that this does not impair the objectivity of the audit.

(c) Recommend EIGHT KPIs which could be used to monitor Bluebell Co's social and environmental performance, and outline the nature of evidence that should be available to provide assurance on the accuracy of the KPIs recommended. Your answer should be in the form of briefing notes to be used at a meeting with Daisy Rosepetal. **(10 marks)**

Note: Requirement (c) includes 2 professional marks.

(Total: 34 marks)

4   CROCUS CO *Walk in the footsteps of a top tutor*

(a)   **Define the following terms:**

(i)   **Forensic Accounting;**

(ii)   **Forensic Investigation;**

(iii)   **ForensicAuditing.**   **(6 marks)**

You are a manager in the forensic investigation department of your audit firm. The directors of a local manufacturing company, Crocus Co, have contacted your department regarding a suspected fraud, which has recently been discovered operating in the company, and you have been asked to look into the matter further. You have held a preliminary discussion with Gita Thrales, the finance director of Crocus Co, the notes of this conversation are shown below:

> **Notes of discussion with Gita Thrales**
>
> Four months ago Crocus Co shut down one of its five factories, in response to deteriorating market conditions, with all staff employed at the factory made redundant on the date of closure.
>
> While monitoring the monthly management accounts, Gita performs analytical procedures on salary expenses. She found that the monthly total payroll expense had reduced by 3% in the months following the factory closure – not as much as expected, given that 20% of the total staff of the company had been made redundant. Initial investigations performed last week by Gita revealed that many of the employees who had been made redundant had actually remained on the payroll records, and salary payments in respect of these individuals were still being made every month, with all payments going into the same bank account. As soon as she realised that there may be a fraud being conducted within the company, Gita stopped any further payments in respect of the redundant employees. She contacted our firm as she is unsure how to proceed, and would like our firm's specialist department to conduct an investigation.
>
> Gita says that the senior accountant, Miles Rutland, has been absent from work since she conducted her initial investigation last week, and it has been impossible to contact him. Gita believes that he may have been involved with the suspected fraud.

Gita has asked whether your department would be able to provide a forensic investigation, but is unsure what this would involve. Crocus Co is not an audit client of your firm.

Required:

(b)   **Prepare a report to be sent to Gita Thrales (the finance director), in which you:**

(i)   **Describe the objectives of a forensic investigation; and**

(ii)   **Explain the steps involved in a forensic investigation into the payroll fraud, including examples of procedures that could be used to gather evidence.**

Note: Requirement (b) includes 3 professional marks.   **(14 marks)**

(c)   **Assess how the fundamental ethical principles of IFAC's Code of Ethics for Professional Accountants should be applied to the provision of a forensic investigation service.**   **(6 marks)**

(Total: 26 marks)

5 MEDIX CO *Walk in the footsteps of a top tutor*

You are a senior audit manager in Mitchell & Co, a firm of Chartered Certified Accountants. You are reviewing some information regarding a potential new audit client, Medix Co, a supplier of medical instruments. Extracts from notes taken at a meeting that you recently held with the finance director of Medix Co, Ricardo Feller, are shown below:

Meeting notes – meeting held 1 June 2008 with Ricardo Feller

Medix Co is a provider of specialised surgical instruments used in medical procedures. The company is owner managed, has a financial year ending 30 June 2008, and has invited our firm to be appointed as auditor for the forthcoming year end. The audit is not going out to tender. Ricardo Feller has been with the company since January 2008, following the departure of the previous finance director, who is currently taking legal action against Medix Co for unfair dismissal.

Company background

Medix Co manufactures surgical instruments which are sold to hospitals and clinics. Due to the increased use of laser surgery in the last four years, demand for traditional metal surgical instruments, which provided 75% of revenue in the year ended 30 June 2007, has declined rapidly. Medix Co is expanding into the provision of laser surgery equipment, but research and development is at an early stage. The directors feel confident that the laser instruments currently being designed will eventually receive the necessary licence for commercial production, and that the laser product will replace surgical instruments as a leading source of revenue. There is currently one scientist working on the laser equipment, subcontracted by Medix Co on a freelance basis. The building in which the research is being carried out has recently been significantly extended by the construction of a large laboratory.

A considerable revenue stream is derived from agents who are not employed by Medix Co. The agents earn a commission based on the value of sales they have secured for Medix Co during the year. There are many suppliers into the market and agents are used by all manufacturers as a means of marketing and distributing their products.

The company's manufacturing facility is located in another country, where operating costs are significantly lower. The facility is under the control of a local manager who visits the head office of Medix Co annually for a meeting with senior management. Products are imported via aeroplane. The overseas plant and equipment is owned by the company and was constructed 12 years ago specifically for the manufacture of metal surgical instruments.

The company has a bank overdraft facility and makes use of the facility most months. A significant bank loan, which will carry a variable interest rate, is currently being negotiated. The terms of the loan will be finalised once the audited financial statements have been viewed by the bank.

After receiving permission from Medix Co, you held a discussion with the current audit partner of Medix Co, Mick Evans, who runs a small accounting and audit practice of which he is one of two partners. Mick told you the following:

'Medix Co has been an audit client for three years. We took over from the previous auditors following a disagreement between them and the directors of Medix Co over fees. As we are a small practice with low overheads we could offer lower fees than our predecessors. We

could also do the audit very quickly, which pleased the client, as they like to keep costs as low as possible.

During our audits we have found the internal systems and controls to be quite weak. Despite our recommendations, there always seemed to be a lack of interest in making improvements to the accounting systems, as this was seen to be a 'waste of money'. There have been two investigations by the tax authorities, which we did not deal with, as we are not tax experts. In the end the directors sorted it all out, and I believe that the tax matter is now resolved.

We never had a problem getting access to accounting books and records. However, the managing director, Jon Tate, once gave us what he described as 'the wrong cash book' by mistake, and replaced it with the 'proper version' later in the day. We never found out why he was keeping two cash books, but cash was an immaterial asset so we didn't worry about it too much.

We are resigning as auditors because the work load is too much for our small practice, and as Medix Co is our only audit client we have decided to focus on providing non-audit services in the future.'

You have also found a recent press cutting regarding Medix Co:

Extract from local newspaper – business section, 2 June 2008

It appears that local company Medix Co has breached local planning regulations by building an extension to its research and development building for which no local authority approval has been given. The land on which the premises is situated has protected status as a 'greenfield' site which means approval by the local authority is necessary for any modification to commercial buildings.

A representative of the local planning office stated today: 'We feel that this is a serious breach of regulations and it is not the first time that Medix Co has deliberately ignored planning rules. The company was successfully sued in 2003 for constructing an access road without receiving planning permission, and we are considering taking legal action in respect of this further breach of planning regulations. We are taking steps to ensure that these premises should be shut down within a month. A similar breach of regulations by a different company last year resulted in the demolition of the building.'

Required:

(a)   Using the information provided, identify and explain the principal business risks facing Medix Co.   **(12 marks)**

(b)   (i)   Discuss the relationship between the concepts of 'business risk' and 'financial statement risk'; and   **(4 marks)**

   (ii)   Identify and explain the potential financial statement risks caused by the breach of planning regulations discussed in the press cutting.   **(6 marks)**

(c)   Prepare briefing notes, to be used by an audit partner in your firm, assessing the professional, ethical and other issues to be considered in deciding whether to proceed with the appointment as auditor of Medix Co.

   Note: Requirement (c) includes 2 professional marks.   **(12 marks)**

(Total: 34 marks)

6   ROSIE CO   *Walk in the footsteps of a top tutor*

Rosie Co is the parent company of an expanding group of companies. The group's main business activity is the manufacture of engine parts. In January 2008 the acquisition of Dylan Co was completed, and the group is currently considering the acquisition of Maxwell Co, a large company which would increase the group's operating facilities by around 40%. All subsidiaries are wholly owned. The group structure is summarised below:

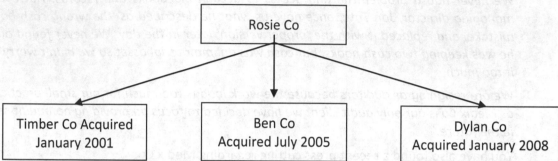

You are an audit manager in Chien & Co, a firm of Chartered Certified Accountants, and you are reviewing the working papers completed on the final audit of Rosie Co and the Rosie Group for the year ended 31 January 2008. Your firm has audited all current components of the group for several years, but the target company Maxwell Co is audited by a different firm.

The management of Rosie Co has provided the audit team with some information about Maxwell Co to aid business understanding, but little audit work is considered necessary as the acquisition, if it goes ahead, will be after the audit report has been issued. Information provided includes audited financial statements for the year ended 31 January 2008, an organisational structure, several customer contracts, and prospective financial information for the next two years. This seems to be all of the information that the directors of Rosie Co have available. The finance director, Leo Sabat is hoping that the other directors will agree that an externally provided due diligence investigation should be carried out urgently, before any investment decision is made, however the other directors feel this is not needed, as the financial statements of Maxwell Co have already been audited. Leo has asked you to prepare a report to explain to the other directors the purpose of due diligence, and the difference between due diligence and an audit of financial statements, which will be presented at the next board meeting.

Goodwill on the acquisition of Dylan Co is recognised in the consolidated statement of financial position (balance sheet) at $750,000. The calculation provided by the client is shown below:

	$000
Cost of Investment:	
Cash consideration	2,500
Deferred consideration payable 31 January 2009	1,500
Contingent consideration payable 31 January 2012 if Dylan Co's revenue grows 5% per annum	1,000
	5,000
Net assets acquired	(4,250)
Goodwill on acquisition	750

All of the figures in the schedule above are material to the financial statements of Rosie Co and the Rosie Group.

Required:

(a) **Prepare a report to Leo Sabat (the finance director), in which you should:**

    (i) **Describe the purpose, and evaluate the benefits of a due diligence investigation to the potential purchaser of a company; and** **(10 marks)**

    (ii) **Compare the scope of a due diligence investigation with that of an audit of financial statements.** **(4 marks)**

    Note: Requirement (a) includes 2 professional marks.

(b) (i) **Explain the matters you should consider, and the evidence you would expect to find in respect of the carrying value of the cost of investment of Dylan Co in the financial statements of Rosie Co; and** **(7 marks)**

    (ii) **State the principal audit procedures to be performed on the consolidation schedule of the Rosie Group.** **(4 marks)**

(c) Maxwell Co is audited by Lead & Co, a firm of Chartered Certified Accountants. Leo Sabat has enquired as to whether your firm would be prepared to conduct a joint audit in cooperation with Lead & Co, on the future financial statements of Maxwell Co if the acquisition goes ahead. Leo Sabat thinks that this would enable your firm to improve group audit efficiency, without losing the cumulative experience that Lead & Co has built up while acting as auditor to Maxwell Co.

Required:

Define 'joint audit', and assess the advantages and disadvantages of the audit of Maxwell Co being conducted on a 'joint basis'. **(7 marks)**

(Total: 32 marks)

 Online question assistance

---

7   **ISLAND CO (A)** *Walk in the footsteps of a top tutor*

Your client, Island Co, is a manufacturer of machinery used in the coal extraction industry. You are currently planning the audit of the financial statements for the year ended 30 November 2007. The draft financial statements show revenue of $125 million (2006 – $103 million), profit before tax of $5.6 million (2006 – $5.1 million) and total assets of $95 million (2006 – $90 million). Your firm was appointed as auditor to Island Co for the first time in June 2007.

Island Co designs, constructs and installs machinery for five key customers. Payment is due in three instalments: 50% is due when the order is confirmed (stage one), 25% on delivery of the machinery (stage two), and 25% on successful installation in the customer's coal mine (stage three). Generally it takes six months from the order being finalised until the final installation.

At 30 November, there is an amount outstanding of $2.85 million from Jacks Mine Co. The amount is a disputed stage three payment. Jacks Mine Co is refusing to pay until the machinery, which was installed in August 2007, is running at 100% efficiency.

One customer, Sawyer Co, communicated in November 2007, via its lawyers with Island Co, claiming damages for injuries suffered by a drilling machine operator whose arm was severely injured when a machine malfunctioned. Kate Shannon, the chief executive officer of Island Co, has told you that the claim is being ignored as it is generally known that Sawyer Co has a poor health and safety record, and thus the accident was their fault. Two orders which were placed by Sawyer Co in October 2007 have been cancelled.

Work in progress is valued at $8.5 million at 30 November 2007. A physical inventory count was held on 17 November 2007. The chief engineer estimated the stage of completion of each machine at that date. One of the major components included in the coal extracting machinery is now being sourced from overseas. The new supplier, Locke Co, is located in Spain and invoices Island Co in Euros. There is a trade payable of $1.5 million owing to Locke Co recorded within current liabilities.

All machines are supplied carrying a one year warranty. A warranty provision is recognised on the statement of financial position at $2.5 million (2006 – $2.4 million). Kate Shannon estimates the cost of repairing defective machinery reported by customers, and this estimate forms the basis of the provision.

Kate Shannon owns 60% of the shares in Island Co. She also owns 55% of Pacific Co, which leases a head office to Island Co. Kate is considering selling some of her shares in Island Co in late January 2008, and would like the audit to be finished by that time.

Required:

(a)   **Using the information provided, identify and explain the principal audit risks, and any other matters to be considered when planning the final audit for Island Co for the year ended 30 November 2007.**

   Note: **Your answer should be presented in the format of briefing notes to be used at a planning meeting. Requirement (a) includes 2 professional marks.   (13 marks)**

(b)   **Explain the principal audit procedures to be performed during the final audit in respect of the estimated warranty provision in the statement of financial position of Island Co as at 30 November 2007.   (5 marks)**

(c)   (i)   **Identify and describe FOUR quality control procedures that are applicable to the individual audit engagement; and   (8 marks)**

   (ii)   **Discuss TWO problems that may be faced in implementing quality control procedures in a small firm of Chartered Certified Accountants, and recommend how these problems may be overcome.   (4 marks)**

(Total: 30 marks)

 Online question assistance

8   SCI-TECH CO *Walk in the footsteps of a top tutor*

You are the manager responsible for the audit of Sci-Tech Co, a pharmaceutical research company. You are planning the substantive audit procedures to be used in the forthcoming audit of intangible assets and operating expenses. Relevant extracts from the financial statements are as follows:

	30 November 2007 (draft)	30 November 2006
	$000	$000
Statement of financial position		
Intangible assets: Development costs		
Cost	2,750	2,000
Accumulated amortisation	(1,450)	(850)
	1,300	1,150
Total assets	**18,500**	**15,000**
Statement of comprehensive income		
Revenue	4,500	3,800
Operating expenses include:		
Research costs	160	200
Amortisation of development costs	600	450
Salary expenses	380	400
Profit before tax	**1,800**	**1,530**

The following is an extract from the notes to the draft financial statements:

'Expenditure on product development is capitalised as an intangible asset from the point at which it is probable that future economic benefits will result from the product once completed. Any product development costs which do not meet the above criteria are expensed as incurred as research costs. Two products are currently in the development phase: Medex, an antiseptic cream; and Flortex, a medicine to reduce the symptoms of fever.

Amortisation of development costs commences with commercial production, the amortisation period being the estimated life span of the product. Currently two products are being amortised over the following periods:

(1)   Plummet Cold Cure five years

(2)   Blingo Cough Cure three years.'

During the initial planning of the audit, the audit senior made the following note on the working papers:

'Bio-Cert Co is the main competitor of our client. It appears that Bio-Cert Co is developing a rival product to Flortex. This rival product is expected to be launched in June 2008, six months prior to the expected launch of Flortex.'

Sci-Tech Co decided to outsource its payroll function, commencing in June 2007. The service is being provided by ProPay Co, a small local company. All of the accounting records relating to payroll are maintained and kept by ProPay Co. In previous years the audit of salary expenses was performed using a systems based approach with limited substantive procedures.

Sci-Tech Co receives funding from governmental health departments, as well as several large charitable donations. This funding represents on average 25% of the company's research and development annual expenditure. The amount of funding received is dependent on three key performance indicator (KPI) targets being met annually. All three of the targets must be met in order to secure the government funding.

Extracts from Sci-Tech Co's operating and financial review are as follows:

KPI target	Draft KPI 2007	Actual KPI 2006
Pharmaceutical products donated free of charge to health care charities: 1% revenue	0.8% revenue	1.2% revenue
Donations to, and cost of involvement with, local community charities: 0.5% revenue	0.6% revenue	0.8% revenue
Accidents in the work place: Less than 5 serious accidents per year	4 serious accidents	2 serious accidents

In addition to performing the financial statement audit, your firm is engaged to provide an assurance opinion on the KPIs disclosed in the operating and financial review.

Required:

(a) Define 'outsourcing' and explain the matters to be considered in planning the audit of salary expense.

Note: Requirement (a) includes 2 professional marks. **(9 marks)**

(b) (i) Explain the matters you should consider to determine whether capitalised development costs are appropriately recognised; and **(5 marks)**

(ii) Describe the evidence you would seek to support the assertion that development costs are technically feasible. **(3 marks)**

(c) Describe the audit procedures you should perform to determine the validity of the amortisation rate of five years being applied to development costs in relation to Plummet. **(5 marks)**

(d) (i) Discuss why it may not be possible to provide a high level of assurance over the stated key performance indicators; and **(4 marks)**

(ii) Describe the procedures to verify the number of serious accidents in the year ended 30 November 2007. **(4 marks)**

(Total: 30 marks)

9 MURRAY

You are an audit manager in Ross & Co, a firm of Certified Public Accountants. The principal activity of one of your audit clients, Murray Co, is the manufacture and retail sale of women's fashions and menswear throughout the capital cities of Western Europe.

The following financial information has been extracted from Murray's most recent consolidated financial statements:

	Year ended 31 March	
	2007	**2006**
	$000	**$000**
Revenue	36,367	27,141
Gross profit	22,368	16,624
Profit before tax	5,307	4,405
Intangible assets		
– goodwill	85	85
– trademarks	52	37
Property, plant and equipment	7,577	4,898
Current assets	13,803	9,737
Total assets	21,517	14,757
Equity	13,226	10,285
Non-current liabilities – provisions	201	87
Current liabilities – trade and other payables		8,090
	4,385	
Total equity and liabilities	21,517	14,757

In May 2007 Murray purchased 100% of the shareholding of Di Rollo Co. Di Rollo manufactures fashion accessories (for example, jewellery, scarves and bags) in South America that are sold throughout the world by mail order. Murray's management is now planning that clothes manufacture will expand into South America and sold into Di Rollo's mail order market. Additionally, Di Rollo's accessories will be added to the retail stores' product range.

Murray is a member of an ethical trade initiative that aims to improve the employment conditions of all workers involved in the manufacture of its products. Last week Di Rollo's chief executive was dismissed following allegations that he contravened Di Rollo's policy relating to the environmentally-friendly disposal of waste products. The former chief executive is now suing Di Rollo for six months' salary in lieu of notice and a currently undisclosed sum for damages.

Ross & Co has recently been invited to accept nomination as auditor to Di Rollo. Murray's management has indicated that the audit fee for the enlarged Murray group should not exceed 120% of the fee for the year ended 31 March 2007. You have been provided with the following information relating to the acquisition of Di Rollo:

	Carrying amount $000	Fair value adjustment $000	Fair value to the group $000
Di Rollo brand name	–	–	600
Plant and equipment	95	419	514
Current assets	400	–	400
Current liabilities	(648)	–	(648)
Net assets at date of acquisition	(153)	419	866
Goodwill arising on acquisition			859
Cash consideration			1,725

Required:

(a) Using the information provided, explain the matters that should be considered before accepting the engagement to audit the financial statements of Di Rollo Co for the year ending 31 March 2008. **(8 marks)**

(b) Explain what effect the acquisition of Di Rollo Co will have on the planning of your audit of the consolidated financial statements of Murray Co for the year ending 31 March 2008. **(10 marks)**

You have been making preliminary inquiries regarding matters arising from the previous year's audit of Di Rollo. It has been revealed that no action has been taken in response to the management letter prepared by the previous auditors. Di Rollo's management has explained that this was because it was 'poorly prepared' and 'unhelpful'.

Required:

(c) Briefly describe various criteria against which the effectiveness of a management letter may be assessed. **(7 marks)**

(Total: 25 marks)

10 YATES

Your firm has successfully tendered for the audit of Yates Co, a private national haulage and distribution company with over 2,000 employees. This long-established company provides refrigerated, bulk and heavy haulage transport services to time-sensitive delivery schedules.

You have obtained the following financial information from Yates:

	For the year to 30 June	
	2006 Draft	2005 Actual
Statement of comprehensive income	$m	$m
Revenue (Note 1)	161.5	144.4
Materials expense (Note 2)	88.0	74.7
Staff costs	40.6	35.6
Depreciation and amortization	8.5	9.5
Other expenses	19.6	23.2
Finance costs	2.9	2.2

Total expenses	159.6	145.2
Profit/(loss) before taxation	1.9	(0.8)
Statement of financial position		
Intangible assets (Note 3)	7.2	6.2
Tangible assets (Note 4)		
Property	55.1	57.8
Vehicles and transport equipment	16.4	16.0
Other equipment	7.4	9.3
Inventories	0.6	0.5
Trade receivables (Note 5)	13.7	13.4
Cash and cash equivalents	3.4	2.8
Total assets	103.8	106.0
Provisions		
Restructuring (Note 6)	9.7	10.8
Tax provision	3.0	3.3
Liabilities		
Finance lease liabilities (Note 7)	5.4	4.4
Trade payables	13.8	13.1
Other liabilities (Note 8)	8.5	7.9
Total liabilities	40.4	39.5

Notes:

(1) Revenue is net of rebates to major customers that increase with the volume of consignments transported.

Rebates are calculated on cumulative sales for the financial year and awarded quarterly in arrears.

(2) Materials expense includes fuel, repair materials, transportation and vehicle maintenance costs.

(3) Purchased intangible assets, including software and industrial licences, are accounted for using the cost model.

Internally generated intangible assets, mainly software developed for customers to generate consignment documents, are initially recognized at cost if the asset recognition criteria are satisfied.

(4) Movements on tangible non-current assets have been drafted as follows:

	Property	Vehicles and transport equipment	Other equipment	Total
Historical cost	$m	$m	$m	$m
Opening balance at 1 July 2005	75.7	25.6	17.8	119.1
Additions	1.4	2.7	1.1	5.2
Disposals	(2.5)	(2.6)	(1.4)	(6.5)
Closing balance at 30 June 2006	74.6	25.7	17.5	117.8

Depreciation and impairment losses				
Opening balance at 1 July 2005	17.9	9.6	8.5	36.0
Depreciation and impairment loss	2.4	1.9	2.5	6.8
Disposals	(0.8)	(2.2)	(0.9)	(3.9)
Closing balance at 30 June 2006	19.5	9.3	10.1	38.9
Carrying amount at 30 June 2006	55.1	16.4	7.4	78.9
Carrying amount at 30 June 2005	57.8	16.0	9.3	83.1

Depreciation is charged using the straight-line method assuming the following useful lives:

	Years
Property	6 to 60
Vehicles and transport equipment	3 to 8
Other equipment	3 to 15

(5)   Trade receivables are carried at their principal amount, less allowances for impairment.

(6)   The restructuring provision relates to employee termination and other obligations arising on the closure and relocation of distribution depots in December 2004.

(7)   Finance leases are capitalized at the date of inception of the lease at fair value or the present value of the minimum lease payments, if less.

(8)   Other liabilities include amounts due to employees for accrued wages and salaries, overtime, sick leave, maternity pay and bonuses.

Required:

In respect of the financial statements audit of Yates Co for the year ending 30 June 2006:

(a)   Calculate preliminary materiality and justify the suitability of your assessment.

(6 marks)

(b)   Identify and explain the financial statement risks to be taken into account in planning the final audit.   (12 marks)

(c)   Explain the extent to which you should plan to place reliance on analytical procedures as audit evidence.   (6 marks)

(d)   Briefly describe the principal audit work to be performed in respect of the carrying amount of the following items in the statement of financial position:

   (i)   trade receivables; and   (3 marks)

   (ii)   vehicles.   (3 marks)

(Total: 30 marks)

11   SHIRE OIL

Shire Oil Co ('Shire'), a listed company, is primarily an oil producer with interests in the North Sea, West Africa and South Asia. Shire's latest interim report shows:

	30 June 2005	30 June 2004	31 December 2004
			Unaudited
	Unaudited	Audited	
	$000	$000	$000
Revenue	22,000	18,300	37,500
Profit before tax	5,500	4,200	7,500
Total assets	95,900	92,300	88,400
Earnings per share (basic)	$1.82	$2.07	$3.53

In April 2005, the company was awarded a new five-year licence, by the central government, to explore for oil in a remote region. The licence was granted at no cost to Shire. However, Shire's management has decided to recognize the licence at an estimated fair value of $3 million.

The most significant of Shire's tangible non-current assets are its 17 oil rigs (2004 – 15). Each rig is composed of numerous items including a platform, buildings thereon and drilling equipment. The useful life of each platform is assessed annually on factors such as weather conditions and the period over which it is estimated that oil will be extracted. Platforms are depreciated on a straight line basis over 15 to 40 years.

A provision for the present value of the expected cost of decommissioning an oil rig Is recognized in full at the commencement of oil production. One of the rigs in South Asia sustained severe cyclone damage in October 2005. Shire's management believes the rig is beyond economic recovery and that there will be no alternative but to abandon it where it is. This suggestion has brought angry protests from conservationists.

In July 2005, Shire entered into an agreement to share in the future economic benefits of an extensive oil pipeline.

You are the manager responsible for the audit of Shire. Last year your firm modified its auditor's report due to a lack of evidence to support management's schedule of proven and probable oil reserves to be recoverable from known reserves.

Required:

(a)   **Using the information provided, identify and explain the audit risks to be addressed when planning the final audit of Shire Oil Co for the year ending 31 December 2005.**

(12 marks)

(b)   **Describe the principal audit work to be performed in respect of the useful lives of Shire Oil Co's rig platforms.**   **(6 marks)**

You have just been advised of management's intention to publish its yearly marketing report in the annual report that will contain the financial statements for the year ending 31 December 2005. Extracts from the marketing report include the following:

'Shire Oil Co sponsors national school sports championships and the 'Shire Ward' at the national teaching hospital. The company's vision is to continue its investment in health and safety and the environment.

'Our health and safety, security and environmental policies are of the highest standard in the energy sector. We aim to operate under principles of no-harm to people and the environment.

'Shire Oil Co's main contribution to sustainable development comes from providing extra energy in a cleaner and more socially responsible way. This means improving the environmental and social performance of our operations. Regrettably, five employees lost their lives at work during the year.'

Required:

(c) Suggest performance indicators that could reflect the extent to which Shire Oil Co's social and environmental responsibilities are being met, and the evidence that should be available to provide assurance on their accuracy. **(6 marks)**

(d) Explain the nature and value of a social report, and draft out the typical contents of a social report attestation. **(10 marks)**

(Total: 34 marks)

12 GENO VESA FARM

Geno Vesa Farm (GVF), a limited liability company, is a cheese manufacturer. Its principal activity is the production of a traditional 'Farmhouse' cheese that is retailed around the world to exclusive shops, through mail order and web sales. Other activities include the sale of locally produced foods through a farm shop and cheese-making demonstrations and tours.

The farm's herd of 700 goats is used primarily for the production of milk. Kids (i.e. goat offspring), which are a secondary product, are selected for herd replacement or otherwise sold. Animals held for sale are not usually retained beyond the time they reach optimal size or weight because their value usually does not increase thereafter.

There are two main variations of the traditional farmhouse cheese; 'Rabida Red' and 'Bachas Blue'. The red cheese is coloured using Innittu, which is extracted from berries found only in South American rain forests. The cost of Innittu has risen sharply over the last year as the collection of berries by local village workers has come under the scrutiny of an international action group. The group is lobbying the South American government to ban the export of Innittu, claiming that the workers are being exploited and that sustaining the forest is seriously under threat.

Demand for Bachas Blue, which is made from unpasteurized milk, fell considerably in 2003 following the publication of a research report that suggested a link between unpasteurized milk products and a skin disorder. The financial statements for the year ended 30 September 2004 recognized a material impairment loss attributable to the equipment used exclusively for the manufacture of Bachas Blue. However, as the adverse publicity is gradually being forgotten, sales of Bachas Blue are now showing a steady increase and are currently expected to return to their former level by the end of September 2005.

Cheese is matured to three strengths – mild, medium and strong – depending on the period of time it is left to ripen, which is six, 12 and 18 months respectively. When produced, the cheese is sold to a financial institution, Abingdon Bank, at cost. Under the terms of sale, GVF has the option to buy the cheese on its maturity at cost plus 7% for every six months which has elapsed.

All cheese is stored to maturity on wooden boards in GVF's cool and airy sheds. However, recently enacted health and safety legislation requires that the wooden boards be replaced with stainless steel shelves with effect from 1 July 2005. The management of GVF has petitioned the government health department that to comply with the legislation would interfere with the maturing process and the production of medium and strong cheeses would have to cease.

In 2003, GVF applied for and received a substantial regional development grant for the promotion of tourism in the area. GVF's management has deferred its plan to convert a disused barn into holiday accommodation from 2004 until at least 2006.

Required:

(a) **Identify and explain the principal audit risks to be considered when planning the final audit of GVF for the year ending 30 September 2005.** **(14 marks)**

(b) **Describe the audit work to be performed in respect of the carrying amount of the following items in the statement of financial position of GVF as at 30 September 2005:**

   (i) **goat herd;** **(4 marks)**

   (ii) **equipment used in the manufacture of Bachas Blue; and** **(4 marks)**

   (iii) **cheese.** **(4 marks)**

   (Total: 26 marks)

13 CERISE

Cerise, a limited liability company, manufactures computer-controlled equipment for production-line industries such as cars, washing machines, cookers, etc. On 1 September 2004 the shareholder-managers decided, unanimously, to accept a lucrative offer from a multi-national corporation to buy the company's patented technology and manufacturing equipment.

By 10 September 2004 management had notified all the employees, suppliers and customers that Cerise would cease all manufacturing activities on 31 October 2004. The 200-strong factory workforce and the majority of the accounts department and support staff were made redundant with effect from that date, when the sale was duly completed.

The marketing, human resources and production managers will cease to be employed by the company at 31 December 2004. However, the chief executive, sales manager, finance manager, accountant and a small number of accounting and other support staff expect to be employed until the company is wound down completely.

Cerise's operations extend to fourteen premises, nine of which were put on the market on 1 November 2004. Cerise accounts for all tangible, non-current assets under the cost model (i.e. at depreciated cost). Four premises are held on leases that expire in the next two to seven years and cannot be sold or sub-let under the lease terms. The small head office premises will continue to be occupied until the lease expires in 2007. No new lease agreements were entered into during 2004.

All Cerise's computer-controlled products carry a one-year warranty. Extended warranties of three and five years, previously available at the time of purchase, have not been offered on sales of remaining inventory from 1 November onwards.

Cerise has three-year agreements with its national and international distributors for the sale of equipment. It also has annual contracts with its major suppliers for the purchase of components. So far, none of these parties have lodged any legal claim against Cerise. However, the distributors are withholding payment of their account balances pending settlement of the significant penalties which are now due to them.

Required:

You are required to answer the following in the context of the final audit of the financial statements of Cerise for the year ending 31 December 2004:

(a) **Using the information provided, identify and explain the financial statement risks to be taken into account in planning the audit.** **(12 marks)**

(b) **Explain how the extent of the reliance to be placed on:**

    (i) **analytical procedures; and** **(4 marks)**

    (ii) **management representations,** **(4 marks)**

    should compare with that for the prior year audit.

(c) **Describe the principal audit work to be performed in respect of the carrying amount of the following items in the statement of financial position:**

    (i) **amounts due from distributors; and** **(3 marks)**

    (ii) **lease liabilities.** **(3 marks)**

(Total: 26 marks)

14 HYDRASPORTS

Hydrasports, a limited liability company and national leisure group, has sixteen centres around the country and a head office. Facilities at each centre are of a standard design which incorporates a heated swimming pool, sauna, air-conditioned gym and fitness studio with supervised childcare. Each centre is managed on a day-to-day basis, by a centre manager, in accordance with company policies. The centre manager is also responsible for preparing and submitting monthly accounting returns to head office.

Each centre is required to have a licence from the local authority to operate. Licences are granted for periods between two and five years and are renewable subject to satisfactory reports from local authority inspectors. The average annual cost of a licence is $900.

Members pay a $100 joining fee, plus either $50 per month for 'peak' membership or $30 per month for 'off-peak', payable quarterly in advance. All fees are stated to be non-refundable.

The centre at Verne was closed from July to September 2003 after a chemical spill in the sauna caused a serious accident. Although the centre was re-opened, Hydrasports has recommended to all centre managers that sauna facilities be suspended until further notice.

In response to complaints to the local authorities about its childcare facilities, Hydrasports has issued centre managers with revised guidelines for minimum levels of supervision. Centre managers are finding it difficult to meet the new guidelines and have suggested that childcare facilities should be withdrawn.

Staff lateness is a recurring problem and a major cause of 'early bird' customer dissatisfaction with sessions which are scheduled to start at 07.00. New employees are generally attracted to the industry in the short-term for its non-cash benefits, including free use of the facilities – but leave when they require increased financial rewards. Training staff to be qualified life-guards is costly and time-consuming and retention rates are poor. Turnover of centre managers is also high, due to the constraints imposed on them by company policy.

Three of the centres are expected to have run at a loss for the year to 31 December 2003 due to falling membership. Hydrasports has invested heavily in a hydrotherapy pool at one of these centres, with the aim of attracting retired members with more leisure time. The building contractor has already billed twice as much and taken three times as long as budgeted for the work. The pool is now expected to open in February 2004.

Cash flow difficulties in the current year have put back the planned replacement of gym equipment for most of the centres.

Insurance premiums for liability to employees and the public have increased by nearly 45%. Hydrasports has met the additional expense by reducing its insurance cover on its plant and equipment from a replacement cost basis to a net realisable value basis.

Required:

(a) (i)   **Identify and explain the business risks which should be assessed by the management of Hydrasports.**   **(8 marks)**

     (ii) **Explain how each of the business risks identified in (i) may be linked to financial statement risk.**   **(8 marks)**

(b) **Describe the principal audit work to be performed in respect of the carrying amount of the following items in the statement of financial position of Hydrasports as at 31 December 2003:**

     (i)   **deferred income; and**   **(3 marks)**

     (ii) **hydrotherapy pool.**   **(3 marks)**

(c) **Suggest performance indicators that could be set to increase the centre managers' awareness of Hydrasports' social and environmental responsibilities and the evidence which should be available to provide assurance on their accuracy.**

                                                                                          (8 marks)

                                                                                    (Total: 30 marks)

Section 2

PRACTICE QUESTIONS – SECTION B

PROFESSIONAL/ETHICAL CONSIDERATIONS AND PRACTICE MANAGEMENT

15   CLIFDEN & CO   *Walk in the footsteps of a top tutor*

   Timed question with Online tutor debrief

(a)   IFAC's Code of Ethics for Professional Accountants states that a professional accountant is required to comply with five fundamental principles, one of which is the principle of 'professional competence and due care'.

Required:

Explain what is meant by the term 'professional competence and due care', and outline how firms of Chartered Certified Accountants can ensure that the principle is complied with.   **(4 marks)**

(b)   You are a senior manager in Clifden & Co, and you are responsible for the audit of Headford Co, a manufacturer of plastic toys which are exported all over the world. The following matter has been brought to your attention by the audit senior, who has just completed the planning of the forthcoming audit for the year ending 30 June 2009:

During a discussion with the production manager, it was revealed that there have been some quality control problems with the toys manufactured between March and May 2009. It was discovered that some of the plastic used in the manufacture of the company's products had been contaminated with a dangerous chemical which has the potential to explode if it is exposed to high temperatures. Headford Co did not recall any of the products which had been manufactured during that time from customers, as management felt that the risk of any injury being caused was remote.

Your firm has been invited to tender for the provision of the external audit service to Cong Co. You are aware that Cong Co operates in the same industry as Headford Co, and that the two companies often enter into highly publicised, aggressive advertising campaigns featuring very similar products. Cong Co is a much larger company than Headford Co, and there would be the opportunity to offer some non-audit services as well as the external audit.

Required:

Assess the ethical and professional issues raised, and recommend any actions necessary in respect of:

(i)   the contaminated plastic used by Headford Co; and   (8 marks)

(ii)   the invitation to audit Cong Co.   (5 marks)

                                                                        (Total: 17 marks)

 Calculate your allowed time, allocate the time to the separate parts..............

---

16   BECKER & CO *Walk in the footsteps of a top tutor*

You are a senior manager in Becker & Co, a firm of Chartered Certified Accountants offering audit and assurance services mainly to large, privately owned companies. The firm has suffered from increased competition, due to two new firms of accountants setting up in the same town. Several audit clients have moved to the new firms, leading to loss of revenue, and an over staffed audit department. Bob McEnroe, one of the partners of Becker & Co, has asked you to consider how the firm could react to this situation. Several possibilities have been raised for your consideration:

(1)   Murray Co, a manufacturer of electronic equipment, is one of Becker & Co's audit clients. You are aware that the company has recently designed a new product, which market research indicates is likely to be very successful. The development of the product has been a huge drain on cash resources. The managing director of Murray Co has written to the audit engagement partner to see if Becker & Co would be interested in making an investment in the new product. It has been suggested that Becker & Co could provide finance for the completion of the development and the marketing of the product. The finance would be in the form of convertible debentures. Alternatively, a joint venture company in which control is shared between Murray Co and Becker & Co could be established to manufacture, market and distribute the new product.

(2)   Becker & Co is considering expanding the provision of non-audit services. Ingrid Sharapova, a senior manager in Becker & Co, has suggested that the firm could offer a recruitment advisory service to clients, specialising in the recruitment of finance professionals. Becker & Co would charge a fee for this service based on the salary of the employee recruited. Ingrid Sharapova worked as a recruitment consultant for a year before deciding to train as an accountant.

(3)   Several audit clients are experiencing staff shortages, and it has been suggested that temporary staff assignments could be offered. It is envisaged that a number of audit managers or seniors could be seconded to clients for periods not exceeding six months, after which time they would return to Becker & Co.

Required:

Identify and explain the ethical and practice management implications in respect of:

(a)   **A business arrangement with Murray Co.**   (7 marks)

(b)   **A recruitment service offered to clients.**   (7 marks)

(c)   **Temporary staff assignments.**   (6 marks)

                                                                        (Total: 20 marks)

17   SMITH & CO *Walk in the footsteps of a top tutor*

You are an audit manager in Smith & Co, a firm of Chartered Certified Accountants. You have recently been made responsible for reviewing invoices raised to clients and for monitoring your firm's credit control procedures. Several matters came to light during your most recent review of client invoice files:

Norman Co, a large private company, has not paid an invoice from Smith & Co dated 5 June 2007 for work in respect of the financial statement audit for the year ended 28 February 2007. A file note dated 30 November 2007 states that Norman Co is suffering poor cash flows and is unable to pay the balance. This is the only piece of information in the file you are reviewing relating to the invoice. You are aware that the final audit work for the year ended 28 February 2008, which has not yet been invoiced, is nearly complete and the audit report is due to be issued imminently.

Wallace Co, a private company whose business is the manufacture of industrial machinery, has paid all invoices relating to the recently completed audit planning for the year ended 31 May 2008. However, in the invoice file you notice an invoice received by your firm from Wallace Co. The invoice is addressed to Valerie Hobson, the manager responsible for the audit of Wallace Co. The invoice relates to the rental of an area in Wallace Co's empty warehouse, with the following comment handwritten on the invoice: *'rental space being used for storage of Ms Hobson's speedboat for six months – she is our auditor, so only charge a nominal sum of $100'*. When asked about the invoice, Valerie Hobson said that the invoice should have been sent to her private address. You are aware that Wallace Co sometimes uses the empty warehouse for rental income, though this is not the main trading income of the company.

In the 'miscellaneous invoices raised' file, an invoice dated last week has been raised to Software Supply Co, not a client of your firm. The comment box on the invoice contains the note *'referral fee for recommending Software Supply Co to several audit clients regarding the supply of bespoke accounting software'*.

Required:

Identify and discuss the ethical and other professional issues raised by the invoice file review, and recommend what action, if any, Smith & Co should now take in respect of:

(a)   **Norman Co;**   **(8 marks)**

(b)   **Wallace Co; and**   **(5 marks)**

(c)   **Software Supply Co.**   **(4 marks)**

                                                                                    (Total: 17 marks)

18   NATE & CO *Walk in the footsteps of a top tutor*

You are an audit manager in Nate & Co, a firm of Chartered Certified Accountants. You are reviewing three situations, which were recently discussed at the monthly audit managers' meeting:

(1)   Nate & Co has recently been approached by a potential new audit client, Fisher Co. Your firm is keen to take the appointment and is currently carrying out client acceptance procedures. Fisher Co was recently incorporated by Marcellus Fisher, with its main trade being the retailing of wooden storage boxes.

(2)   Nate & Co provides the audit service to CF Co, a national financial services organisation. Due to a number of errors in the recording of cash deposits from new customers that have been discovered by CF Co's internal audit team, the directors of CF Co have requested that your firm carry out a review of the financial information technology systems. It has come to your attention that while working on the audit planning of CF Co, Jin Sayed, one of the juniors on the audit team, who is a recent information technology graduate, spent three hours providing advice to the internal audit team about how to improve the system. As far as you know, this advice has not been used by the internal audit team.

(3)   LA Shots Co is a manufacturer of bottled drinks, and has been an audit client of Nate & Co for five years. Two audit juniors attended the annual inventory count last Monday. They reported that Brenda Mangle, the new production manager of LA Shots Co, wanted the inventory count and audit procedures performed as quickly as possible. As an incentive she offered the two juniors ten free bottles of 'Super Juice' from the end of the production line. Brenda also invited them to join the LA Shots Co office party, which commenced at the end of the inventory count. The inventory count and audit procedures were completed within two hours (the previous year's procedures lasted a full day), and the juniors then spent four hours at the office party.

Required:

(a)   Define 'money laundering' and state the procedures specific to money laundering that should be considered before, and on the acceptance of, the audit appointment of Fisher Co.   **(5 marks)**

(b)   With reference to CF Co, explain the ethical and other professional issues raised.
                                                                                                                                         (9 marks)

(c)   Identify and discuss the ethical and professional matters raised at the inventory count of LA Shots Co.   **(6 marks)**

                                                                                                                                (Total: 20 marks)

 Online question assistance

19   FOX & STEEPLE – THREE AUDIT ASSIGNMENTS

You are an audit manager in Fox & Steeple, a firm of Chartered Certified Accountants, responsible for allocating staff to the following three audits of financial statements for the year ending 31 December 2006:

(a)   Blythe Co is a new audit client. This private company is a local manufacturer and distributor of sportswear. The company's finance director, Peter, sees little value in the audit and put it out to tender last year as a cost-cutting exercise. In accordance with the requirements of the invitation to tender your firm indicated that there would not be an interim audit.

(b)   Huggins Co, a long-standing client, operates a national supermarket chain. Your firm provided Huggins Co with corporate financial advice on obtaining a listing on a recognized stock exchange in 2005. Senior management expects a thorough examination of the company's computerized systems, and are also seeking assurance that the annual report will not attract adverse criticism.

(c)   Gray Co has been an audit client since 1999 after your firm advised management on a successful buyout. Gray provides communication services and software solutions. Your firm provides Gray with technical advice on financial reporting and tax services. Most recently you have been asked to conduct due diligence reviews on potential acquisitions.

Required:

For these assignments, compare and contrast:

(i)   the threats to independence;

(ii)   the other professional and practical matters that arise; and

(iii)   the implications for allocating staff.

(Total: 15 marks)

20   EBONY

You are an audit manager in Ebony, a firm of Chartered Certified Accountants. Your specific responsibilities include planning the allocation of professional staff to audit assignments. The following matters have arisen in connection with the audits of three client companies:

(a)   **The Finance Director of Almond, a private limited company, has requested that only certain staff are to be included on the audit team to prevent unnecessary disruption to Almond's accounting department during the conduct of the audit. In particular, that Xavier be assigned as accountant in charge (AIC) of the audit and that no new trainees be included in the audit team. Xavier has been the AIC for this client for the last two years.** (5 marks)

(b)   **Alex was one of the audit trainees assigned to the audit of Phantom, a private limited company, for the year ended 31 March 2004. Alex resigned from Ebony with effect from 30 November 2004 to pursue a career in medicine. Kurt, another AIC, has just told you that on the day Alex left he told Kurt that he had ticked schedules of audit work as having been performed when he had not actually carried out the tests.** (5 marks)

(c)   **During the recent interim audit of Magenta, a private limited company, the AIC, Jamie, has discovered a material error in the prior year financial statements for the year ended 31 December 2003. These financial statements had disclosed an unquantifiable contingent liability for pending litigation. However, the matter was settled out of court for $4.5 million on 14 March 2004. The auditor's report on the financial statements for the year ended 31 December 2003 was signed on 19 March 2004. Jamie believes that Magenta's management is not aware of the error and has not drawn it to their attention.** (5 marks)

Required:

Comment on the ethical, quality control and other professional issues raised by each of the above matters and their implications, if any, for Ebony's staff planning.

Note: **The mark allocation is shown against each of the three issues.** (Total: 15 marks)

21   SEPIA

You are an audit manager in Sepia, a firm of Chartered Certified Accountants. Your specific responsibilities include advising the senior audit partner on the acceptance of new assignments. The following matters have arisen in connection with three prospective client companies:

(a)   Your firm has been nominated to act as auditor to Squid, a private limited company. You have been waiting for a response to your letter of 'professional enquiry' to Squid's auditor, Krill & Co, for several weeks. Your recent attempts to call the current engagement partner, Anton Fargues, in Krill & Co have been met with the response from Anton's personal assistant that 'Mr Fargues is not available'.   (5 marks)

(b)   Sepia has been approached by the management of Hatchet, a company listed on a recognized stock exchange, to advise on a take-over bid which they propose to make. The target company, Vitronella, is an audit client of your firm. However, Hatchet is not.   (5 marks)

(c)   A former colleague in Sepia, Edwin Stenuit, is now employed by another audit firm, Keratin. Sepia and Keratin and three other firms have recently tendered for the audit of Benthos, a limited liability company. Benthos is expected to announce the successful firm next week. Yesterday, at a social gathering, Edwin confided to you that Keratin 'lowballed' on their tender for the audit as they expect to be able to provide Benthos with lucrative other services.   (5 marks)

Required:

Comment on the professional issues raised by each of the above matters and the steps, if any, that Sepia should now take.

Note: The mark allocation is shown against each of the three issues.   (Total: 15 marks)

22   RAINBOW

(a)   Explain the importance of the role of objectivity to the auditor-client relationship.   (5 marks)

(b)   You are the audit partner in a firm which provides a variety of accountancy-related services to a large portfolio of clients. The firm's gross practice income is $1 million. The firm has a particularly successful tax department, which carries out a great deal of recurring and special tax work for both audit and non-audit clients. The tax manager has recently involved you in discussions with a major tax client who is considering changing its auditors. The client, Rainbow, would expect audit fees of around $100,000 (which is a reasonable fee for the audit). Your adult daughter has been working as an administrative assistant in the sales department of Rainbow for a year, after being introduced by the tax manager. She has just joined an employee share benefit scheme.

The client is keen to use the firm to provide audit services as he is pleased with the taxation services they provide. The managing director and major shareholder, Mr Parkes, has therefore offered an incentive to the audit fee of an additional 1% of profits in excess of $20 million, annually where relevant. The current recurring taxation fees from Rainbow are $35,000, and last year special tax work amounted to $25,000. Last year's fees remain outstanding.

The managing director has suggested that you give consideration to the matter while staying for the weekend at his villa in Tenerife. He has arranged flights for both you and your spouse.

Required:

Comment on the matters that you should consider in deciding whether or not your audit firm can accept appointment as auditors of Rainbow. **(10 marks)**

(Total: 15 marks)

ASSIGNMENTS

23 **ROBSTER CO** *Walk in the footsteps of a top tutor*

 Timed question with Online tutor debrief

Robster Co is a company which manufactures tractors and other machinery to be used in the agricultural industry. You are the manager responsible for the audit of Robster Co, and you are reviewing the audit working papers for the year ended 28 February 2009. The draft financial statements show revenue of $10·5 million, profit before tax of $3·2 million, and total assets of $45 million.

Two matters have been brought to your attention by the audit senior, both of which relate to assets recognised in the statement of financial position for the first time this year:

Leases

In July 2008, Robster Co entered into five new finance leases of land and buildings. The leases have been capitalised and the statement of financial position includes leased assets presented as non-current assets at a value of $3·6 million, and a total finance lease payable of $3·2 million presented as a non-current liability.

Financial assets

Non-current assets include financial assets recognised at $1·26 million. A note to the financial statements describes these financial assets as investments classified as 'fair value through profit or loss', and the investments are described in the note as 'held for trading'. The investments are all shares in listed companies. A gain of $350,000 has been recognised in net profit in respect of the revaluation of these investments.

Required:

(a) **In your review of the audit working papers, comment on the matters you should consider, and state the audit evidence you should expect to find in respect of:**

(i) **the leases; and** **(8 marks)**

(ii) **the financial assets.** **(5 marks)**

You are aware that Robster Co is seeking a listing in September 2009. The listing rules in this jurisdiction require that interim financial information is published half-way through the accounting period, and that the information should be accompanied by a review report issued by the company's independent auditor.

Required:

(b) Explain the principal analytical procedures that should be used to gather evidence in a review of interim financial information. **(4 marks)**

(Total: 17 marks)

 Calculate your allowed time, allocate the time to the separate parts..............

24 POPPY CO (A) *Walk in the footsteps of a top tutor*

(a) Financial statements often contain material balances recognised at fair value. For auditors, this leads to additional audit risk.

Required:

Discuss this statement. **(7 marks)**

(b) You are the manager responsible for the audit of Poppy Co, a manufacturing company with a year ended 31 October 2008. In the last year, several investment properties have been purchased to utilise surplus funds and to provide rental income. The properties have been revalued at the year end in accordance with IAS 40 *Investment Property*, they are recognised on the statement of financial position at a fair value of $8 million, and the total assets of Poppy Co are $160 million at 31 October 2008. An external valuer has been used to provide the fair value for each property.

Required:

(i) Recommend the enquiries to be made in respect of the external valuer, before placing any reliance on their work, and explain the reason for the enquiries; **(7 marks)**

(ii) Identify and explain the principal audit procedures to be performed on the valuation of the investment properties. **(6 marks)**

(Total: 20 marks)

25 PULP CO *Walk in the footsteps of a top tutor*

(a) Discuss why the identification of related parties, and material related party transactions, can be difficult for auditors. **(5 marks)**

You are an audit manager responsible for providing hot reviews on selected audit clients within your firm of Chartered Certified Accountants. You are currently reviewing the audit working papers for Pulp Co, a long standing audit client, for the year ended 31 January 2008. The draft statement of financial position (balance sheet) of Pulp Co shows total assets of $12 million (2007 – $11.5 million).The audit senior has made the following comment in a summary of issues for your review:

'Pulp Co's statement of financial position (balance sheet) shows a receivable classified as a current asset with a value of $25,000. The only audit evidence we have requested and obtained is a management representation stating the following:

(1)   that the amount is owed to Pulp Co from Jarvis Co,

(2)   that Jarvis Co is controlled by Pulp Co's chairman, Peter Sheffield, and

(3)   that the balance is likely to be received six months after Pulp Co's year end.

The receivable was also outstanding at the last year end when an identical management representation was provided, and our working papers noted that because the balance was immaterial no further work was considered necessary. No disclosure has been made in the financial statements regarding the balance. Jarvis Co is not audited by our firm and we have verified that Pulp Co does not own any shares in Jarvis Co.'

Required:

(b)   **In relation to the receivable recognised on the statement of financial position (balance sheet) of Pulp Co as at 31 January 2008:**

     (i)   **Comment on the matters you should consider.**   **(5 marks)**

     (ii)   **Recommend further audit procedures that should be carried out.**   **(4 marks)**

(c)   **Discuss the quality control issues raised by the audit senior's comments.**   **(3 marks)**

                                                     (Total: 17 marks)

26   MULLIGAN CO   *Walk in the footsteps of a top tutor*

You are an audit manager in Webb & Co, a firm of Chartered Certified Accountants. Your audit client, Mulligan Co, designs and manufactures wooden tables and chairs. The business has expanded rapidly in the last two years, since the arrival of Patrick Tiler, an experienced sales and marketing manager.

The directors want to secure a loan of $3 million in order to expand operations, following the design of a completely new range of wooden garden furniture. The directors have approached LCT Bank for the loan. The bank's lending criteria stipulate the following:

'Loan applications must be accompanied by a detailed business plan, including an analysis of how the finance will be used. LCT Bank need to see that the finance requested is adequate for the proposed business purpose. The business plan must be supported by an assurance opinion on the adequacy of the requested finance.'

The $3 million finance raised will be used as follows:

	$000
Construction of new factory	1,250
Purchase of new machinery	1,000
Initial supply of timber raw material	250
Advertising and marketing of new product	500

Your firm has agreed to review the business plan and to provide an assurance opinion on the completeness of the finance request. A meeting will be held tomorrow to discuss this assignment.

Required:

(a)   **Identify and explain the matters relating to the assurance assignment that should be discussed at the meeting with Mulligan Co.**   **(8 marks)**

(b)   **State the enquiries you would make of the directors of Mulligan Co to ascertain the adequacy of the $3 million finance requested for the new production facility.**

(7 marks)

During the year the internal auditor of Mulligan Co discovered several discrepancies in the inventory records. In a statement made to the board of directors, the internal auditor said:

'I think that someone is taking items from the warehouse. A physical inventory count is performed every three months, and it has become apparent that about 200 boxes of flat-packed chairs and tables are disappearing from the warehouse every month. We should get someone to investigate what has happened and quantify the value of the loss.'

Required:

(c)   **Define 'forensic accounting' and explain its relevance to the statement made by the internal auditor.**   **(5 marks)**

(Total: 20 marks)

27   CUSITER

You are a manager in a firm of Chartered Certified Accountants. You have been assigned to review and report on the following prospective financial information produced by one of your audit clients, Cusiter Co. The information has been produced to support an application for a $250,000 long-term loan from a bank. The funds from the loan will be invested, on 1 January 2008, in new plant and equipment that will be used to manufacture a new product range following a recent purchase of a patented technology.

	Actual Year to 31 December 2006 $000	Actual Quarter to 31 March 2007 $000	Forecast Year to 31 December 2007 $000	Forecast Year to 31 December 2008 $000
Non-current assets				
Intangible asset – Patent	0	0	10	10
Property, plant and equipment	257	262	289	569
Accumulated depreciation	−123	−128	−139	−191
Net book value	134	134	150	378
Investments	7	6	7	7
Current assets				
Accounts receivable	71	65	84	100
Inventory	50	59	59	69
Cash and cash equivalents	6	7	7	0
	127	131	150	169
Total assets	268	271	317	564

Equity				
Share capital	1	1	1	1
Retained earnings	26	30	67	109
	27	31	68	110
Non-current liabilities				
Term borrowings	174	174	151	343
Current liabilities				
Accounts payable	23	21	27	32
Accrued expenses	21	22	25	28
Short-term borrowings	23	23	46	51
	67	66	98	111
Total equity and liabilities	268	271	317	564

Statement of comprehensive income	$000	$000	$000	$000
Revenue	394	86	466	556
Cost of goods sold	(278)	(61)	(329)	(390)
Gross profit	116	25	137	166
Gross profit %	29.4%	29.1%	29.4%	29.9%
Operating expenses	(47)	(12)	(55)	(80)
Earnings before interest & tax	69	13	82	86
EBIT%	17.5%	15.1%	17.6%	15.5%
Interest expense	(21)	(4)	(18)	(44)
Earnings before tax	48	9	64	42

Required:

(a)   Explain the term 'prospective financial information' ('PFI').   (3 marks)

(b)   Explain the matters that should be considered when planning the nature and scope of the examination of Cusiter Co's forecast statement of financial position and statement of comprehensive income as prepared for the bank.   (7 marks)

(c)   Describe the examination procedures you should use to verify Cusiter Co's prospective financial information.   (9 marks)

(d)   Discuss the professional accountant's liability for reporting on prospective financial information and the measures that the professional accountant might take to reduce that liability.   (6 marks)

(Total: 25 marks)

28   SEYMOUR

You are the manager responsible for the audit of Seymour Co. The company offers information, proprietary foods and medical innovations designed to improve the quality of life. (Proprietary foods are marketed under and protected by registered names.) The draft consolidated financial statements for the year ended 30 September 2006 show revenue of $74.4 million (2005 – $69.2 million), profit before taxation of $13.2 million (2005 – $15.8 million) and total assets of $53.3 million (2005 – $40.5 million).

The following issues arising during the final audit have been noted on a schedule of points for your attention:

(a)   In 2001, Seymour had been awarded a 20-year patent on a new drug, Tournose, that was also approved for food use. The drug had been developed at a cost of $4 million which is being amortized over the life of the patent. The patent cost $11,600. In September 2006 a competitor announced the successful completion of preliminary trials on an alternative drug with the same beneficial properties as Tournose. The alternative drug is expected to be readily available in two years time.   **(7 marks)**

(b)   Seymour offers health-related information services through a wholly-owned subsidiary, Aragon Co. Goodwill of $1.8 million recognized on the purchase of Aragon in October 2004 is included at cost in the consolidated statement of financial position. At 30 September 2006 Seymour's investment in Aragon is shown at cost, $4.5 million, in its separate financial statements. Aragon's draft financial statements for the year ended 30 September 2006 show a loss before taxation of $0.6 million (2005 – $0.5 million loss) and total assets of $4.9 million (2005 – $5.7 million). The notes to Aragon's financial statements disclose that they have been prepared on a going concern basis that assumes that Seymour will continue to provide financial support.   **(7 marks)**

(c)   In November 2006 Seymour announced the recall and discontinuation of a range of petcare products. The product recall was prompted by the high level of customer returns due to claims of poor quality. For the year to 30 September 2006, the product range represented $8.9 million of consolidated revenue (2005 – $9.6 million) and $1.3 million loss before tax (2005 – $0.4 million profit before tax). The results of the 'petcare' operations are disclosed separately on the face of the statement of comprehensive income.   **(6 marks)**

Required:

For each of the above issues:

(i)   comment on the matters that you should consider; and

(ii)   state the audit evidence that you should expect to find,

in undertaking your review of the audit working papers and financial statements of Seymour Co for the year ended 30 September 2006.

Note: The mark allocation is shown against each of the three issues.

(Total: 20 marks)

29 RBG

The activities of the Retail and Business Group (RBG) comprise retailing of general merchandize and luxury goods. RBG has developed an internal audit function over many years. Employee turnover in the internal audit department has risen, with high performing employees moving to other departments and less successful ones moving out. The external auditors, Grey & Co have suggested that RBG outsources its internal audit function to experienced auditors.

Your firm, York & Co, has been invited to tender for the provision of internal audit services to RBG for the three years to 31 December 2009. The appointment will include an evaluation of organizational risk, financial compliance, information technology control and systems audits, and fraud investigation. As the prospective assignment manager, you have been asked to identify the principal matters to be presented in your firm's written submission. The invitation to tender indicates that written submissions will be used as a means of shortlisting candidates to make a detailed presentation to RBG's Audit and Risk Management Committee.

You have obtained the following information from RBG:

(1)   The Audit and Risk Management Committee receives annual reports from the head of internal audit on the controls over operational, financial and compliance risks.

(2)   RBG has a comprehensive system of budgetary control including monthly performance reviews of both financial and non-financial indicators.

(3)   Financial extracts ($m):

	Six months to 30 June 2006 Draft	Year to 31 December 2005 Actual
Revenue	387	751
Profit before tax	46	83

(4)   A substantial proportion of RBG's revenue is generated through retail outlets in department stores and shopping centres. Many of the rents payable for these premises are contingent on revenues earned.

Required:

(a)   Briefly describe potential advantages and disadvantages to RBG of outsourcing its internal audit services.   (6 marks)

(b)   Describe the principal matters that should be included in your firm's submission to provide internal audit services to RBG.   (10 marks)

(c)   Explain the possible impact of RBG outsourcing its internal audit services on the audit of the financial statements by Grey & Co.   (4 marks)

(Total: 20 marks)

30 KEFFLER CO

You are the manager responsible for the audit of Keffler Co, a private limited company engaged in the manufacture of plastic products. The draft financial statements for the year ended 31 March 2006 show revenue of $47.4 million (2005 – $43.9 million), profit before taxation of $2 million (2005 – $2.4 million) and total assets of $33.8 million (2005 – $25.7 million).

The following issues arising during the final audit have been noted on a schedule of points for your attention:

(a)   In April 2005, Keffler bought the right to use a landfill site for a period of 15 years for $1.1 million. Keffler expects that the amount of waste that it will need to dump will increase annually and that the site will be completely filled after just ten years. Keffler has charged the following amounts to the statement of comprehensive income for the year to 31 March 2006:

- $20,000 licence amortization calculated on a sum-of-digits basis to increase the charge over the useful life of the site; and

- $100,000 annual provision for restoring the land in 15 years' time.   (9 marks)

(b)   A sale of industrial equipment to Deakin Co in May 2005 resulted in a loss on disposal of $0.3 million that has been separately disclosed on the face of the statement of comprehensive income. The equipment cost $1.2 million when it was purchased in April 1996 and was being depreciated on a straight-line basis over 20 years.   (6 marks)

(c)   In April 2006, Keffler was banned by the local government from emptying waste water into a river because the water did not meet minimum standards of cleanliness. Keffler has made a provision of $0.9 million for the technological upgrading of its water purifying process and included $45,000 for the penalties imposed in 'other provisions'.   (5 marks)

Required:

For each of the above issues:

(i)   comment on the matters that you should consider; and

(ii)   state the audit evidence that you should expect to find,

in undertaking your review of the audit working papers and financial statements of Keffler Co for the year ended 31 March 2006.

Note: The mark allocation is shown against each of the three issues.   (20 marks)

31   PRESCOTT CO

Your audit client, Prescott Co, is a national hotel group with substantial cash resources. Its accounting functions are well managed and the group accounting policies are rigorously applied. The company's financial year end is 31 December.

Prescott has been seeking to acquire a construction company for some time in order to bring in-house the building and refurbishment of hotels and related leisure facilities (e.g. swimming pools, squash courts and restaurants).

Prescott's management has recently identified Robson Construction Co as a potential target and has urgently requested that you undertake a limited due diligence review lasting two days next week.

Further to their preliminary talks with Robson's management, Prescott has provided you with the following brief on Robson Construction Co:

The chief executive, managing director and finance director are all family members and major shareholders. The company name has an established reputation for quality constructions.

Due to a recession in the building trade the company has been operating at its overdraft limit for the last 18 months and has been close to breaching debt covenants on several occasions.

Robson's accounting policies are generally less prudent than those of Prescott (e.g. assets are depreciated over longer estimated useful lives).

Contract revenue is recognized on the percentage of completion method, measured by reference to costs incurred to date. Provisions are made for loss-making contracts.

The company's management team includes a qualified and experienced quantity surveyor. His main responsibilities include:

(1)   supervising quarterly physical counts at major construction sites;

(2)   comparing costs to date against quarterly rolling budgets; and

(3)   determining profits and losses by contract at each financial year end.

Although much of the labour is provided under subcontracts all construction work is supervized by full-time site managers.

In August 2005, Robson received a claim that a site on which it built a housing development in 2002 was not properly drained and is now subsiding. Residents are demanding rectification and claiming damages. Robson has referred the matter to its lawyers and denied all liability, as the site preparation was subcontracted to Sarwar Services Co. No provisions have been made in respect of the claims, nor has any disclosure been made.

The auditor's report on Robson's financial statements for the year to 30 June 2005 was signed, without modification, in March 2006.

Required:

(a)   **Identify and explain the specific matters to be clarified in the terms of engagement for this due diligence review of Robson Construction Co.** **(6 marks)**

(b)   **State, with reasons, the principal additional information that should be made available for your review of Robson Construction Co.** **(8 marks)**

(c)   **State the specific inquiries you should make of Robson Construction Co's management relevant to its accounting for construction contracts.** **(6 marks)**

(Total: 20 marks)

32 ALBREDA

You are the manager responsible for the audit of Albreda Co, a limited liability company, and its subsidiaries. The group mainly operates a chain of national restaurants and provides vending and other catering services to corporate clients. All restaurants offer 'eat-in', 'take-away' and 'home delivery' services. The draft consolidated financial statements for the year ended 30 September 2005 show revenue of $42.2 million (2004 – $41.8 million), profit before taxation of $1.8 million (2004 – $2.2 million) and total assets of $30.7 million (2004 – $23.4 million).

The following issues arising during the final audit have been noted on a schedule of points for your attention:

(a)   **In September 2005 the management board announced plans to cease offering 'home delivery' services from the end of the month. These sales amounted to $0.6 million for the year to 30 September 2005 (2004 – $0.8 million). A provision of $0.2** million has been made as at 30 September 2005 for the compensation of redundant employees (mainly drivers). Delivery vehicles have been classified as non-current assets held for sale as at 30 September 2005 and measured at fair value less costs to sell, $0.8 million (carrying amount, $0.5 million).   (8 marks)

(b) Historically, all owned premises have been measured at cost depreciated over 10 to 50 years. The management board has decided to revalue these premises for the year ended 30 September 2005. At the statement of financial position date two properties had been revalued by a total of $1.7 million. Another 15 properties have since been revalued by $5.4 million and there remain a further three properties which are expected to be revalued during 2006. A revaluation surplus of $7.1 million has been credited to equity.   (7 marks)

(c) During the year Albreda paid $0.1 million (2004 – $0.3 million) in fines and penalties relating to breaches of health and safety regulations. These amounts have not been separately disclosed but included in cost of sales.   (5 marks)

Required:

For each of the above issues:

(i)   comment on the matters that you should consider; and

(ii) state the audit evidence that you should expect to find,

in undertaking your review of the audit working papers and financial statements of Albreda Co for the year ended 30 September 2005.

Note: The mark allocation is shown against each of the three issues.   (Total: 20 marks)

33   VOLCAN

You are the manager responsible for the audit of Volcan, a long-established limited liability company. Volcan operates a national supermarket chain of 23 stores, five of which are in the capital city, Urvina. All the stores are managed in the same way with purchases being made through Volcan's central buying department and product pricing, marketing, advertising and human resources policies being decided centrally. The draft financial statements for the year ended 31 March 2005 show revenue of $303 million (2004 – $282 million), profit before taxation of $9.5 million (2004 – $7.3 million) and total assets of $178 million (2004 – $173 million).

The following issues arising during the final audit have been noted on a schedule of points for your attention:

(a) On 1 May 2005, Volcan announced its intention to downsize one of the stores in Urvina from a supermarket to a 'City Metro' in response to a significant decline in the demand for supermarket-style shopping in the capital.

The store will be closed throughout June, re-opening on 1 July 2005. Goodwill of $5.5 million was recognized three years ago when this store, together with two others, was bought from a national competitor. 60% of the goodwill has been written off due to impairment   (7 marks)

(b) On 1 April 2004 Volcan introduced a 'reward scheme' for its customers. The main elements of the reward scheme include the awarding of a 'store point' to customers' loyalty cards for every $1 spent, with extra points being given for the purchase of each week's special offers. Customers who hold a loyalty card can convert their points into cash discounts against future purchases on the basis of $1 per 100 points.   (6 marks)

(c)   In October 2004, Volcan commenced the development of a site in a valley of 'outstanding natural beauty' on which to build a retail 'megastore' and warehouse in late 2005. Local government planning permission for the development, which was received in April 2005, requires that three 100-year-old trees within the valley be preserved and the surrounding valley be restored in 2006. Additions to property, plant and equipment during the year include $4.4 million for the estimated cost of site restoration. This estimate includes a provision of $0.4 million for the relocation of the 100-year-old trees.

In March 2005 the trees were chopped down to make way for a car park. A fine of $20,000 per tree was paid to the local government in May 2005.   **(7 marks)**

Required:

For each of the above issues:

(i)   comment on the matters that you should consider; and

(ii)   state the audit evidence that you should expect to find,

in undertaking your review of the audit working papers and financial statements of Volcan for the year ended 31 March 2005.

Note: The mark allocation is shown against each of the three issues.   **(Total: 20 marks)**

COMPLETION AND REPORTING

34   PLUTO CO (A) *Walk in the footsteps of a top tutor*

 Timed question with Online tutor debrief

(a)   Explain the term 'fraudulent financial reporting', illustrating your explanation with examples.   **(4 marks)**

You are the partner responsible for performing an engagement quality control review on the audit of Pluto Co, a listed company. You are currently reviewing the engagement partner's proposed audit report on the financial statements of Pluto Co for the year ended 31 March 2009. During the year the company has undergone significant reorganisation, involving the discontinuance of two major business segments. Extracts of the proposed audit report are shown below:

Adverse opinion arising from disagreement about application of IAS 37

The directors have not recognised a provision in relation to redundancy costs associated with the reorganisation during the year. The reason is that they do not feel that a reliable estimate of the amount can be made, and so the recognition criteria of IAS 37 have not been met. We disagree with the directors as we feel that an estimate can be made. This matter is more fully explained in a note to the financial statements. We feel that this is a material misstatement as the profit for the year is overstated.

In our opinion, the financial statements do not show a true and fair view of the financial position of the company as of 31 March 2009, and of its financial performance and its cash flows for the year then ended in accordance with International Financial Reporting Standards.

Emphasis of matter paragraph

The directors have decided not to disclose the Earnings per Share for 2009, as they feel that the figure is materially distorted by significant discontinued operations in the year. Our opinion is not qualified in respect of this matter.

Required:

(a) Critically appraise the proposed audit report of Pluto Co for the year ended 31 March 2009.

Note: you are NOT required to re-draft the extracts from the audit report. **(9 marks)**

(b) Explain the matters to be considered in deciding who is eligible to perform an engagement quality control review for a listed client. **(4 marks)**

(Total: 17 marks)

 Calculate your allowed time, allocate the time to the separate parts...............

---

35 DEXTER CO (A) *Walk in the footsteps of a top tutor*

(a) Compare and contrast the responsibilities of management, and of auditors, in relation to the assessment of going concern. You should include a description of the procedures used in this assessment where relevant. **(7 marks)**

You are the manager responsible for performing hot reviews on audit files where there is a potential disagreement between your firm and the client regarding a material issue. You are reviewing the going concern section of the audit file of Dexter Co, a client with considerable cash flow difficulties, and other, less significant operational indicators of going concern problems. The working papers indicate that Dexter Co is currently trying to raise finance to fund operating cash flows, and state that if the finance is not received, there is significant doubt over the going concern status of the company. The working papers conclude that the going concern assumption is appropriate, but it is recommended that the financial statements should contain a note explaining the cash flow problems faced by the company, along with a description of the finance being sought, and an evaluation of the going concern status of the company. The directors do not wish to include the note in the financial statements.

Required:

(b) Consider and comment on the possible reasons why the directors of Dexter Co are reluctant to provide the note to the financial statements. **(5 marks)**

(c) Identify and discuss the implications for the audit report if:

(i) the directors refuse to disclose the note; **(4 marks)**

(ii) the directors agree to disclose the note. **(4 marks)**

(Total: 20 marks)

 Online question assistance

---

36 BLOD CO (A) *Walk in the footsteps of a top tutor*

You are the manager responsible for the audit of Blod Co, a listed company, for the year ended 31 March 2008. Your firm was appointed as auditors of Blod Co in September 2007. The audit work has been completed, and you are reviewing the working papers in order to draft a report to those charged with governance. The statement of financial position (balance sheet) shows total assets of $78 million (2007 – $66 million). The main business activity of Blod Co is the manufacture of farm machinery.

During the audit of property, plant and equipment it was discovered that controls over capital expenditure transactions had deteriorated during the year. Authorisation had not been gained for the purchase of office equipment with a cost of $225,000. No material errors in the financial statements were revealed by audit procedures performed on property, plant and equipment.

An internally generated brand name has been included in the statement of financial position (balance sheet) at a fair value of $10 million. Audit working papers show that the matter was discussed with the financial controller, who stated that the $10 million represents the present value of future cash flows estimated to be generated by the brand name. The member of the audit team who completed the work programme on intangible assets has noted that this treatment appears to be in breach of IAS 38 *Intangible Assets*, and that the management refuses to derecognise the asset.

Problems were experienced in the audit of inventories. Due to an oversight by the internal auditors of Blod Co, the external audit team did not receive a copy of inventory counting procedures prior to attending the count. This caused a delay at the beginning of the inventory count, when the audit team had to quickly familiarise themselves with the procedures. In addition, on the final audit, when the audit senior requested documentation to support the final inventory valuation, it took two weeks for the information to be received because the accountant who had prepared the schedules had mislaid them.

Required:

(a) (i) **Identify the main purpose of including 'findings from the audit' (management letter points) in a report to those charged with governance.** **(2 marks)**

(ii) **From the information provided above, recommend the matters which should be included as 'findings from the audit' in your report to those charged with governance, and explain the reason for their inclusion.** **(7 marks)**

The finance director of Blod Co, Uma Thorton, has requested that your firm type the financial statements in the form to be presented to shareholders at the forthcoming company general meeting. Uma has also commented that the previous auditors did not use a liability disclaimer in their audit report, and would like more information about the use of liability disclaimer paragraphs.

Required:

(b) **Discuss the ethical issues raised by the request for your firm to type the financial statements of Blod Co.** **(3 marks)**

(c) **In the context of a standard unmodified audit report, describe the content of a liability disclaimer paragraph, and discuss the main arguments for and against the use of a liability disclaimer paragraph.** **(5 marks)**

(Total: 17 marks)

37 BERTIE & CO (A) *Walk in the footsteps of a top tutor*

You are the audit manager for three clients of Bertie & Co, a firm of Chartered Certified Accountants. The financial year end for each client is 30 September 2007.

You are reviewing the audit senior's proposed audit reports for two clients, Alpha Co and Deema Co.

Alpha Co, a listed company, permanently closed several factories in May 2007, with all costs of closure finalised and paid in August 2007. The factories all produced the same item, which contributed 10% of Alpha Co's total revenue for the year ended 30 September 2007 (2006 – 23%). The closure has been discussed accurately and fully in the chairman's statement and Directors' Report. However, the closure is not mentioned in the notes to the financial statements, nor separately disclosed on the financial statements.

The audit senior has proposed an unmodified audit opinion for Alpha Co as the matter has been fully addressed in the chairman's statement and Directors' Report.

In October 2007 a legal claim was filed against Deema Co, a retailer of toys. The claim is from a customer who slipped on a greasy step outside one of the retail outlets. The matter has been fully disclosed as a material contingent liability in the notes to the financial statements, and audit working papers provide sufficient evidence that no provision is necessary as Deema Co's lawyers have stated in writing that the likelihood of the claim succeeding is only possible. The amount of the claim is fixed and is adequately covered by cash resources.

The audit senior proposes that the audit opinion for Deema Co should not be qualified, but that an emphasis of matter paragraph should be included after the audit opinion to highlight the situation.

Hugh Co was incorporated in October 2006, using a bank loan for finance. Revenue for the first year of trading is $750,000, and there are hopes of rapid growth in the next few years. The business retails luxury hand made wooden toys, currently in a single retail outlet. The two directors (who also own all of the shares in Hugh Co) are aware that due to the small size of the company, the financial statements do not have to be subject to annual external audit, but they are unsure whether there would be any benefit in a voluntary audit of the first year financial statements. The directors are also aware that a review of the financial statements could be performed as an alternative to a full audit. Hugh Co currently employs a part-time, part-qualified accountant, Monty Parkes, who has prepared a year end statement of financial position and statement of comprehensive income, and who produces summary management accounts every three months.

Required:

(a) **Evaluate whether the audit senior's proposed audit report is appropriate, and where you disagree with the proposed report, recommend the amendment necessary to the audit report of:**

    (i)   **Alpha Co;**   **(6 marks)**

    (ii)   **Deema Co.**   **(4 marks)**

(b) **Describe the potential benefits for Hugh Co in choosing to have a financial statement audit.**   **(4 marks)**

(c) With specific reference to Hugh Co, discuss the objective of a review engagement and contrast the level of assurance provided with that provided in an audit of financial statements. **(6 marks)**

(Total: 20 marks)

38   CLEEVES (A)

(a) The purpose of ISA 250 *Consideration of Laws and Regulations in an Audit of Financial Statements* is to establish standards and provide guidance on the auditor's responsibility to consider laws and regulations in an audit of financial statements.

Explain the auditor's responsibilities for reporting non-compliance that comes to the auditor's attention during the conduct of an audit. **(5 marks)**

(b) You are an audit manager in a firm of Chartered Certified Accountants currently assigned to the audit of Cleeves Co for the year ended 30 September 2006. During the year Cleeves acquired a 100% interest in Howard Co. Howard is material to Cleeves and audited by another firm, Parr & Co. You have just received Parr's draft auditor's report for the year ended 30 September 2006. The wording is that of an unmodified report except for the opinion paragraph which is as follows:

Audit opinion

As more fully explained in notes 11 and 15 impairment losses on non-current assets have not been recognized in profit or loss as the directors are unable to quantify the amounts.

In our opinion, provision should be made for these as required by International Accounting Standard 36 (Impairment). If the provision had been so recognized the effect would have been to increase the loss before and after tax for the year and to reduce the value of tangible and intangible non-current assets. However, as the directors are unable to quantify the amounts we are unable to indicate the financial effect of such omissions.

In view of the failure to provide for the impairments referred to above, in our opinion the financial statements do not present fairly in all material respects the financial position of Howard Co as of 30 September 2006 and of its loss and its cash flows for the year then ended in accordance with International Financial Reporting Standards.

Your review of the prior year auditor's report shows that the 2005 audit opinion was worded identically.

Required:

(i) **Critically appraise the appropriateness of the audit opinion given by Parr & Co on the financial statements of Howard Co, for the years ended 30 September 2006 and 2005.** **(7 marks)**

(ii) **Briefly explain the implications of Parr & Co's audit opinion for your audit opinion on the consolidated financial statements of Cleeves Co for the year ended 30 September 2006.** **(3 marks)**

(Total: 15 marks)

39   JOHNSTON CO (A)

(a)   The purpose of ISA 510 *Initial Audit Engagements – Opening Balances* is to establish standards and provide guidance regarding opening balances when the financial statements are audited for the first time or when the financial statements for the prior period were audited by another auditor.

Required:

Explain the auditor's reporting responsibilities that are specific to initial engagements.   **(5 marks)**

(b)   You are the audit manager of Johnston Co, a private company. The draft consolidated financial statements for the year ended 31 March 2006 show profit before taxation of $10.5 million (2005 – $9.4 million) and total assets of $55.2 million (2005 – $50.7 million).

Your firm was appointed auditor of Tiltman Co when Johnston Co acquired all the shares of Tiltman Co in March 2006. Tiltman's draft financial statements for the year ended 31 March 2006 show profit before taxation of $0.7 million (2005 – $1.7 million) and total assets of $16.1 million (2005 – $16.6 million). The auditor's report on the financial statements for the year ended 31 March 2005 was unmodified.

You are currently reviewing two matters that have been left for your attention on the audit working paper files for the year ended 31 March 2006:

(i)   In December 2004 Tiltman installed a new computer system that properly quantified an overvaluation of inventory amounting to $2.7 million. This is being written off over three years.

(ii)   In May 2006, Tiltman's head office was relocated to Johnston's premises as part of a restructuring. Provisions for the resulting redundancies and non-cancellable lease payments amounting to $2.3 million have been made in the financial statements of Tiltman for the year ended 31 March 2006.

Required:

Identify and comment on the implications of these two matters for your auditor's reports on the financial statements of Johnston Co and Tiltman Co for the year ended 31 March 2006.   **(10 marks)**

(Total: 15 marks)

40   BEIGE INTERIORS (A)

(a)   **Compare and contrast the auditor's considerations of materiality at the planning stage and the overall review stage of an audit.**   **(6 marks)**

(b)   You are the manager in charge of the audit of Beige Interiors, a limited liability company. Your auditor's report for the year to 30 September 2003 was signed, without modification, in January 2004.

The scope of the audit for the year to 30 September 2004 has however been limited as the former chief executive fled the country in early February 2004, taking the accounting records with him. As a training exercise you have asked one of the trainees assigned to the audit, Jade, to draft the extracts for the basis of opinion and opinion paragraphs that would not be standard wording in an unmodified auditor's report. Jade has drafted the following:

Basis of opinion (extract)

'However, the evidence available to us was limited because accounting records were missing at the beginning of the period and it was not possible to completely reconstruct them.'

Opinion (extract)

'Because of the possible effect of the limitation in evidence available to us, we do not express an opinion on the financial statements.'

Required:

Discuss the suitability of Jade's draft. Your answer should identify and comment on the principal matters relevant to forming an appropriate opinion on the financial statements of Beige Interiors for the year ended 30 September 2004.   (9 marks)

Note: You are NOT required to redraft the extracts.   (Total: 15 marks)

41 JINACK (A)

(a)   Explain the auditor's responsibilities in respect of subsequent events.   (5 marks)

(b)   You are the audit manager of Jinack Co, a private limited liability company. You are currently reviewing two matters that have been left for your attention on the audit working paper file for the year ended 30 September 2005:

(i)   Jinack holds an extensive range of inventory and keeps perpetual inventory records. There was no full physical inventory count at 30 September 2005 as a system of continuous inventory checking is operated by warehouse personnel under the supervision of an internal audit department.

A major systems failure in October 2005 caused the perpetual inventory records to be corrupted before the year-end inventory position was determined. As data recovery procedures were found to be inadequate, Jinack is reconstructing the year-end quantities through a physical count and 'rollback'. The reconstruction exercise is expected to be completed in January 2006.   (6 marks)

(ii)   Audit work on after-date bank transactions identified a transfer of cash from Batik Co. The audit senior has documented that the finance director explained that Batik commenced trading on 7 October 2005, after being set up as a wholly-owned foreign subsidiary of Jinack. No other evidence has been obtained.   (4 marks)

Required:

Identify and comment on the implications of the above matters for the auditor's report on the financial statements of Jinack Co for the year ended 30 September 2005 and, where appropriate, the year ending 30 September 2006.

Note: The mark allocation is shown against each of the matters.

(Total: 15 marks)

42   HEGAS (A)

(a)   Explain the auditor's responsibilities for other information in documents containing audited financial statements.   **(5 marks)**

(b)   You are an audit manager with specific responsibility for reviewing other information in documents containing audited financial statements before your firm's auditor's report is signed.   The financial statements of Hegas, a privately-owned civil engineering company, show total assets of $120 million, revenue of $261 million, and profit before tax of $9.2 million for the year ended 31 March 2005. Your review of the Annual Report has revealed the following:

(i)   The statement of changes in equity includes $4.5 million under a separate heading of 'miscellaneous item' which is described as 'other difference not recognized in income'. There is no further reference to this amount or 'other difference' elsewhere in the financial statements. However, the Management Report, which is required by statute, is not audited. It discloses that 'changes in shareholders' equity not recognized in income includes $4.5 million arising on the revaluation of investment properties'.

The notes to the financial statements state that the company has implemented IAS 40 *Investment Property* for the first time in the year to 31 March 2005 and also that 'the adoption of this standard did not have a significant impact on Hegas's financial position or its results of operations during 2005'.

(ii)   The chairman's statement asserts 'Hegas has now achieved a position as one of the world's largest generators of hydro-electricity, with a dedicated commitment to accountable ethical professionalism'. Audit working papers show that 14% of revenue was derived from hydro-electricity (2004: 12%). Publicly available information shows that there are seven international suppliers of hydro-electricity in Africa alone, which are all at least three times the size of Hegas in terms of both annual turnover and population supplied.

Required:

Identify and comment on the implications of the above matters for the auditor's report on the financial statements of Hegas for the year ended 31 March 2005.

(10 marks)

(Total: 15 marks)

43   KITE ASSOCIATES (A)

(a)   **Explain why quality control may be difficult to implement in a smaller audit firm and illustrate how such difficulties may be overcome.**   **(5 marks)**

(b)   Kite Associates is an association of small accounting practices. One of the benefits of membership is improved quality control through a peer review system. Whilst reviewing a sample of auditor's reports issued by Rook & Co, a firm only recently admitted to Kite Associates, you come across the following modified opinion on the financial statements of Lammergeier Group:

Qualified opinion arising from material misstatement accounting treatment relating to the non-adoption of IAS 7

The management has not prepared a group statement of cashflows and its associated notes. In the opinion of the management it is not practical to prepare a group statement of cashflows due to the complexity involved. In our opinion the reasons for the departure from IAS 7 are sound and acceptable and adequate disclosure has been made concerning the departure from IAS 7. The departure in our opinion does not impact on the truth and fairness of the financial statements.

'In our opinion, except for the non-preparation of the group statement of cashflows and associated notes, the financial statements give a true and fair view of the financial position of the Company as at 31 December 2003 and of the profit of the group for the year then ended, and have been properly prepared in accordance with …'

Your review of the prior year auditor's report has revealed that the 2002 year-end audit opinion was identical.

Required:

Critically appraise the appropriateness of the audit opinion given by Rook & Co on the financial statements of Lammergeier Group for the years ended 31 December 2003 and 2002. **(10 marks)**

(Total: 15 marks)

Section 3

ANSWERS TO PRACTICE QUESTIONS – SECTION A

Tutorial note

These model answers are considerably longer and more detailed than would be expected from any candidate in the examination. They should be used as a guide to the form, style and technical standard (but not in length) of answer that candidates should aim to achieve. However, these answers may not include all valid points mentioned by a candidate – credit will be given to candidates mentioning such points.

1   CHAMPERS CO (A) *Walk in the footsteps of a top tutor*

Key answer tips

The focus of this question is business risk, i.e.: the unique risks Champers faces due to operating in it's chosen industry and due to the manner in which it operates.

Part (a) simply asks you to consider what aspects of the business you need to consider when assessing business risk and what methods/procedures you can use. It is NOT asking for a risk assessment at this point!

Part (b) asks you to perform the risk assessment for Champers. It is unlikely that you will receive marks here for repetition of points made in part (a). This highlights the importance of reading the whole requirement before answering any part of the question. With 13 marks available you need to present a minimum of 7 explained risks. Do not assume that generic risks to the restaurant industry will necessarily score well. You must be specific to the scenario and justify your assessment by bringing some of the information given into your answer.

Part (c) requires audit tests for construction assets and advertising expenses. It is important that you describe the tests. A useful tip is to imagine you are setting a piece of work for a first time audit junior. You need to ensure you explain the test fully so that they can follow your instructions. "Review invoice" simply will not suffice and, hence, would score no marks. You should work on the basis of 1 mark per explained procedure.

The highlighted words are key phases that markers are looking for.

(a)   (i)   **Briefing notes**
To: Audit Juniors
From: Audit manager
Subject: Understanding a client's business and environment

Introduction

Gaining an understanding of the business of a client, and the environment in which it operates is a crucial part of the audit planning process. ISA 315 *Identifying and Assessing the Risks of Material Misstatement Through Understanding The Entity and Its Environment* provides guidance on this matter. The issue is that the auditor must have a thorough understanding of many aspects of the client's business and environment in order to be able to assess risk, decide on an appropriate audit strategy, and be able to design and perform effective audit procedures.

Aspects to be considered

ISA 315 states that there are certain key aspects of the client and its environment which the auditor should understand:

(1)   **Relevant industry, regulatory and other external factors including the applicable financial reporting framework**

This means having an understanding of the industry in which the company operates, including the level of competition, the nature of the relationships with suppliers and customers, and the level of technology used in the industry. The industry may have specific laws and regulations which impact on the business. The auditor should also consider wider economic factors such as the level and volatility of interest rates and exchange rates and their potential impact on the client.

The importance of these issues is their potential impact on the financial statements and on the planning of the audit. For example, if a client operates in a highly regulated industry, it may be worth considering the inclusion in the audit team of a person with specific experience or knowledge of those regulations. Regulations include the financial reporting framework, for example, whether the company uses local or international financial reporting standards.

(2)   **Nature of the entity**

This includes having an understanding of the legal structure of the company (and group where relevant), the ownership and governance structure, and the main sources of finance used by the company. Complex ownership structures with multiple subsidiaries and/or locations may increase the risk of material misstatement.

(3)   **The entity's selection and application of accounting policies**

The auditor should evaluate whether the accounting policies are appropriate to the business and consistent with the financial reporting framework applied. Specifically the auditor should consider: the methods used to account for significant and unusual transactions; the effect of significant accounting policies in controversial or emerging areas; changes in accounting policy; and areas that are new to the entity.

(4) **Objectives and strategies and related business risks**

The management of the company should define the objectives of the business, which are the overall plans for the company. Strategies are the operational approaches by which management intend to meet the defined objectives. For example, an objective could be to maximise market share, and the strategy to achieve this could be to launch a new brand or product every year. Business risks are factors which could stop the company achieving its stated objectives, for example, launching a product for which there is limited demand. Most business risks will eventually have financial consequences, and thus an effect on the financial statements. This is why auditors perform a business risk assessment as part of their planning procedures.

(5) **Measurement and review of the entity's financial performance**

Here the auditor is looking to gain an understanding of the performance measures which management and others consider to be of importance. Performance measures can create pressure on management to take action to improve the financial statements through deliberate misstatement. For example, a bonus payable to the management based on revenue growth could create pressure for revenue to be overstated. Thus the auditor must gain an understanding of the company's financial and non-financial key performance indicators, targets, budgets and segmental information.

(6) **Internal control**

The auditor must gain knowledge of internal control in order to consider how different aspects of internal control could impact on the audit. Internal control includes the control environment, the entity's risk assessment procedures, information systems, control activities, and the monitoring of controls. Put simply, the evaluation of the strength or weakness of internal control is a crucial consideration in the assessment of audit risk, and so will have a significant impact on the audit strategy. The design and implementation of controls should be considered as part of gaining an understanding. The auditor should also understand whether controls are manual or automated. ISA 315 contains a great deal of detailed guidance on the understanding of controls, which these briefing notes do not cover.

(ii) **Procedures used to gain understanding**

(1) **Enquiries of management and others within the company**

A discussion with management is often the starting point in gaining understanding. A meeting is usually held with management to talk about all of the aspects of the company and its environment referred to in the first part of the briefing notes. However, inquiries can also be made of others, who may be able to provide a different perspective or provide specific insights into certain matters. For example, internal auditors would be able to comment specifically on internal controls.

(2) **Analytical procedures**

Auditors perform analytical procedures at the planning stage in order to identify unusual transactions or events, and to understand the main trends reflected in the financial statements for the year. This will enable the auditor, for example, to see if the company has experienced a growth or decline in revenue or profits in the year, which when reviewed in the context of industry or economic trends, may indicate a risk of material misstatement. Analytical procedures should be performed in accordance with ISA 520 *Analytical Procedures*.

(3) **Observation**

Observation may help to support inquiries of management and others, and could involve, for example, physical observation of the internal control operations, and visits to premises such as factories, warehouses and head office.

(4) **Inspection**

Inspection may support inquiries made of management and others. It could include, for example, an inspection of business plans, internal control manuals, reports made by management such as interim financial statements, the minutes of board meetings, and reviewing the company's website and brochures.

Conclusion

Auditors must make sure that they have gained and documented an understanding of five main aspects of the client's business and the environment in which it operates, and a variety of procedures can be used. Without a thorough knowledge of the business and its environment, an auditor would be unable to effectively assess the risk of material misstatement in the financial statements, and therefore could not plan the audit to minimise audit risk.

Business risks include the following:

Health and safety regulations

Champers Co operates in a highly regulated industry, and the risk of non-compliance with various laws and regulations is high. The industry has strict health and safety regulations which must be complied with, and there will be regular health and safety inspections to ensure that regulations are being adhered to. One of the Happy Monkeys restaurants failed a heath and safety inspection during the year. This could lead to bad publicity and damage to the brand name. As the Happy Monkeys business segment contributes the highest proportion of revenue to the company, damage to this brand name could be significant for the company. In addition, damage to one brand name could be easily transferred to the other brand names used by Champers Co.

Child play areas

There was an incident during the year where a child was injured at a Happy Monkeys restaurant. This could have significant repercussions for the company. It is essential that the play areas are perceived as a safe environment in which children can be placed by their parents. If this is not the case, then visits to these restaurants will fall in number, leading to loss of revenue and cash inflows. The Happy Monkeys business segment contributes 53% to total revenue (2008 – 49%), so any loss of revenue from this brand could have a major impact on the performance of the company as a whole. Any bad publicity surrounding this incident could cause major damage to the Happy Monkeys brand.

In addition, this incident could provoke action by regulatory bodies, such as an investigation into health and safety procedures at all Happy Monkeys child care facilities. Any breaches in regulation could result in the facility and possibly the associated restaurant being shut down. As discussed above, damage to any one of the brand names could easily transfer across to the other brand names used by Champers Co.

As a result of the accident, the company may have to spend a significant amount on the play areas to bring them in line with the required health and safety standards. Funds may have to be diverted from other projects e.g. the advertising campaign for the Quick-bite brand, or the development of new Green George cafés.

Quick-bite chain – revenue reduction

Revenue from the Quick-bite business segment has fallen by 6%. This is significant given that the business segment contributes 25% to total revenue in 2009 (2008 – 30%). The reduction in demand is likely to be linked to the increased awareness of the importance of healthy eating. Champers Co has responded to this issue by publishing nutritional information, but new business strategies will need to be put in place to avert further any decline in revenue. Perhaps the company should consider carrying healthier product lines to attract any customers they have lost. These new product lines could be part of the advertising campaign for the brand.

Expenditure on advertising to support the Quick-bite brand name is material at 10% of the total revenue of the company, and the expenditure amounts to 40% of the revenue generated by the Quick-bite business segment. Given the company's relatively poor cash position at the year end, this level of expenditure is unlikely to be sustainable. This is a competitive market with a huge number of suppliers, so brand awareness in important, but supporting the brand name using expensive advertising techniques could prove to be prohibitively expensive.

Further problems lie ahead for the Quick-bite brand, as new regulations will prohibit the advertising of food to children from September 2009. Half of the revenue of Quick-bite is derived from the sale of 'chuckle boxes' to children. The advertising ban will detrimentally affect a significant revenue and cash flow stream for the company. Champers Co needs to consider the development of alternative menus and consider how to support the brand name given the restriction imposed by the government.

Expansion plans – City Sizzler grills

Champers Co has ambitious plans to dramatically increase the number of City Sizzler restaurants from 250 to 500 within the next 12 months. It may be that the expansion plans are unrealistic, and that a different strategy should be used in order to expand the company. The risk is that the company could begin to expand the City Sizzler chain but then run out of cash and be unable to complete the expansion. The risk is increased by the fact that the grills are located in prime city centre locations, which will be expensive to acquire.

The company may need to borrow significantly to carry out this expansion. It is essential that a realistic business plan is prepared to assess if the expansion is financially viable. Given the scale of the expansion plans in relation to both the City Sizzler and the Green George chains, it is likely that the company will struggle to raise all of the necessary finance.

The on-going refurbishment costs are also a potential problem. If Champers Co does not have the cash to spend on refurbishing the restaurants every two years, then customers with high expectations regarding luxury surroundings are likely to switch their preference to other chains of restaurants. In addition, the closure of the restaurants during the refurbishment every two years would lead to a loss of revenue. Possibly the period between refurbishments should be extended to reduce future costs and prevent the loss of revenue on such a frequent basis.

Expansion plans – Green George cafés

To compound the problems discussed above, there are plans to open another 30 Green George cafés during the year. The cafés are located in affluent areas, so the site acquisition costs are likely to be expensive.

It would seem that Champers Co is trying to expand two business segments at the same time, which would be feasible given sufficient finance being raised, but it may be wise for the company to focus on the expansion of one business segment at a time.

Green George cafés

A new business segment has been launched during the year, and further expansion of the brand is planned, which has been discussed above.

One particular risk with this business segment is the guarantee that the produce is chemical-free, and that it has been produced in a sustainable way. Champers Co will have to be extremely vigilant in monitoring the supply chain of ingredients. Any perceived breaches of these claims with associated bad publicity could totally destroy the integrity of the brand name.

Profit before tax has fallen by 13%

Despite an overall increase in revenue of 11%, profits have fallen by 13%. This may indicate poor cost control by the company, or it could be that some one-off expenses (for example, set up costs for the new Green George cafés) during this year have caused a distorting effect in the financial statements. In either case, the management of Champers Co should consider how costs are managed and monitored.

This is especially important given the increase in minimum wage which is going to come into force a few months after the year end. The regulation will have the effect of increasing operating expenses and thus causing a further reduction in profits.

Reduction in cash

The cash position is now only one third of the amount as at last year end. If this trend were to continue, Champers Co will run out of cash within the next financial year. The company has increased revenue during the year, so it seems that poor cash management techniques are being used for such a reduction in the cash balance to have occurred. Possibly the company is overtrading – attention is being focused on maximising revenue with little attention being paid to working capital and cash management.

The cash flow problem is a priority and should be addressed immediately if the company is to successfully expand in the way that management plans.

Cash based business

Restaurants in general, and especially fast food outlets such as the Quick-bite branches, tend to be cash based businesses. This can lead to a high risk of fraud, as cash can easily be misappropriated by staff when dealing with cash sales.

Internal structure

The company is already facing financial problems – namely the fall in profit and a reduction in cash. Yet there are ambitious plans for significant growth which will rely on funds being available. These problems will become worse as the expansion proceeds unless high calibre management and employees can be put into place as soon as possible. The company should review its internal structure and the skills and experience of key management personnel before proceeding with expansion plans. It seems that management is planning large scale expansion at a time when the company is facing regulatory pressures, which may not be an appropriate prioritisation of, and reaction to, the issues facing the company at this time.

Tutorial note

Credit will be awarded for other relevant business risks discussed in the answer to this requirement, for example, the competitive nature of the industry.

(c) (i) **Audit procedures for costs capitalised:**

- Obtain a breakdown of the total amount capitalised and agree the total to the general ledger.

- Agree a sample of costs to supporting documentation:
  - Site acquisition costs to purchase invoice and legal papers/ surveyor's report (if any),
  - Labour costs to approved payroll records, time sheets, etc,
  - Materials (such as cement, bricks, and fittings) to suppliers' invoice.

- Compare the amounts capitalised restaurant to restaurant and discuss as above.

- Review any relevant signed contracts e.g. from building contractors, electricians, architects, etc, and discuss any significant deviations from the amounts stated in the contract and the amount capitalised.

- Review the list of amounts capitalised to ensure that revenue items have not been capitalised by mistake (e.g. staff training costs, consumable items such as cutlery and plates – these are operating expenses which should not be capitalised).

- For any sites still in construction at the year end, obtain a stage of completion certificate from the building contractor.

- For the capitalised finance cost:
  - Recalculate the amount, agreeing that the capitalisation period ceases on completion of the restaurant.
  - The completion date should be verified by evidence from building inspectors of the date the building was signed off as complete.
  - Agree the rate of interest to the terms of finance.
  - Read the terms of finance to see that the finance was taken out specifically in relation to the construction of the restaurants.

Tutorial note

The procedures described above will provide evidence that finance costs have been capitalised in accordance with IAS 23 (revised) Borrowing costs, which states that finance costs should be capitalised only up until the point when the asset is ready for its intended use.

(ii) **Audit work for the advertising and marketing expense:**

- Discuss the nature of the advertising with the appropriate employee, e.g. brand manager, marketing director, in order to gain an understanding of the specific type of advertising campaigns conducted during the year e.g. TV or radio, magazine or newspaper advertising. This should help the auditor to form an expectation of the expense.

- Review business plans which outline the marketing strategy to be used to support the brand name (again to develop an understanding).

- Perform analytical review comparing current year expense to prior year and budget.

- Inspect advertising and marketing budgets and check for approval of the amount.

- Agree a sample of advertising costs to supporting documentation, e.g. invoices for newspaper or television advertising.

- Physically inspect the marketing documents e.g. newspaper advertisements, flyers.

- Review after-date invoices received in connection with advertising to ensure that the £150 million expense is complete and that all outstanding amounts have been accrued for.

- Inspect the dates when advertising took place to gain assurance that costs and benefits have been matched in the correct accounting period. Any costs incurred for which advertising has not yet taken place should be treated as a prepayment.

Examiner's comments

Requirement (a)

Most candidates attempted the first part of the requirement well, being able to identify various aspects that contribute towards business understanding, such as relevant laws and regulations, and industry factors such as suppliers and competitive forces. Fewer candidates recognised the need to understand the internal control environment, and fewer still mentioned the importance of understanding the relevant financial reporting framework and performance measures of the client. Only a very few candidates were aware of the relevance of ISA 315, on which the question requirement was based. In terms of procedures, most candidates recognised the importance of a meeting with management, but fewer commented on the need for analytical procedures, or a visit to the client to observe activities. In addition, the **procedures were usually not well explained**, for example, enquiries of management had to be inferred from 'I will have a chat with the directors', and inspection from comments 'read press cuttings' and 'get a copy of the organisational chart'.

Candidates tended **not** to gain the professional mark available for the clarity of their answer, because explanations were often confused, repetitive, or non-existent. Some candidates did not separate their answers into (ai) and (aii), which, as well as making the answer hard to mark, meant that professional marks were hard to award, as the answers were often confusing and would not have been clear enough for the audit team to follow.

Regarding the use of professional language, candidates need to bear in mind that professional marks are awarded partly for the quality of language used. This requirement asked for briefing notes to be used at a meeting with your audit team. So comments such as 'you need to Google the client', 'the client may be facing massive risks that need to get sorted', and 'ask the client whether they have any integrity' will detract from the quality of the answer provided.

Many answers seemed disproportionately long given the marks available. This usually meant that the answers to (b) and (c) were rushed and not detailed enough to score well.

Requirement (b) asked for an evaluation of business risks facing the company. The scenario contained a variety of business risks, and most candidates covered a range of these risks in their answer. There were some **common weaknesses** to the business risk evaluation, outlined below:

- Failure to use the financial information provided to identify risks – candidates should have used the figures provided to calculate profit margins, consider the declining level of cash, and to calculate the trend in revenue for each of the brands

- Focusing on financial statement risk, which was NOT a requirement of the question, for example, discussion of the impact on the financial statements of provisions, impairment, etc was not relevant to the requirement

- Trying to link every risk identified to a going concern risk – it is true that Champers had a number of serious business risks which could culminate in business failure, however, candidates should appreciate that there are many risks which business face prior to going out of business

- Some risks that amounted to general speculation, for example 'the risk of lorries from the busy road crashing into restaurants and killing people, leading to a loss of customers and revenue'. There were enough clear indications of risk in the scenario to make such speculation unnecessary.

Requirement (c) tended to produce the weakest answers to this question. (ci) asked for principal audit procedures relevant to the amount capitalised in relation to the construction of new restaurants. Few candidates could suggest anything other than 'check the relevant invoices' or 'check the amount was approved'. These comments are simply **not specific enough** to be given credit. Some candidates suggested procedures based on verifying the capitalised borrowing costs to finance agreements, and analytical procedures such as comparisons of the amounts capitalised in each restaurant.

(cii) asked for audit procedures in relation to the amount recognised as an expense for advertising of a brand. Most candidates here **failed to read the requirement**, and the scenario, both of which stated that the advertising costs had been **expensed**. Most candidates however, ignored this fact and discussed the merits of recognising the amount as an intangible asset, which as well as being completely irrelevant is also technically incorrect. Only the best answers provided any relevant audit procedures at all for this expense.

Candidates are reminded to restrict their comments to those which are specific to the question requirement; in this case ONLY principal audit procedures were required in both parts of (c). Therefore discussions of materiality, relevant financial reporting standards, and implications for the audit opinion were irrelevant. Again, most procedures, when provided, were too vague to be awarded credit, typical examples being 'check for the accuracy of the expense', or 'check correct classification of the expense'.

Finally, candidates should remember that written representations from management as a source of audit evidence should generally be reserved for situations where evidence is not available from other sources. It was disappointing to see that for both (ci) and (cii), management representations were commonly recommended as a principal audit procedure, usually along with 'check for board approval'.

		Marking scheme	Marks
(a)	(i)	**Identify and explain aspects of understanding business and environment** NB Professional marks to be awarded for format, use of introduction and conclusion, use of language that an audit junior could understand. Generally ½ mark for identification and 1 mark for explanation - External factors - Entity and accounting policies - Objectives, strategies and business risks - Performance measures - Internal control 1/2 mark ref ISA 315	2
		Maximum marks	6
	(ii)	**Recommend procedures to gain understanding** Generally 1 mark per procedure described: - Enquiry - Analytical procedure - Observation - Inspection	
		Maximum marks	4
(b)		**Business risk** Generally ½ mark for identification, 1 further mark for explanation, from ideas list. 1 mark to be given for each appropriate calculation, e.g. trends, materiality - Risk of damage to brand/bad publicity - Investment needed to prevent health and safety problems - Compliance risk re health and safety regulations – food preparation - Fall in revenue from Quick-bite business segment - Reduced demand for fast food/emphasis on healthy eating - Advertising ban could reduce revenue - Rapid expansion plans for City Sizzler chain – danger of overtrading - Potential lack of cash for the capital expenditure - Potential lack of cash for continued advertising - Green George chain – need to monitor supply chain - PBT fallen 13% – poor cost control? - Minimum wage legislation will increase costs significantly next year - Cash position worsened during year - Cash based business – risk of fraud - Internal structure may need addressing	
		Maximum marks	13

(c)	(i)	**Audit procedures on amounts capitalised**	
		Generally 1 mark per specific audit procedure.	
		Ideas list	
		- Agree sample of costs to invoice/tender documents	
		- Review capex budget and discuss variances actual v budget	
		- Agree interest rate of finance cost to terms of finance	
		- Agree period of capitalisation correct by reference to date of completion of restaurants	
		- Review list of items capitalised to ensure all capital in nature	
		Maximum marks	**5**
	(ii)	**Audit work for advertising expense**	
		Generally 1 mark per specific audit procedure.	
		Ideas list	
		- Agree sample of costs to invoices/reports from consultants	
		- Analytical review	
		- Discuss with relevant personnel/review of business plan	
		- Inspect budgets	
		- Physically inspect the advertising	
		- After-date invoice review	
		- Assess date advertising conducted	
		Maximum marks	**4**
		Total	**34**

2 DRAGON GROUP *Walk in the footsteps of a top tutor*

Key answer tips

This question based upon the principles of appointing an auditor.

Part (a) requires little more than common sense regarding why auditors may not wish to continue auditing a particular client.

Part (b) requires a basic knowledge fo the contents of a tender document. You then need to flesh this out by applying this knowledge to the specific information given. For ten marks you need to make at least 7 explained points.

Part (c) asks you to consider what professional issues you need to consider before accepting a new client. This could include any aspect of audit quality control, ethics or general practice management/administration.

Part (d) required some basic knowledge and then some common sense suggestions about the difficulty of cross-border audit.

The highlighted words are key phases that markers are looking for.

(a) **Reasons why a firm of auditors may decide not to seek re-election – any FOUR of the following:**

Disagreement with the client

The audit firm may have disagreed with the client for a number of reasons, for example, over accounting treatments used in the financial statements. A disagreement over a significant matter is likely to cause a breakdown in the professional relationship between auditor and client, meaning that the audit firm could lose faith in the competence of management. The auditor would be reluctant to seek re-election if the disagreement were not resolved.

Lack of integrity of client

The audit firm may feel that management is not acting with integrity, for example, the financial statements may be subject to creative accounting, or dubious business ethics decisions could be made by management, such as the exploitation of child labour. The auditor would be likely not to seek re-election (or to resign) in this case to avoid being associated with the client's poor decisions.

Fee level

The audit firm could be unable to demand a high enough audit fee from the client to cover the costs of the audit. In this situation the audit firm may choose not to offer itself for re-election, to avoid continuing with a loss making audit engagement, and consequently to use resources in a more commercially advantageous way.

Fee payments

The audit firm could have outstanding fees which may not be fully recovered due to a client's poor cash flow position. Or, the client could be slow paying, causing the audit firm to chase for payment and possibly affecting the relationship between the two businesses. In such cases the audit firm may make the commercial decision not to act for the client any longer.

Resources

The audit firm may find that it lacks the resources to continue to provide the audit service to a client. This could happen if the client company grows rapidly, financially or operationally, meaning that a larger audit team is necessary. The audit firm may simply lack the necessary skilled staff to expand the audit team.

Competence

The audit firm could feel that it is no longer competent to perform an audit service. This could happen for example if a client company diversified into a new and specialised business operation of which the audit firm had little or no experience. The audit firm would not be able to provide a high quality audit without building up or buying in the necessary knowledge and skills, and so may decide not to be considered for re-election.

Overseas expansion

A client could acquire one or several material overseas subsidiaries. If the audit firm does not have an associate office in the overseas location, the firm may feel that the risk and resources involved in relying on the work of other auditors is too great, and so decide not to act for the client any longer.

Independence

There are many ethical guidelines in relation to independence which must be adhered to by auditors, and in the event of a potential breach of the guidelines, the audit firm may decide not to seek re-election. For example, an audit firm may need to increase the audit fee if a client company grows in size. This could have the effect of increasing the fee received from the client above the allowed thresholds. As there would be no ethical safeguard strong enough to preserve the perception of independence, in this case the audit firm would not be able to continue to provide the audit service.

Tutorial note

Other examples may be used to explain why the issue of independence could cause an audit firm not to seek re-election, e.g. audit firm takes on a financial interest in the client, close personal relationships develop between the firm and the client.

Conflicts of interest

An audit firm may become involved in a situation where a conflict of interest arises between an existing audit client and another client of the firm. For example, an audit firm could take on a new audit client which is a competitor of an existing audit client. Although with the use of appropriate safeguards this situation could be successfully managed, the audit firm may decide that stepping down as auditor of the existing firm is the best course of action.

(b) **Matters to be included in tender document**

Brief outline of Unicorn & Co

This should include a short history of the firm, a description of its organisational structure, the different services offered by the firm (such as audit, tax, corporate finance, etc), and the locations in which the firm operates. The document should also state whether it is a member of any international audit firm network. The geographical locations in which Unicorn & Co operates will be important given the multi national structure of the Dragon Group.

Specialisms of the firm

Unicorn & Co should describe the areas in which the firm has particular experience of relevance to the Dragon Group. It would be advantageous to stress that the firm has an audit department dedicated to the audit of clients in the retail industry, as this emphasises the experience that the firm has relevant to the specific operations of the group.

Identification of the needs of the Dragon Group

The tender document should outline the requirements of the client, in this case, that each subsidiary is required to have an individual audit on its financial statements, and that the consolidated financial statements also need to be audited. Unicorn & Co may choose to include here a brief clarification of the purpose and legal requirements of an audit. The potential provision of non-audit services should be discussed, either here, or in a separate section of the tender document (see below).

Outline of the proposed audit approach

This is likely to be the most detailed part of the tender document. Here the firm will describe how the audit would be conducted, ensuring that the needs of the Dragon Group (as discussed above) have been met. Typically contained in this section would be a description of the audit methodology used by the firm, and an outline of the audit cycle including the key deliverables at each phase of work. For example:

- How the firm would intend to gain business understanding at group and subsidiary level.
- Methods used to assess risk and to plan the audits.

- Procedures used to assess the control environment and accounting systems.
- Techniques used to gather evidence, e.g. the use of audit software.

How the firm would structure the audit of the consolidation of the group financial statements and how they would liaise with subsidiary audit teams.

The firm should clarify its adherence to International Standards on Auditing, ethical guidelines and any other relevant laws and regulations operating in the various jurisdictions relevant to the Dragon Group. The various financial reporting frameworks used within the group should be clarified.

Quality control

Unicorn & Co should emphasise the importance of quality control and therefore should explain the procedures that are used within the firm to monitor the quality of the audit services provided. This should include a description of firm-wide quality control policies, and the procedures applied to individual audits. The firm may wish to clarify its adherence to International Standards on Quality Control.

Communication with management

The firm should outline the various reports and other communication that will be made to management as part of the audit process. The purpose and main content of the reports, and the timing of them, should be outlined. Unicorn & Co may provide some 'added value' bi-products of the audit process. For example, the business risks identified as part of the audit planning may be fed back to management in a written report.

Timing

Unicorn & Co should outline the timeframe that would be used. For example, the audits of the subsidiaries' financial statements should be conducted before the audit of the consolidated financial statements. The firm may wish to include an approximate date by which the group audit opinion would be completed, which should fit in, if possible, with the requirements of the group. If Unicorn & Co feel that the deadline requested by the client is unrealistic, a more appropriate deadline should be suggested, with the reasons for this clearly explained.

Key staff and resources

The document should name the key members of staff to be assigned to the audit, in particular the proposed engagement partner. In addition, the firm should clarify the approximate number of staff to be used in the audit team and the relevant experience of the key members of the audit team. If the firm considers that external specialists could be needed, then this should be explained in this section of the document.

Fees

The proposed fee for the audit of the group should be stated, and the calculation of the fee should be explained, i.e. broken down by grade of staff and hourly/daily rates per grade. In addition, invoicing and payment terms should be described, e.g. if the audit fee is payable in instalments, the stages when each instalment will fall due.

Extra services

Unicorn & Co should ensure that any non-audit services that it may be able to offer to the Dragon Group are described. For example, subject to ethical safeguards, the firm may be able to offer corporate finance services in relation to the stock exchange listing that the group is seeking, although the provision of this non-audit service would need to be carefully considered in relation to independence issues.

(c) **Evaluation of matters to be considered:**

Size and location of the group companies

The Dragon Group is a large multi-national group of companies. It is extremely important that Unicorn & Co assesses the availability of resources that can be allocated to the audit team. The assignment would comprise the audit of the financial statements of all 20 current subsidiaries, the audit of the parent company's and the group's financial statements. This is a significant engagement which will demand a great deal of time.

The location of half of the group's subsidiaries in other countries means that the overseas offices of Unicorn & Co would be called upon to perform some or all of the audit of those subsidiaries. In this case the resource base of the relevant overseas offices should be considered to ensure there is enough staff with appropriate skills and experience available to perform the necessary audit work.

Unicorn & Co must consider if they have offices in all of the countries in which the Dragon Group has a subsidiary.

Depending on the materiality of the overseas subsidiaries to the group financial statements, it is likely that some overseas visits would be required to evaluate the work of the overseas audit teams. Unicorn & Co should consider who will conduct the visits (presumably a senior member of the audit team), and whether that person has the necessary skills and experience in evaluating the work of overseas audit teams.

Planned expansion of the group

In light of the comments above, Unicorn & Co should consider that the planned further significant expansion of the group will mean more audit staff will be needed in future years, and if any subsidiaries are acquired in other countries, the audit is likely to be performed by overseas offices. The firm should therefore consider not only its current resource base in the local and overseas offices, but whether additional staff will be available in the future if the group's expansion goes ahead as planned.

Relevant skills and experience

Unicorn & Co has an audit department specialising in the audit of retail companies, so it should not be a problem to find audit staff with relevant experience in this country.

On consolidation, the financial statements of the subsidiaries will be restated in line with group accounting policies and financial reporting framework, and will also be retranslated into local presentational currency. All of this work will be performed by the management of the Dragon Group. Unicorn & Co must evaluate the availability of staff experienced in the audit of a consolidation including foreign subsidiaries.

Timing

It is important to consider the timeframe when conducting a group audit. The audit of each subsidiary's financial statements should be carried out prior to the audit of the consolidated financial statements. Unicorn & Co should consider the expectation of the Dragon Group in relation to the reporting deadline, and ensure that enough time is allowed for the completion of all audits. The deadline proposed by management of 31 December is only three months after the year end, which may be unrealistic given the size of the group and the multi-national location of the subsidiaries. The first year auditing a new client is likely to take longer, as the audit team will need to familiarise themselves with the business, the accounting systems and controls, etc.

Mermaid Co – prior year qualification

If Unicorn & Co accepts the engagement, the firm will take on the audit of Mermaid Co, whose financial statements in the prior year were in breach of financial reporting standards. This adds an element of risk to the engagement. Unicorn & Co should gather as much information as possible about the contingent liability, and the reason why the management of Mermaid Co did not amend the financial statements last year end. This could hint at a lack of integrity on the part of the management of the company.

The firm should also consider whether this matter could be significant to the consolidated financial statements, by assessing the materiality of the contingent liability at group level.

Further discussions should be held with the management of the Dragon Group in order to understand their thoughts on the contingency and whether it should be disclosed in the individual financial statements of Mermaid Co, and at group level. Contacting the incumbent auditors (after seeking relevant permission from the Dragon Group) would also be an important procedure to gather information about the qualification.

Minotaur Co – different business activity

The acquisition of Minotaur Co represents a new business activity for the group. The retail business audit department may not currently have much, if any, experience of auditing a distribution company. This should be easily overcome, either by bringing in staff from a different department more experienced in clients with distribution operations, or by ensuring adequate training for staff in the retail business audit department.

Highly regulated/reliance on financial statements and audit report

The Group is listed on several stock exchanges, and is therefore subject to a high degree of regulation. This adds an element of risk to the engagement, as the management will be under pressure to publish favourable results. This risk is increased by the fact that a new listing is being sought, meaning that the financial statements and audit report of the group will be subject to close scrutiny by the stock exchange regulators.

There may be extra work required by the auditors due to the listings, for example, the group may have to prepare reconciliations of financial data, or additional narrative reports on which the auditors have to express an opinion under the rulings of the stock exchange. The firm must consider the availability of staff skilled in regulatory and reporting listing rules to perform such work.

Previous auditors of Dragon Group

Unicorn & Co should consider the reason why the previous audit firm is not seeking re-appointment, and whether the reason would impact on their acceptance decision. After seeking permission from the Dragon Group, contact should be made with the previous auditors to obtain confirmation of the reason for them vacating office (amongst other matters).

In conclusion, this is a large scale, multi-national group, which carries a fairly high level of risk. Unicorn & Co must be extremely careful to only commit to the group audit if it has the necessary resources, can manage the client's expectation in relation to the reporting deadline, is convinced of the integrity of management, and is confident to take on a potentially high profile client.

Tutorial note

Credit will be awarded in this requirement for discussion of ethical matters which would be considered prior to accepting the appointment as auditor of the Dragon Group. However, as the scenario does not contain any reference to specific ethical matters, marks will be limited to a maximum of 2 for a general discussion of ethical matters on acceptance.

(d) (i) **Definition:** A transnational audit means an audit of financial statements which are or may be relied upon outside the audited entity's home jurisdiction for the purpose of significant lending, investment or regulatory decisions.

Relevance: The Dragon Group is listed on the stock exchange of several countries, (and is planning to raise more finance by a further listing). This means that the group is subject to the regulations of all stock exchanges on which it is listed, and so is bound by listing rules outside of its home jurisdiction. The group also contains many foreign subsidiaries, meaning that it operates in a global business and financial environment.

(ii) **Transnational audit and audit risk** – any TWO of the following:

Application of auditing standards

Although many countries of the world have adopted International Standards on Auditing (ISAs), not all have done so, choosing instead to use locally developed auditing regulations. In addition, some countries use modified versions of ISAs. This means that in a transnational audit, some components of the group financial statements will have been audited using a different auditing framework, resulting in inconsistent audit processes within the group, and potentially reducing the quality of the audit as a whole.

Regulation and oversight of auditors

Similar to the previous comments on the use of ISAs, across the world there are many different ways in which the activities of auditors are regulated and monitored. In some countries the audit profession is self-regulatory, whereas in other countries a more legislative approach is used. This also can impact on the quality of audit work in a transnational situation.

Financial reporting framework

Some countries use International Financial Reporting Standards, whereas some use locally developed accounting standards. Within a transnational group it is likely that adjustments, reconciliations or restatements may be required in order to comply with the requirements of the jurisdictions relevant to the group financial statements (i.e. the jurisdiction of the parent company in most cases). Such reconciliations can be complex and require a high level of technical expertise of the preparer and the auditor.

Corporate governance requirements and consequent control risk

In some countries there are very prescriptive corporate governance requirements, which the auditor must consider as part of the audit process. In this case the auditor may need to carry out extra work over and above local requirements in order to ensure group wide compliance with the requirements of the jurisdictions relevant to the financial statements. However, in some countries there is very little corporate governance regulation at all and controls are likely to be weaker than in other components of the group. Control risk is therefore likely to differ between the various subsidiaries making up the group.

Examiner's comments

Requirement (a) was a short factual requirement, not related to the detail of the question scenario, which asked candidates to explain four reasons why a firm of auditors may decide not to seek re-election as auditor. There were two main problems with answers to this requirement. Firstly, too few candidates actually provided an **explanation of the reasons** they gave. For example, an answer stated that the auditor had a disagreement with the client over something in the financial statements. While this is indeed a reason why the auditor may chose not to seek re-election, it is not an explanation, which would entail going on to say that the disagreement had caused a breakdown in the working relationship between the auditor and client, and that the auditor had lost faith in the competence and /or integrity of management.

Secondly, the requirement asked for **FOUR** reasons. It is a waste of time and effort to provide more than the required number of reasons.

The **second requirement** focussed on the audit tendering process, and asked for matters to be included in a tender document to be presented to the Dragon Group. This requirement seemed to polarise candidates. Those candidates who tailored their answer to the question scenario tended to do well, with a significant proportion achieving close to the maximum marks available. However, candidates who provided a list of points to be included in ANY tender, regardless of the information provided about the prospective client, and about your audit firm, scored inadequately. In other words, it is important to **apply knowledge** to score well, as is true for any scenario-based question.

Sound answers to (b) appreciated that the point of the tender document is to sell your audit firm's services to the client, and recommended points to include such as the global positioning of both audit firm and prospective client, the specialism of the audit firm in retail, and the firm's ability to potentially provide services relating to the expansion plans of the group, such as due diligence.

Weak answers simply stated vague comments: 'we should discuss fees', 'we should set a deadline,' etc. Some answers confused a tender document with an engagement letter, and included points more suited to that document, such as a statement of responsibilities or a legal disclaimer.

Inadequate answers to (b) were those that seemed to confuse the requirements with those of (c). Candidates are reminded that it is important to **read ALL of the requirements** of a question before beginning their answer, to avoid such confusion. Examples of statements commonly seen in answers to (b) which are more relevant to (c) are:

- 'are we competent to audit the group'
- 'can we audit the goodwill and foreign exchange transactions which are complex'

- 'will any of our audit staff want to go abroad to work'
- 'do any of our partners hold shares in Dragon Group'.

These comments definitely do not belong in a tender document, which should highlight the audit firm's capabilities to service the prospective client, rather than question the firm's competence or ability to take on the assignment. Such comments indicate a failure to read and understand the question requirement, as well as a lack of commercial awareness.

Requirement (c) asked candidates to evaluate the matters that should be considered before accepting the audit engagement. Answers here were weak, despite this being a **regularly examined syllabus area**. Most answers were not tailored to the question, and just provided a list of questions or actions, such as 'get permission to contact previous auditor', or 'check the integrity of management', and 'do we have the skill to audit foreign currencies'.

Providing a list of such comments will not generate enough marks to pass the question requirement. Better answers discussed, amongst other points:

- the risk posed by the numerous stock exchange listings of the potential client, and whether the audit fee would be enough to compensate for that risk
- the practical difficulties entailed in co-ordinating an audit of more than 20 companies across many different countries
- the tight deadline imposed by the potential client, especially in light of this being a first year audit, and the learning curve that the audit firm would need to go through.

Some candidates appeared to think that the audit would be too much trouble – a sizeable number of scripts contained comments such as 'auditing a company far from our main office would be tedious and inconvenient'. I would suggest that most audit firms, on being successful in a tender for an audit as significant as this, would consider the inconvenience worthwhile.

Requirement (c) had 2 professional marks associated, awarded for the clarity and presentation of the evaluation provided. It was not necessary to present the answer in a particular format, the presentation mark was awarded to candidates who used headings and a logical structure. An evaluation should contain prioritisation, and a conclusion, but very few candidates suggested that some of the matters they had considered were more important than others, and even fewer concluded as to whether the firm should accept the appointment as group auditor.

Requirement (d) was the worst answered on the paper. Clearly, very few candidates had studied the issue of transnational audits, and answers displayed a lack of knowledge. (di) asked for a definition of transnational audit, and an explanation as to why the term was applicable to the Dragon Group audit. Only a small minority of candidates could provide the correct definition, the rest guessing from the scenario that it was 'an audit covering many countries', or 'an audit performed by several audit firms from different countries', neither of which is true. (dii) asked for two features of a transnational audit that contribute to a high level of audit risk. Answers again appeared to be based mainly on guesswork, with common suggestions being 'language difficulties' and 'communication barriers'. However, some candidates could identify variations in auditing standards and financial reporting frameworks as issues contributing to high risk, but these points were rarely developed to their full potential.

		Marking scheme	
			Marks
(a)		**Identify and explain using examples why an audit firm may not seek re-election**	
		Generally ½ mark for identification and 1 mark for explanation/example, any FOUR:	
		- Disagreement	
		- Lack of integrity	
		- Fee level	
		- Late payment of fees	
		- Resources	
		- Overseas expansion	
		- Competence	
		- Independence	
		- Conflict of interest	
		Maximum marks	**6**
(b)		**Contents of tender document**	
		Up to 1½ marks per matter described:	
		- Outline of firm	
		- Specialisms	
		- Audit requirement of Dragon Group	
		- Outline audit approach (max 3 marks if detailed)	
		- QC	
		- Communication with management	
		- Timing	
		- Key staff/resources	
		- Fees	
		- Extra services	
		Maximum marks	**10**
(c)		**Matters to consider re. acceptance**	
		Professional marks to be awarded for clarity of evaluation, use of headings and conclusion based on points discussed	**2**
		Generally ½ mark for identification, 1 further mark for explanation, from ideas list:	
		- Large and expanding group – availability of staff now and in the future	
		- Use of overseas offices	
		- Visits to overseas audit teams	
		- Skills/experience in retail/foreign subsidiaries consolidation	
		- Timing – tight deadline	
		- Mermaid Co – implication of prior year qualification	
		- Minotaur Co – implication of different business activity	
		- Highly regulated – risk/additional reporting requirements	
		- Reason for previous auditors leaving office	
		Maximum marks	**7**
(d)	**(i)**	**Define transnational audit and relevance to Dragon Group**	
		1 mark for definition	
		2 marks for relevance to Dragon Group	
		Maximum marks	**3**
	(ii)	**Audit risk factors in a transnational audit**	
		2 marks per point explained	
		- Auditing standards	
		- Regulation of auditors	
		- Financial reporting standards	
		- Corporate governance/control risk	
		Maximum marks	**4**
		Total	**32**

3   BLUEBELL CO *Walk in the footsteps of a top tutor*

Key answer tips

The main element of the question focuses on financial statement risk, i.e. the risk that the accounts contain errors, and the procedures that would be employed to gather evidence on the final audit. This question marks a significant step up in the complexity of financial reporting matters covered. Therefore knowledge retained from P2 is vital. In this case the question focuses on share options and deferred tax. That said, there are many simple areas of this question, such as: revenue recognition, provision and impairments.

For part (a) students must focus their discussion on issues referred to in the scenario. General discussion of problems facing the hotel industry will not score.

For part (b) students must focus on the *specific* wording of the question, i.e. *measuring* the share based expense and *recoverability* of the deferred tax asset. Discussions of authorisation of the share options and the calculation of deferred tax are irrelevant.

Part (c) requires little more than business common sense. The question asks for some social and environmental KPIs. These must be *measurable*, i.e. targets in $ or %. Simply stating "environmentally friendly" is not a KPI. Evidence should (preferably) be written and external.

Part (c) has 2 professional marks attached. Pay close attention to format and presentation.

The highlighted words are key phases that markers are looking for.

(a)   **Financial Statement Risks**

Revenue Recognition

Bluebell Co has an accounting policy of recognising revenue when a room is occupied. The deposits (and possibly sometimes even full payment) are received when the room is booked. Revenue will be overstated if it is recognised too early. On receipt of a deposit prior to the occupation of the room, the revenue should be deferred and disclosed as a liability, per IAS 18 *Revenue*. Liabilities may therefore be understated and profit overstated.

Further indication of possible overstatement of revenue is shown by Bluebell Co's 24.8% increase in revenue compared to industry average of only 20%.

Share-based payment

The expense could be overstated if the assumption regarding all of the shares vesting is incorrect. The expense should be calculated by considering whether performance conditions attached to the share options will be met. It is unlikely that every single employee granted an option will meet the required performance criteria and therefore a more realistic, lower estimate should be made of the expense. The expense should be adjusted each year end to account for staff turnover. If the expense is overstated due to an incorrect assumption, then the corresponding credit to equity is also overstated.

In addition, the calculation of the total cost of the share-based payment is complex, and if any of the components of the calculation are incorrect, then the expense will be over or understated. For example, the fair value used to calculate the expense should be the fair value of the granted share options calculated at the grant date, the use of fair value at any other date is incorrect. The model used to calculate fair value (e.g. the Black-Scholes Model) must comply with IFRS 2 *Share-based Payment*.

It is also important for the measurement of the expense that it has been calculated based on the share options being granted mid way through the accounting period.

Provisions

The provisions for repairing flood damage should only be recognised if Bluebell Co has an obligation to perform the repairs at the year end. There is unlikely to be any legal or constructive obligation attached to this situation so a provision should not have been recognised in this accounting period. Operating expenses (and property, plant and equipment if the portion of the provision relating to refurbishment has been capitalised) and liabilities are therefore overstated.

Disclosure should be made in a note to the financial statements for any capital commitment entered into before the year end.

In addition, it is important to consider that the buildings are covered by an insurance policy, which will pay out for repair and refurbishment costs to the assets. The fact that Bluebell Co has recognised a repair expense of $100 million indicates that either the buildings were not covered by adequate insurance (a business risk), or that the accounting implication of the reimbursement has been ignored.

Impairment of flood damaged properties

The net book value of the properties will be overstated if the carrying value has not been fully written down to recoverable amount. It is not stated whether or not the damaged properties have been tested for impairment, but it would seem likely that given the amount of damage caused by flooding, that some impairment loss should have been recognised this year.

Potential understatement of operating expenses

A comparison of operating expenses for the two years reveals an unusual trend. The operating expenses for 2008 include two new items – the share-based payment expense of $138 million, and the repairs of $100 million. Once these have been eliminated to enable a meaningful comparison to the previous year, the 2008 operating expenses is $597 million ($835 − 138 − 100). This is a reduction in operating expenses compared to the prior year of $93 million i.e. 13.5% (93/690 × 100).

Given that revenue has increased by 24·8% (as discussed above), it would appear likely that operating expenses for the current year are understated.

Property disposals

It is correct that profit on asset disposals should be recognised within other operating income, or alternatively, if material, be disclosed separately on the face of the statement of comprehensive income. However, it appears that the substance of this transaction is more a financing arrangement than a genuine sale. Bluebell Co has retained operational control of the assets and is still exposed to the risk and the reward associated with the properties, as shown by the financial return received each year based on the performance of the hotels. In addition, the option to repurchase in 15 years time indicates that at that time Bluebell Co will be repaying the long term finance secured on the properties 'sold'.

Therefore the assets should remain on the statement of financial position, with the proceeds received on the 'sale' recognised as a liability. There should be no profit recorded on the transaction. Currently other operating income is overstated by the 'profit' of $125 million. Property plant and equipment are understated by the value of the properties 'sold', and liabilities understated by the amount of finance raised.

In addition, Bluebell Co will need to continue to depreciate the properties. Operating expenses are currently understated due to the lack of depreciation on the disposed properties since the date of disposal.

Finally, as the 'sale' is in reality a finance arrangement, it is likely that Bluebell Co should accrue finance charges. The total finance charge associated with the sale and repurchase arrangement should be allocated over the period of the finance. It is likely that finance charges are understated due to the lack of inclusion of finance cost in relation to the sale and repurchase arrangement.

Property revaluations

Property, plant and equipment is a highly material figure, representing 44% of total assets (2007 – 51%). The revaluation during the year introduces financial statement risk to the carrying value of the assets given the subjective nature of establishing the fair value of properties. As Bluebell Co is trying to raise finance in order to improve liquidity, there is a definite incentive for overvaluation of the properties, as this will strengthen the statement of financial position and make Bluebell Co more attractive to potential providers of finance.

Under IAS 12 *Income Taxes*, a deferred tax provision must be recognised on the revaluation of a property, with the debit recorded within equity. If the properties have been overvalued in the financial statements then the corresponding deferred tax liability and equity entry will be similarly misstated.

Tutorial note

Note 6 shows a deferred tax entry of $88 million charged to equity during the year, representing 35.2% of the $250 million revaluation gain recognised (note 4). Therefore the financial statement risk is not that the deferred tax has not been recognised, but that its value will be incorrect if the revaluation itself is misstated.

Deferred tax asset

IAS 12 states that a deferred tax asset can only be recognised where the recoverability of the asset can be demonstrated. Unutilised tax losses can be carried forward for offset against future taxable profits, so Bluebell Co must demonstrate using budgets and forecasts, that future tax profits will be available for the losses to be fully utilised. If this cannot be demonstrated then the deferred tax asset recognised should be restricted to the level of future profits that can be measured with reasonable certainty.

The financial statements currently show a profit before tax of $145 million, indicating healthy performance. However, when the profit on asset disposal is removed from profit before tax, if adjustments are necessary in respect of the impaired properties (as discussed above), and if finance costs and depreciation charges need to be expensed in respect of the sale and repurchase agreement, then it could be that

Bluebell Co's profitability has actually substantially decreased from last year, and is likely to be a loss.

Tutorial note

credit will be awarded where candidates calculate a new profit before tax figure based on the adjustments suggested in their answer.

Given this detrimental underlying trend in profitability, and given the past losses generated by the company, it could be difficult to demonstrate that the tax losses are recoverable against future profits. If this is the case then the deferred tax asset is overstated.

Going concern

Given poor liquidity, and an underlying trend of falling profits, the company could face going concern problems. Disclosure regarding the availability of long-term finance may be necessary for the financial statements to show a true and fair view.

(b) (i) **Principal audit procedures – measurement of share-based payment expense**

– Obtain management calculation of the expense and agree the following from the calculation to the contractual terms of the scheme:

– Number of employees and executives granted options

– Number of options granted per employee

– The official grant date of the share options

Vesting period for the scheme

– Required performance conditions attached to the options.

– Recalculate the expense and check that the fair value has been correctly spread over the stated vesting period.

– Agree fair value of share options to specialist's report and calculation, and evaluate whether the specialist report is a reliable source of evidence.

– Agree that the fair value calculated is at the grant date.

Tutorial note

A specialist such as a chartered financial analyst would commonly be used to calculate the fair value of non-traded share options at the grant date, using models such as the Black-Scholes Model

– Obtain and review a forecast of staffing levels or employee turnover rates for the duration of the vesting period, and scrutinise the assumptions used to predict level of staff turnover.

– Discuss previous levels of staff turnover with a representative of the human resources department and query why 0% staff turnover has been predicted for the next three years.

– Check the sensitivity of the calculations to a change in the assumptions used in the valuation, focusing on the assumption of 0% staff turnover.

– Obtain written representation from management confirming that the assumptions used in measuring the expense are reasonable.

Tutorial note

A high degree of scepticism must be used by the auditor when conducting the final three procedures due to the management assumption of 0% staff turnover during the vesting period.

(ii) **Principal audit procedures – recoverability of deferred tax asset**

– Obtain a copy of Bluebell Co's current tax computation and deferred tax calculations and agree figures to any relevant tax correspondence and/or underlying accounting records.

– Develop an independent expectation of the estimate to corroborate the reasonableness of management's estimate.

– Obtain forecasts of profitability and agree that there is sufficient forecast taxable profit available for the losses to be offset against. Evaluate the assumptions used in the forecast against business understanding. In particular consider assumptions regarding the growth rate of taxable profit in light of the underlying detrimental trend in profit before tax.

– Assess the time period it will take to generate sufficient profits to utilise the tax losses. If it is going to take a number of years to generate such profits, it may be that the recognition of the asset should be restricted.

– Using tax correspondence, verify that there is no restriction on the ability of Bluebell Co to carry the losses forward and to use the losses against future taxable profits.

Tutorial note

In many tax jurisdictions losses can only be carried forward to be utilised against profits generated from the same trade. Although in the scenario there is no evidence of such a change in trade, or indeed any kind of restriction on the use of losses, it is still a valid audit procedure to verify that this is the case.

(c) **Briefing notes Guidance on the establishment of social and environmental Key Performance Indicators (KPIs) within Bluebell Co For discussion with Daisy Rosepetal, internal auditor of Bluebell Co**

Introduction

Many companies use social and environmental KPIs as a means of establishing performance targets and measuring actual results against the performance target set. Social KPIs involve performance relating to employees, customers, and the wider community. Environmental KPIs are focussed on the environmental impact of the company's activities.

The following table recommends some KPIs and suggests the evidence that should be available in relation to each KPI:

KPI	Nature of evidence
Social – employees	
% female employees, % ethnic minority employees.	Personnel files, starters and leavers documentation.
Staff absentee rates – number of days of absenteeism compared to total labour days per year.	Payroll records, medical certificates, supporting sick leave.
Employee satisfaction/engagement index.	Internal audit could prepare a questionnaire/survey of Bluebell Co's staff. Alternatively, summaries of staff appraisal records could provide evidence.
Monetary value of staff training and development.	Cash book to verify amount. Also documents authorising the training and outlining the need for the training.
Staff turnover	Personnel files, leavers' documentation from payroll records, exit interview records.
Social – customers	
Customer satisfaction rates - % satisfaction with service provided, cleanliness of room, quality of food, etc.	Surveys or questionnaires completed by customers after staying at a hotel or using a room for an event.
Level of repeat bookings – repeat bookings as % of total bookings.	Customer account details from the sales system would indicate multiple bookings. Bluebell Co may operate a loyalty reward scheme to attract multiple bookings – this would provide detailed evidence.
Level of complaints – number of customers who have demanded refunds or have made a formal written complaint.	Management log book of complaints received. Sales system could provide evidence of refunds via credit notes issued.

Number of customers reporting accidents while on Bluebell Co premises (this point could also be made in relation to staff).	Accident log book describing the nature of the injury, seriousness, whether emergency services called.

Social – wider community

Monetary value of any donations made to local or other charities, could be expressed as % profit.	Cash book will show value of any donations. Board minutes should contain evidence of authorisation.
Number of times Bluebell Co has made its hotels available for use free of charge for local community or charity events.	Register of events – Bluebell Co will have some kind of diary or timetable indicating date and reason for use of facilities. Approval by manager of free use.

Environmental

% change in water use, electricity use, etc compared to prior year.	Comparison of utilities costs using suppliers bills received. Review of actual to budgeted consumption of water, electricity, etc.
Monetary amount of investment in or purchase of environmentally friendly items, e.g. energy efficient light bulbs, recycled paper, water efficient dishwashers.	List of preferred suppliers and products. Observation by internal auditor or products used in the hotels.
Quantification of carbon footprint, and % change from to prior years.	Review energy supplier contracts for evidence that energy used is from renewable source. Board authorisation of any payments made for carbon offsetting.
% waste recycled compared to non-recycled.	Cash book should show amounts invested in recycling facilities at each hotel. Observation of the use of recycling facilities.

Conclusion

The specific KPIs set by Bluebell Co should reflect the priorities of the company. There is an extremely wide range of measures that could be used – **the important thing is to make each measure quantifiable** and to ensure that evidence will be readily available to support the stated KPI. In the absence of this, the KPIs may lack credibility if disclosed in the future as part of Bluebell Co's annual report or in any publicly available information.

Tutorial note

The answer states more than the required number of KPIs to illustrate the wide variety of points that could have been made in answering the question. As indicated in the conclusion to the briefing notes, there are many alternative KPIs which could have been suggested for use by Bluebell Co. Credit will be awarded for any suitable KPI and associated evidence.

Examiner's comments

Requirement (a) asked the candidate to 'identify and explain financial statement risks to be addressed when planning the final audit'. This requirement should not have been a surprise, as financial statement risk had appeared in the previous exam, and a recent examiner's article had discussed how financial reporting issues impacted on the auditor at the planning stage of the audit. However, some common failings in answers to requirement (a) are noted below:

- Describing a financial reporting issue but then failing to develop the point to provide a financial statement risk. For example, most candidates appreciated that the property sale was some kind of financing arrangement. However, too few candidates discussed the risk of non-current assets being understated due to the properties being incorrectly removed from the statement of financial position, or the risk of finance charges being understated.

- Clutching at straws – many candidates seemed not to know what the exact financial statement risk was, and so put that the risk was 'over or understatement' of a balance.

- Vague answers – many candidates simply explained a risk as 'risk of incorrect accounting treatment' or 'risk that accounting standard not followed'. These answers unfortunately highlight to markers a lack of knowledge rather than an application of knowledge.

- A propensity for asking questions was apparent in many scripts. For example a risk explained by asking 'is the accounting treatment for the provision correct?' or 'has the property been valued correctly?' These are not financial statement risks and are definitely not explanations of such risks.

- Failure to think about the figures provided. Very few candidates looked at the trends shown by the draft financial statements. For example; only a small minority recognised that after removing the share-based payment and property repair expenses, the company's underlying operating expenses had decreased by 13.5%, whereas revenue had increased by 24.8%. This should have prompted a discussion that either revenue was overstated, expenses understated, or both.

- Lack of basic accounting knowledge. One of the more worrying features of many answers to Q1(a) was a display of inadequate basic accounting knowledge. For example, many claimed that 'the repairs should be a provision not an expense' or that 'the revaluation should be a reserve, not on the balance sheet'.

Requirement (b) asked candidates to describe principal audit procedures in respect of specific assertions relevant to the share- based payment expense, and deferred tax asset. Unfortunately, candidates still fail to answer the specific requirement. Requirement (bi) focussed on the measurement of the expense, (bii) on the recoverability of the asset. The majority of candidates ignored these assertions and instead provided procedures irrelevant to the requirement, for example, on the calculation of tax rather than the likelihood of it providing a future benefit to the company.

The second problem was that many so-called procedures provided were not actually audit procedures at all, but a vague hint as to what the auditor might do. For example, 'check calculation of share -based payment expense' – yes, the auditor would need to do this, but how? The 'how' is the audit procedure. Other examples of inadequate answers include 'ensure appropriate disclosure' and 'check last year's figure' – both are too vague and not relevant to the assertions required.

Finally, many candidates seemed not to understand the nature of the items in question. Some seemed to think that the deferred tax asset was a tangible asset, with many claims that it should be 'physically verified to ensure existence', and for the share- based payment, the auditor should 'count the share certificates' even though the question is about share options rather then shares. Candidates must take a little time to stop and think about whether their answer is logical before putting pen to paper.

Requirement (c) tended to be either extremely well answered, or extremely inadequately answered. Inadequate answers usually attempted to recommend KPIs relevant to hotels, but they usually described the policies that a company should have in place rather than the KPI that would measure the success of such a policy. For example, there were many calls for the company to be environmentally friendly, for example by recycling waste. This is a policy. A relevant KPI might be to increase the proportion of waste recycled by 30% in the next 12 months.

A significant minority of candidates failed to give even one KPI, and many provided no specific sources of evidence at all. For example, a candidate may have identified a staff turnover rate as a KPI, which is fine, but then went on to say that evidence would be to 'check with human resources'. This is much too vague to gain credit. Some answers seemed a little far fetched – for example, a potential KPI being the 'courtesy displayed to royal guests in the hotel', and some answers irrelevant to a hotel chain – a potential KPI being 'deaths due to toxic gasses escaping from the factory'. Candidates should remember that most of the marks awarded in the paper are for application skills. Such comments indicate that no application to the scenario provided has been performed.

Marking scheme		Marks
(a)	**Financial Statement Risks** Generally ½ mark each risk/matter identified. ½ mark for reference to correct IFRS / IAS – maximum 2 marks. Maximum 2 marks for materiality calculations. - Share-based payment (3 marks) IFRS 2 - Revenue recognition (2 marks + 1 mark for trend/calc) *IAS 18* - Provision for repairs (2 marks) *IAS 37* - Insurance reimbursement (1 mark) - Understatement of operating expenses (2 marks) - Impairment of properties (1 mark) *IAS 36* - Property disposals (3½ marks) - Property revaluation (1½ marks) *IAS 16* - Deferred tax on property revaluation (11/2 marks) IAS 12 - Deferred tax asset (2 marks + 1 mark for recalculating) *IAS 12* - Going concern (1 mark)	
	Maximum marks	14
(b)	**(i) Audit Procedures – share options** Generally 1 mark per procedure - Agree components of calculation to scheme documentation (½ mark per item agreed, max 2) - Recalculate + check vesting period - Agreement of grant date, fair values, etc to specialist report - Review of forecast staffing levels - Management representation - Discussion with HR re assumptions used	
	Maximum marks	6
	(ii) Audit Procedures – deferred tax Generally 1 mark per procedure - Obtain client tax comp + deferred tax schedules, recalculate - Form independent estimate of amount - Profitability forecasts – assumptions - Profitability forecast – time period for losses to be utilised - Tax authority agreement on c/f of losses	
	Maximum marks	4

(c)	Social and environmental KPIs	
	Up to 2 professional marks for format, logical structure and use of language appropriate to internal auditor i.e. free from jargon, all comments clearly explained. Tabular format not required. **Specifically: ½ heading, ½ introduction, 1 for whether KPIs are specific to hotels, easy to quantify, sensible etc.**	
	Generally ½ mark per KPI, ½ mark per evidence point. Can increase to 1 mark (for either) if the point is very specific to a hotel business.	
	Ideas list	
	Employees:	
	- Training spend	
	- Absenteeism rates	
	- Employee engagement index	
	Customers	
	- Customer satisfaction rate	
	- Number of complaints	
	- Number of accidents	
	- Repeat business rates	
	Community	
	- Charitable donations	
	- Free use of hotel facilities	
	Environment	
	- Waste recycling	
	- Energy efficient items purchased	
	- Carbon footprint	
	Maximum marks	**10**
	Total	**34**

4 CROCUS CO *Walk in the footsteps of a top tutor*

Key answer tips

Prior to attempting this question students may find it helpful to read the examiner's article "Forensic Auditing" from September 2008 as the question followed its publication.

Firstly, it is important to note that the question contains 3 professional marks. Once again students must take care to present their work accordingly to secure these valuable marks. The question asks you to respond directly to a client who suspects a fraud at her work place. You are asked to discuss the objectives of an investigation and the steps involved. The objectives require little more than repetition of basic knowledge. The steps involved require the student to apply themselves more to the scenario by tailoring their answer to the style of fraud being committed. It should be noted that part b (ii) requires *examples of procedures as a sub-element* to the question. Simply discussing tests you would perform would not obtain a good mark. The question requires you to consider the whole investigation from the planning stage all the way through to the ultimate court case.

The highlighted words are key phases that markers are looking for.

(a) (i) Forensic accounting utilises accounting, auditing, and investigative skills to conduct an examination into a company's financial statements. The aim of forensic accounting is to provide an accounting analysis that is potentially suitable for use in court. Forensic accounting is an umbrella term encompassing both forensic investigations and forensic audits. It includes the audit of financial information to prove or disprove a fraud, the interview process used during an investigation, and the act of serving as an expert witness.

Tutorial note

Forensic accounting can be used in a very wide range of situations, e.g. settling monetary disputes in relation to a business closure, marriage break up, insurance claim, etc. Credit will be awarded for any reasonable examples provided

---

(ii)   A forensic investigation is a process whereby a forensic accountant carries out procedures to gather evidence, which could ultimately be used in legal proceedings or to settle disputes. This could include, for example an investigation into money laundering. A forensic investigation involves many stages (similar to an audit), including planning, evidence gathering, quality control reviews, and finally results in the production of a report.

(iii)   Forensic auditing is the specific use of audit procedures within a forensic investigation to find facts and gather evidence, usually focused on the quantification of a financial loss. This could include, for example, the use of analytical procedures, and substantive procedures to determine the amount of an insurance claim.

(h)   **Report to Gita Thrales**

Subject: Forensic investigation into alleged payroll fraud

Introduction

This report has been requested in order to outline and explain the operation of a forensic investigation into an alleged payroll fraud. The report will outline the steps taken in such an investigation and provide an explanation of the expected output of the work performed.

Objectives of a forensic investigation

The first objective is to decide if a deliberate fraud with the intention of stealing cash from the company has actually taken place. There is a possibility that the employees made redundant have remained on the payroll records by error rather than fraud. The investigation should uncover whether the situation has arisen through mistake or through deliberate criminal action.

Secondly, the investigation will aim to discover the perpetrator(s) of the fraud, and ultimately to assist in their prosecution. The investigation will gather evidence, which may include an interview with the suspected fraudster, which can then be used in criminal procedures against the individual(s) concerned. In this case there is an individual suspected of involvement in the alleged fraud. It will be an important part of the investigation to discover if there were other people involved, as frauds often involve collusion between several individuals.

Thirdly, the investigation should quantify the financial loss suffered by Crocus Co as a result of the fraud. The evidence gathered will determine the amount which has been stolen from the company as a result of the fraud. It is important for the loss to be quantified; as legally a crime has only been committed if a victim (i.e. Crocus Co) has suffered a financial loss.

Steps in investigating a suspected fraud

The first step will be to determine the type of fraud that has taken place. The fact that employees no longer employed by the company have not been removed from the payroll indicates a fraud known as a 'ghost employee' scheme, whereby the fraudster diverts the payroll of the non-existent employees into their own possession.

Then the investigator will need to consider how the fraud could have taken place. This would normally be due to the fraudster(s) circumventing internal controls and concealing their actions from their colleagues and supervisors. For example, there should be a control in place to ensure that any amendments made to payroll data (in this case an amendment appears to have been made to re-route the ex-employees pay into the bank account of the fraudster) must be approved by a senior manager, and should be flagged by an exception report.

The investigator will also need to establish how long the fraud has been operating – in this case it is likely that the fraud began at the same time as the factory closure, but this will need to be clarified.

The next step would be to gather evidence – this is a crucial part of the investigation as it should determine both the identity of the perpetrator(s) and the monetary value of the fraud. Gathering evidence could include an examination of accounting records and other documentation, the use of computer-assisted auditing techniques (CAATs), interviewing employees of the company, and discussions with management. A key issue here is to ensure that the evidence will be sufficient to prove three matters:

- That a fraud has taken place,

- The identity of the fraudster, and

- The amount of the loss to the company.

This is essential because the legal framework will require clear evidence in order for a prosecution to be instigated against the perpetrator(s) of the fraud.

Evidence must be sufficient and relevant to the accusations being made. For example, the legal framework is likely to require evidence of the following:

- The motive for the fraud,

- The ability of the alleged fraudster to conduct the fraud,

- Any attempt made by the alleged to conceal the crime.

Investigative procedures could include, for example:

- Review of authorisation of monthly payroll.

- Use of CAATs to determine any alteration of payroll details.

- Use of CAATs to determine:

  - Any individual on the payroll who has no contact details.

  - Any bank account receiving the pay of more than one individual.

  - Employees who have not taken holiday or sick leave.

- Reconciliation of employees in the payroll database with employees in the human resources database.

The purpose of the above is to establish how the controls that should have been operating in the payroll system were circumvented. It would seem that authorisations to alter payroll details, i.e. altering payments so that they all go into one bank account, have not taken place.

The investigation should also involve an interview with the suspect(s), with the aim of extracting a confession. This would form a key part of the evidence to be ultimately presented at court.

The investigator will produce a report for the attention of the management of Crocus Co, summarising all findings and concluding on the identity of the fraudster(s) and the amount of financial loss suffered. This report is also likely to be presented as part of evidence during court proceedings.

Though not strictly part of the investigation, which ends on the production of the report described above, it is worth mentioning that the investigator would be likely to be called as an expert witness during the legal process, whereby the evidence gathered and report produced as part of the investigation would be explained to those involved in the legal proceedings, and the investigator may be asked questions regarding the investigation performed.

Finally, advice can be provided to management, as to how to prevent this kind of fraud from occurring again. Recommendations would be likely to focus on improvements in internal systems and controls in the specific part of the business where the fraud occurred.

Conclusion

This report has explained that the objective of a forensic investigation is to clarify whether a fraud has taken place, to discover the identity of the fraudster, and to quantify the financial loss suffered. The specialist skills of the investigation team will produce evidence which is sufficient and relevant enough to be used to assist legal proceedings against those involved with the fraud.

(c) **Application of ethical principles to a fraud investigation**

IFAC's *Code of Ethics for Professional Accountants* applies to all ACCA members involved in professional assignments, including forensic investigations. There are specific considerations in the application of each of the principles in providing such a service.

Integrity

The forensic investigator is likely to deal frequently with individuals who lack integrity, are dishonest, and attempt to conceal the true facts from the investigator. It is imperative that the investigator recognises this, and acts with impeccable integrity throughout the whole investigation.

Objectivity

As in an audit engagement, the investigator's objectivity must be beyond question. The report that is the outcome of the forensic investigation must be perceived as independent, as it forms part of the legal evidence presented at court. The investigator must adhere to the concept that the overriding objective of court proceedings is to deal with cases fairly and justly. Any real or perceived threats to objectivity could undermine the credibility of the evidence provided by the investigator.

This issue poses a particular problem where an audit client requests its auditors to conduct a forensic investigation. In this situation, the audit firm would be exposed to threats to objectivity in terms of advocacy, management involvement and self-review. The advocacy threat arises because the audit firm may feel pressured into promoting the interests and point of view of their client, which would breach the overriding issue of objectivity in court proceedings. Secondly, the investigators could be perceived to be involved in management decisions regarding the implications of the fraud, especially where the investigator acts as an expert witness. It is however the self-review threat that would be the most significant threat to objectivity. The self-review threat arises because the investigation is likely to involve the estimation of an amount (i.e. the loss), which could be material to the financial statements.

For the reasons outlined above, The Code states that the firm should evaluate threats and put appropriate safeguards in place, and if safeguards cannot reduce the threats to an acceptable level, then the firm cannot provide both the audit service and the forensic investigation.

Professional competence and due care

Forensic investigations will involve very specialist skills, which accountants are unlikely to possess without extensive training. Such skills would include:

– Detailed knowledge of the relevant legal framework surrounding fraud,

– An understanding of how to gather specialist evidence,

– Skills in the safe custody of evidence, including maintaining a clear 'chain' of evidence,

– Strong personal skills in, for example, interview techniques, presentation of material at court, and tactful dealing with difficult and stressful situations.

It is therefore essential that forensic work is only ever undertaken by highly skilled individuals, under the direction and supervision of an experienced fraud investigator. Any doubt over the competence of the investigation team could severely undermine the credibility of the evidence presented at court.

Confidentiality

Normally accountants should not disclose information without the explicit consent of their client. However, during legal proceedings arising from a fraud investigation, the court will require the investigator to reveal information discovered during the investigation. There is an overriding requirement for the investigator to disclose all of the information deemed necessary by the court.

Outside of the court, the investigator must ensure faultless confidentiality, especially because much of the information they have access to will be highly sensitive.

Professional behaviour

Fraud investigations can become a matter of public interest, and much media attention is often focused on the work of the forensic investigator. A highly professional attitude must be displayed at all times, in order to avoid damage to the reputation of the firm, and of the profession. Any lapse in professional behaviour could also undermine the integrity of the forensic evidence, and of the credibility of the investigator, especially when acting in the capacity of expert witness.

During legal proceedings, the forensic investigator may be involved in discussions with both sides in the court case, and here it is essential that a courteous and considerate attitude is presented to all parties.

Examiner's comments

Requirement (a) asked for definitions of forensic accounting, forensic investigation, and forensic auditing. There were many sound displays of this factual knowledge, though some candidates who did not know the difference between the three tended to write the same thing for each one.

Requirement (b) was the core of the question. A scenario was provided in which a potential fraud had been discovered, and a report was required, describing the objectives of a forensic investigation, and explaining the steps involved. Encouragingly, the vast majority of candidates produced their answer in an appropriate format and included an introduction and conclusion, enabling at least some of the professional marks available to be awarded. The majority of answers successfully described the objectives of a forensic investigation, and most adequately explained the steps involved in such an investigation. It was clear that most candidates appreciated that this is a very different engagement to an audit, with many mentioning the potential role as an expert witness, and the importance of evidence being admissible in court. However two common problems detracted from the quality of many answers for this requirement:

Firstly, providing tactless and unnecessary comments regarding whether the assignment should be accepted. For example, discussing whether the firm had sufficient competence to perform the work (presumably this is the case, as the question stated that 'you are a manager in the forensic investigation department of your firm', or considering whether there were any ethical issues to consider prior to acceptance (presumably not given that the question stated that Crocus Co is not an audit client)). Such comments show that candidates had failed to read and understand the scenario. However the more significant issue is that such comments would not be made in a report to a potential client, they are internal issues, inappropriate for an external communication.

Secondly, the procedures suggested where often too vague, or not even procedures at all. It was common to see 'procedures' suggested such as 'obtain a list of the current payroll' or 'use CAATs to get payroll data on those made redundant'. What the investigator should do with this information was not discussed. Some candidates recognised that information about the system in use and the ownership of the bank account should be gathered before the suspect was interviewed, but few recognised this as a priority.

As in Q1(c), some candidates got a little carried away with the scenario, providing some far-fetched discussions of getting DNA evidence and blood samples, and using the police to 'hunt and capture' the suspect. Such comments are clearly based more on popular TV shows than the scenario provided, and can detract from an otherwise professional answer.

Requirement (c) was not often well answered. This requirement asked for the application of the fundamental ethical principles to the provision of a forensic investigation service. The best answers went through each ethical principle in turn, explaining its specific application to this type of service. Some candidates recognised the vital importance of confidentiality in the context of a fraud investigation, and others realised the significance of acting with utmost integrity when dealing with criminal activity.

However, many answers were just not applied in any way, making little or no reference to forensics. A significant number of candidates simply wrote the principles down with a brief definition of each, not answering the question requirement at all.

A lot of candidates were unable to identify the fundamental ethical principles, and focussed purely on independence.

Marking scheme			
(a)	**Definitions**		*Marks*
	2 marks per definition (general principle rather than exact wording. Examples can be used to illustrate definition – **give ½ mark per example**)		
	Maximum marks		6
(b)	**Report**		
	Up to 3 marks for use of professional business English, language appropriate to client and to finance director (i.e. not patronising), tactful (i.e. does not criticise client). **Specifically ½ for headings, 1 for introduction, then up to 1½ for remainder.**		
	Up to 1½ marks per comment:		
	– Intro ref. reason for report and to clarify contents (1 mark)		
	– Aim – clarify fraud taken place		
	– Aim – discover the perpetrator(s)		
	– Aim – prosecute the perpetrator(s)		
	– Aim – quantify losses		
	– Method – consider type of fraud – ghost employee		
	– Method – identify opportunity – controls override		
	– Method – collect evidence – + up to 2 for examples		
	– Method – interview suspect		
	– Method – produce reports		
	– Expert witness		
	– Advice and recommendations to prevent another fraud		
	Maximum marks		14
(c)	**Ethics**		
	Up to 1½ marks per comment		
	– Integrity (max 1 mark)		
	– Objectivity (max 3 marks)		
	– Professional competence and due care		
	– Confidentiality		
	– Professional behaviour		
	1 mark for recognition that principles apply to all professional engagements		
	Maximum marks		6
	Total		26

5 MEDIX CO *Walk in the footsteps of a top tutor*

Key answer tips

The question is based on a scenario within the context of a potential new audit client for the firm. The question focusses on the analysis of business risk, and financial statement risk, and also requires an assessment of acceptance issues in the form of notes to be used by an audit partner. Risk assessment is a key part of the syllabus, as highlighted in the Examiner's Approach article, and this part of the question should not have been a surprise to candidates. However, it should be noted that the requirements to discuss business risk and financial statement risk are split. A number of candidates failed to read the full requirement and repetition in part (a) and (b) was a common problem. It is also important to note that the outgoing auditor has already been contacted and has responded to the professional etiquette letter.

The highlighted words are key phases that markers are looking for.

(a)   **Business risks include the following:**

Product life cycle

Demand is declining for the main revenue generating product. The market is moving such that demand for laser surgical instruments is increasing, while demand for traditional metal instruments is declining. The continued loss of a main revenue stream will have significant detrimental profit and cash flow implications.

Demand has been declining for four years, yet it seems that research has only recently commenced into a new source of revenue. The management appears not to be focused on the long term strategy needed for survival in this competitive market.

Research is at an early stage. It may take many years for the development stage to be reached. Research and development necessitates a significant cash outflow, and this is happening at the same time as loss of cash inflows from the main revenue stream. As the company is already short of liquid funds, as evidenced by the on-going use of an overdraft facility, it could be that there will be insufficient funds to continue to develop the new product.

The research is being conducted by only one scientist, who is not employed by the company. The scientist is critical for the successful development of a replacement revenue stream. If the scientist were to leave, Medix Co would lose the knowledge base of the new technology, hindering progress into the new market. Given that this is a very specialist role, it may be a difficult and lengthy process to find a new scientist to work on the project. It is a significant risk to rely so heavily on a person not employed by the company for such a crucial role in the future success of the business.

There may also be confidentiality issues – if the scientist is freelancing for any competitor of Medix Co, the new laser equipment designs could be copied and used unless Medix Co secures protection of the design e.g. by taking out a patent.

Finally, the industry is highly regulated, and licences are necessary in order to take medical instruments to market. If the licence is not granted, the research and development funds will have been wasted and the continuation of the business as a going concern could be jeopardised.

New research premises

An extremely important problem is shown in the press cutting. If the local authority is successful in shutting down the newly constructed research laboratory, the company will have to find new premises, which could be expensive and take time. Any delay in the development of the new products will compound the cash flow pressures the company is already suffering.

There is also the possibility that fines or penalties could be imposed on the company, and that the extension, or even the whole building may have to be demolished, which Medix Co may have to pay for, putting the company into further financial distress.

The potential impairment of the building at the year end would have a detrimental impact on the company's net asset position at the year end, in turn affecting the ability to raise finance and causing potential going concern problems.

Further bad publicity could follow, and demand for Medix Co's products may suffer as a result.

Tutorial note

Planning regulations have already been breached. Candidates should not focus their answer on the breach itself, which has already occurred, but on the possible consequences of the breach i.e. financial risk of fines having to be paid, the need to find new premises, and operational risk of further decline in demand for products.

Use of agents for marketing and distribution

Medix Co appears to rely heavily on agents to secure sales to hospitals and clinics. If the agents are unsuccessful, or decide to reduce the effort they put into promoting Medix Co's products in preference for products from an alternative supplier, then the company will face a substantial reduction in revenue and cash inflows.

A second risk associated with the use of agents is that there is a scope for fraud – the agents could deliberately overstate the value of sales in order to maximise the commission they receive. When this point is linked to the poor internal systems and controls as indicated by Mick Evans, it is likely that such frauds would not be detected.

Overseas location of manufacturing facility

The fact that products are manufactured abroad could lead to problems in controlling and monitoring production. Decisions made locally may not be compatible with the overall operating strategy of the company. Also, if communication channels are not operating efficiently then decisions made at the head office may take time to be relayed to the foreign manager. This could lead to production inefficiencies, e.g. if an agent secures a contract to supply a particular product, it may take time for this to be communicated to the manufacturing facility, and delays in fulfilling the order will then be inevitable, leading to loss of agent and customer goodwill.

Having the production facility operating abroad could also lead to problems with monitoring the quality of output. This is a highly regulated industry, where suppliers of faulty equipment could face fines and bad publicity in the event of supplying a poor quality item. Agents would withdraw their support for the products immediately in preference to those of competitors.

Importing goods using aeroplanes exposes the company to fluctuating overhead costs as fuel prices and freight costs are notoriously difficult to predict. Higher levels of tax could also be imposed on imported goods.

Finally, as the company manufactures abroad, it is inevitable that it will make payments in foreign currency and will therefore be exposed to exchange rate risk.

Capital expenditure and financial management

Plant and equipment appears to be fairly old, constructed twelve years ago. In the future, if the research and development into new laser equipment is successful, then capital expenditure will be needed to create the capacity to manufacture the new products. The risk is that finance may not be available to invest in new plant.

The company appears to have a problem managing liquidity. Continually operating using an overdraft is expensive in terms of finance costs. A bank loan carrying a variable interest rate exposes the company to the economic risk of fluctuations in the interest rate, making planning and budgeting cash flows difficult.

Internal systems and controls

The comments made by Mick Evans show that the company has a weak control environment and poor systems. Frauds are more likely to occur in the absence of controls and the quality of financial information used by the directors for planning and reviewing business performance could be inadequate. Medix Co is an owner-managed business, and it appears that Jon Tate, the managing director, has a dominant style leading to frequent disagreements (with previous auditors and finance director) and flouting of rules (tax and local authority investigations). This increases the likelihood of management disregard for, and override of, controls.

Tax investigations

Recent tax investigations could indicate that the company is not complying with relevant tax regulations, which in turn leads to the risk of fines and penalties, which could be severe if this is a recurring breach of regulations which has not been resolved.

(b) (i) *Business risk* is defined as a threat which could mean that a business fails to meet an ongoing business objective. Business risks represent problems which are faced by the management of a business, and these problems should be identified and assessed for their possible impact on the business.

Financial statement risk is the risk that components of the financial statements could be misstated, through inaccurate or incomplete recording of transactions or disclosure. Financial statement risks therefore represent potential errors or deliberate misstatements in the published accounts of a business.

There is usually a direct relationship between business risk and financial statement risk. Generally a business risk, if not addressed by management, will have an impact on specific components of the financial statements. For example, for Medix Co, declining demand for metal surgical equipment has been identified as a business risk. An associated financial statement risk is the potential over-valuation of obsolete inventory.

Sometimes business risks have a more general effect on the financial statements. Weak internal systems and controls are often identified as a business risk. Inadequacies in systems and controls could lead to errors or misstatements in any area of the financial statements so auditors would perceive this as a general audit risk factor.

Business risks are often linked to going concern issues, because if a business is failing to meet objectives such as cash generation, or revenue maximisation, then it may struggle to continue in operational existence. In terms of financial statement risk, going concern is a very specific issue, and the risk is normally the inadequate disclosure of going concern problems. In the extreme situation where a business is definitely not a going concern, then the risk is that the financial statements have been prepared on the wrong basis, as in this case the 'break up basis' should be used.

Business risk and financial statement risk concepts can both be used by auditors in order to identify areas of the financial statements likely to be misstated at the year end. The business risk approach places the auditor 'in the shoes' of management, and therefore provides deeper insight into the operations of the business and generates extensive business understanding.

(ii) Several significant financial statement risks are indicated by the press cutting.

Overstatement of property, plant and equipment

Medix Co has constructed a research laboratory which is likely to be impaired at the year end. The local authority has the power to shut down the facility, and it is clear from the press cutting that this is likely to happen before the year end. Following IAS 36 *Impairment of Assets*, the premises should be written down to recoverable amount, and the impairment loss recognised as an expense. The directors should carry out an impairment review before the year end. If the premises cannot be used as intended then the recoverable amount (measured using the higher of value in use and fair value less selling cost) is likely to be less than current carrying value. In this case, assuming the local authority is successful in shutting down the research laboratory, the recoverable amount is likely to be nil, as the premises have no value in use, as it will never be used commercially, and has no market value as it is likely to be demolished.

In addition, any tangible assets such as laboratory equipment located at the premises should be tested for impairment as if the company cannot use the premises then the assets contained within it are likely to have a lower recoverable amount than carrying value.

Contingency – fines or penalties imposed by local authority

The press cutting indicates that Medix Co has been sued before, and that the local authority may again take legal action against the company. IAS 37 *Provisions, Contingent Liabilities and Contingent Assets* states that a provision should be recognised if the company has a probable obligation at the year end which can be measured reliably. If payment is deemed only possible at the year end, then disclosure of the contingent liability should be made in a note to the financial statements.

If the local authority commences legal proceedings against Medix Co before the year end of 30 June 2008, then management should assess the probability of payment. The financial statement risk is not recognising a provision (and associated expense within the statement of comprehensive income), or not disclosing a contingency.

Demolition costs

The local authority may require Medix Co to demolish the premises. If this demand is made before the year end, Medix Co should recognise a provision for demolition costs as an unavoidable legal obligation would have been created. The financial statement risk is that in this situation, Medix Co fails to recognise a provision and associated expense within the statement of comprehensive income.

Going concern

The above issues could indicate that the company may not continue in operational existence. The potential lack of disclosure of these issues represents a financial statement risk.

(c) **Briefing notes**
To: Audit partner
From: Audit manager
Subject: Issues to consider regarding appointment as auditor of Medix Co

Introduction

Medix Co has recently invited our firm to become appointed as auditor. These briefing notes summarise the main issues we should consider in deciding whether to take the appointment a stage further. My comments are based on a discussion held with Ricardo Feller, finance director of Medix Co, a discussion with the current audit partner, and information provided in the local newspaper.

Legal actions and investigations

There are several indications that Medix Co has a history of non compliance with law and regulations. The former finance director is claiming unfair dismissal, and in the past the local authority has successfully taken legal action against the company and has a current case pending. In addition, there have been two tax investigations in recent years hinting at non-compliance with relevant tax regulations.

There are two problems for us in taking on a client with a propensity for legal actions and investigations. Firstly, the reputation of the company must be considered. If we become associated with the company through being appointed as auditor, we could be 'tarred with the same brush' and our own reputation also tarnished.

Secondly, we could become quickly exposed to an advocacy independence threat, which clearly should be avoided. Our ethical status should not be compromised for the sake of gaining a new audit client. Mick Evans only 'believes' that the tax matter has been resolved by the directors, and we should avoid taking on a new client which is involved in an on-going investigation.

Public interest

The problems noted above are compounded by the bad publicity which the company is currently receiving. The local press contained a recent article discussing Medix Co's past and current breach of planning regulations. Given the current level of public interest in environmental issues, and emphasis on corporate responsibility, it would seem that Medix Co has a poor public perception, which we would not want to be associated with.

Potential liability to lender

The company is currently negotiating a significant bank loan, and the lender will be using the audited financial statements to make a decision on whether to advance a loan, and the terms of any finance that might be advanced to Medix Co. This means that our audit opinion for the forthcoming year end will be scrutinised by the lender, and our firm is exposed to a relatively high risk of liability to a third party. Given that this will be our first audit, and the limited time we have available (discussed below) our firm may feel that the risk of this audit engagement is too high. Should the appointment be accepted, disclaimers should be put in place to ensure that we could not be sued in the event of the bank suffering a financial loss as a result of their lending decision.

Timeframe and resources

It is currently the last month of the financial year. If we are appointed as auditor we need to work quickly to develop a thorough understanding of the business, and to begin to plan the assignment. We need to consider whether our firm has sufficient resources to put together an audit team so quickly without detracting from other client work currently being conducted.

To make this matter worse, Mick Evans states that Medix Co likes 'a quick audit', and we need to consider how to manage this expectation, as first year audit procedures such as systems documentation, and developing business understanding tend to take a long time. We must be careful that the client does not pressure us into a 'quick audit', which could compromise quality.

Medix Co operates in a reasonably specialist and highly regulated industry, so our firm should take care to ensure we have expertise in this industry.

Potentially aggressive management style

There are several indicators that the management may take a confrontational approach, such as the unfair dismissal claim brought against the company by the ex-finance director. In addition, the auditors prior to Mick Evans resigned following a disagreement with management. This history shows that we may find it difficult to establish a good working relationship with the management. As the company is owner managed the presence of a dominant managing director exacerbates this problem.

Management bias

There is incentive for the financial statements to be manipulated in order to secure bank finance. There is considerable risk of material misstatement which our firm may consider to be unacceptably high.

Internal systems and controls

The current auditors have found systems and controls to be poor, and management has not acted upon recommendations made by the auditors. Of course this does not mean that we should not take on the assignment – many companies have weak controls. However, if we did take on the appointment, we would not be able to rely on controls or use a controls based approach for the audit. We would need to take a substantive approach to the audit. One practical issue here is availability of staff to conduct the audit testing, as substantive procedures tend to be more time consuming than if we could have taken a systems based approach.

Opening balances

In all new audit assignments, work must be conducted to verify the opening balances. Given the possible fraud and poor controls described above, we would need to perform detailed testing on the opening balances as there is a high risk of fraud and/or error in previous accounting periods. We may also wish to consider the competence of the previous auditors, who appeared to disregard potential fraud indicator (two cash books) and had only one audit client.

Fees

Mick Evans has made it clear that Medix Co's management likes to keep a tight control on costs, and it may put pressure on us to charge a low audit fee. We need to bear in mind the risks associated with this engagement, as discussed above, and only take on this high risk audit if the audit fee is high enough to compensate.

We should also consider the cash flow problems being experienced by the company. As a business we need to ensure that we only take on clients with a good credit rating, and it seems that Medix Co, operating with an overdraft, may not be able to pay our invoices.

Indication of fraud or money laundering

Surely the most serious issue to consider is that Jon Tate, the managing director, has kept two cash books. We need further detail on this, but it clearly could indicate a fraud being perpetrated at the highest level of management. The fact that he has maintained two cash books could indicate money laundering activities taking place, especially when considered in the context of an owner-managed business with overseas operations. If this were the ONLY problem discovered it could be deemed serious enough to bring to an end our appointment process. It would be reckless for our firm to take on a client where the managing director is a fraudster.

Conclusion

Further information is needed in many areas before a final decision is made. However, from the information we have gathered so far, it appears that Medix Co would represent a high risk client, and our firm must therefore be very careful to assess each problem noted above before deciding whether to proceed with the appointment.

Examiner's comments

Common problems in answers to **requirement (a)** included:

- Confusion between business risk and financial statement risk;

- Providing recommendations or solutions to the risks – **NOT** a requirement of the question;

- Discussion of audit risk, for example, the fact that this is a potential new audit client giving rise to detection risk – again, this was **NOT** a requirement;

- Trying to link every risk identified to a going concern risk;

- Identification of risks which are unlikely to materialise, for example, the potential death of the scientist or the plane crashing and destroying inventories, and while I agree these events could happen; there are plenty of other, more pressing risks to be discussed.

- Many candidates spent too long on this section.

Requirement (b) produced the worst answers to Question 1. The first part of the requirement asked for a discussion of the relationship between business risk and financial statement risk. Most candidates attempted a definition of the two terms, but the discussion of the link between them was weak. Some candidates drifted into a description of 'top down auditing', which did not answer the question requirement, though was awarded credit if the discussion demonstrated an understanding of the link between the two types of risk. Candidates are reminded that in questions which relate to auditing concepts, it is recommended that the answer begins with a definition of the concept. In this case, marks were awarded for definition of the terms and any relevant supporting example provided.

In (bii), candidates were asked to 'identify and explain potential financial statement risks'. Some sound answers were given here, where candidates understood the financial reporting implications of Medix's breach of planning regulations, and clearly explained the risk in terms of specific balances in the financial statements being under or overstated, or the risk of non-disclosure.

However, many answers simply stated that the company 'might need to make a provision', or should 'consider the value of the property', comments which are much too vague to score well.

Common weaknesses in **answers to (c)** included:

- Failure to produce the answer in the required format

- Listing general acceptance considerations, often as questions ('have we got shares in the client? Do we have any personal relationships with the client?')

- Making comments wholly inappropriate to the scenario. E.g. many answers urged the audit partner to 'make contact with the previous auditor to find out matters we should be aware of'. It should have been noted that 1/3 of the scenario is a based on a duscussion with the outgoing auditor.

- Answers which concentrated on what the outgoing auditors had done wrong rather than problems for the new audit firm.

- Lack of prioritisation.

- Failure to reach a conclusion as to whether or not the appointment should go ahead.

	Marking scheme	
(a)	**Identify and explain business risks**	*Marks*
	Generally 1/2 mark for identification, and 1/2–1 mark for explanation	
	Ideas list:	
	Declining demand for main product and revenue/cash flow implication	
	R+D represents cash drain	
	Lack of management focus on long term strategy	
	Breach of planning – risk of facility being shut down and bad publicity	
	Regulated industry and reliance on licence for commercial production	
	Over reliance on scientist	
	Reliance on agents	
	Commission payments – high risk of fraud	
	Overseas manufacturing plant – hard to control and maintain quality	
	High and volatile costs of importing goods	
	Capital expenditure likely in near future	
	Future exposure to fluctuating interest rates	
	Non compliance with tax regulations – fines and penalties	
	Legal action – finance director and planning office	
	Weak controls, risk of fraud	
	Owner-managed business	
	Maximum marks	**12**
(b) (i)	**Discuss relationship between business risk and financial statement risk**	
	1/2 mark for definition of business risk	
	1/2 mark for definition of financial statement risk	
	1 mark for each comment made from ideas list:	
	Business risk leads to specific FS risk	
	Business risk leads to general FS risk	
	Relationship regarding going concern	
	Maximum marks	**4**
(ii)	**Financial statement risk**	
	Generally 1/2 mark for identification, 1 further mark for explanation, from ideas list:	
	Overstatement of non-current assets	
	Overstatement of other assets (max 1 mark)	
	Possible understatement of provision/non disclosure of contingency	
	Possible understatement of provision for demolition costs	
	Going concern (max 1 mark)	
	Reference IAS 36, IAS 37 (1/2 mark each)	
	Maximum marks	**6**

(c)	**Briefing notes regarding invitation to become appointed auditor** Up to 1 professional mark for clarity of discussion, style appropriate for audit partner 1 professional mark for format, introduction and conclusion provided 1–2 marks per issue discussed, from ideas list: **NB:** comments must be derived from the information provided in order to be awarded marks Poor reputation of Medix Co Potential advocacy threat from frequent litigation Public interest in the company Potential liability to lender Short timeframe to build business knowledge Aggressive management style Incentive to manipulate financial statements Poor systems and controls Extra work on opening balances (max 1 mark) Need expertise in this regulated industry Fee pressure Creditworthiness Possible management fraud Indicator of money laundering Question competence of previous auditors		
	Maximum marks		**12**
	Total		**34**

6 ROSIE CO *Walk in the footsteps of a top tutor*

Key answer tips

The question features an expanding group of companies. The question followed an examiner's article entitled 'Group Audit Issues,' published in March 2008 and well prepares students, who have read the article should not find this question too challenging. Group audit is an important part of the syllabus and candidates should expect to see it examined on a regular basis. The question also combines discussion of due diligence. This should be considered in the context of non-audit review engagements or agreed upon procedures and is linked closely to engagements reporting on prospective financial information.

The highlighted words are key phases that markers are looking for.

(a) **Report to Leo Sabat outlining the purpose and scope of a due diligence assignment.**

Introduction

Before purchasing a company, it is crucial that the purchaser undertake a comprehensive survey of the business in order to avoid any operational or financial surprises post-acquisition. Due diligence can simply be seen as 'fact finding', and as a way to minimise the risk of making a bad investment. This report provides a summary of the purpose of due diligence and also contrasts the scope of a due diligence assignment with the scope of an audit of financial statements.

Purpose of due diligence

Information gathering

Investigative due diligence is the process by which information is gathered about a target company, for the purpose of ensuring that the acquirer has full knowledge of the operations, financial performance and position, legal and tax situation, as well as general commercial background. Essentially the aim is to uncover any 'skeletons in the closet' and therefore to reveal any potential problem areas before a decision regarding the acquisition is made.

For example, Maxwell Co may have taken out debt finance. It is crucial for the acquirer to understand the terms of any debt covenant attached to such finance, and to know if there is a history of Maxwell Co defaulting on payment to the provider of that finance. This information is unlikely to be available unless a detailed due diligence investigation is carried out.

Verification of specific management representations

Additionally, the vendor may make representations to the potential acquirer which it is essential to verify. For example, the vendor of Maxwell Co may state that the company has never been the subject of a tax investigation, or that the company fully complies with all relevant health and safety regulations. Due diligence work should substantiate such claims.

Identification of assets and liabilities

From an accounting perspective it is crucial that all of the assets of the target company are identified. This is important because internally generated intangibles such as customer databases, trade dress, and brand names are unlikely to be recognised in the individual company statement of financial position (balance sheet), but should be identified and valued for the purpose of calculating goodwill on acquisition. As these assets are, by definition, without physical substance, only a detailed due diligence investigation will uncover them.

As well as being important for the goodwill calculation, it is crucial to identify these assets as they represent 'hidden wealth' within the target company, and should be taken into account when negotiating the acquisition price.

Contingent liabilities must also be identified, as the acquirer will need to understand the likelihood of the liability crystallising, and the potential financial consequence. Intangible assets and contingent liabilities are notoriously difficult to value, and the directors of Rosie Co could choose to have the valuation performed as part of the due diligence exercise, as they themselves are likely to lack this expertise.

Operational issues

As discussed above, one of the key benefits of due diligence is to discover problems or risks within the entity. These risks may not necessarily arise in the context of a contingent liability, but could instead be operational issues such as high staff turnover, or the need to renegotiate contract terms with suppliers or customers. The directors of the acquiring company will need to carefully consider whether such matters constitute deal breakers, in which case the investment would be considered too risky and so would not go ahead. Alternatively, the risks uncovered could be useful in negotiation to reduce the consideration paid, or the target company could be asked to provide assurance that these problems will be resolved pre-acquisition.

Acquisition planning

The due diligence investigation will also **assess** the commercial benefits, and potential drawbacks, of the acquisition. On the positive side, it will highlight matters such as expected operational synergies to be created post acquisition, and potential economies of scale to be exploited. On the downside there will be acquisition expenses to pay, costs in terms of reorganisation and possible redundancies, as well as the important but hard to quantify issue of change management. The due diligence provider may be able to offer recommendations as to the best way to integrate the new company into the group.

Management involvement

Due diligence investigations can be performed internally, by the directors of the acquiring company. However, this can be time consuming, and the directors may lack sufficient specialist knowledge to perform the investigation. Therefore one of the purposes of an externally provided due diligence service is to reduce time spent by the directors on fact finding, leaving more time to focus on strategic matters to do with the acquisition and on running the existing group.

Credibility

An external investigation will also provide an independent, impartial view on the situation, enhancing the credibility of the investment decision, and the amount paid for the investment.

Rosie Co has only recently acquired Dylan Co, with a cash outflow of $2.5 million in January 2008. The group may already be short of liquid resources, and may be stretched financially and in terms of change management coping with this new addition to the group. Acquiring Maxwell Co in July 2008 would potentially worsen any cash flow problems and operational issues arising from additions to the group. For this reason it is important for the directors of Rosie Co to carefully consider the benefits and timing of the proposed acquisition of Maxwell Co so soon after the acquisition of Dylan Co. It may be that senior management should concentrate in the short term on the successful integration of Dylan Co into the existing group structure, and leave the due diligence investigation to external providers, or even postpone the investigation and potential acquisition.

Scope of a due diligence assignment compared to an audit

When conducting a due diligence assignment, the scope is focused, as discussed above, primarily on fact finding. This means that although the most recent set of financial statements will form a crucial source of information, the investigation will draw on a much wider range of sources of information, including:

–   Several years prior financial statements

–   Management accounts

–   Profit and cash flow forecasts

–   Any business plans recently prepared

–   Discussions with management, employees and third parties.

The aim of due diligence, in contrast to an audit, is **NOT** to provide assurance that financial data is free from material misstatement, but rather to provide the acquirer with a set of information that has been reviewed. Consequently no detailed audit procedures will be performed unless there are specific issues which either cause concern, or have been specifically selected for further verification. For example, the acquirer may specifically request that the due diligence exercise provides an estimate of the valuation of acquired intangible assets, as discussed above.

The type of work performed will therefore be quite different, as a due diligence investigation will primarily use analytical procedures as a means of gathering information. Very few, if any substantive procedures would be carried out, unless they had been specifically requested by the client.

Due diligence is much more 'forward looking' than an audit. Much of the time during a due diligence investigation will be spent assessing forecasts and predictions. In comparison audit procedures only tend to cover future events if they are directly relevant to the year end financial statements, for example, contingencies, or going concern problems.

In contrast to an audit, when it is essential to evaluate systems and controls, the due diligence investigation will not conduct detailed testing of the accounting and internal control systems, unless specifically requested to do so.

Conclusion

To summarise, it can be seen that due diligence provides necessary information for the directors of an acquiring company to decide whether to go ahead with an acquisition, the timing of the acquisition, the value of consideration to be paid, and to assess the operational impact of the acquisition. Due diligence should be viewed as a risk management tool, which is crucial when a significant acquisition is being considered. That a due diligence exercise has taken place will increase stakeholder confidence in the acquisition decision.

(b) (i) **Cost of investment on acquisition of Dylan Co**

Matters to consider

According to the schedule provided by the client, the cost of investment comprises three elements. One matter to consider is whether the cost of investment is complete.

It appears that no legal or professional fees have been included in the cost of investment (unless included within the heading 'cash consideration'). Directly attributable costs should be included per IFRS 3 *Business Combinations*, and there is a risk that these costs may be expensed in error, leading to understatement of the investment.

The cash consideration of $2.5 million is the least problematical component. The only matter to consider is whether the cash has actually been paid. Given that Dylan Co was acquired in the last month of the financial year it is possible that the amount had not been paid before the year end, in which case the amount should be recognised as a current liability on the statement of financial position (balance sheet). However, this seems unlikely given that normally control of an acquired company only passes to the acquirer on cash payment.

IFRS 3 states that the cost of investment should be recognised at fair value, which means that deferred consideration should be discounted to present value at the date of acquisition. If the consideration payable on 31 January 2009 has not been discounted, the cost of investment, and the corresponding liability, will be overstated. It is possible that the impact of discounting the $1.5 million payable one year after acquisition would be immaterial to the financial statements, in which case it would be acceptable to leave the consideration at face value within the cost of investment.

Contingent consideration should be accrued if it is probable to be paid. Here the amount is payable if revenue growth targets are achieved over the next four years. The auditor must therefore assess the probability of the targets being achieved, using forecasts and projections of Maxwell Co's revenue. Such information is inherently subjective, and could have been manipulated, if prepared by the vendor of Maxwell Co, in order to secure the deal and maximise consideration. Here it will be crucial to be sceptical when reviewing the forecasts, and the assumptions underlying the data. The management of Rosie Co should have reached their own opinion on the probability of paying the contingent consideration, but they may have relied heavily on information provided at the time of the acquisition.

Audit evidence

- Agreement of the monetary value and payment dates of the consideration per the client schedule to legal documentation signed by vendor and acquirer.

- Agreement of $2.5 million paid to Rosie Co's bank statement and cash book prior to year end. If payment occurs after year end confirm that a current liability is recognised on the individual company and consolidated statement of financial position (balance sheet).

- Board minutes approving the payment.

- Recomputation of discounting calculations applied to deferred and contingent consideration.

- Agreement that the discount rate used is pre-tax, and reflects current market assessment of the time value of money (e.g. by comparison to Rosie Co's weighted average cost of capital).

- Revenue and profit projections for the period until January 2012, checked for arithmetic accuracy.

- A review of assumptions used in the projections, and agreement that the assumptions are comparable with the auditor's understanding of Dylan Co's business.

Tutorial note

As the scenario states that Chien & Co has audited Dylan Co for several years, it is reasonable to rely on their cumulative knowledge and understanding of the business in auditing the revenue projections.

(ii) Audit procedures on the consolidation schedule of the Rosie Group:

- Agree correct extraction of individual company figures by reference to individual company audited financial statements.

- Cast and cross cast all consolidation schedules.

–   Recalculate all consolidation adjustments, including goodwill, elimination of pre acquisition reserves, cancellation of intercompany balances, fair value adjustments and accounting policy adjustments.

–   By reference to prior year audited consolidated accounts, agree accounting policies have been consistently applied.

–   Agree brought down figures to prior year audited consolidated accounts and audit working papers (e.g. goodwill figures for Timber Co and Ben Co, consolidated reserves).

–   Agree that any post acquisition profits consolidated for Dylan Co arose since the date of acquisition by reference to date of control passing per the purchase agreement.

–   Reconcile opening and closing group reserves and agree reconciling items to group financial statements.

(c)   A joint audit is when two or more audit firms are jointly responsible for giving the audit opinion. This is very common in a group situation where the principal auditor is appointed jointly with the auditor of a subsidiary to provide a joint opinion on the subsidiary's financial statements. There are several advantages and disadvantages in a joint audit being performed.

Advantages

It can be beneficial in terms of audit efficiency for a joint audit to be conducted, especially in the case of a new subsidiary. In this case, Lead & Co will have built up an understanding of Maxwell Co's business, systems and controls, and financial statement issues. It will be time efficient for the two firms of auditors to work together in order for Chien & Co to build up knowledge of the new subsidiary. This is a key issue, as Chien & Co need to acquire a thorough understanding of the subsidiary in order to assess any risks inherent in the company which could impact on the overall assessment of risk within the group. Lead & Co will be able to provide a good insight into the company, and advise Chien & Co of the key risk areas they have previously identified.

On the practical side, it seems that Maxwell Co is a significant addition to the group, as it is expected to increase operating facilities by 40%. If Chien & Co were appointed as sole auditors to Maxwell Co it may be difficult for the audit firm to provide adequate resources to conduct the audit at the same time as auditing the other group companies. A joint audit will allow sufficient resources to be allocated to the audit of Maxwell Co, assuring the quality of the opinion provided.

If there is a tight deadline, as is common with the audit of subsidiaries, which should be completed before the group audit commences, then having access to two firms' resources should enable the audit to be completed in good time.

The audit should also benefit from an improvement in quality. The two audit firms may have different points of view, and would be able to discuss contentious issues throughout the audit process. In particular, the newly appointed audit team will have a 'fresh pair of eyes' and be able to offer new insight to matters identified. It should be easier to challenge management and therefore ensure that the auditors' position is taken seriously.

Tutorial note

Candidates may have referred to the recent debate over whether joint audits increase competition in the profession. In particular, joint audits have been proposed as a way for 'mid tier' audit firms to break into the market of auditing large companies and groups, which at the moment is monopolised by the 'Big 4'. Although this does not answer the specific question set, credit will be awarded for demonstration of awareness of this topical issue.

Disadvantages

For the client, it is likely to be more expensive to engage two audit firms than to have the audit opinion provided by one firm. From a cost/benefit point of view there is clearly no point in paying twice for one opinion to be provided. Despite the audit workload being shared, both firms will have a high cost for being involved in the audit in terms of senior manager and partner time. These costs will be passed on to the client within the audit fee.

The two audit firms may use very different audit approaches and terminology. This could make it difficult for the audit firms to work closely together, negating some of the efficiency and cost benefits discussed above. Problems could arise in deciding which firm's method to use, for example, to calculate materiality, design and pick samples for audit procedures, or evaluate controls within the accounting system. It may be impossible to reconcile two different methods and one firm's methods may end up dominating the audit process, which then eliminates the benefit of a joint audit being conducted. It could be time consuming to develop a 'joint' audit approach, based on elements of each of the two firms' methodologies, time which obviously would not have been spent if a single firm was providing the audit.

There may be problems for the two audit firms to work together harmoniously. Lead & Co may feel that ultimately they will be replaced by Chien & Co as audit provider, and therefore could be unwilling to offer assistance and help.

Potentially, problems could arise in terms of liability. In the event of litigation, because both firms have provided the audit opinion, it follows that the firms would be jointly liable. The firms could blame each other for any negligence which was discovered, making the litigation process more complex than if a single audit firm had provided the opinion. However, it could be argued that joint liability is not necessarily a drawback, as the firms should both be covered by professional indemnity insurance.

Examiner's comments

Requirement (a) focussed on due diligence. Some candidates seemed not to know what a due diligence investigation involves. Although most answers picked up on the fact that due diligence is carried out in a potential business combination (a fact which was itself given in the question scenario), very few answers discussed the fact-finding nature of the investigation, and that the result of the investigation can help the management make a decision about whether or not to go ahead with the acquisition (which again is given in the scenario).

Comparison of the scope with that of an audit was poorly attempted. Most candidates simply discussed 'negative assurance' compared with 'true and fair view', and hardly any answers mentioned the fact that due diligence is forward looking, and makes use of a wide range of information about the company being investigated.

Some answers were extremely disparaging in their attitude towards due diligence investigations, many claiming that it would be 'very expensive and not as good as an audit' and that 'you don't even get an opinion' or 'you can't place any reliance on due diligence'. These comments display a lack of commercial awareness. The tone of the report should have been more positive towards the benefits of such investigations – ultimately the directors in the scenario should be provided with a report which encourages them to initiate due diligence on the target company Maxwell, but many answers would have persuaded the directors even more against it.

Requirement (b) was probably the worst answered section of the whole paper. Most candidates were completely unable to restrict their answer to the cost of investment as shown in the scenario, and most launched into a discussion of the accounting treatment of goodwill. This was NOT asked for. Candidates at this level in their examinations should be able to distinguish between the cost of an investment in the parent company's financial statements, and the goodwill which arises on consolidation. The requirement clearly referred to the financial statements of the parent company and no marks were awarded for irrelevant discussions of net assets acquired or goodwill impairment or amortisation, as these balances only arise in the group consolidated financial statements.

The majority of candidates seemed not to know the contents of a consolidation schedule, or how to audit it. However, those candidates who had read the relevant article in student accountant tended to score well on this requirement. However even these answers were not always tailored to the scenario. For example, some answers described an audit procedure to determine the accuracy of the calculation of the minority interest in the group, despite the scenario clearly stating 'all subsidiaries are wholly owned.' Making irrelevant comments not only wastes time in the exam, but also detracts from the overall quality of an answer.

Some answers to this requirement digressed into general matters that a group auditor should bear in mind (organising group audit instructions, checking the competence of other auditors in the group). Again, such comments were irrelevant.

Thankfully, **requirement (c)** was well attempted by the majority of candidates. This requirement differentiated clearly between strong and weak candidates.

Marking scheme			
(a)	**Report on due diligence – purpose and benefit of investigation**		*Marks*
	Award up to 2 professional marks for good style of report with clear explanations and logical flow		
	1–1½ marks per point from ideas list:		
	Introduction		
	Fact finding		
	Verify specific representations		
	Identify and value assets, especially intangibles, and contingencies		
	Tool to aid negotiation of consideration		
	Operational issues identified – staff, suppliers, customers, contracts		
	Consideration of commercial impact – synergies and drawbacks		
	Benefit of external provision – free up management time, independent investigation		
	Enhanced credibility		
	Maximum marks		**10**

(ii)	**Report on due diligence – scope compared to audit of financial statements** ½ mark for identification and 1 mark for explanation: Wider scope – more information sources No detailed testing of transactions/balances – unless specifically agreed No detailed evaluation of internal systems and controls Greater use of analytical procedures, reduced scope for substantive procedures Forward looking	
	Maximum marks	4
(b)	**Matters and evidence for cost of investment on acquisition of Dylan Co:** Generally 1 mark per matter and specific audit procedure: Completeness – missing professional fees Agree consideration to legal documentation Agree cash consideration to bank statement Deferred consideration – discounted per IFRS 3 Recalculate (1/2 mark only) Agree reasonable discount factor used Contingent consideration – accrue if probable per IFRS 3 Review forecasts and assumptions **NB:** no marks to be awarded for discussion of materiality as scenario states that all figures are material no marks for discussion of goodwill – this is not asked for	
	Maximum marks	7
(ii)	**Principal audit procedures on consolidation schedule:** Generally 1 mark per specific audit procedure: Agree figures to individual co financial statements Cast and cross cast schedule Agree brought down figures Recalculate consolidation adjustments – award ½ mark for each adjustment clearly identified, max 2 marks Reconcile opening and closing reserves Agree post acquisition reserves consolidated for Dylan Co	
	Maximum marks	4
(c)	**Joint audit** 1 mark for definition 1 mark for each ad and disad – cap at max 3 for each Advantages: Knowledge sharing Increase resource availability Easier to meet tight deadline Improve audit quality New insight of new auditor Current issue – increase competition Disadvantages: Higher cost for client Bureaucracy Difference in audit approach Problems in working together Joint liability	
	Maximum marks	7
	Total	32

7   ISLAND CO (A) *Walk in the footsteps of a top tutor*

Key answer tips

This question tests the ability to perform an audit risk assessment at the planning stage of an audit and to suggest audit procedures relevant to a provision. These have been identified as core examinable elements of P7. It is important in (a) to discuss audit risk, i.e. the risk that the auditor fails to detect material misstatement, specifically in Island Co's accounts. Discussion of general business risks will not score unless linked to the potential for fraud or error. In part (b) it is vital to consider tests relevant to the warranty provision referred to in the question. General discussions of provision tests will likely only score basic marks. Finally part (c) draws from another part of the syllabus. Part of the marks are for factual recall but some marks encourage students to think for themselves about practical, commercial issues facing small/medium practices. This is something Lisa Weaver appears keen to encourage.

The highlighted words are key phases that markers are looking for.

(a)   **Briefing Notes**

Subject: Principal Audit Risks – Island Co

Revenue Recognition – timing

Island Co raises sales invoices in three stages. There is potential for breach of IAS 18 *Revenue*, which states that revenue should only be recognised once the seller has the right to receive it, in other words the seller has performed its contractual obligations. This right does not necessarily correspond to amounts falling due for payment in accordance with an invoice schedule agreed with a customer as part of a contract. Island Co appears to receive payment from its customers in advance of performing any obligation, as the stage one invoice is raised when an order is confirmed i.e. before any work has actually taken place. This creates the potential for revenue to be recognised too early, in advance of any performance of contractual obligation. When a payment is received in advance of performance, a liability should be recognised equal to the amount received, representing the obligation under the contract. Therefore a significant risk is that revenue is overstated and liabilities understated.

Tutorial note

Equivalent guidance is also provided in IAS 11 Construction Contracts and credit will be awarded where candidates discuss revenue recognition under IAS 11 as Island Co is providing a single substantial asset for a customer under the terms of a contract.

Disputed receivable

The amount owed from Jacks Mine Co is highly material as it represents 50.9% of profit before tax, 2.3% of revenue, and 3% of total assets. The risk is that the receivable is overstated if no impairment of the disputed receivable is recognised.

Legal claim

The claim should be investigated seriously by Island Co. The chief executive officer's (CEO) opinion that the claim will not result in any financial consequence for Island Co is naïve and flippant. Damages could be awarded against Island Co if it is found that the machinery is faulty. The recurring high level of warranty provision implies that machinery faults are fairly common and therefore the accident could be the result of a defective machine being supplied to Sawyer Co. The risk is that no provision is created for the potential damages under IAS 37 *Provisions, Contingent Liabilities and Contingent Assets*, if the likelihood of paying damages is considered probable. Alternatively, if the likelihood of damages being paid to Sawyer Co is considered a possibility then a disclosure note should be made in the financial statements describing the nature and possible financial effect of the contingent liability. As discussed below, the CEO, Kate Shannon, has an incentive not to make a provision or disclose a contingent liability due to the planned share sale post year end.

A further risk is that any legal fees associated with the claim have not been accrued within the financial statements. As the claim has arisen during the year, the expense must be included in this year's statement of comprehensive income, even if the claim is still ongoing at the year end.

The fact that the legal claim is effectively being ignored may cast doubts on the overall integrity of senior management, and on the integrity of the financial statements. Management representations should be approached with a degree of professional scepticism during the audit.

Sawyer Co has cancelled two orders. If the amounts are still outstanding at the year end then it is highly likely that Sawyer Co will not pay the invoiced amounts, and thus receivables are overstated. If the stage one payments have already been made, then Sawyer Co may claim a refund, in which case a provision should be made to repay the amount, or a contingent liability disclosed in a note to the financial statements.

Sawyer Co is one of only five major customers, and losing this customer could have future going concern implications for Island Co if a new source of revenue cannot be found to replace the lost income stream from Sawyer Co. If the legal claim becomes public knowledge, and if Island Co is found to have supplied faulty machinery, then it will be difficult to attract new customers.

A case of this nature could bring bad publicity to Island Co, a potential going concern issue if it results in any of the five key customers terminating orders with Island Co. The auditors should plan to extend the going concern work programme to incorporate the issues noted above.

Inventories

Work in progress is material to the financial statements, representing 8.9% of total assets. The inventory count was held two weeks prior to the year end. There is an inherent risk that the valuation has not been correctly rolled forward to a year end position.

The key risk is the estimation of the stage of completion of work in progress. This is subjective, and knowledge appears to be confined to the chief engineer. Inventory could be overvalued if the machines are assessed to be more complete than they actually are at the year end. Absorption of labour costs and overheads into each machine is a complex calculation and must be done consistently with previous years.

It will also be important that consumable inventories not yet utilised on a machine, e.g. screws, nuts and bolts, are correctly valued and included as inventories of raw materials within current assets.

Overseas supplier

As the supplier is new, controls may not yet have been established over the recording of foreign currency transactions. Inherent risk is high as the trade payable should be retranslated using the year end exchange rate per IAS 21 *The Effects of Changes in Foreign Exchange Rates*. If the retranslation is not performed at the year end, the trade payable could be significantly over or under valued, depending on the movement of the dollar to euro exchange rate between the purchase date and the year end. The components should remain at historic cost within inventory valuation and should not be retranslated at the year end.

Warranty provision

The warranty provision is material at 2.6% of total assets (2006 – 2.7%). The provision has increased by only $100,000, an increase of 4.2%, compared to a revenue increase of 21.4%. This could indicate an underprovision as the percentage change in revenue would be expected to be in line with the percentage change in the warranty provision, unless significant improvements had been made to the quality of machines installed for customers during the year. This appears unlikely given the legal claim by Sawyer Co, and the machines installed at Jacks Mine Co operating inefficiently. The basis of the estimate could be understated to avoid charging the increase in the provision as an expense through the statement of comprehensive income. This is of special concern given that it is the CEO and majority shareholder who estimates the warranty provision.

Majority shareholder

Kate Shannon exerts control over Island Co via a majority shareholding, and by holding the position of CEO. This greatly increases the inherent risk that the financial statements could be deliberately misstated, i.e. overvaluation of assets, undervaluation of liabilities, and thus overstatement of profits. The risk is severe at this year end as Kate Shannon is hoping to sell some Island Co shares post year end. As the price that she receives for these shares will be to a large extent influenced by the statement of financial position of the company at 30 November 2007, she has a definite interest in manipulating the financial statements for her own personal benefit. For example:

- not recognising a provision or contingent liability for the legal claim from Sawyer Co

- not providing for the potentially irrecoverable receivable from Jacks Mines Co

- not increasing the warranty provision

- Recognising revenue earlier than permitted by IAS 18 *Revenue*.

Related party transactions

Kate Shannon controls Island Co and also controls Pacific Co. Transactions between the two companies should be disclosed per IAS 24 *Related Party Disclosures*. There is risk that not all transactions have been disclosed, or that a transaction has been disclosed at an inappropriate value. Details of the lease contract between the two companies should be disclosed within a note to the financial statements, in particular, any amounts owed from Island Co to Pacific Co at 30 November 2007 should be disclosed.

Other issues

- Kate Shannon wants the audit to be completed as soon as possible, which brings forward the deadline for completion of the audit. The audit team may not have time to complete all necessary procedures, or there may not be time for adequate reviews to be carried out on the work performed. Detection risk, and thus audit risk is increased, and the overall quality of the audit could be jeopardised.

- This is especially important given that this is the first year audit and therefore the audit team will be working with a steep learning curve. Audit procedures may take longer than originally planned, yet there is little time to extend procedures where necessary.

- Kate Shannon may also exert considerable influence on the members of the audit team to ensure that the financial statements show the best possible position of Island Co in view of her share sale. It is crucial that the audit team members adhere strictly to ethical guidelines and that independence is beyond question.

- Due to the seriousness of the matters noted above, a final matter to be considered at the planning stage is that a second partner review (Engagement Quality Control Review) should be considered for the audit this year end. A suitable independent reviewer should be indentified, and time planned and budgeted for at the end of the assignment.

Conclusion

From the range of issues discussed in these briefing notes, it can be seen that the audit of Island Co will be a relatively high risk engagement.

(b) ISA 540 *Auditing Accounting Estimates, Including Fair Value Accounting Estimates and Related Disclosures* requires that auditors should obtain sufficient audit evidence as to whether an accounting estimate, such as a warranty provision, is reasonable given the entity's circumstances, and that disclosure is appropriate. One, or a combination of the following approaches should be used:

Review and test the process used by management to develop the estimate

- Review contracts or orders for the terms of the warranty to gain an understanding of the obligation of Island Co.

- Review correspondence with customers during the year to gain an understanding of claims already in progress at the year end.

- Perform analytical procedures to compare the level of warranty provision year on year, and compare actual to budgeted provisions. If possible disaggregate the data, for example, compare provision for specific types of machinery or customer by customer.

- Re-calculate the warranty provision.

- Agree the percentage applied in the calculation to the stated accounting policy of Island Co.

- Review board minutes for discussion of on-going warranty claims, and for approval of the amount provided.

- Use management accounts to ascertain normal level of warranty rectification costs during the year.

- Discuss with Kate Shannon the assumptions she used to determine the percentage used in her calculations.

- Consider whether assumptions used are consistent with the auditors' understanding of the business.

- Compare prior year provision with actual expenditure on warranty claims in the accounting period.

- Compare the current year provision with prior year and discuss any fluctuation with Kate Shannon.

Review subsequent events which confirm the estimate made

- Review any work carried out post year end on specific faults that have been provided for. Agree that all costs are included in the year end provision.

- Agree cash expended on rectification work in the post reporting period to the cash book.

- Agree cash expended on rectification work post year end to suppliers' invoices, or to internal cost ledgers if work carried out by employees of Island Co.

- Read customer correspondence received post year end for any claims received since the year end.

(c) (i) ISQC 1 *Quality Control for Firms That Perform Audits and Reviews of Historical Financial Information and Other Assurance and Related Services* Engagements provides guidance on the overall quality control systems that should be implemented by an audit firm. ISA 220 *Quality Control for an Audit of Financial Statements* specifies the quality control procedures that should be applied by the engagement team in individual audit assignments.

Procedures include the following:

Client acceptance procedures

There should be full documentation, and conclusion on, ethical and client acceptance issues in each audit assignment. The engagement partner should consider whether members of the audit team have complied with ethical requirements, for example, whether all members of the team are independent of the client. Additionally, the engagement partner should conclude whether all acceptance procedures have been followed, for example, that the audit firm has considered the integrity of the principal owners and key management of the client. Other procedures on client acceptance should include:

- obtaining professional clearance from previous auditors

- consideration of any conflict of interest

- money laundering (client identification) procedures.

Engagement team

Procedures should be followed to ensure that the engagement team collectively has the skills, competence and time to perform the audit engagement. The engagement partner should assess that the audit team, for example:

- has the appropriate level of technical knowledge

- has experience of audit engagements of a similar nature and complexity

- has the ability to apply professional judgement
- understands professional standards, and regulatory and legal requirements.

Direction

The engagement team should be directed by the engagement partner. Procedures such as an engagement planning meeting should be undertaken to ensure that the team understands:

- their responsibilities
- the objectives of the work they are to perform
- the nature of the client's business
- risk related issues
- how to deal with any problems that may arise; and
- the detailed approach to the performance of the audit.

The planning meeting should be led by the partner and should include all people involved with the audit. There should be a discussion of the key issues identified at the planning stage.

Supervision

Supervision should be continuous during the engagement. Any problems that arise during the audit should be rectified as soon as possible. Attention should be focused on ensuring that members of the audit team are carrying out their work in accordance with the planned approach to the engagement. Significant matters should be brought to the attention of senior members of the audit team. Documentation should be made of key decisions made during the audit engagement.

Review

The review process is one of the key quality control procedures. All work performed must be reviewed by a more senior member of the audit team. Reviewers should consider for example whether:

- rork has been performed in accordance with professional standards
- the objectives of the procedures performed have been achieved
- work supports conclusions drawn and is appropriately documented.

The review process itself must be evidenced.

Consultation

Finally the engagement partner should arrange consultation on difficult or contentious matters. This is a procedure whereby the matter is discussed with a professional outside the engagement team, and sometimes outside the audit firm. Consultations must be documented to show:

- the issue on which the consultation was sought; and
- the results of the consultation.

(ii) Consultation – it may not be possible to hold extensive consultations on specialist issues within a small firm, due to a lack of specialist professionals. There may be a lack of suitably experienced peers to discuss issues arising on client engagements. Arrangements with other practices for consultation may be necessary.

Training/Continuing Professional Development (CPD) – resources may not be available, and it is expensive to establish an in-house training function. External training consortia can be used to provide training/CPD for qualified staff, and training on non-exam related issues for non-qualified staff.

Review procedures – it may not be possible to hold an independent review of an engagement within the firm due to the small number of senior and experienced auditors. In this case an external review service may be purchased.

Lack of specialist experience – where special skills are needed within an engagement; the skills may be bought in, for example, by seconding staff from another practice. Alternatively if work is too specialised for the firm, the work could be sub-contracted to another practice.

Working papers – the firm may lack resources to establish an in-house set of audit manuals or standard working papers. In this case documentation can be provided by external firms or professional bodies.

Examiner's comments

It was pleasing to see many candidates scoring well on **part (a)**. However, many candidates clearly misunderstood the concept of audit risk, confusing it with business risk, leading to inappropriate comments. Examples included:

Suggesting 'foreign exchange' as an audit risk with no discussion of the potential for misstatement of liabilities or exchange gains or losses in the financial statements.

Suggesting 'going concern' as an audit risk, but with no explanation of the impact of this at the transaction or disclosure level.

Suggesting 'potential for litigation or claims' as an audit risk, with no indication of how this could result in liabilities or the need for disclosure within the financial statements.

It is disappointing that at this level candidates seem unable to distinguish between audit risk and business risk, meaning that a significant minority of candidates failed to answer the question requirement. In addition, many candidates wasted valuable time in the examination by producing a detailed discussion of the coal mining industry, how the industry is in decline, and how environmentally unfriendly the industry is. This may be true, but it does not answer the question. Firstly, these comments could be classified as business risks, but they are not audit risks, and so are irrelevant. Secondly, your client is not actually a coal mining business, it is a engineering firm which designs, manufactures and installs machinery – a fundamental fact that it appears a lot of candidates did not pick up on.

In addition, some candidates included irrelevant discussion of audit acceptance issues in their answer to part (a), with comments such as 'do we have enough competent staff', 'we need to sign an engagement letter', and 'we need to decide on a fee level' commonly seen. Candidates need to make sure that they read the question carefully and understand the 'time line' in the question. Here, your firm has already been appointed auditor, and you are in the process of planning the audit. It is too late to be wondering whether your firm should have accepted the appointment, and how much you might charge for the engagement.

Some financial data was provided in the scenario, and many candidates used the figures to ascertain the materiality of some of the financial statement balances that were discussed. However, just stating 'we need to consider materiality' earns no marks when it is possible to actually calculate it from information in the scenario.

The marking guide for part (a) included 2 professional marks. The requirement was to prepare briefing notes, and professional marks were awarded where candidates used an appropriate format, such as a clear heading indicating that the document was indeed briefing notes, a brief introduction and conclusion, and the use of headings and sections within the document to display a logical structure. Candidates should be aware that ignoring the instruction to produce the answer in a certain format means that the professional marks cannot be awarded.

In **part (b)** candidates were required to suggest audit procedures relevant to an estimated warranty provision. There were some sound answers here, indicating that many candidates had prepared well for this type of requirement. However, there were many vague suggestions, such as 'get a management representation', 'get an expert opinion' and 'compare with industry average'. All of these suggestions are not specific enough to answer the requirement, and in the case of an industry average I would be surprised if such a statistic existed, and if it did, how appropriate any comparison between Island Co's provision and an industry average would be.

The final section of the question focussed on quality control. On the whole answers were reasonable for the first part of the requirement. My first comment here would be to remind candidates to read the requirement carefully, and when asked for FOUR quality control procedures, they should restrict their comments to FOUR procedures. It is a waste of time to write any extra. Additionally, candidates should have picked up on the fact that they should have discussed procedures relevant to the individual audit engagement. Hence, discussions of firm-wide quality control procedures, such as appointing an ethics partner, and conducting firm-wide training on ethics were totally irrelevant. Candidates must only answer the specific question that has been set.

The **final requirement** was by far the least well answered in Question 1. Candidates were asked to discuss the particular problems faced by small firm of Chartered Certified Accountants in implementing quality control procedures. Although some candidates provided a logical discussion and some reasonable, practical recommendations, many candidates displayed an appalling lack of tack and professionalism in answering the question, seeming to condemn small firms as totally incompetent, and having no ability to produce good quality work at all. Typical comments along these lines included:

- 'small firms cannot attract competent staff'

- 'small firms have no resources'

- 'small firms focus on getting new business and ignore quality controls'

...and the most common suggestion as to how small firms can overcome these alleged 'problems' was for small firms to merge with each other and thus avoid being small.

Candidates must appreciate that these types of comments are wholly inappropriate and display a real lack of any kind of commercial awareness.

			Marking scheme		
(a)			**Principal audit risks/planning matters**		*Marks*
			Generally ½ mark each risk/matter identified.		
			Up to 1 further mark for significant issues explained:		
			Revenue recognition		
			Legal claim		
			Going concern		
			Valuation of inventories		
			Warranty provision		
			CEO incentive to manipulate figures and disclosures		
			Disputed receivable		
			Cancelled orders		
			Overseas supplier		
			Related party disclosure		
			CEO influence on audit team		
			Up to ½ further mark for obvious matters explained:		
			New client		
			Tight deadline		
			Up to 2 marks for format of briefing notes and clarity of explanation		13
(b)			**Audit procedures for warranty provision**		
			Generally 1 mark per procedure:		
			Review contracts		
			Review correspondence		
			Recalculate (max ½ mark)		
			Review board minutes		
			Consider assumptions		
			Compare actual current year expenditure to prior year provision		
			Post year end expenditure		5
(c)	(i)		**Four QC procedures for individual audit assignment**		
			2 marks per procedure described (½ mark max if only identified and not described):		
			– Client acceptance		
			– Engagement team		
			– Direction		
			– Supervision		
			– Review		
			– Consultation		
			– Ref ISQC 1/ISA 220 – 1 mark max		
	(ii)		**Two QC problems in small firm**		
			2 marks per problem = 1 mark for problem, 1 mark for recommendation:		
			Ideas list:		
			– Consultation		
			– Training/CPD		
			– Review procedures		
			– Specialist experience		
			– Working papers		12
Total					30

8   SCI-TECH CO *Walk in the footsteps of a top tutor*

Key answer tips

The questions mixes a number of elements of the syllabus. As well as being framed in the context of planning the final year end audit the question also requires consideration of the impact of outsourcing accounting functions and providing an assurance opinion on Key Performance Indicators. The question also requires a sound knowledge of accounting treatment of intangible development costs. The key to scoring well in this question is to ensure you identify the specific requirements of the questions and do not slip into general considerations of payroll accounting and development costs. There are many issues in the narrative that must be considered in a well balanced answer.

(a)   Outsourcing is when an external specialist organisation (also known as a service organisation) is used to carry out functions which would normally be performed within the entity. Service organisations usually operate in one of two ways:

- The service organisation fully maintains the outsourced function, dealing with all aspects of the function including establishing accounting records, maintaining those records and initiating transactions relevant to the function. Here the reporting entity may hold no internal records at all in relation to the function other than those provided from the service organisation.

- The service organisation executes transactions only at the request of the entity, or acts as a custodian of assets. Here the reporting entity will maintain internal records relating to the outsourced function.

It is increasingly common for functions such as data processing, payroll, and internal audit to be outsourced. ISA 402 *Audit Considerations Relating to an Entity Using a Service Organisation* contains guidance for auditors on how outsourcing should be considered during the audit process.

The matters to be considered in planning the audit approach of payroll are as follows:

Materiality

Salary expense is material at 8.4% of revenue in 2007 (2006 – 10.5%). In addition to the salary expense separately disclosed as part of operating expenses, the capitalised development costs will also contain an element of salary expenses, being the salary of employees working directly on development projects. Payroll represents a significant transaction cycle and therefore the audit of payroll is significant within the audit process.

Accessibility

A key issue is that the auditors' terms of agreement are with Sci-Tech Co, not ProPay Co. This means that the auditors do not necessarily have the right of access to books and records held at ProPay Co. It is essential for auditors to be allowed access to the payroll records held at ProPay Co in order to conduct necessary audit procedures. The contractual terms containing access arrangements between Sci-Tech Co and ProPay Co should be reviewed and documented. Contact will need to be made with the service organisation to arrange the time when the auditor can have access to the relevant books and records.

Control risk

In previous years the audit of payroll was systems based, implying a strong control environment and good control procedures when payroll was internally operated. Now the payroll function is outsourced the auditor will have to determine the strength of the controls operated by ProPay Co. The following should be considered:

- extent of controls operated by ProPay Co

- extent of quality assurance within ProPay Co (e.g. internal audit)

- degree of monitoring by Sci-Tech Co (e.g. monthly review of payroll records maintained by ProPay Co)

- experience of errors within payroll data since outsourcing commenced.

As the salary expense is material to the financial statements, the accounting systems of ProPay Co should be fully documented and the controls tested to determine the extent of any reliance to be placed upon them.

Existence of independent records

If Sci-Tech Co does not maintain independent back up records relating to payroll then the figures in the financial statements are simply those taken from the records of ProPay Co. In this case the risk of error is heightened as there is no independent check by Sci-Tech Co that the figures are accurate, and the only audit evidence available will be from the records of ProPay Co.

Compliance

It is essential to determine whether proper accounting records have been maintained by the service organisation. Payroll records must comply with tax as well as accounting regulations, and could therefore be subject to periodic regulatory inspections.

Initiation of transactions

A crucial issue is whether salary payments to employees and deductions paid to tax authorities and pension plans are initiated by Sci-Tech Co or by ProPay Co. If ProPay Co initiates such transactions then detailed substantive procedures should be performed on the records of ProPay Co, and detailed understanding must be gained on how the data is transferred into the accounting records of Sci-Tech Co.

(b) (i) **Materiality**

The net book value of capitalised development costs represent 7% of total assets in 2007 (2006 – 7.7%), and is therefore material. The net book value has increased by 13%, a significant trend.

The costs capitalised during the year amount to $750,000. If it was found that the development cost had been inappropriately capitalised, the cost should instead have been expensed. This would reduce profit before tax by $750,000, representing 42% of the year's profit. This is highly material. It is therefore essential to gather sufficient evidence to support the assertion that development costs should be recognised as an asset.

In 2007, $750,000 capitalised development costs have been incurred, when added to $160,000 research costs expensed, total research and development costs are $910,000 which represents 20.2% of total revenue, again indicating a high level of materiality for this class of transaction.

Relevant accounting standard

Development costs should only be capitalised as an intangible asset if the recognition criteria of IAS 38 *Intangible Assets* have been demonstrated in full.

- Intention to complete the intangible asset and use or sell it.

- Technical feasibility and ability to use or sell.

- Ability to generate future economic benefit.

- Availability of technical, financial and other resources to complete.

- Ability to measure the expenditure attributable to the intangible asset.

Research costs must be expensed, as should development costs which do not comply with the above criteria. The auditors must consider how Sci-Tech Co differentiates between research and development costs.

There is risk that not all of the criteria have been demonstrated, especially due to the subjective nature of the development itself.

- Pharmaceutical development is highly regulated. If the government does not license the product then the product cannot be sold, and economic benefits will therefore not be received.

- Market research should justify the commercial viability of the product. The launch of a rival product to Flortex means that market share is likely to be much lower than anticipated, and the ability to sell Flortex is reduced. This could mean that Flortex will not generate an overall economic benefit if future sales will not recover the research and development costs already suffered, and yet to be suffered, prior to launch. The existence of the rival product could indicate that Flortex is no longer commercially viable, in which case the capitalised development costs relating to Flortex should be immediately expensed.

- The funding on which development is dependent may be withdrawn, indicating that there are not adequate resources to complete the development of the products. Sci-Tech has failed to meet one of its required key performance indicators (KPI) in the year ended 30 November 2007, as products valued at 0.8% revenue have been donated to charity, whereas the required KPI is 1% revenue.

Given that there is currently a breach of the target KPIs, this is likely to result in funding equivalent to 25% of research and development expenditure being withdrawn. If Sci-Tech Co is unable to source alternative means of finance, then it would seem that adequate resources may not be available to complete the development of new products.

(ii) Evidence supporting the assertion that development costs are technically feasible would include the following.

- Review the results of scientific tests performed on the products, for example, the results of animal or human testing of the products.

- Discuss any detrimental results of these tests, e.g. harmful side effects, with the scientists working on the project to determine what corrective action is being taken.

- Enquire whether any licences necessary for continued development and/or commercial production have been granted by the appropriate regulatory body.

- Compare expected to actual development costs incurred per product being developed. Where actual costs are in excess of expected costs investigate whether the extra costs have been incurred in order to make good any problems identified in the development process.

- Review board minutes for relevant discussion of the product development taking place during the year.

(c) **Audit procedures to determine the validity of the amortisation rate of five years** being applied to development costs in relation to the product Plummet would include the following.

- Obtain the papers documenting market research carried out on Plummet. Review and ascertain that the market research supports a product life span of five years.

- Review actual sales patterns since the launch of Plummet and compare to the predicted sales per the market research document.

Tutorial note

This will help to demonstrate the accuracy of the predicted sales forecast of Plummet

- Read the assumptions underpinning the market research sales projections, and consider whether these assumptions agree with the auditors' understanding of the business.

- Discuss sales trends with the sales/marketing directors and ascertain whether sales are in line with management's expectations.

- Read correspondence with retail outlets to ensure there is continued support for selling Plummet.

- Obtain marketing/advertising budgets and ascertain enough expenditure is continuing on Plummet to support continued sales.

(d) (i) The main reason why it may not be possible to provide a high level of assurance is that the KPIs are not defined precisely.

- The value of donated pharmaceutical products is compared to revenue to provide a percentage. However, it will be difficult to accurately value the donated products – are they valued at cost, or at sales price? Are delivery costs included in the valuation? The intrinsic value may be lower than sales value as Sci-Tech Co may decide to donate products which are not useful or relevant to the charities they are donated to.

- The value of 'cost of involvement with local charities' is also not defined. If the donations are purely cash, then it should be easy to verify donations using normal audit procedures to verify cash payments. However, the 'involvement with local charities' is not defined and will be difficult to quantify as a percentage of revenue. For example, involvement may include:
  - time spent by Sci-Tech Co employees at local charity events
  - education and training provided to members of the local community in health care matters.

- Number of serious accidents is also difficult to quantify as what constitutes a 'serious' accident is subjective. For example, is an accident serious if it results in a hospitalisation of the employee? Or serious if it results in more than five days absence from work while recovering?

In addition, the sufficiency of evidence available is doubtful, as such matters will not form part of the accounting records and thus there may be limited and possibly only unreliable sources of evidence available.

- Donated goods may not be separately recorded in inventory movement records. It may not be possible to distinguish donated goods from sold or destroyed items.

- Unless time sheets are maintained, there is unlikely to be any detailed records of 'involvement' in local charities.

(ii) Procedures to verify the number of serious accidents during 2007 could include the following:

Tutorial note

Procedures should focus on the completeness of the disclosure as it is in the interest of Sci-Tech Co to understate the number of serious accidents.

- Review the accident log book and count the total number of accidents during the year.

- Discuss the definition of 'serious accident' with the directors and clarify exactly what criteria need to be met to satisfy the definition.

- For serious accidents identified:
  - review HR records to determine the amount of time taken off work
  - review payroll records to determine the financial amount of sick pay awarded to the employee
  - review correspondence with the employee regarding the accident.

Tutorial note

The above will help to clarify that the accident was indeed serious.

- Review board minutes where the increase in the number of serious accidents has been discussed.

- Review correspondence with Sci-Tech Co's legal advisors to ascertain any legal claims made against the company due to accidents at work.

- Enquire as to whether any health and safety visits have been conducted during the year by regulatory bodies, and review any documentation or correspondence issued to Sci-Tech Co after such visits.

Tutorial note

It is highly likely that in a regulated industry such as pharmaceutical research, any serious accident would trigger a health and safety inspection from the appropriate regulatory body.

- Discuss the level of accidents with representatives of Sci-Tech Co's employees to reach an understanding as to whether accidents sometimes go unreported in the accident log book.

Examiner's comments

Part (a) concerned the outsourced payroll function, with candidates required to discuss the matters to be considered in planning the audit of payroll. This was a broad requirement, and many candidates produced good answers covering a variety of 'matters', including the materiality of the payroll expense, the audit approach to be considered, and the need to contact, and very likely visit, the service organisation providing the payroll function. The best answers used the data provided to perform some simple analytical review, leading them to discuss why the salary expense figure had decreased from the previous year, when the turnover had increased. It was however disappointing to see that very few candidates really discussed in any depth the requirements and guidance contained in ISA 402 *Audit Considerations Relating to an Entity Using a Service Organisation*. Some answers to part (a) simply stated a list of audit procedures relating to payroll, totally ignoring the fact that the function was now outsourced, and many answers provided a list of pros and cons of outsourcing which clearly was not asked for. Some candidates assumed that they would be able to rely on Propay's records without any further work, some thought that they could rely on the work of Propay's auditors, neither of which is true.

Professional marks were awarded in part (a) for the breadth of topics discussed, and for displaying a sensible prioritisation of the issues contained in the scenario, including an appreciation that outsourcing would have a significant impact on the planning and the execution of the audit of payroll.

Part (b) focussed on the audit of development costs which had been capitalised as an intangible asset. The answers were on the whole rather disappointing. Requirement (bi) required a discussion of matters to be considered in deciding on the appropriateness of capitalising the development costs. Most candidates could reel off the criteria for capitalisation under IAS 38 *Intangible Assets*, which is relevant, but few candidates then went on to apply the criteria to the scenario provided. It is very important that candidates appreciate that at this level of professional examination, few marks can be awarded for the rote-learning and regurgitating of facts, such as accounting standards criteria, without any application to the question.

Candidates who discussed the possible impairment of the development intangible asset due to a competitor's actions performed well, as did candidates who questioned the continued availability of government funding which was dependent on KPI targets being met. Examiners do not provide detailed information such as this in scenario questions for no reason – the information is there to be read, understood, and used in answering the question. Some answers didn't contain any relevant points from the question scenario.

Answers were also unsatisfactory for requirement (bii), where candidates were asked for the evidence they would seek to support the assertion that the capitalised development costs related to projects that were technically feasible. Most candidates ignored this requirement and instead gave a list of evidence that would be relevant to other assertions, for example, that the development was commercially viable (market research being the most common source of evidence quoted here), or that the projects' costs were separately identifiable (the evidence commonly referred to here was the mysterious 'management approval'). Technical feasibility is nothing to do with commercial viability or management approval. Candidates should have asked themselves 'what would give me evidence that Sci-Tech can actually make this product' (e.g. scientific test results), not 'will they be able to sell this product' (e.g. positive results from market research).

Requirement (c) focussed on audit procedures relevant to the amortisation of capitalised development costs. Many candidates appeared to have confused this with the previous requirement, or simply gave unclear examples of audit procedures along the same lines as discussed above with reference to question 1(b), for example 'get management representation', 're-perform calculation', and 'compare with industry average'. As discussed above, these vague comments are not detailed audit procedures and are not worthy of credit at this stage in the professional examinations.

The final section of the question covered the provision of an assurance engagement on the company's published KPIs. The inclusion of this part of the syllabus in a compulsory question should not have been a surprise, as the Examiner's Approach article clearly states that non-audit assignments are likely to feature in every examination. In addition the Examiner's articles Continue to Rest Assured, and in particular Clear Thinking both covered the issue of KPIs being increasingly disclosed by companies. It was clear that those candidates who had taken the time to read through these articles as part of their preparation for the examination performed well here. However, there were common mistakes. Many candidates seemed to misread 'key performance indicator' as 'prospective financial information' and the word 'target' as 'future', and proceeded to provide a wholly inappropriate discussion of gathering evidence in relation to forecasts. Some candidates focussed on the KPIs being 'immaterial' and therefore not worth auditing. Only the best scripts identified that KPIs are hard to define, and suffer from a lack of evidence.

In answering the final requirement, which invited candidates to suggest procedures used to verify the number of serious accidents reported, the marks awarded to scripts were polarised. Many candidates seemed to think that the auditor has access to absolutely any kind of evidence that they could wish for. Common sources of evidence referred to included:

- The private medical records of employees
- Police reports on 'dangerous' incidents
- Hospital admissions data
- Interviews with ambulance drivers / paramedics / doctors
- Death certificates

Candidates need to appreciate that although the auditor will have access to books and records held by their client, they will not be able to access external and possibly highly confidential information as a means to gather evidence. The above examples show of a lack of commercial, or even, common sense.

	Marking scheme	
(a)	**Outsourcing – definition and matters to be considered**	*Marks*
	Definition – 1 mark	
	Matters to be considered – generally 1½ marks for each matter explained:	
	– Materiality	
	– Accessibility	
	– Control issues (extend to 2 marks for detailed answer)	
	– Independent records	
	– Compliance	
	– Transactions	
	– Ref ISA 402 (½ mark max)	
	Up to 2 marks for clarity of explanation	9
(b)	(i) **Recognition of development costs**	
	– Materiality – max 2 marks	
	– IAS 38 criteria – max 1 mark	
	– Application of criteria to scenario – max 3 marks	
	(ii) **Evidence on technical feasibility**	
	Generally 1 mark per procedure:	
	– Review documentary evidence of scientific test results	
	– Discuss test results	
	– Licences	
	– Analytical procedures	
	– Board minute review	8
(c)	**Evidence on amortisation rate**	
	Generally 1 mark per procedure:	
	– Market research results	
	– Actual sales patterns	
	– Management assumptions	
	– Discussion of sales trends	
	– Correspondence with retail outlets	
	– Advertising budgets	5
(d)	(i) **KPI assurance difficulties**	
	– Discussion of problems in defining KPI terms – max 2 marks	
	– Discussion of difficulty in gathering evidence – max 2 marks	
	(ii) **Procedures on number of accidents**	
	Generally 1 mark per procedure:	
	Ideas list:	
	– Review log book	
	– Discuss and clarify criteria	
	– HR/payroll records	
	– Employee correspondence	
	– Board minute review	
	– Legal letter review	
	– Discuss with employees	8
	Total	30

9 MURRAY

Key answer tips

This question is unusual in that it doesn't ask about risk! However matters to consider in taking on an engagement includes risk, so it's examined indirectly. This question is also a great question to revise groups, but make sure you restrict your answer to the planning of the audit, not the whole audit process.

(a) **Matters to consider**

- Ross & Co should be sufficiently competent and experienced to undertake the audit of Di Rollo as it has similar competence and experience in auditing the larger Murray Co. However, Ross needs knowledge of conducting businesses in South America including legal and tax regulations.

Tutorial note

Candidates should not be querying their competence and experience in the field of retailing as though they were dealing with highly regulated or specialist industries such as banking or insurance.

- Any factors that might impair Ross's objectivity in forming an opinion on the financial statements of Di Rollo (and the consolidated financial statements of Murray). For example, if Ross was involved in any due diligence review of Di Rollo, the same senior staff should not be assigned to the audit.

Tutorial note

Candidates will not be awarded marks for going into 'autopilot' on independence issues. For example, Ross holding shares in Di Rollo is not possible (since 100%-owned).

- Whether Ross has sufficient, if any, resources in South America (e.g. in representative/associated offices). Ross must have sufficient time to report on Di Rollo within the timeframe for reporting on the consolidated financial statements of Murray.

- Ross should not accept the nomination if any limitation imposed by management would be likely to result in the need to issue a disclaimer of opinion on Di Rollo's financial statements.

- Whether the proposed restriction in audit fee compromises the quality of the audit of Di Rollo and/or the Murray group. The 20% increase needs to be sufficient to cover the cost of the audit of Di Rollo and the incremental costs associated with auditing Murray's consolidated financial statements (as well as any general annual price increase that might be applied to audit fees).

- Di Rollo is material to the Murray group. At acquisition the fair values of Di Rollo's tangible non-current assets, current assets and current liabilities represent 6.8%, 2.9% and 8%, respectively, of those in Murray's consolidated financial statements at 31 March 2007.

- It is usual that a parent company should want its auditors to audit its subsidiaries. If Ross were to decline the nomination, Murray's management may seek an alternative auditor for the group.

Tutorial note

Credit will not be awarded for merely querying why the current auditor is not being retained.

- Murray should give Ross written permission to communicate with Di Rollo's current auditor to enquire if there is any professional reason why they should not accept this assignment.

- Murray may provide Ross with additional fee-earning opportunities (e.g. due diligence reviews, tax consultancy, etc) if it continues to expand in future.

(b) **Effect of acquisition on planning the audit of Murray's consolidated financial statements for the year ending 31 March 2008**

Group structure

The new group structure must be ascertained to identify all entities that should be consolidated into the Murray group's financial statements for the year ending 31 March 2008.

Materiality assessment

Preliminary materiality for the group will be much higher, in monetary terms, than in the prior year. For example, if a % of total assets is a determinant of the preliminary materiality, it may be increased by 10% (as the fair value of assets acquired, including goodwill, is $2,373,000 compared with $21.5m in Murray's consolidated financial statements for the year ended 31 March 2007).

The materiality of each subsidiary should be re-assessed, in terms of the enlarged group as at the planning stage. For example, any subsidiary that was just material for the year ended 31 March 2007 may no longer be material to the group.

This assessment will identify, for example:

– those entities requiring an audit visit; and

– those entities for which substantive analytical procedures may suffice.

As Di Rollo's assets are material to the group Ross should plan to inspect the South American operations. The visit may include a meeting with Di Rollo's previous auditors to discuss any problems that might affect the balances at acquisition and a review of the prior year audit working papers, with their permission.

Di Rollo was acquired two months into the financial year therefore its post-acquisition results should be expected to be material to the consolidated statement of comprehensive income.

Goodwill acquired

The assets and liabilities of Di Rollo at 31 March 2008 will be combined on a line-by-line basis into the consolidated financial statements of Murray and goodwill arising on acquisition recognized.

Audit work on the fair value of the Di Rollo brand name at acquisition, $600,000, may include a review of a brand valuation specialist's working papers and an assessment of the reasonableness of assumptions made.

Significant items of plant are likely to have been independently valued prior to the acquisition. It may be appropriate to plan to place reliance on the work of expert valuers. The fair value adjustment on plant and equipment is very high (441% of carrying amount at the date of acquisition). This may suggest that Di Rollo's depreciation policies are over-prudent (e.g. if accelerated depreciation allowed for tax purposes is accounted for under local GAAP).

As the amount of goodwill is very material (approximately 50% of the cash consideration) it may be overstated if Murray has failed to recognize any assets acquired in the purchase of Di Rollo in accordance with IFRS 103 *Business Combinations*. For example, Murray may have acquired intangible assets such as customer lists or franchises that should be recognized separately from goodwill and amortized (rather than tested for impairment).

Subsequent impairment

The audit plan should draw attention to the need to consider whether the Di Rollo brand name and goodwill arising have suffered impairment as a result of the allegations against Di Rollo's former chief executive.

Liabilities

Proceedings in the legal claim made by Di Rollo's former chief executive will need to be reviewed. If the case is not resolved at 31 March 2008, a contingent liability may require disclosure in the consolidated financial statements, depending on the materiality of amounts involved. Legal opinion on the likelihood of Di Rollo successfully defending the claim may be sought. Provision should be made for any actual liabilities, such as legal fees.

Group (related party) transactions and balances

A list of all the companies in the group (including any associates) should be included in group audit instructions to ensure that intra-group transactions and balances (and any unrealized profits and losses on transactions with associates) are identified for elimination on consolidation. Any transfer pricing policies (e.g. for clothes manufactured by Di Rollo for Murray and sales of Di Rollo's accessories to Murray's retail stores) must be ascertained and any provisions for unrealized profit eliminated on consolidation.

It should be confirmed at the planning stage that inter-company transactions are identified as such in the accounting systems of all companies and that inter-company balances are regularly reconciled. (Problems are likely to arise if new inter-company balances are not identified/reconciled. In particular, exchange differences are to be expected.)

Other auditors

If Ross plans to use the work of other auditors in South America (rather than send its own staff to undertake the audit of Di Rollo), group instructions will need to be sent containing:

- proforma statements;
- a list of group and associated companies;
- a statement of group accounting policies (see below);
- the timetable for the preparation of the group accounts (see below);
- a request for copies of management letters;
- an audit work summary questionnaire or checklist;
- contact details (of senior members of Ross's audit team).

Accounting policies

Di Rollo may have material accounting policies which do not comply with the rest of the Murray group. As auditor to Di Rollo, Ross will be able to recalculate the effect of any non-compliance with a group accounting policy (that Murray's management would be adjusting on consolidation).

Timetable

The timetable for the preparation of Murray's consolidated financial statements should be agreed with management as soon as possible. Key dates should be planned for:

- agreement of inter-company balances and transactions;
- submission of proforma statements;
- completion of the consolidation package;
- tax review of group accounts;
- completion of audit fieldwork by other auditors;
- subsequent events review;
- final clearance on accounts of subsidiaries;
- Ross's final clearance of consolidated financial statements.

Tutorial note

The order of dates is illustrative rather than prescriptive.

(c) Management letter effectiveness criteria

Tutorial note

Candidates at this level must know that a management letter is a letter of weakness (also called post-audit letter). NO marks will be awarded for consideration of any other letters (e.g. management representation letters, engagement letters).

- Timeliness – a management letter should be issued as soon as possible after completion of the audit procedures giving rise to comment. This is particularly important when audit work is carried out on more than one audit visit and where it is a matter of urgency that management make improvements to their procedures (e.g. where there is evidence of serious weakness).

- Clarity – wording must be clear so that recipients understand the significance of weaknesses that are being drawn to their attention. It is particularly important that implications are explained clearly in terms that will prompt management to respond positively (e.g. drawing attention to the risks of financial loss arising).

- Illustrative – specific illustrative examples (e.g. of where controls have not been evidenced) should aid management in understanding the nature of the problem(s).

- Constructive comments/advice – recommendations for improvements must be practicable (i.e. appropriate and cost effective in the light of the client's resources) if the client is to take corrective action.

- Conciseness – unnecessary volume will distract management from new/additional matters that require their attention. For example, matters adequately dealt with in the internal auditor's report should not be repeated.

- Factual accuracy is essential. Inaccuracies will not only aggravate the client and appear unprofessional but could, in rare circumstances, result in liability. Similarly, the letter should not criticize (or 'cast aspersions') on individual staff members if it is the system that is inadequate.

- A suitable structure – for example 'tiered', where the report contains matters of varying levels of significance. By directing different classes of matters to the appropriate level or area of responsibility action by management can be taken more speedily and constructively.

Tutorial note

An alternative structure might be one that sequences those recommendations that improve profitability/cash flows before those that deal with information systems.

- Inclusion of staff responses – both to advise senior management of action proposed/being taken by their staff and to give credit to recommendations for improvements where it is due (e.g. where client's staff have proposed recommendations).

- Inclusion of management's response – an indication of the actions that management intends to take is more likely to result in action being taken. Discussing findings with management first should also ensure their factual accuracy.

- Client's perspective – implications from the client's viewpoint (e.g. in terms of cost savings) are more likely to be acted on than those expressed from an audit perspective (e.g. in terms of lowered audit risk).

- Professional tone – should not be offensive. Comments that fault management's knowledge, competence, motives or integrity are likely to provoke defensive reactions. Comments should be positive/constructive by emphasizing solutions/benefits.

Tutorial note

Other points that candidates may include:

- Inclusion of matters of future relevance
- Cost effectiveness – minutes of discussions with management instead of a formal weakness letter
- Not raising 'people problems' in such a formal communication (a confidential discussion is preferable).

10 YATES

Key answer tips

Part (a) – First think of the bases used to calculate planning materiality (Revenue; Assets; Profits) and the range of calculations; to justify your assessment consider the relevance of the results. i.e. Are profits a good indicator in this case?

Part (b) – Remember that business risks do not necessarily result in financial statement risks – your objective is to identify those risks that may result in the financial statements being materially misstated. A review of the components in the 'draft' (contain errors?) financial statements on a line by line basis is a good starting point.

Part (c) – Think about the plausible relationships between financial and non-financial information that will exist in this type of business. E.g. Mpg calculation? What 'proof in total' figures can be estimated?

Part (d) – Whilst having regard to the risk of misstatement, consider the principal financial statement assertions that need to be supported by audit evidence, the likely nature of evidence available and the testing techniques to be used.

(a) **Preliminary materiality**

	1/2%	1%
Revenue		
2006	$0.8m	$1.6m
2005	$0.7m	$1.4m
Profit before taxation	5%	10%
2006	$0.1m	$0.2m
2005	n/a	n/a
Total assets	1%	2%
2006	$1.0m	$2.1m
2005	$1.1m	$2.1m

A suitable range for preliminary materiality is $1.0m – $1.6m.

Tutorial note

As the financial statements are presented to a precision of $0.1m it is meaningless to suggest a preliminary materiality to a greater level of precision since this suggests a level of accuracy that will not be achieved.

Justification

- It is not meaningful to base preliminary materiality on a small profit (or a loss) as this will result in over-auditing of the financial statements.

- More than $1.6m revenue is material to the statement of comprehensive income, therefore preliminary materiality is likely to be set so as not to exceed this amount. Less than $0.8m is not material to revenue (or the statement of financial position) so preliminary materiality should not be less than this amount.

- A suitable preliminary materiality level is most likely to be one that lies within the overlap of the ranges calculated for revenue and total assets. $1m (1% of total assets) represents 0.6% revenue. This would be a prudent estimate of materiality (resulting in a higher level of audit work).

- $1.6m (1% of revenue) represents 1.5% of total assets. Preliminary materiality might be set at this end of the range had this been a recurring audit. However, as this is a first audit (and caution would generally result in over-auditing) preliminary materiality is likely to be lower.

- Total assets have fallen (marginally) since the prior year, whereas revenue has increased (by 11.8%). As draft figures for the statement of financial position appear more stable than for the statement of comprehensive income, preliminary materiality is more likely to be set in relation to statement of financial position amounts.

- The 2006 financial statements are draft for an unexpired period of time. Therefore greater errors should be expected than if they were actual. So, relatively, sample sizes for audit testing should be increased (i.e. preliminary materiality should be set at a relatively lower level).

(b) **Financial statement risks**

Tutorial note

Note the timeframe. Financial statements for the year to 30 June 2006 are draft. Certain misstatements may therefore exist due to year-end procedures not yet having taken place.

Revenue/(Receivables)

- Revenue has increased by 11.8% ((161.5 − 144.4)/ 144.4 × 100). Overstatement could arise if rebates due to customers have not yet been accounted for in full (as they are calculated in arrears). If rebates have still to be accounted for trade receivables will be similarly overstated.

Materials expense

- Materials expense has increased by 17.8% ((88.0 − 74.7) /74.7 × 100). This is more than the increase in revenue. This could be legitimate (e.g. if fuel costs have increased significantly). However, the increase could indicate misclassification of:

  - revenue expenditure (see fall in other expenses below);

  - capital expenditure (e.g. on overhauls or major refurbishment) as revenue;

  - finance lease payments as operating lease.

Depreciation/amortization

- This has fallen by 10.5% ((8.5 − 9.5) / 9.5 × 100). This could be valid (e.g. if Yates has significant assets already fully depreciated or the asset base is lower since last year's restructuring). However, there is a risk of understatement if, for example:

  - not all assets have been depreciated (or depreciated at the wrong rates, or only for 11 months of the year);

  - cost of non-current assets is understated (e.g. due to failure to recognize capital expenditure).

  This may be unlikely as other expenses have fallen also;

  - impairment losses have not been recognized (as compared with the prior year).

Tutorial note

Depreciation on vehicles and transport equipment represents only 7% of cost. If all items were being depreciated on a straight-line basis over eight years this should be 12.5%. The depreciation on other equipment looks more reasonable as it amounts to 14% which would be consistent with an average age of vehicles of seven years (i.e. in the middle of the range 3 − 13 years).

Other expenses

- These have fallen by 15.5% ((19.6 − 23.2)/23.2 × 100). They may have fallen (e.g. following the restructuring) or may be understated due to:

  - expenses being misclassified as materials expense;

  - underestimation of accrued expenses (especially as the financial reporting period has not yet expired).

Intangibles

- Intangible assets have increased by $1m (16% on the prior year). Although this may only just be material to the financial statements as a whole (see (a)) this is the net movement, therefore additions could be material.

- Internally-generated intangibles will be overstated if:

  - any of the IAS 38 recognition criteria cannot be demonstrated;

  - any impairment in the year has not yet been written off in accordance with IAS 36 *Impairment of Assets*.

Tangible assets

- The net book value of property (at cost) has fallen by 5%, vehicles are virtually unchanged (increased by just 2.5%) and other equipment (though the least material category) has fallen by 20.4%.

- Vehicles and equipment may be overstated if:

  - disposals have not been recorded;

  - depreciation has been undercharged (e.g. not for a whole year);

  - impairments have not yet been accounted for.

- Understatement will arise if finance leases are treated as operating leases.

Receivables

- Trade receivables have increased by just 2.2% (although sales increased by 11.8%) and may be understated due to a cut off error resulting in overstatement of cash receipts.

- There is a risk of overstatement if sufficient allowances have not been made for the impairment of individually significant balances and for the remainder assessed on a portfolio or group basis.

Restructuring provision

- The restructuring provision that was made last year has fallen/been utilized by 10.2%. There is a risk of overstatement if the provision is underutilized/not needed for the purpose for which it was established.

Finance lease liabilities

- Although finance lease liabilities have increased (by $1m) there is a greater risk of understatement than overstatement if leased assets are not recognized on the statement of financial position (i.e. capitalized).

- Disclosure risk arises if the requirements of IAS 17 *Leases* (e.g. in respect of minimum lease payments) are not met.

Trade payables

- These have increased by only 5.3% compared with the 17.8% increase in materials expense. There is a risk of understatement as notifications (e.g. suppliers' invoices) of liabilities outstanding at 30 June 2006 may have still to be received (the month of June being an unexpired period).

Other (employee) liabilities

- These may be understated as they have increased by only 7.6% although staff costs have increased by 14%. For example, balances owing in respect of outstanding holiday entitlements at the year end may not yet be accurately estimated.

Tutorial note

Credit will be given to other financial statements risks specific to the scenario. For example, 'time-sensitive delivery schedules' might give rise to penalties or claims, that could result in understated provisions or undisclosed contingent liabilities. Also, given that this is a new audit and the result has changed significantly (from loss to profit) might suggest a risk of misstatement in the opening balances (and hence comparative information).

(c) **Extent of reliance on analytical procedures as audit evidence**

Tutorial note

In the requirement '… reliance … as audit evidence' is a direction to consider only substantive analytical procedures. Answer points concerning planning and review stages were not asked for and earn no marks.

- Although there is likely to be less reliance on analytical procedures than if this had been an existing audit client, the fact that this is a new assignment does not preclude placing some reliance on such procedures.

- Analytical procedures will not be relied on in respect of material items that require 100% testing. For example, additions to property is likely to represent a very small number of transactions.

- Analytical procedures alone may provide sufficient audit evidence on line items that are not individually material. For example, inventory (less than 1/2% revenue and less than 1% total assets) may be shown to be materially correctly stated through analytical procedures on consumable stores (i.e. fuel, lubricants, materials for servicing vehicles etc).

- Substantive analytical procedures are best suited to large volume transactions (e.g. revenue, materials expense, staff costs). If controls over the completeness, accuracy and validity of recording transactions in these areas are effective then substantive analytical procedures showing that there are no unexpected fluctuations should reduce the need for substantive detailed tests.

- The extent of planned use will be dependent on the relationships expected between variables. (e.g. between items of financial information and between items of financial and non-financial information). For example, if material costs rise due to an increase in the level of business then a commensurate increase in revenue and staff costs might be expected also.

- 'Proofs in total' (or reasonableness tests) provide substantive evidence that statement of comprehensive income items are not materially misstated. In the case of Yates these might be applied to staff costs (number of employees in each category × wage/salary rates, grossed up for social security, etc) and finance expense (interest rate × average monthly overdraft balance).

- However, such tests may have limited application, if any, if the population is not homogenous and cannot be subdivided. For example, all the categories of non-current asset have a wide range of useful life. Therefore it would be difficult/meaningless to apply an 'average' depreciation rate to all assets in the class to substantiate the total depreciation expense for the year. (Although it might highlight a risk of potential over or understatement requiring further investigation.)

- Substantive analytical procedures are more likely to be used if there is relevant information available that is being used by Yates. For example, as fuel costs will be significant, Yates may monitor consumption (e.g. miles per gallon (MPG)).

- Analytical procedures may supplement alternative procedures that provide evidence regarding the same assertion. For example, the review of after-date payments to confirm the completeness of trade payables may be supplemented by calculations of average payment period on a monthly basis.

Tutorial note

Credit will be given for other relevant points drawn from the scenario. For example, the restructuring during the previous year is likely to have caused fluctuations that may result in less reliance being placed on analytical procedures.

(d) **Principal audit work**

(i) **Trade receivables**

- Review of agreements to determine the volume rebates terms. For example,

    – the % discounts;

    – the volumes to which they apply;

    – the period over which they accumulate;

    – settlement method (e.g. by credit note or other off-set or repayment).

- Direct positive confirmation of a value-weighted sample of balances (i.e. larger amounts) to identify potential overstatement (e.g. due to discounts earned not being awarded).

- Monitoring of after-date cash receipts and matching against amounts due as shortfalls may indicate disputed amounts.

- Review of after-date credit notes to ensure adequate allowance (accrual) is made for discounts earned in the year to 30 June 2006.

- Credit risk analysis of individually significant balances and assessment of impairment losses (where carrying value is less than the present value of the estimated cash flows discounted at the effective interest rate).

(ii)   **Vehicles**

- Agreeing opening ledger balances of cost and accumulated depreciation (and impairment losses) to the non-current asset register to confirm the comparative amounts.

- Physically inspecting a sample of vehicles (selected from the asset register) to confirm existence and condition (for evidence of impairment). If analytical procedures use management information on mileage records this should be checked (e.g. against millimetres) at the same time.

- Agreeing additions to purchase invoices to confirm cost.

- Reviewing the terms of all lease contracts entered into during the year to ensure that finance leases have been capitalized.

- Agreeing the depreciation rates applied to finance lease assets to those applied to similar purchased assets.

- Reviewing repairs and maintenance accounts (included in materials expense) to ensure that there are no material items of capital nature that have been expensed (i.e. a test for completeness).

11   SHIRE OIL

Key answer tips

Part (a) asks for audit risks to be identified. One approach, illustrated here, is to consider overall risks and risks specific to individual items.

Part (b) is about the useful lives of rig platforms, so ensure you restrict your answer to that area of non-current assets only.

Part (c) is a fairly common question about performance indicators.

(a)   **Audit risks**

Inherent – financial statements level

- As Shire is a listed company there will be pressures on its management to meet the expectations of users, in particular shareholders and analysts, thereby increasing inherent risk.

- The oil industry is exposed to a volatile market (e.g. in futures trading).   This increases going concern (failure) risk.

- Shire operates in different regions with exposure to economic instability, currency devaluation and high inflation. Increased disclosure risk arises as IAS 1 *Presentation of Financial Statements* requires that key assumptions concerning the future of such sources of estimation uncertainty be disclosed.

- Disclosure risk is increased as Shire is required to comply with the extensive disclosure requirements of IAS 14 *Segment Reporting*.

- The fall in basic EPS (as compared with the first six months of the previous half year) may increase management bias to overstate performance in the second half year (to 31 December 2005).

Inherent – assertion level

- The grant of a licence may be valued at either cost or fair value (IAS 20 *Accounting for Government Grants and Disclosure of Government Assistance*). However, valuation other than at cost ($nil) is inherently risky as fair value has been estimated by management. The licence may be unique (being for five years in a remote region) and in the absence of an active market in them – or recent transactions for which prices can be observed – it seems unlikely that any estimate of fair value made by management can be substantiated.

- The licence is an intangible asset. If recognized other than at cost it should be amortized on a straight-line basis over five years (IAS 38 *Intangible Assets*).

- Item replacements (e.g. of drilling equipment) should be recognized as items of property, plant and equipment (and the replaced items as disposals) in accordance with (IAS 16 *Property, Plant and Equipment*). Constituent items of each rig should be depreciated over their useful lives.

- If management is properly re-assessing the useful life of each rig annually then this should be reflected in the change, from time to time, of the number of years over which each rig is depreciated.

Tutorial note

A change in estimate – not policy. It is NOT a risk that the useful life of a platform is not the same for all rigs.

- Although the treatment of decommissioning provisions (Debit Asset/Credit Provision) appears to be correct (IAS 16 and IAS 37 *Provisions, Contingent Liabilities and Contingent Assets*) abandoning the cyclone-damaged rig calls into question Shire's recognition of such provisions. In the absence of a legal or constructive obligation there is no liability to be provided for.

- The abandoned rig may be overstated. Depreciation should cease and the rig tested for impairment. In particular, the decommissioning provision should be reversed against the undepreciated balance included in cost (and any difference included in profit or loss).

Tutorial note

The difference is between depreciation charge and finance cost (on 'unwinding of the discount').

- Actual and/or contingent liabilities may arise if Shire is exposed to fines/penalties as a result of abandoning the rig (IAS 37). As the rig was damaged before the year end, provisions should be made as at 31 December 2005 unless they cannot be reliably measured (unlikely). (This could include provision for redundancy of rig workers)

- The oil pipeline is a jointly controlled asset that should be accounted for to reflect its economic substance (IAS 31 *Interests in Joint Ventures*). Shire must recognize its share of the asset, liabilities and expenditure incurred and any income from the sale of its share of the oil output (as well as its own liabilities and expenses separately incurred).

- The prior year modification would have been 'qualified – except for'. If there is a similar lack of evidence in the current year the auditor's report should be similarly qualified. Even if the correct position at 31 December 2005 is determinable, the audit opinion at that date should be modified in respect of the impact, if any, on the opening position and comparative information (unless the opening oil reserves position has since been ascertained and can be corrected with a prior period adjustment).

Tutorial notes

Modification could not have been an emphasis of matter as there was a lack of scope. The matter was evidently material but not pervasive.

Credit will be given for additional answer points relevant to the scenario and the industry. For example:

- Going concern (failure) risk is increased if significant operating licences (withdrawal of the new licence would not create a going concern issue) are withdrawn from oil-producing areas (e.g. as a result of non-compliance with environmental legislation).

- Research and development (may also be described as 'exploration and evaluation' costs or 'discovery and assessment') costs must be expensed unless/until Shire has a legal right to explore the area in which they are incurred. So, in the remote region, Shire can only capitalize costs incurred from April. (Risk is asset overstatement)

- Exploration and evaluation assets should be classified as tangible (e.g. rigs) or intangible (e.g. drilling rights) according to their nature (IFRS 6 *Exploration for and Evaluation of Mineral Resources*).

- When a technical feasibility and commercial viability of extracting oil from an area of interest can be demonstrated, exploration and evaluation assets must be tested for impairment before reclassification (as tangible/intangible assets).

(b) **Principal audit work – useful life of rig platforms**

Tutorial notes

The platforms are just one item of each rig. Candidates should not be awarded marks here for the matters to be considered in the assessment of useful lives (since this is illustrated in the scenario). No marks will be awarded for criticising management for estimating useful lives on a per platform basis or for audit work on depreciation charges/carrying amounts unrelated to the determination of useful lives.

- Review of management's annual assessment of the useful life of each rig at 31 December 2005 and corroboration of any information that has led to a change in previous estimates. For example, for the abandoned rig, where useful life has been assessed to be at an end, obtain:

  - weather reports;

    –   incident report supported by photographs;

    –   insurance claim, etc.

- Consider management's past experience and expertise in estimating useful lives. For example, if all lives initially assessed as short (c. 15 years) are subsequently lengthened (or long lives consistently shortened) this would suggest that management is being over (under) prudent in its initial estimates.

- Review of industry comparatives as published in the annual reports of other oil producers.

- Comparison of actual maintenance costs against budgeted to confirm that the investment needed in maintenance, to achieve expected life expectancy, is being made.

- Comparison of actual output (oil extracted) against budgeted. If actual output is less than budgeted the economic life of the platform may be:

    –   shorter (e.g. because there is less oil to be extracted than originally surveyed); or

    –   longer (e.g. because the rate of extraction is less than budgeted).

- A review of the results of management's impairment testing of each rig (i.e. the cash-generating unit of which each platform is a part).

- Recalculations of cash flow projections (based on reasonable and supportable assumptions) discounted at a suitable pre-tax rate.

Tutorial note

As the rigs will not have readily determinable net selling prices (each one being unique and not available for sale) any impairment will be assessed by a comparison of value in use against carrying amount.

- Review of working papers of geologist/quantity surveyor(s) employed by Shire supporting estimations of reserves used in the determination of useful lives of rigs.

(c)   **Social and environmental responsibilities**

Performance indicators

- Absolute ($) and relative (%) level of investment in sports sponsorship, and funding to the Shire Ward.

- Increasing number of championship events and participating schools/students as compared with prior year.

- Number of medals/trophies sponsored at events and/or number awarded to Shire sponsored schools/students.

- Number of patients treated (successfully) a week/month. Average bed occupancy (daily/weekly/monthly and cumulative to date).

- Staffing levels (e.g. of volunteers for sports events, Shire Ward staff and the company):

    –   ratio of starters to leavers/staff turnover;

    –   absenteeism (average number of days per person per annum).

- Number of:

    - breaches of health and safety regulations and environmental regulations;

    - oil spills;

    - accidents and employee fatalities;

    - insurance claims.

Evidence

- Actual level of investment ($) compared with budget and budget compared with prior period.

- Physical evidence of favourable increases on prior year, for example:

    - medals/cups sponsored;

    - number of beds available.

- Increase in favourable press coverage/reports of sponsored events. (Decrease in adverse press about accidents/fatalities.)

- Independent surveys (e.g. by marine conservation organizations, welfare groups, etc) comparing Shire favourably with other oil producers.

- A reduction in fines paid compared with budget (and prior year).

- Reduction in legal fees and claims being settled as evidenced by fee notes and correspondence files.

- Amounts settled on insurance claims and level of insurance cover as compared with prior period.

(d) Many companies now publish social and environmental reports, but few attach audit reports to these. However it is possible to:

- conduct an audit on social, environmental or health and safety issues, and/or

- attest to the report to add assurance to its authenticity.

Whether an audit firm is the right agent to perform a 'social audit' is debatable. There are specialized firms which carry out such audits.

The benefit of such a report to the company is to enable it to demonstrate its responsible social attitude and be compared (hopefully favourably) to other companies.

The benefit of the attestation report issued by reporting accountants is to add credibility to the statements made by the company, thereby enhancing its standing from a social and ethical point of view.

Audit firms may provide an attestation on a social report issued by the company; the report might be framed as follows:

SOCIAL REPORT ATTESTATION

To: The Board of Directors, Shire Oil

We have examined the information which has been included in the Social Report on pages XX to XX in accordance with the instructions set out in your letter of (date).

In accordance with our terms of reference, the purpose of the attestation is to test the assertions and statements made in the Social Report in order to give assurance to the reader from an independent third party regarding the information in the report. The report has been prepared by the directors, who are responsible for the collection and presentation of information within it. The attestation statement in itself should not be taken as a basis for interpreting Shire Oil's performance in relation to its non-financial policies.

There are currently no statutory requirements or generally accepted standards in (country) relating to the preparation, public reporting and attestation of corporate social reports.

We have therefore developed an attestation approach which addresses the requirements of our terms of reference and which involves challenging the Social Report's contents in detail. The approach has three main components. These are summarized below:

- Challenging and substantiating the assertions and claims made in the Social Report to ensure that the information as reported is consistent with the evidence obtained. We carry out a number of specific procedures to gain this assurance.

- Reviewing the consistency of social performance data collection and reporting processes in order to gain assurance of the reliability of data reported.

- Reviewing implementation of the non-financial policies through a sample of site visits and discussions with executives and senior managers to gather supporting evidence relating to the data, statements and assertions made in the report.

In our opinion the information is fairly stated.

Signed

Reporting accountants

Address

Date

If an attesting accountant found that the work done revealed an inconsistency or misstatement in the social report then clearly the matter would need to be discussed with management and the report amended. An attest report would not be issued if the matter could not be resolved. A qualified report is probably not an option.

12 GENO VESA FARM

Key answer tips

Yet another risk question, this one about audit risk, so think of risks from the perspective of the auditor rather than the business. Part (b) tests a relatively unusual standard , agriculture, emphasising that any of the standards from P2 can be examined and that it's therefore important not to question spot.

(a) **Principal audit risks**

Industry

'Farming' is an inherently risky business activity – being subject to conditions (e.g. disease, weather) outside management's control. In some jurisdictions, where the industry is highly regulated, compliance risk may be high.

The risks of mail order retailing 'exclusive' products are higher (than for 'essential' products, say) as demand fluctuations are more dramatic (e.g. in times of recession). However, the Internet has provided GVF with a global customer base.

The planned audit approach should be risk-based combined with a systems approach to (say) controls in the revenue cycle.

Goat herd

The goat herd will consist of:

- mature goats held for use in the production of milk (i.e. accounted for as depreciable non-current tangible assets – IAS 16 *Property, Plant and Equipment*);

- kids which are held for replacement purposes (accounted for as biological assets under IAS 41 *Agriculture*); and

- kids which are to be sold (held as inventory under IAS 2).

Therefore, the number of animals in each category must be accurately ascertained to determine:

- the statement of financial position carrying amounts analysed between current and non-current assets; and

- the charge to the statement of comprehensive income (e.g. for depreciation and fair value adjustments).

There is a risk that the carrying amount of the production animals will be misstated if, for example:

- useful lives/depreciation rates are unreasonable;

- estimates of residual values are not kept under review.

Animals raised during the year should be recognized initially and at each statement of financial position date at fair value less estimated point-of-sale costs. Such biological assets will be understated in the statement of financial position if they are not recorded on birth.

The net realisable value of animals held for sale may fall below cost if they are not sold soon after reaching optimal size and weight.

Unrecorded revenue

Raised (bred) animals are not purchased and, in the absence of documentation supporting their origination, could be sold for cash (and the revenue unrecorded).

Although the controls over retailing around the world are likely to be strong, there are other sources of income – the shop and other activities at the farm. Although revenue from these sundry sources may not be material, there is a risk that it could go unrecorded due to lack of effective controls.

'Rabida Red'

The cost of an ingredient which is essential to the manufacturing process has increased significantly. If the cost is passed on to the customers, demand may fall (increasing going concern risk).

Supplies of the ingredient, Innittu, may be restricted – further increasing going concern risk.

Any disclosure of GVF's socio-environmental policies (e.g. in other information presented with the audited financial statements), if any, should be scrutinized to ensure that it does not mislead the reader and/or undermine the credibility of the financial statements.

'Bachas Blue'

If 'Bachas Blue' has been specifically cited as a cause of a skin disorder then GVF could face contingent liabilities for pending litigation. However, it is more likely that the fall in demand has threatened GVF's going concern. As the fall in demand has not been permanent, this threat has been removed for the time being.

The impairment loss previously recognized in respect of the equipment used exclusively in the manufacture of Bachas Blue should be reversed if there has been a change in the estimates used to determine their recoverable amount (IAS 36 *Impairment of Assets*).

The recoverable amount would have been based on value in use (since net selling price would not have been applicable). GVF's management will have to provide evidence to support their best estimates of future cash flows for the recalculation of value in use at 30 September 2005.

Maturing cheese

The substance of the sale and repurchase of cheese is that of a loan secured on the inventory. Therefore revenue should not be recognized on 'sale' to Abingdon Bank. The principal terms of the secured borrowings should be disclosed, including the carrying amount of the inventory to which it applies.

Borrowing costs should all be recognized as an expense in the period unless it is GVF's policy to capitalize them (the allowed alternative treatment under IAS 23 *Borrowing Costs*). Since the cost of inventories should include all costs incurred in bringing them to their present location and condition (of maturity), the cost of maturing cheese should include interest at 7% per six months (as clearly the borrowings are specific). There is a risk that, if the age of maturing cheeses is not accurately determined, the cost of cheese will be misstated.

Health and safety legislation

At 30 September 2005 the legislation will have been in effect for three months. If GVF's management has not replaced the shelves, a provision should be made for the penalties/fines accruing from non-compliance.

If the legislation is complied with:

- plant and equipment may be overstated e.g.:
    - if the replaced shelves are not written off;
    - if the value of equipment, etc is impaired because the maturing cheese business is to be downsized;
- inventory may be overstated (e.g. if insufficient allowance is made for the deterioration in maturing cheese resulting from handling it to replace the shelves);
- GVF may no longer be a going concern if it does not have the produce to sell to its exclusive customers.

Grant

There is a risk that the grant received has become repayable. For example, if the terms of the grant specified a timeframe for the development which is now to be exceeded. In this case the grant should be presented as a payable in the statement of financial position.

If the reason for deferring the implementation is related to cash flow problems, this could have implications for the going concern of GVF.

(b) **Audit work on carrying amounts**

(i) *Goat herd*

- Physical inspection of the number and condition of animals in the herd and confirming, on a test basis, that they are tagged (or otherwise 'branded' as being owned by GVF).

- Tests of controls on management's system of identifying and distinguishing held-for-sale animals (inventory) from the production herd (depreciable non-current assets).

- Comparison of GVF's depreciation policies (including useful lives, depreciation methods and residual values) with those used by other farming entities.

- 'Proof in total', or other reasonableness check, of the depreciation charge for the herd for the year.

- Observing test counts or total counts of animals held for sale.

- Market values of kids, according to their weight and age, as at 30 September 2005 – for both held-for-sale and held-for-replacement animals.

- For held-for-sale animals only, vouching (on a sample basis) management's schedule of point-of-sale costs (e.g. market dealers' commissions).

(ii) *Equipment used in the manufacture of Bachas Blue*

- Agree cost less accumulated depreciation and impairment losses at the beginning of the year to prior year working papers (and/or last year's published financial statements).

- Recalculate the current year depreciation charge based on the carrying amount (as reduced by the impairment loss).

- Calculate the carrying amount of the equipment as at 30 September 2005 without deduction of the impairment loss.

- Agree management's schedule of future cash flows estimated to be attributable to the equipment for a period of up to five years (unless a longer period can be justified) to approved budgets and forecasts.

- Recalculate:

  - on a sample basis, the make up of the cash flows included in the forecast;

  - GVF's weighted average cost of capital.

- Review production records and sales orders for the year, as compared with the prior period, to confirm a 'steady increase'.

- Compare sales volume at 30 September 2005 with the pre-'scare' level to assess how much of the previously recognized impairment loss it would be prudent to write back (if any).

- Scrutinize sales orders in the post statement of financial position event period. Sales of such produce can be very volatile and another 'incident' could have sales plummeting again – in which case the impairment loss should not be reversed.

(iii) *Cheese*

- Examine the terms of sales to Abingdon Bank – confirm the bank's legal title (e.g. if GVF were to cease to trade and so could not exercise buy-back option).

- Obtain a direct confirmation from the bank of the cost of inventory sold by GVF to Abingdon Bank and the amount re-purchased as at 30 September 2005 (the net amount being the outstanding loan).

- Inspect the cheese as at 30 September 2005 (e.g. during the physical inventory count) paying particular attention to the factors which indicate the age (and strength) of the cheese (e.g. its location or physical appearance).

- Observe how the cheese is stored – if on steel shelves discuss with GVF's management whether its net realisable value has been reduced below cost.

- Test check, on a sample basis, the costing records supporting the cost of batches of cheese.

- Confirm that the cost of inventory sold to the bank is included in inventory as at 30 September 2005 and the nature of the bank security adequately disclosed.

- Agree the repurchase of cheese which has reached maturity at cost plus 7% per six months to purchase invoices (or equivalent contracts) and cash book payments.

- Test check GVF's inventory-ageing records to production records. Confirm the carrying amount of inventory as at 30 September 2005 that will not be sold until after 30 September 2006, and agree to the amount disclosed in the notes to inventory as a 'non-current' portion.

13   CERISE

Key answer tips

Part (a) asks for financial statement risks so be sure to relate your answer to items in the financial statements that may be materially misstated.

In part (b), ensure that you compare with the previous year, using relevant information from the question, and don't just talk generally about analytical procedures/management representations.

(a)   **Financial statement risks – planning the final audit 31 December 2004**

Computer-controlled equipment for production-line industries

- Cerise is manufacturing a relatively high-tech range of products. Inventory will be overstated if sufficient allowance is not made for technical obsolescence and slow-moving items (i.e. writing inventory down to lower of cost and net realisable value).

- As Cerise is ceasing manufacture two months prior to the year end the items remaining in inventory at the year end are likely to require being written down in value. The amount of write down is required to be disclosed in accordance with IAS 2 *Inventories*.

Cessation of trade

- Cerise ceased to trade during the year. The financial statements should not therefore be prepared on a going concern basis, but on a 'break-up' or other 'realisable' basis.

  This has implications for:

  - the reclassification of assets and liabilities (from non-current to current);

  - the carrying amount of assets (at recoverable amount); and

  - the completeness of recorded liabilities.

Redundant workforce

- Liabilities may not be disclosed (if contingent) or provided for, if there are claims arising from the redundant workers (e.g. if their statutory or contractual rights have been breached).

- Although statutory redundancy pay, holiday pay, accrued overtime etc may well have all been settled before the year end there may be additional liabilities in respect of former employees (e.g. pension obligations).

Sale of patented technology and manufacturing equipment

- All assets sold should be derecognized and the profit on disposal disclosed as an exceptional item arising from the discontinuance of operations.

- Plant and equipment will be overstated if:

  - manufacturing equipment that has been sold is left 'on the books';

  - assets that were not part of the sale are not:

    tested for impairment (in accordance with IAS 36 *Impairment of Assets*);

    written down to the higher of net selling price and value in use.

Accounts department

- Fewer ('skeleton') staff being employed in the accounts department may increase the risk of errors arising as staff assume wider areas of responsibility as the volume of transactions is reduced.

- The risk of errors arising not being detected (i.e. control risk) is also likely to increase. For example, levels of supervision and degrees of segregation of duties may be reduced and adherence to control procedures may slacken.

Premises

- If the unsold properties meet all the criteria of IFRS 5 *Non-current Assets Held for Sale and Discontinued Operations* at the statement of financial position date they should be:

  - separately classified as held for sale.

  - carried at the lower of carrying amount (i.e. depreciated cost) and fair value less estimated costs to sell.

- Any after-date losses on disposal would provide evidence of impairment. (However, as it is Cerise's policy to carry non-current assets at depreciated cost, impairment is less likely than if they were carried at revalued amounts.)

- Unoccupied premises may fall into disrepair with time. The financial statements would be misstated if the management of Cerise sought to provide for:

  - dilapidations on the properties arising after the statement of financial position date; and/or

  - future expectation of repairs on unsold properties.

Such provisions are contrary to IAS 37 *Provisions, Contingent Liabilities and Contingent Assets.*

Tutorial note

Consider a property with carrying amount $1 million (depreciated cost) and fair value $16 million. Repair costs of $0.5 million incurred for deterioration after 31 December 2004 cannot be provided for, nor is the carrying amount impaired.

Onerous contracts

- Full provision should be made for the lease obligations under onerous contracts on four premises in accordance with IAS 37. This should not be extended to the head office premises.

Product warranties

- Adequate provision must be made for warranties of:

  - one year (sales in the year to 31 December 2004);

  - up to three years (sales between 1 January 2002 and 31 October 2004); and

  - up to five years (sales between 1 January 2000 and 31 October 2004).

- The provision may be understated if the basis of its calculation is no longer appropriate. For example, if Cerise must now outsource warranty work as it no longer has an in-house capability.

Breach of agreements/contracts

- Since Cerise no longer has the means of fulfilling contracts with distributors, provision should be made for any compensation or penalties arising. Where the penalties due to distributors for breach of supply agreements exceed the amounts due from them, the receivables should be written down and provision made for any excess.

- Adequate provision should be made for breaches of contracts with suppliers (non-purchase). If suppliers do not exercise their rights to invoke penalty clauses disclosure of the contingent liability may be more appropriate than a provision.

(b) **Reliance on audit work**

(i) *Analytical procedures*

Note: Reliance on analytical procedures is only obtained through those that provide substantive audit evidence. This question therefore concerns substantive analytical procedures as evidence – which are optional – not those at the planning and review stages (which are mandatory).

- Overall the extent of reliance on analytical procedures is likely to be less than that for the prior year audit as the scale and nature of Cerise's activities will differ from the prior year.

- There are a number of individually material transactions in the current year which will require detailed substantive testing (e.g. sale of patented technology and manufacturing equipment and sale of premises).

- Budgetary information used for analytical procedures in prior periods (e.g. budgeted production/sales) will have less relevance in the current year as the cessation of trade is unlikely to have been forecast.

- Information will be comparable with the prior year for at most 10 months (i.e. January to October). Costs incurred in November/December will relate to winding down operations – rather than operational activities.

- The impact of the 'one-off' circumstance on carrying amounts is more likely to be assessed through detailed substantive testing (e.g. after-date realization) than reliance on ratios and past history.

- For example, analytical procedures on an aged-trade receivables analysis and calculation of average collection period used in prior years will not be relevant to assessing the adequacy of the write-down now needed. Similarly, inventory turnover ratios will no longer be comparable when inventory is no longer being replenished.

- However, some reliance will still be placed on certain analytical procedures. For example, in substantiating charges to the statement of comprehensive income for the 10 months of operations.

(ii) *Management representations*

- Overall the extent of reliance on management representations is likely to be increased as compared with the prior year audit.

- The magnitude of matters of judgement and opinion is greater than in prior years. For example, inventory/trade receivable write-downs, impairment losses and numerous provisions. The auditor will seek to obtain as much corroborative evidence as is available. However, where amounts of assets have still to be recovered and liabilities settled, management will be asked to make representations on the adequacy of write-downs, provisions, etc and the completeness of disclosures (e.g. for claims and other contingent liabilities).

- Where negotiations are under discussion but not yet formalized (e.g. with a prospective buyer for premises), management may be the only source of evidence (e.g. for the best estimate of sale proceeds).

- However, the extent to which reliance can be placed on representations depends on the extent to which those making the representation can be expected to be well-informed on the particular matters. Therefore, as the human resources and production directors will not be available after the statement of financial position date particular thought should be given to obtaining representations on matters pertaining to employee obligations and product warranties (say).

(c) **Principal audit work – carrying amount**

(i) *Amounts due from distributors*

- Agreeing gross amounts due to accounts receivable balances (for sales made in the normal course of business up to 31 October 2004 and in the 'running down' of inventory to 31 December 2004).

- As a significant portion of account balances outstanding will already be two months old at 31 December 2004, all receipts of after-date cash (if any) should be monitored for evidence of recoverability.

- Review of agreements with distributors to confirm the unexpired period (up to three years) and the penalties stipulated.

- Recalculation of amounts due to distributors for the early termination of the agreements with them.

- Review of Cerise's correspondence to the distributors (e.g. offering financial settlement) and responses received.

(ii) *Lease liabilities*

- Confirm the leases as operating leases to prior period working papers/disclosures in the previous year's financial statements.

- To confirm contracts as onerous and justify full provision:

    - review Cerise's correspondence with the lessors requesting terms for an early exit from the lease period;

    - visit premises to confirm that Cerise is not receiving any economic benefit from them (i.e. they are not still occupied or sub-let).

- Agree/reconcile the amounts provided for liabilities under onerous contracts to the present value of the future minimum lease payments under non-cancellable operating leases.

- Agree/reconcile the future minimum lease payments used in the calculation of the provision to those disclosed (under IAS 17 *Leases*) in the financial statements to 31 December 2003 as:

    - later than one year and not later than five years; plus

    - later than five years.

14   HYDRASPORTS

Key answer tips

For part (a) remember that anything that threatens the business from achieving its goals is a business risk. These will usually translate into the overstatement of assets or understatement of liabilities. Any control weaknesses will ultimately have the same effect.

For part (b) you should bring to mind the definition of an asset, the recognition and measurement criteria to be used and the relevant accounting standard IAS 16 and IAS 23.

For part (c) think about how the centre impacts upon the community it serves and the environment in which it operates.

(a)

(i) **Business risks**	(ii) **Financial statement risk**
• The standard design of facilities increases operational risk as any difficulties encountered in one facility will be compounded by the number of other facilities (potentially all) which are similarly affected. This is illustrated by the closure of the saunas.	• The carrying amount of the associated non-current assets (i.e. equipment, fixtures and fittings) is likely to be overstated as they are likely to be impaired if they are not in use.
• Centralized control through company policy is resulting in inefficient and ineffective operations as managers cannot respond on a timely basis to local needs.	• Management circumvention or override of control procedures laid down by head office may result in system weaknesses. If errors arising are not detected and corrected the risk of misstatement in the financial statements is increased.
• Business reporting risk is likely to be increased by centre managers preparing monthly accounting returns. Operational risk may be increased if centre managers cannot fulfil their day-to-day responsibilities (e.g. relating to customer satisfaction, human resources, health and safety).	• Information processing risk is increased as accounting information flowing into the financial statements may not be properly captured, input, processed or output by the centre managers.
	• Inherent risk, of errors arising, in monthly 'branch' returns is high.
• Advanced payments contribute to business reporting and financial (cash flow) risk. Cash received must be available to meet the costs of providing future services.	• Revenue may be overstated if an accurate cut-off is not achieved. In particular, there is an estimate risk in determining the amount of deferred income at the statement of financial position date.
	• An error of principle may also arise if Hydrasports' revenue recognition policy does not comply with IAS 18 *Revenue*.
• Hydrasports cannot operate a centre if a licence is suspended, withdrawn or not renewed (e.g. through failing a local authority inspection or failing to apply for renewal).	• An error of principle arises if licences are not capitalized as intangible assets (but instead written off as expenses when incurred).
	• Intangible assets (licences) should be reviewed for impairment at each statement of financial position date (e.g. for centres which are closed).
• Closure may result in customers finding alternative facilities with permanent loss of fee revenue.	• Failure risk (i.e. that Hydrasports will not continue to operate as a going concern) is increased.

(i) **Business risks**

- 'Early bird' customers dissatisfaction similarly increases operational risk.

- Serious accidents may prompt investigation by local authority – resulting in penalties, fines and/or withdrawal of licence to operate.

- Although fees are non-refundable, suspension of a facility (e.g. sauna) may result in customers asking for partial refund. In particular Hydrasports may have an obligation to refund fees paid in advance when centres are closed (e.g. the Verne centre from July–September 2003).

- Permanent loss of customers requiring childcare facilities increases operating risk. Compliance risk is increased if the new guidelines are not met.

- Similarly, inability to retain lifeguards increases operational risk that pools cannot open (due to health and safety regulations). Compliance risk is increased by the possibility that pools may be operated without a lifeguard being on duty.

- High staff turnover indicates increased operational risk (poor human resource management, inefficiency in working practices, reduced capacity, etc).

- Limitations on centre managers' levels of authority may not be commensurate with their responsibilities. Empowerment risk arises if managers are not properly led (and if they, in turn, do not properly lead their centre staff).

- More centres may become loss-making if the reasons for falling membership are not addressed.

(ii) **Financial statement risk**

- This creates disclosure risk if the disclosures relating to going concern as the basis of accounting do not meet the requirements of IAS 1 *Presentation of Financial Statements*.

- If licences are withdrawn, the intangible asset (amounts prepaid) should be written off to the extent that monies are not refundable.

- The likelihood of contingent (if not actual) liabilities increases disclosure risk.

- Provisions may be understated at 31 December 2003 if Hydrasports has a legal obligation to refund fees where it has failed to provide services.

- Disclosure risk is (again) increased if fines/penalties arising are material and not disclosed.

- Staff costs may be overstated as the risk that payments may be made to leavers is increased.

- Any lack of integrity may increase the risk of management and/or employee fraud, illegal acts and unauthorized use of company assets. In particular the assertion of existence of assets may be at risk (resulting in overstatement).

- Loss-making centres should be tested for impairment as cash-generating units.

(i) Business risks

- The hydrotherapy pool cannot operate until construction is complete, which may be threatened by cash flow problems.
- Cash flow difficulties increase liquidity/financial risk.
- Obsolete gym equipment increases operational risk as customer satisfaction decreases and health and safety risks are increased.

- The reduction in insurance cover reduces the recoverable amount of assets in the event of loss through fire (for example). Inability to replace lost/damaged assets increases operational risk (see obsolete gym equipment above).
- Operational risk is increased if the substantial increase in liability insurance premiums is a reflection of an increase in the level of claims being made.

(ii) Financial statement risk

- The value of the asset in construction should be written down if it is impaired (even if it has not yet been brought into use)
- See above reference to going concern and disclosure risk.
- Depreciation may be overstated if Hydrasports continues to calculate depreciation on fully-depreciated assets.
- Disclosures for capital commitments (e.g. to replace equipment) in the financial statements may be inappropriate if Hydrasports does not have funds to finance such commitments.
- See above reference to going concern and disclosure risk.

- Disclosure risk is increased in relation to contingent assets (for reimbursement under insurance policies).

(b) Principal audit work

   (i) Deferred income

- Agreeing Hydrasports' analysis of joining fee and peak/off-peak membership fees on a sample basis.

- Reconciling membership income to fees paid. If customers can renew their membership without payment there should be no deferral of income (unless the debt for unpaid fees is also recognized).

- Assessing the collectibility of unpaid fees (if any) by reviewing after date receipts and correspondence with members.

- Recomputing the deferred income element of fees received in the three months before the statement of financial position date.

- Comparison of year-end balance with prior year and investigation of variance.

   (ii) Hydrotherapy pool

- Verifying the initial cost of this constructed asset will include an examination of:

  - the contract with the builder

  - contractors billings; and

  - stage payments.

- Hydrasports is likely to be advised by its own expert (a quantity surveyor) on how the contract is progressing. Audit work will include a review of the expert's assessment of stage of completion as at the statement of financial position date, estimated costs to completion, etc.

- Physical inspection of the construction at the year end to confirm work to date and assess the reasonableness of stage of completion.

- Borrowing costs associated with this substantial ('heavy') investment should be agreed to finance terms and payments. The calculation of any amount capitalized should be recomputed to confirm accuracy.

- The basis of capitalization, if any, should be agreed to comply with IAS 23 *Borrowing Costs* (e.g. interest accruing during any suspension of building work should not be capitalized).

- As the construction has already cost twice as much as budgeted, its value in use (when brought into use) may be less than cost. Management's assessment of possible impairment (of the hydrotherapy pool and the centre) should be critically appraised.

(c) **Performance indicators – social/environmental responsibility**

Member satisfaction

- Number of people on membership waiting lists (if any).
- Number of referrals/recommendations to club membership by existing members.
- Proportion of renewed memberships.
- Actual members: 100% capacity membership (sub-analysed between 'peak' and 'off-peak').

Membership dissatisfaction

- Proportion of members requesting refunds per month/quarter.
- Proportion of memberships 'lapsing' (i.e. not renewed).

Staff

- Average number of staff employed per month.
- Number of starters/leavers per month.
- Staff turnover/average duration of employment.
- Number of training courses for lifeguards per annum.

Predictability

- Number of late openings (say more than 5, 15 and 30 minutes after advertised opening times).
- Number of days closure per month/year of each facility (i.e. pool, crèche, sauna, gym) and centre.

Safety

- Incidents reports documenting the date, time and nature of each incident, the extent of damage and/or personal injury, and action taken.
- Number of accident free days.

Other society

- Local community involvement (e.g. facilities offered to schools and clubs at discount rates during 'off-peak' times).
- Range of facilities offered specifically to pensioners, mothers and babies, disabled patrons, etc.
- Participation in the wider community (e.g. providing facilities to support sponsored charity events).

Environment

- Number of instances of non-compliance with legislation/regulations (e.g. on chemical spills).
- Energy efficiency (e.g. in maintaining pool at a given temperature throughout the year).
- Incentives for environmental friendliness such as discouraging use of cars/promoting use of bicycles (e.g. by providing secure lock-ups for cycles and restricted car parking facilities).

Evidence

- Membership registers clearly distinguishing between new and renewed members, also showing lapsed memberships.
- Pool/gym timetables – showing sessions set aside for 'over 60s', 'ladies only', schools, clubs, special events, etc.
- Staff training courses and costs.
- Staff timesheets – showing arrival/departure times and adherence to staff rotas.
- Documents supporting additions to/deletions from payroll standing data (e.g. new joiner/leaver notifications).
- Engineer's inspection reports – confirming gym equipment, etc is in satisfactory working order. Also, engineer and safety check manuals and the maintenance program.
- Levels of expenditure on repairs and maintenance.
- Energy saving equipment/measures (e.g. insulated pool covering).
- Safety drill reports (e.g. alarm tests, pool evacuations).
- Accident report register – showing date, nature of incident, personal injury sustained (if any), action taken (e.g. emergency services called in).
- Any penalties/fines imposed by the local authorities and the reasons for them.
- Copies of reports of local authority investigations.
- The frequency and nature of insurance claims (e.g. to settle claims of injury to members and/or staff).

Section 4

ANSWERS TO PRACTICE QUESTIONS – SECTION B

PROFESSIONAL/ETHICAL CONSIDERATIONS AND PRACTICE MANAGEMENT

15   CLIFDEN & CO *Walk in the footsteps of a top tutor*

Key answer tips

This question is a typical "ethics/professional issues" question. To plan your answer remember that such questions can be subdivided into the following categories:

-    Ethics (code of ethics + threats): use the standard language, e.g. familiarity, self-interest etc

-    Quality control: ISQC 1 e.g. leadership, human resources;

-    Practice management: e.g. staffing

-    Legal issues: e.g. money laundering, negligence, ISA 250

By considering all of these areas when planning your answer (rather than the typical response that goes no further than ehtics) you should be able to draft a suitable, relevant response.

The highlighted words are key phases that markers are looking for.

(a)   'Professional competence and due care' is one of the fundamental ethical principles explained as part of the Code's conceptual framework. It can be broken down into two parts.

Professional competence

This is the concept that a professional accountant must firstly achieve, and subsequently maintain, professional knowledge and skill at the level required to ensure that clients and employers receive competent professional service.

Attaining professional knowledge is achieved through a mixture of formal professional qualifications, informal 'on the job' training, and gaining experience of a range of professional work.

Maintaining professional knowledge is achieved through continuing professional development. Professional accountants must ensure that they are aware of changes in technical fields such as tax, auditing and financial reporting regulations where relevant to the services they offer to clients. Professional accountants should also be aware of general business developments, such as the use of information technology and e-commerce.

Due care

This is about acting diligently in accordance with applicable technical and professional standards when providing professional services. This means applying knowledge to a specific situation with careful consideration, minimising the chance of mistakes being made. It may also include wider issues such as making sure that there is enough time to complete work with due care, and ensuring that staff fully understand the objectives of the work they are being asked to perform.

Compliance with the principle

Attaining and maintaining professional knowledge:

Firms can offer training on specific technical matters, such as changes to tax rules or new auditing guidelines, which could be provided by senior members of the firm or by external consultants.

Due care

Adherence to quality control guidelines will help ensure that due care has been exercised. Particularly the supervision and review of work by more senior members of the firm should act as a preventative and detective control to pick up any errors made in the work.

In addition, formal and informal staff appraisals will enable members of staff to raise issues with more senior members of staff, e.g. if they felt under too much time pressure to properly perform their work.

Reviews carried out as part of the normal audit cycle (i.e. hot and cold reviews) can also help to identify where the firm may need to organise more training for staff.

(i) **Contaminated plastic**

It appears that Headford Co has manufactured items which potentially could cause serious injury or even death to a consumer. Management has decided not to recall any products, which indicates a lack of integrity. Even though the risk of this happening has been assessed by management as low, it would still be ethically appropriate to announce the problem, allowing customers to return potentially harmful products. As the contaminated products were made in the last few months of the year, it is likely that some items are still held within the company as finished goods inventory, in which case the company is putting its own staff and assets in danger. The assertion by management that the risk of injury is 'remote' should be treated with scepticism.

Firstly, Clifden & Co should encourage the management of Headford Co to make the problem with the products public. There will obviously be reluctance to do this due to the bad publicity which would follow, especially in the competitive industry in which the company operates. However, the auditors should try to explain to management the reasons why they should disclose, and hopefully convince management that this would be the ethically correct way to proceed.

If management still refuse to make a disclosure, Clifden & Co should consider their duty of confidentiality. Both IFAC and ACCA recognise that information discovered while performing a professional engagement must not be disclosed without proper and specific authority to do so, or unless there is a legal or professional right or duty to disclose. Clifden & Co may wish to disclose the problem with the products in order to protect consumers from potential harm, but the firm must be very careful to consider whether it has a right or duty to disclose.

ISA 250 *Consideration of Laws and Regulations in an Audit of Financial Statements* may provide relevant guidance in this situation. It is likely that children's toys have to be tested in accordance with industry regulations for health and safety. If this is the case, and the use of contaminated ingredients constitutes a non-compliance with law and regulations, the auditor may have a statutory right or duty to report the situation to the appropriate authority.

In the absence of any industry regulation, Clifden & Co should consider if there is a necessary disclosure in the public interest. This is a difficult and subjective decision, as there is little guidance on what is meant by 'public interest', and it would be hard to decide who exactly the recipient of any disclosure should be. In deciding whether to disclose in the public interest, the auditors should consider the reasons for the client's unwillingness to disclose, the seriousness of the matter i.e. the likelihood of harm being caused, and the relevant laws and regulations.

Before making any disclosure, Clifden & Co should obtain information and evidence regarding the contamination, e.g. how the contamination was discovered (did a toy actually explode?) and whether anyone has been injured. If this is the case there could be legal claims already in progress against the company.

As a last resort, Clifden & Co could consider resigning from the audit. The firm could then circularise a 'statement of circumstances' which would describe the reason for the resignation, including details of the faulty products and the lack of management integrity.

In addition Clifden & Co should establish whether the supplier of the plastic raw material has been contacted, the number of products sold which are contaminated and the number still held as inventory (if any). There could be a counter-claim against the supplier in which case the likelihood of the claim's success should be evaluated.

Finally, the situation also impacts on the audit procedures that are currently being planned. Any contaminated inventory still held by Headford Co should be written off, and provisions may be necessary for refunds of returned products, if the matter becomes known. The financial statements may need to contain disclosures relating to contingent liabilities, or provisions may need to be recognised in respect of damages claimed by customers in the event of any injuries occurring and legal action being taken against Headford Co. The audit should be planned to devote sufficient time to these matters.

Careful consideration should be made relating to the year end inventory count. Assuming that some finished goods containing the contaminated ingredient are still held by the company, audit staff may be in danger of injury when they attend the inventory count. Headford Co must take action to make the items safe or to keep them in safe conditions i.e. at low temperatures, in order to prevent any injuries to its own staff and members of the audit team.

(ii) The invitation to audit Cong Co gives rise to a potential conflict of interest between the interests of different clients. There is nothing ethically wrong in having clients operating in the same industry, in fact it is normal for firms of auditors to specialise in the provision of services to companies in a particular industry or market sector, some of whom are likely to be competitors. However, acting for two competing companies can give rise to ethical threats, particularly objectivity and confidentiality. It could be perceived that impartial, objective services and advice cannot be offered to a company where the audit firm also audits a competitor, and the client companies may be concerned that commercially sensitive information may become known to its competitor if the same audit firm is used by both companies.

The main safeguard in this situation is disclosure of the potential conflict to all parties concerned. Therefore, the audit of Cong Co should only be accepted if both companies have been informed of the services provided by Clifden & Co which could be perceived to create a conflict of interest, and if both companies give their consent to act.

If the audit of both companies goes ahead, then the following extra safeguards should be considered:

- The use of separate engagement teams
- Issuing clear guidelines to the teams on issues of security and confidentiality
- The use of confidentiality agreements by audit team members
- Regular review of the safeguards by an independent partner.

In addition, as Cong Co is a large company, an evaluation as to whether Clifden & Co has sufficient resources to carry out both audits using totally separate teams should take place.

It is quite likely that one or both of the companies do not give consent, in which case Clifden & Co will have to decide which company to act for. As Cong Co is a larger company, it is probable that a higher audit fee would be charged. In addition the provision of non-audit services can be lucrative, indicating that it may be commercially advantageous to take on Cong Co as a client, and to resign from the audit of Headford Co.

Examiner's comments

Requirement (a)

A proportion of candidates achieved maximum marks for this requirement. However, some candidates could not provide a definition other than 'professional competence is when you are competent to take on a professional engagement,' which does not add anything to what is given in the question. Due care was sometimes badly defined as just 'being careful' or 'acting professionally'.

Requirement (bi)

Answers were often limited to brief comments relating to the client's lack of integrity, and the need to recall the products. Many candidates missed the main point of the requirement, which was the auditor's duty to maintain confidentiality, and whether that duty should be breached in this case in the public interest. Only the better answers considered the potential impact of the events on the financial statements, or the risk to the audit firm's reputation if the situation is not handled appropriately. A significant proportion of candidates focused entirely on what the client should do in this situation, (better quality control, sack the production manager, put a notice in newspapers, etc), and hardly mentioned the ethical and professional issues relating to the audit firm at all.

Requirement (bii)

Although the mark allocation for (bii) was lower than that of (bi), most candidates wrote the same, or more, for (bii). Answers here tended to be adequate, with the majority of answers identifying the problems of conflict of interest, and client confidentiality, and most were able to recommend appropriate actions such as full disclosure of the situation, and the use of separate teams for the two clients if the audit appointment were to go ahead.

		Marking scheme	Marks
(a)	(i)	**Competence and due care** Generally 1 mark per comment from ideas list: - Definition of competence, including for example: - Competence – attain knowledge/skills - Competence – maintain knowledge/skills - Definition of due care - To ensure compliance: training, study support, QC, appraisals etc Max 2 marks for definition/explanation of term and 2 marks for compliance comments **Maximum marks**	4
(b)	(i)	**Plastic ingredients** Generally 1 mark per comment/specific action to be taken: - Management lack integrity - Encourage management to disclose - Auditors' duty of confidentiality - Consider law and regs - Consider disclosure in public interest - Legal advice - Consider resignation - Seek evidence/information re matter - Impact on financial statements and planned audit procedures - Safety of staff attending inventory count ½ mark ref ISA 250 **Maximum marks**	8
	(ii)	**Audit of Cong Co** Generally 1 mark per comment/specific action to be taken: - Conflict of interest – explain why - Disclosure to both parties - Other safeguards (1 mark each max 3) - Commercial considerations **Maximum marks**	5
		Total	17

16   BECKER & CO *Walk in the footsteps of a top tutor*

Key answer tips

This question is a slight departure from the traditional ethics/professional issues style question in that it asks for ethical and practice management implications. Despite this departure the question should be no more difficult than traditional questions. The examiner is assessing whether students can place themselves in the shoes of a senior manager at an accounting practice and consider practical, as well as ethical, issues.

In addition to self-interest, self review and familiarity threats students should consider issues such as: can the practice afford it? Do staff have requisite knowledge/skills? What will be the impact on the other areas of business? What will be the effect on reputation? What will be the impact on staff morale?

The highlighted words are key phases that markers are looking for.

(a)   Joint business arrangement

The business opportunity in respect of Murray Co could be lucrative if the market research is to be believed.

However, IFAC's *Code of Ethics for Professional Accountants* states that a mutual business arrangement is likely to give rise to self-interest and intimidation threats to independence and objectivity. The audit firm must be and be seen to be independent of the audit client, which clearly cannot be the case if the audit firm and the client are seen to be working together for a mutual financial gain.

In the scenario, two options are available. Firstly, Becker & Co could provide the audit client with finance to complete the development and take the product to market. There is a general prohibition on audit firms providing finance to their audit clients. This would create a clear financial self-interest threat as the audit firm would be receiving a return on investment from their client. The Code states that if a firm makes a loan (or guarantees a loan) to a client, the self-interest threat created would be so significant that no safeguard could reduce the threat to an acceptable level.

The provision of finance using convertible debentures raises a further ethical problem, because if the debentures are ultimately converted to equity, the audit firm would then hold equity shares in their audit client. This is a severe financial self-interest, which safeguards are unlikely to be able to reduce to an acceptable level.

The finance should not be advanced to Murray Co while the company remains an audit client of Becker & Co.

The second option is for a joint venture company to be established. This would be perceived as a significant mutual business interest as Becker & Co and Murray Co would be investing together, sharing control and sharing a return on investment in the form of dividends. IFAC's *Code of Ethics* states that unless the relationship between the two parties is clearly insignificant, the financial interest is immaterial, and the audit firm is unable to exercise significant influence, then no safeguards could reduce the threat to an acceptable level. In this case Becker & Co may not enter into the joint venture arrangement while Murray Co is still an audit client.

The audit practice may consider that investing in the new electronic product is a commercial strategy that it wishes to pursue, either through loan finance or using a joint venture arrangement. In this case the firm should resign as auditor with immediate effect in order to eliminate any ethical problem with the business arrangement. The partners should carefully consider if the potential return on investment will more than compensate for the lost audit fee from Murray Co.

The partners should also reflect on whether they want to diversify to such an extent – this investment is unlikely to be in an area where any of the audit partners have much knowledge or expertise. A thorough commercial evaluation and business risk analysis must be performed on the new product to ensure that it is a sound business decision for the firm to invest.

The audit partners should also consider how much time they would need to spend on this business development, if they decided to resign as auditors and to go ahead with the investment. Such a new and important project could mean that they take their focus off the key business i.e. the audit practice. They should consider if it would be better to spend their time trying to compete effectively with the two new firms of accountants, trying to retain key clients, and to attract new accounting and audit clients rather than diversify into something completely different.

(b) **Recruitment service**

IFAC's *Code of Ethics for Professional Accountants* does not prohibit firms from offering a recruitment service to client companies. However several ethical problems could arise if the service were offered. The severity of these problems would depend on the exact nature of the service provided, and the role of the person recruited into the client's organisation.

Specific ethical threats could include:

Self-interest – clearly the motive for Becker & Co to offer this service is to generate income from audit clients, thereby creating a financial self-interest threat. The amount received for the recruitment service depends on the magnitude of the salary of the person employed. The more senior the person recruited, the higher their salary is likely to be, and therefore the higher the fee to be paid to Becker & Co.

In addition, the firm could be tempted to advise positively on the recruitment of an individual merely to receive the relevant recruitment fee, without properly considering the suitability of the person for the role.

Familiarity – when performing the audit, the auditors may be less likely to criticise or challenge the work performed by a person they helped to recruit, as any significant problems discovered may make the recruitment appear ill-advised.

Management involvement – there is also a threat that the audit firm could be perceived to be making management decisions by selecting employees. The firm could offer services such as reviewing the professional qualifications of a number of applicants, and providing advice on the applicant's suitability for the post. In addition the firm could draw up a short list of candidates for interview, using criteria specified by the client. However in all cases, the final decision as to whom to hire must be made by the client, as the audit firm should not make, or be perceived to be making, management decisions.

The threats discussed above would increase in significance if the recruitee took on a role in key management pertaining to the finance function, such as finance director or financial controller. The threats would be less severe if the audit firm advised on the recruitment of a junior member of the client's finance function.

If these threats could not be reduced to a level less than clearly insignificant, then the recruitment service should not be offered.

Commercial evaluation

The firm should consider whether there is likely to be much demand for the potential service before developing such a resource. Some form of market research is essential.

Offering this type of service represents a significant departure from normal audit services. The firm should consider whether there is sufficient knowledge and expertise to offer a recruitment service. Ingrid Sharapova seems to have some experience, but her skills may be out of date, and may not be specifically relevant to the recruitment of finance professionals. It may be that considerable training, and possibly the attainment of a new professional qualification relevant to recruitment may be necessary for a credible service to be offered to clients.

If the recruitment service proved successful, then Ingrid could be faced with too much work as she is the only person with relevant experience, and has no one to delegate to. If the firm decides to offer this service, then one other person should receive appropriate training, to cover for Ingrid's holidays and any sick leave, and to provide someone for Ingrid to delegate to. The financial cost of such training should be considered.

Finally, Becker & Co should consider the potential damage to the firm's reputation if the service offered is not of a high quality. If the partners decide to pursue this business opportunity, they may wish to consider setting it up as a separate entity, so that if the business fails or its reputation is questioned, the damage to Becker & Co would be minimised.

(c) **Temporary staff assignments**

Lending staff on a temporary basis to an audit client will create the following ethical threats:

Management involvement – Assuming that the manager or senior is seconded to the finance function of the audit client, it is likely that the individual could be in some way involved in decision making in relation to the accounting systems, management accounts or financial statements.

Self-review – On returning to the audit firm, a seconded individual could be a member of the audit team for the client to which they seconded. This would create a self- review threat whereby they would be unlikely to be critical of their own work performed or decisions made. Even if the individual were not assigned to the client where they performed a temporary assignment, the audit team assigned may tend to over rely on areas worked on by a colleague during the period of their temporary assignment.

Familiarity – if the individual is working at the client at any time during the audit, there will be a familiarity threat, whereby audit team members will be unlikely to sufficiently challenge, and therefore not exercise enough professional scepticism when dealing with work performed by the seconded individual.

In addition, due to the over-staffing problem of Becker & Co, the seconded individuals may feel that if they were not on the secondment, they could be made redundant. This may cause them to act in such as way as not to jeopardise the secondment, even if the action were not in the best interests of the firm.

The threats discussed above are increased where a senior person likely to make significant decisions is involved with the temporary assignment, as in this case where audit managers or seniors will be the subjects of the proposed secondment.

In practice, assistance can be provided to clients, especially in emergency situations, but only on the understanding that the firm's personnel will not be involved with:
– Making management decisions,
– Approving or signing agreements or similar documents, and
– Having the authority to enter into commitments on behalf of the company.

In addition, the individual seconded to a client should not then be involved in any way with the audit of that client when they return to the audit firm. This may be a difficult area, as presumably the client would prefer to have an individual seconded to them who has knowledge and experience of their business, i.e. a member of the audit team, and most likely in this scenario to be the audit manager. If this were the case the manager would then have to be reassigned to a different client, causing internal problems for the audit firm. This problem is likely to outweigh any benefits, financial or otherwise, to Becker & Co.

If the temporary staff assignment were to a non-finance department of the client then the threats would be reduced.

If Becker & Co decides to go ahead with the secondment programme, the firm must ensure that the staff are suitably experienced and qualified to carry out the work given to them by the client. There could be a risk to the reputation of Becker & Co if the seconded staff are not competent or do not perform as well as expected by the client.

One advantage of a secondment is that the individual concerned can benefit from exposure to a different type of work and work environment. This will provide some valuable insights into accounting within a business and the individual may bring some new skills and ideas back into the audit firm.

However, the staff seconded could be offered a permanent position at the client. This would lead to the loss of key members of staff, and be detrimental for Becker & Co in the long run.

The other benefit for the audit firm is that a programme of secondments will ease the problem of an over-staffed audit department, and should have cash flow benefits.

Tutorial note

In answering this question it is relevant to briefly mention corporate governance implications i.e. the client may not be able to accept the services offered by their auditor for ethical, particularly objectivity, reasons.

Examiner's comments

Answers tended to be inadequate overall. Problems mainly arose from candidates not answering the part of the requirement dealing with practice management, and simply not explaining their comments in enough depth.

Requirement (a)

Most candidates spotted the obvious ethical problems of making loans to clients, and of having a mutual financial interest. However few candidates really explained why this is a problem. Many candidates would simply state a type of threat – 'self- interest' and 'intimidation' being the most common, with little attempt to explain how the threat arose and if anything could be done to mitigate the threat. Stronger candidates responded well to the practice management issues, discussing whether the audit firm has the relevant skills for such a business venture and whether attention would be better focused on attracting new audit and assurance clients. Unfortunately there were the inevitable requests for the audit partner to be 'disciplined' or 'struck off' because the client had approached him or her with the business opportunity.

Requirement (b)

Similar problems appeared here, with many candidates stating threats but not explaining them. Some candidates devoted much of their answer to the fee based on salary, maintaining that it was a contingent fee, banned under ethical guidelines. The best answers explained the potential management, self-interest and familiarity threats and how they could be avoided using safeguards. Some answers also considered practice management issues such as a commercial evaluation of the proposal (i.e. how much demand would there be for this service) and also the costs of setting up the service.

Requirement (c)

Many candidates simply repeated the same comments they had made for requirement (b), seeming not to realise that the two were entirely different proposals. This shows the importance of explaining the threats, as similar threats may indeed arise from the possibilities described in (b) and in (c), but why they arise and the implication for the audit firm is completely different. The better answers focused on the issue that ethical risk is increased due to the seniority of those who may be seconded to clients.

Generally the answers to question four lacked any depth in either the analysis of the question scenarios, or the quality of explanations provided. Candidates should consider that ethics questions are often very practical in nature, placing the candidate in a real-life audit firm scenario. It is difficult to score well on these questions with little practical experience or commercial awareness.

	Marking scheme	
(a)	**Joint business arrangement**	*Marks*
	Generally 1–1½ marks per comment:	
	– Self-interest independence threats:	
	– Loans to clients generally prohibited	
	– Convertible loan would lead to equity in client – prohibited	
	– Joint venture arrangement is significant business interest	
	– Audit firm would share control of JV with audit client	
	– Finance involved likely to be significant	
	– Can only proceed with business venture if resign as auditors	
	– Potentially lucrative business opportunity	
	– Auditors lack commercial experience in this type of venture	
	– Should spend time on client retention and attraction	
	Maximum marks	**7**

(b)	**Recruitment services**	
	Generally 1–1½ marks per comment:	
	– Explanation of self-interest threat	
	– Explanation of familiarity threat	
	– Explanation of management involvement threat	
	– Threats increase with seniority of recruitee	
	– Can look at CVs but management to take final decision	
	– Ingrid lacks specific, recent experience	
	– May not be much demand for the service	
	– Need to train second person – cost implication	
	– Consider setting up as separate business	
	Maximum marks	**7**
(c)	**Temporary staff assignment**	
	Generally 1–1½ marks per comment:	
	– Explanation of self-review threat	
	– Explanation of management involvement threat	
	– Explanation of familiarity threat	
	– Description of safeguards	
	– Problem when secondee returns – reassign to other client	
	– Individual benefits from different work experience...	
	– But may be offered permanent employment by the client	
	– Issues with competence of people seconded	
	– Eases audit firms over-staffing problem	
	Maximum marks	**6**
	Total	**20**

17 SMITH & CO *Walk in the footsteps of a top tutor*

Key answer tips

This question is typical of the style and wording of ethics/professional issue questions. Each mini scenario must be considered in turn. Ethical issues require consideration of the Code of Ethics and ethical threats. Professional issues require consideration of quality control, legal concerns/responsibilities and other practice management matters. Once concerns are noted the candidate is then asked to identify how the firm should respond to manage the risks identified. It may help improve your scores to break answers down into the headings: 'ethics', 'quality control', 'legal issues', and 'responses'.

It is important to note the marking guide for each scenario. This indicates how much time should be spent on each. Obviously, twice as much time should be devoted to part (a) in comparison to (c). It is also important that the answer contains reference to the key ethics and quality control terms, such as; self-interest, familiarity, leadership, acceptance etc.

The highlighted words are key phases that markers are looking for.

(a) **Norman Co**

The invoice is 12 months old and it appears doubtful whether the amount outstanding is recoverable. The fact that such an old debt is unsettled indicates poor credit control by Smith & Co. Part of good practice management is to run a profitable, cash generating audit function. The debt should not have been left outstanding for such a long period. It seems that little has been done to secure payment since the file note was attached to the invoice in November 2007.

There is also a significant ethical issue raised. Overdue fees are a threat to objectivity and independence. Due to Norman Co not yet paying for the 2007 year end audit, it could be perceived that the audit has been performed for free. Alternatively the amount outstanding could be perceived as a loan to the client, creating a self-interest threat to independence.

The audit work for the year ended 28 February 2008 should not have been carried out without some investigation into the unpaid invoice relating to the prior year audit. This also represents a self-interest threat – if fees are not collected before the audit report is issued, an unmodified report could be seen as enhancing the prospect of securing payment. It seems that a check has not been made to see if the prior year fee has been paid prior to the audit commencing.

It is also concerning that the audit report for the 2008 year end is about to be issued, but no invoice has been raised relating to the work performed. To maximise cash inflow, the audit firm should invoice the client as soon as possible for work performed.

Norman Co appears to be suffering financial distress. In this case there is a valid commercial reason why payment has not been made – the client simply lacks cash. While this fact does not eliminate the problems noted above, it means that the auditors can continue so long as adequate ethical safeguards are put in place, and after the monetary significance of the amount outstanding has been evaluated.

It should also be considered whether Norman Co's financial situation casts any doubt over the going concern of the company. Continued cash flow problems are certainly a financial indicator of going concern problems, and if the company does not resolve the cash flow problem then it may be unable to continue in operational existence.

Action to be taken:

– Discuss with the audit committee (if any) or those charged with governance of Norman Co:

The ethical problems raised by the non-payment of invoices, and a payment programme to secure cash payment in stages if necessary, rather than demanding the total amount outstanding immediately.

– Notify the ethics partner of Smith & Co of the situation – the ethics partner should evaluate the ethical threat posed by the situation and document the decision to continue to act for Norman Co.

– The documentation should include an evaluation of the monetary significance of the amount outstanding, as it will be more difficult to justify the continuance of the audit appointment if the amount is significant.

– The ethics partner should ensure that a firm-wide policy is communicated to all audit managers requiring them to check the payment of previous invoices before commencing new client work. This check should be documented.

– Consider an independent partner review of the working papers prepared for the 28 February 2008 audit.

– The audit working papers on going concern should be reviewed to ensure that sufficient evidence has been gathered to support the audit opinion. Further procedures may be found to be necessary given the continued cash flow problems.

- Smith & Co have already acted to improve credit control by making a manager responsible for reviewing invoices and monitoring subsequent cash collection. It is important that credit control procedures are quickly put into place to prevent similar situations arising.

(b) **Wallace Co**

Being the audit manager, Valerie Hobson is clearly in a position to influence the outcome of the audit. She appears to have entered into a private commercial transaction with her client. IFAC's Code of Ethics for Professional Accountants does not prohibit such commercial transactions so long as they are:

- In the normal course of business,

- At arm's length, and

- The value is not material to either party.

In this case the transaction is in the normal course of business for the client. Rental of storage space is not the main business of Wallace Co, but it appears that this type of transaction is quite common for the company. However the note on the invoice indicates that a substantial discount has been offered and accepted, and so the transaction is not at arm's length. The value is not material to Wallace Co, but could represent a significant discount to normal commercial terms to the audit manager. Goods and services can be received from an audit client, but only if the value is clearly insignificant.

A self-interest threat is clearly established. Valerie Hobson is benefiting financially from her position as audit manager. She may compromise the audit approach – which has recently been planned – and furthermore she may compromise the audit opinion to keep the client happy. She may also have other audit clients where bias could have occurred.

Action to be taken:

- The ethics partner will need to evaluate whether the value of the transaction and the discount received is 'clearly insignificant'.

- Her benefiting from a discount on services provided by Wallace Co, which was not disclosed, could result in disciplinary action.

- Valerie should be removed from the audit immediately, and a new audit manager assigned to Wallace Co.

- The audit planning for year ended 31 May 2008 should be subject to independent review and amendments made where necessary.

- The transaction should be disclosed to the audit committee of Wallace Co, or to those charged with governance.

- The ethics partner may wish to consider Valerie's relationships with other audit clients for any evidence of transactions or other indicators of potential bias.

(c) **Software Supply Co**

Here it seems that Smith & Co has referred the provision of bespoke accounting software to an external provider – Software Supply Co, and that a commission is being paid to Smith & Co for these referrals. It is common for audit firms to recommend other providers to their audit clients.

This could be perceived as an objectivity and self-interest threat, as the audit firm is benefiting financially through recommending clients to a particular provider of goods and services. However, if appropriate safeguards are in place, the referrals and receipt of commissions can continue.

Action to be taken:

–   Verification from all personnel involved with the audit of clients to whom Software Supply Co has provided a service that they have no financial or personal interest in Software Supply Co.

–   Smith & Co must ensure that:

    For each client where a referral is made, full disclosure has been made to the client regarding the arrangement

    Written acknowledgement that Smith & Co is to receive a referral fee should be obtained from the client.

–   Procedures must be put into place to monitor the quality of goods and services provided by Software Supply Co to audit clients.

Examiner's comments

Requirement (a)

The best answers briefly discussed a range of ethical and professional issues. Most discussed the fact that not raising an invoice for this year's audit, and not yet receiving payment for last year's audit is a threat to independence, but only the better answers developed this into the situation being akin to providing a loan to the client, or being perceived as performing the audit for free. It is crucial that in ethics questions, the reason WHY something is a threat to independence is fully explained. Some answers also considered the difficult ethical position that the audit firm was in – could the firm ethically withhold the audit report until some payment had been received from the client? Or should the report be issued despite payment not being received? Only the best answers discussed that it was the failings of the audit firm's own credit control procedures and quality control measures which had resulted in this tricky situation. Weak answers blamed the client entirely. Some answers discussed the urgent need to arrange a payment plan with the client, while weaker answers suggested that the auditors resort to legal action against their client or even 'send the bailiffs round' to recover some benefit from the situation.

Requirement (b)

On the whole, answers here were satisfactory, with most candidates appreciating that the manager's integrity could be questioned due to the financial interest she is receiving from the client. Most answers also picked up on the fact that the threat is more severe as it is the audit manager who is receiving the benefit. The recommended actions tended to be relevant and specific, though as in question 3 (c), there were repeated requests to 'punish' the manager by reporting her to ACCA. (Though this did not affect the marking of the requirement, it was interesting to note that many candidates made the manager a man in their answer, despite the scenario clearly referring to her as a female manager.)

The answers given to requirements (a) and (b) were usually the same length, despite there being more marks available for (a). Again, candidates are reminded to be careful with time allocation within each question that they attempt.

Requirement (c)

Answers were generally inadequate. Most candidates seemed not to appreciate that auditors often make recommendations to clients, and that as long as the client is aware that a commission will be received by the audit firm, the practice is generally seen as acceptable. Many answers seemed horror-struck at the situation as described, and again there were repeated requests to discipline whoever had raised the invoice, without any attempt to consider why the invoice had been raised. Only the best answers identified the threat to objectivity, the potential self-review threat posed by the situation, and the need to carefully consider the quality of the services offered by the recommended software supplier.

	Marking scheme	
(a)	**Norman Co**	*Marks*
	1 mark per matter discussed/*action point*	
	– Poor credit control	
	– Independence threat – free audit/loan	
	– Independence threat – self-interest in 2008 report	
	– Financial distress leads to going concern threat for the company	
	– Non payment due to financial distress does not necessitate resignation	
	– Discuss with client – ethical problem/payment arrangements	
	– Ethics partner notification	
	– Assess significance of amount outstanding	
	– Policy to check prior invoices paid	
	– Continue to improve credit control	
	– Second partner review	
	– Review of audit work performed on going concern	
	Maximum marks	**8**
(b)	**Wallace Co**	
	1 mark per matter discussed/action point	
	– Non arm's length commercial transaction	
	– Material to audit manager	
	– Self-interest/intimidation threat	
	– Question audit manager's integrity	
	– Potential disciplinary action	
	– Remove Valerie from audit team	
	– Review all work performed on Wallace Co	
	– Consider Valerie's relationship with and likelihood of bias towards her other clients	
	– Disclosure of ethical threat to those charged with governance	
	– Provide clear communication to all staff regarding transactions with clients	
	Maximum marks	**5**
(c)	**Software Supply Co**	
	1 mark per matter discussed/action point	
	– Self review threat	
	– Self-interest threat	
	– Independence check	
	– Client disclosure and acknowledgement	
	– QC monitoring	
	Maximum marks	**4**
	Total	**17**

18 NATE & CO *Walk in the footsteps of a top tutor*

Key answer tips

This is another example of a traditional ethics/professional issues question. As with Smith & Co relevant areas of the syllabus include the Code of Ethics, quality control and legal issues, specifically an accountants responsibility regarding money laundering. A sound answer will also consider the accountants response to risks identfied. Breaking the answer down under those four headings will improve the relevance and flow of your response.

Once again a sound answer will refer to the specific elements of ethics and quality control and refer them back to the issues in the scenario. Failure to apply knowledge to the scenrio will lead to vague, low scoring answers. One way, perhaps, to encourage your application skills is to constantly refer points back to the companies and indviduals named in the question.

The highlighted words are key phases that markers are looking for.

(a) • Money laundering is the process by which criminals attempt to conceal the true origin and ownership of the proceeds of criminal activity, allowing them to maintain control over the proceeds, and ultimately providing a legitimate cover for their sources of income. The objective of money laundering is to break the connection between the money, and the crime that it resulted from.

• It is widely defined, to include possession of, or concealment of, the proceeds of any crime.

• Examples include proceeds of fraud, tax evasion and benefits of bribery and corruption.

Client procedures should include the following:

• Client identification:

– Establish the identity of the entity and its business activity e.g. by obtaining a certificate of incorporation.

– If the client is an individual, obtain official documentation including a name and address, e.g. by looking at photographic identification such as passports and driving licences.

– Consider whether the commercial activity makes business sense (i.e. it is not just a 'front' for illegal activities).

– Obtain evidence of the company's registered address e.g. by obtaining headed letter paper.

– Establish the current list of principal shareholders and directors.

• Client understanding:

– Pre-engagement communication may be considered, to explain to Marcellus Fisher and the other directors the nature and reason for client acceptance procedures.

       –   Best practice recommends that the engagement letter should also include a paragraph outlining the auditor's responsibilities in relation to money laundering.

(b)   There are several issues that must be addressed as a matter of urgency:

Extra work must be planned to discover the extent of the breakdown in internal controls that occurred during the year. It is important to decide whether the errors were isolated, or continued through the accounting period and whether similar errors have occurred in other areas e.g. cash receipts from existing customers or cash payments. A review of the working papers of the internal audit team should be carried out as soon as possible. The materiality of the errors should be documented.

Errors discovered in the accounting systems will have serious implications for the planned audit approach of new customer deposits. Nate & Co must plan to expand audit testing on this area as control risk is high. Cash deposits will represent a significant class of transaction in CF Co. A more detailed substantive approach than used in prior year audits may be needed in this material area if limited reliance can be placed on internal controls.

A combination of the time spent investigating the reasons for the errors, their materiality, and a detailed substantive audit on this area means that the audit is likely to take longer than previously anticipated. This may have cost and recoverability implications. Extra staff may need to be assigned to the audit team, and the deadline for completion of audit procedures may need to be extended. This will need to be discussed with CF Co.

Due to the increased audit risk, Nate & Co should consider increasing review procedures throughout the audit. In addition CF Co is likely to be a highly regulated company as it operates in financial services, increasing possible attention focused on the audit opinion. These two factors indicate that a second partner review would be recommended.

A separate issue is that of Jin Sayed offering advice to the internal audit team. The first problem raised is that of quality control. A new and junior member of the audit team should be subject to close direction and supervision which does not appear to have been the case during this assignment.

Secondly, Jin Sayed should not have offered advice to the internal audit team. On being made aware of the errors, he should have alerted a senior member of the audit team, who then would have decided the action to be taken. This implies that he does not understand the limited extent of his responsibilities as a junior member of the audit team. Nate & Co may wish to review the training provided to new members of staff, as it should be made clear when matters should be reported to a senior, and when matters can be dealt with by the individual.

Thirdly, Jin Sayed must be questioned to discover what exactly he advised the internal audit team to do. Despite his academic qualification, he has little practical experience in the financial information systems of CF Co. He may have given inappropriate advice, and it will be crucial to confirm that no action has been taken by the internal audit team.

The audit partner should consider if Nate & Co are at risk because of the advice that has been provided by Jin Sayed. As he is a member of the audit team, his advice would be considered by the client as advice offered by Nate & Co, and the partner should ascertain by discussion with the client whether this advice has been acted upon.

Finally Nate & Co should consider whether as a firm they could provide the review of the financial information technology system, as requested by CF Co. IFAC's Code of Ethics, and ACCA's Code of Ethics and Conduct places restrictions on the provision of non-audit services. Nate & Co must be clear in what exactly the 'review' will involve.

Providing a summary of weaknesses in the system, with appropriate recommendations is considered part of normal audit procedures. However, given the errors that have arisen in the year, CF Co may require Nate & Co to design and implement changes to the system. This would constitute a self-review threat and should only be considered if significant safeguards are put in place, for example, using a separate team to provide the non-audit service and/or having a second partner review of the work.

(c)   There are several ethical and professional issues raised in relation to the inventory count of LA Shots Co.

Firstly, it was inappropriate of Brenda Mangle to offer the incentive to the audit juniors. As she is a new manager, it may be that she didn't realise how the incentive would be perceived. Brenda should be informed that her actions could have serious implications.

The offer could be viewed as a bribe of the audit juniors, and could be perceived as a self-interest independence threat as there is a financial benefit offered to members of the audit team.

The value of the ten bottles of 'Super Juice' should be considered, as it is only appropriate for a member of the audit team to accept any goods or hospitality from the audit client if the value is 'clearly insignificant'. Ultimately it would be the decision of the audit partner as to whether the value is clearly insignificant. It is likely that this does not constitute a significant threat to independence, however the offer should still be referred to the audit partner.

Also, if the juniors took ten bottles of 'Super Juice', this could interfere with the physical count of goods and/or with cut off details obtained at the count. The juniors should therefore have declined the offer and informed a senior member of the audit team of the situation.

There may be a need to adequately train new members of staff on ethical matters if the juniors were unsure of how to react to the offer.

The work performed by the juniors at the inventory count must be reviewed. The audit procedures were performed very quickly compared to last year and therefore sufficient evidence may not have been gathered. In an extreme situation the whole inventory count may have to be reperformed if it is found that the procedures performed cannot be relied upon.

In addition, the juniors should not have attended the audit client's office party without the permission of the audit manager. The party appears to have taken place during work time, when the juniors should have been completing the inventory count procedures. The two juniors have not acted with due professional consideration, and could be considered to lack integrity. The actions of the juniors should be discussed with them, possibly with a view to disciplinary action.

There may also be questions over whether the direction and supervision of the juniors was adequate. As the two juniors are both recent recruits, this is likely to be the first inventory count that they have attended. It appears that they may not have been adequately briefed as to the importance of the inventory count as a source of audit evidence, or that they have disregarded any such briefing that was provided to them. In either case possibly a more senior auditor should have accompanied them to the inventory count and supervised their actions.

Examiner's comments

Requirement (a) asked candidates to define money laundering and to state procedures relevant to money laundering that should take place on the acceptance of a new audit client. Candidates appeared to have prepared for the topic of money laundering, as the definitions were usually sound. Unfortunately, few candidates could provide many, if any, specific procedures. Many answers provided a discussion of the firm-wide money laundering arrangements that should be made, and in particular there were many extensive descriptions of the role of the Money Laundering Reporting Officer (MLRO) – all of which has nothing to do with the procedures specific to the acceptance of a new client. Some candidates referred to the need to contact Fisher Co's existing auditors, an irrelevant point as Fisher Co had only recently been incorporated. A significant minority of answers suggested that Fisher Co should appoint an MLRO, totally misunderstanding the facts of the scenario, i.e. that Fisher Co is a potential audit client, not a firm of auditors. Only the best answers discussed 'know your client' procedures, and the need for clarification in the engagement letter of matters to do with money laundering. Unfortunately, when procedures were referred to, candidates seemed to think the audit firm would have unrestricted access to police records, as there were frequent descriptions of the need to verify that Marcellus Fisher was not known to the police for criminal behaviour in the past.

Requirements (b) and (c) both focused on ethics, providing brief scenarios as a context. Requirement (b) described a situation in which an audit junior had been providing advice to a client's internal audit team, following the discovery of a number of errors in the accounting system. Some answers described a range of issues, including the potential existence of a fraud and the resulting impact on the audit, the lack of supervision and direction of the audit junior, and the appropriateness of your firm conducting a review of the accounting systems. However some answers focussed almost exclusively on the alleged wrong-doings of the audit junior, with repeated requests that he be disciplined by his firm, removed not only from this audit team but from all audits conducted by the firm, and also reported to ACCA for his bad behaviour. The junior was also often advised that he had made the wrong career choice and would be much more suited to a job in an IT department. The real issue here was the lack of quality control over the audit. Why hadn't his senior asked him where he was for three hours when he was supposed to be carrying out audit work? Why hadn't be been briefed as to the limit of his authority and responsibility? Unfortunately few candidates spotted these issues as they were too focussed on taking action against the junior.

This attitude spilled over into answers to requirement (c), where the scenario described two audit juniors who had appeared to rush an inventory count in order to go to a party at the invitation of the client. Answers were again focussed on recommending various types of disciplinary action against the juniors, instead of discussing the deeper issues of a lack of direction and supervision. Few candidates mentioned the major problem in the offering of a gift of inventory wasn't so much that the client was trying to hide a fraud, but more that it would disrupt the count procedures.

Candidates should remember to allocate their time carefully between question requirements. Most scripts contained answers to requirements (a), (b) and (c) of a similar length, when it clear that the mark allocation differs significantly for requirement (b).

	Marking scheme	Marks
(a)	**Money laundering** Definition – 1 mark Procedures – generally 1 mark each Ideas list: – Client identity – Client business activity – Client address – Client principal shareholders and directors – Engagement letter clarification	*Marks* **5**
(b)	**Ethical and professional issues** Generally 1–1½ marks per issue explained – Extra work on control weaknesses – Review work of internal audit – Expand audit testing – Cost/budget implication – 2nd partner review – Lack of supervision and direction – Lack of understanding of extent of responsibilities – Inappropriate advice – Provision of non audit service – Safeguards	 **9**
(c)	**Ethical and professional issues** Generally 1–1½ marks per issue explained – Perception of bribe – Modesty of gift – Interference with count procedures – Review of work performed – Possible reperformance/alternative procedures – Lack of professional behaviour – QC issues	 **6**
	Total	**20**

19 FOX & STEEPLE – THREE AUDIT ASSIGNMENTS

Key answer tips

Because the requirements are to 'compare and contrast the various assignments issues' the answer must be formatted thus:

(i) Threats – comparison of the three clients B, H and G

(ii) Other professional matters to consider – comparison of clients B, H and G

(iii) Staffing implications – comparison of clients B, H and G

A good working knowledge of IFAC/ACCA ethical codes is required and the ability to identify threats and apply safeguards where appropriate. Other professional matters include for example, quality control, logistics, budgets/fees, staffing requirements, etc. Implications for staffing will need to take account of independence safeguards, e.g. separate teams for the different services provided, etc as well as competence and relevant knowledge/specialisms and experience.

(i)   **Threats to independence**

Self-interest

- A self-interest threat could potentially arise in respect of any (or all) of these assignments as, regardless of any fee restrictions (e.g. per IFAC's 'Code of Ethics for Professional Accountants'), the auditor is remunerated by clients for services provided.

- This threat is likely to be greater for Huggins Co (larger/listed) and Gray Co (requires other services) than for Blythe Co (audit a statutory necessity).

- The self-interest threat may be greatest for Huggins Co. As a company listed on a recognized stock exchange it may give prestige and credibility to Fox & Steeple (though this may be reciprocated). Fox & Steeple could be pressurized into taking evasive action to avoid the loss of a listed client (e.g. concurring with an inappropriate accounting treatment).

Self-review

- This threat is also likely to be greater for Huggins and Gray where Fox & Steeple is providing other (non-audit) services.

- A self-review threat may be created by Fox & Steeple providing Huggins with a 'thorough examination' of its computerized systems if it involves an extension of the procedures required to conduct an audit in accordance with International Standards on Auditing (ISAs).

- Appropriate safeguards must be put in place if Fox & Steeple assists Huggins in the performance of internal audit activities. In particular, Fox & Steeple's personnel must not act (or appear to act) in a capacity equivalent to a member of Huggins' management (e.g. reporting, in a management role, to those charged with governance).

- Fox & Steeple may provide Gray with accounting and bookkeeping services, as Gray is not a listed entity, provided that any self-review threat created is reduced to an acceptable level. In particular, in giving technical advice on financial reporting, Fox & Steeple must take care not to make managerial decisions such as determining or changing journal entries without obtaining Gray's approval.

- Taxation services comprise a broad range of services, including compliance, planning, provision of formal taxation opinions and assistance in the resolution of tax disputes. Such assignments are generally not seen to create threats to independence.

- The due diligence reviews for Gray may create a self-review threat (e.g. on the fair valuation of net assets acquired).

- However, safeguards may be available to reduce these threats to an acceptable level.

- If staff involved in providing other services are also assigned to the audit, their work should be reviewed by more senior staff not involved in the provision of the other services (to the extent that the other service is relevant to the audit).

- The reporting lines of any staff involved in the audit of Huggins and the provision of other services for Huggins should be different. (Similarly for Gray.)

Familiarity

- Long association of a senior member of an audit team with an audit client may create a familiarity threat. This threat is likely to be greatest for Huggins, a long-standing client. It may also be significant for Gray as Fox & Steeple have had dealings with this client for seven years now.

- As Blythe is a new audit client this particular threat does not appear to be relevant.

- Senior personnel should be rotated off the Huggins and Gray audit teams. If this is not possible (for either client), an additional professional accountant who was not a member of the audit team should be required to independently review the work done by the senior personnel.

- The familiarity threat of using the same lead engagement partner on an audit over a prolonged period is particularly relevant to Huggins, which is now a listed entity. IFAC's *Code of Ethics for Professional Accountants* requires that the lead engagement partner should be rotated after a pre-defined period, normally no more than seven years. Although it might be time for the lead engagement partner of Huggins to be changed, the current lead engagement partner may continue to serve for the 2006 audit.

Intimidation

- This threat is most likely to come from Blythe as auditors are threatened with a tendering process to keep fees down.

- Peter may have already applied pressure to reduce inappropriately the extent of audit work performed in order to reduce fees, by stipulating that there should not be an interim audit.

- The audit senior allocated to Blythe will need to be experienced in standing up to client management personnel such as Peter.

Tutorial note

Correct classification under 'ethical', 'other professional', 'practical' or 'staff implications' is not as important as identifying the matters.

(ii) **Other professional and practical matters**

- The experience of staff allocated to each assignment should be commensurate with the assessment of associated risk. For example, there may be a risk that insufficient audit evidence is obtained within the budget for the audit of Blythe. Huggins, as a listed client, carries a high reputational risk.

- Sufficient appropriate staff should be allocated to each audit to ensure adequate quality control (in particular in the direction, supervision, review of each assignment). It may be appropriate for a second partner to be assigned to carry out a 'hot review' (before the auditor's report is signed) of:

  – Blythe, because it is the first audit of a new client; and

  – Huggins, as it is listed.

- Existing clients (Huggins and Gray) may already have some expectation regarding who should be assigned to their audits. There is no reason why there should not be some continuity of staff providing appropriate safeguards are put in place (e.g. to overcome any familiarity threat).

- Senior staff assigned to Blythe should be alerted to the need to exercise a high degree of professional skepticism (in the light of Peter's attitude towards the audit).

- New staff assigned to Huggins and Gray would perhaps be less likely to assume unquestioned honesty than staff previously involved with these audits.

Logistics (practical)

- All three assignments have the same financial year end, therefore there will be an element of 'competition' for the staff to be assigned to the year-end visits and final audit assignments. As a listed company, Huggins is likely to have the tightest reporting deadline and so have a 'priority' for staff.

- Blythe is a local and private company. Staff involved in the year-end visit (e.g. to attend the physical inventory count) should also be involved in the final audit. As this is a new client, staff assigned to this audit should get involved at every stage to increase their knowledge and understanding of the business.

- Huggins is a national operation and may require numerous staff to attend year-end procedures. It would not be expected that all staff assigned to year-end visits should all be involved in the final audit.

Time/fee/staff budgets

- Time budgets will need to be prepared for each assignment to determine manpower requirements (and to schedule audit work).

(iii) **Implications for allocating staff**

- Fox & Steeple should allocate staff so that those providing other services to Huggins and Gray (that may create a selfreview threat) do not participate in the audit engagement.

Competence and due care (Qualifications/Specialization)

- All audit assignments will require competent staff.

- Huggins will require staff with an in-depth knowledge of their computerized system.

- Gray will require senior audit staff to be experienced in financial reporting matters specific to communications and software solutions (e.g. in revenue recognition issues and accounting for internally-generated intangible assets).

- Specialists providing tax services and undertaking the due diligence reviews for Gray may not be required to have any involvement in the audit assignment.

20 EBONY

Key answer tips

Although a good working knowledge of the professional codes is required here and an ability to apply them, students must be able to deal with these situations in a way which satisfies the professional requirements, maintains audit quality and is satisfactory in maintaining a mutually beneficial relationship with the clients concerned. A common sense approach is required. In situation (c) the accounting/reporting implications must be considered.

(a) **Audit team**

- There are many factors to be taken into account when allocating staff to an assignment, for example:

    - the number of staff and levels of technical expertise required;

    - logistics of time and place;

    - the needs of staff (e.g. for study leave); and

    - what is in the client's (i.e. the shareholders') best interest (e.g. an expeditious audit).

- As a matter of practice management, a client should not dictate who staffs their audit. If the Finance Director's requests are based solely on the premise that to have staff other than as requested would cause disruption then he should be assured that anyone assigned to the audit will be:

    - technically competent to perform the tasks delegated to them;

    - adequately briefed and supervised; and

    - mindful of the need not to cause unnecessary disruption.

- Ebony may have other (more complex) assignments on which Xavier (and other staff previously involved in the audit of Almond) could be better utilized.

- To re-assign Xavier to the job may be to deny him other on-the-job training necessary to his personal development. For example, he may be ready to assume a more demanding supervisory role with another client – or he may wish to expand the client base on which he works to obtain a practising certificate (say).

- To keep Xavier with Almond for a third year may also increase the risk of familiarity with the client's staff – a threat to the independence of the audit.

- If it is usual to assign new trainees to Almond then the Finance Director should be advised that to assign a higher grade of staff is likely to increase the audit fee (as more experienced staff cannot necessarily do the work of more junior staff in any less time).

Conclusion

The Finance Director's requests should be granted only if:

(1) it is in the interests of Almond's shareholders (primarily);

(2) meets the needs of Ebony's staff; and

(3) Almond agrees to the commensurate audit fee.

(b) **'Phantom ticking'**

- Ebony's quality control procedures should be such that:

    - the work delegated to Alex was within his capability;

    - Alex was supervised in its execution; and

    - the work performed by Alex was reviewed by appropriate personnel (i.e. someone of at least equal competence).

- Alex's working papers for the audit of Phantom should be re-reviewed to confirm that there is evidence of his work having been properly directed, supervised and reviewed. If there is nothing which appears untoward – it should be discussed with Alex's supervisor on the assignment whether Alex's confession to Kurt could have been 'a joke'.

- As Alex has already left not only the firm, but the profession, it may not seem worth the effort taking any disciplinary action against him (e.g. reporting the [alleged] misconduct to ACCA). However, ACCA's disciplinary committee would investigate such a matter and take appropriate action.
- It is likely that Ebony will have given Alex's new employer a reference. This should be reviewed in the light of any evidence which may cast aspersions on Alex's work ethics.
- As there are now doubts about the integrity of Alex, his work should now be re-reviewed, to determine the risk (if any) that the conclusions drawn on his work may be unsubstantiated (in terms of the relevance, reliability and sufficiency of audit evidence).
- It should also be considered whether the reviewer of Alex's work should have seen the problem. (For example, in a purchase test, the reviewer should have been put upon enquiry if a test indicated that a goods received note had been inspected where a purchase was clearly for services provided and not goods received.) If the reviewer did not detect an evident problem they should be (re)trained as necessary.
- The work undertaken by Alex for audit clients other than Phantom should also be subject to scrutiny.

Conclusion

As Kurt is already aware of the potential problem, it may be appropriate that he be assigned as AIC to audits on which Alex undertook audit work, as he will be alert to any ramifications. It is possible that Ebony should not want to make the situation known to its staff generally.

(c) **Prior year audit failure**

- It appears that the subsequent events review was inadequate in that an adjusting event (the out-of-court settlement) was not taken account of.
- The financial statements for the year ended 31 December 2003 contained a material error in that they disclosed a contingent liability (of unspecified amount) when a provision should have been made (for a known liability).
- The reasons for the error/oversight should be ascertained. For example:

  – who was responsible for signing off on the post statement of financial position event review?

  – when was the review completed?

  – for what reason, if any, was it not extended to the date of signing the audit report?

  – on what date was the management representation letter signed?

  – did the management representation letter cover the outcome of pending litigation (for example)?

- The error has implications for the firm's quality control procedures. For example:

  – was the AIC adequately directed and supervised in the completion of the post statement of financial position event review?

  – was the work of the AIC adequately reviewed, to notice (for example) that it was not extended up until the date on which the auditor's report was signed?

Ebony may need to review and improve on its procedures for the audit of provisions, contingent liabilities and post statement of financial position events.

- If the AIC (or other staff) involved in the prior year audit of Magenta were not as thorough as they should have been, with respect to the post statement of financial position event review, then other audit clients may be similarly affected.

- The auditor has a duty of care to draw the error/oversight to Magenta's attention. This would be an admission of fault for which Ebony should be liable if Magenta were to take action against the firm.

- If Ebony were to remain silent and hope the error is unnoticed there is the risk that Magenta will find out anyway.

- As the matter is material it warrants a prior period adjustment (IAS 8 *Accounting Policies, Changes in Accounting Estimates and Errors*). If this is not made the financial statements will be materially misstated with respect to the current year and comparatives – because the expense of the out-of-court settlement should be attributed to the prior period and not the current year's net profit or loss.

- The most obvious implication for the current year audit of Magenta is that a more thorough post statement of financial position event review will be required than the previous year. This may have a consequent effect on the time/fee/staff budgets of Magenta for the year ended 31 December 2004.

- As the matter is material, it needs to be brought to the attention of Magenta's management, so that a prior year adjustment is made. In the absence of which a qualified auditor's report 'except for' should be required.

Conclusion

The staffing of the final audit of Magenta should be reviewed and perhaps a more experienced person assigned to the post statement of financial position event review than in the prior year. The assignments allocated to the staff responsible for the oversight in Magenta's prior period should be reviewed and their competence/capability re-assessed.

21 SEPIA

Key answer tips

This question addresses the question of client confidentiality, conflicts of interest and the practice of lowballing to obtain other services. Whilst a knowledge of the professional codes is essential, the examiner is looking for the ability of students to apply them in a practical manner and reach a satisfactory solution. There may be alternatives, so consider all the options available before reaching a conclusion.

(a) **'Professional enquiry'**

Professional issues raised

Krill has a professional duty of confidentiality to its client, Squid. If Krill's lack of response is due to Squid not having given them permission to respond, Sepia should not accept the appointment. However, in this case, Anton Fargues should have:

– notified Squid's management of the communication received from Sepia; and

– written to Sepia to decline to give information and state his reasons.

Krill should not have simply failed to respond.

Krill may have suspicions of some unlawful act (e.g. defrauding the taxation authority), but no proof, which they do not wish to convey to Sepia in a written communication. However, Krill has had the opportunity of oral discussion with Sepia to convey a matter which may provide grounds for the nomination being declined by Sepia.

Steps by Sepia

- Obtain written representation from Squid's management, that Krill & Co has been given Squid's written permission to respond to Sepia's communication.

- Send a further letter to Krill by a recorded delivery service (i.e. requiring a signature) which states that if a reply is not received in the next seven days (say) Sepia will assume that there are no matters of which they should be aware and so proceed to accept the appointment. (Advise also that unless a response is received, a written complaint will be made to the relevant professional body.)

- Make a written complaint to the disciplinary committee of the professional body of which Anton Fargues is a member – so that his unprofessional conduct can be investigated.

(b) **Take-over bid**

Professional issues raised

- Sepia has a professional duty of confidentiality to its existing audit client, Vitronella.

- Vitronella may ask Sepia to give corporate finance advice on Hatchet's take-over bid which would be incidental to the audit relationship. Providing Sepia can maintain and demonstrate integrity and objectivity throughout, there would be no objection to Sepia providing such an additional service, to advance their existing clients' case.

- It is often in a company's best interests to have financial advice provided by their auditors, and there is nothing ethically improper in this. So it seems unusual that Hatchet should have approached Sepia, rather than their current auditors.

- ACCA's '*Code of Ethics and Conduct* ' consider that it would not be improper for an audit firm to audit two parties, even if the take-over is contested, and that to cease to act could damage the client's interests. However, the situation is different here in that Sepia is not Hatchet's auditor.

- Sepia should take all reasonable steps to avoid conflicts of interest arising from new engagements and the possession of confidential information. Sepia cannot therefore resign from Vitronella in order to undertake the advisory role for Hatchet. (A relationship which has ended only in the last two years is still likely to constitute a conflict.)

Steps by Sepia

- As it is clear that a material conflict of interest exists, Sepia should decline to act as adviser to Hatchet.

- Advise Vitronella's management that Hatchet's approach has been declined.

(c) **Lowballing**

Professional issues raised

'Lowballing' is a practice in which auditors compete for clients by reducing their fees for statutory audits. Lower audit fees are compensated by the auditor carrying out more lucrative non-audit work (e.g. consultancy and tax advice).

The fact that Keratin has quoted a lower fee than the other tendering firms (if that is the case) is not improper providing that the prospective client, Benthos, is not misled about:

– the precise range of services that the quoted fee is intended to cover; and

– the likely level of fees for any other work undertaken.

Although an admission to lowballing 'Setting the early price in an arrangement at a low amount to secure business with the intent later to raise the price' may sound improper, it does not breach current ethical guidance providing Benthos understands the situation. So, for example, Keratin could offer Benthos a 'free' first-year audit, providing Benthos appreciates what the cost of future audits would be.

The risk is, that if the non-audit work does not materialize, Keratin may be under pressure to cut corners or resort to irregular practices (e.g. the falsification of audit working papers) in order to 'keep within budget'. If a situation of negligence (say) were then to arise, Keratin could be found guilty of incompetence.

As the provision of other services is under scrutiny and becoming increasingly restricted this risk is likely to be high. For example, non-audit services which are prohibited in the US include bookkeeping, financial information systems design and implementation, valuation services, actuarial services, internal audit (outsourced), human resource services for executive positions, investment and legal services.

Keratin may not be just lowballing on the first year audit fee, but in the longer term. Perhaps indicating that future increases might only be in line with inflation. In this case if, rather than comprise the quality of the audit, Keratin were to substantially increase Benthos' audit fees, a fee dispute could arise. In this event Benthos could refuse to pay the higher fee. It might be difficult then for Keratin to take the matter to arbitration if Benthos was misled.

Steps by Sepia

- There are no steps which Sepia can take to prevent Benthos from awarding the tender to whichever firm it chooses.

- If Keratin is successful in being awarded the tender, Sepia should consider its own policy on pricing in future competitive tendering situations.

22 RAINBOW

Key answer tips

The area of goods and services and hospitality arises regularly in a variety of guises so make sure you can discuss it.

(a)   Objectivity is one of the fundamental principles for a member of ACCA. It is defined as being 'The state of mind which has regard to all considerations relevant to the task in hand and no other. It presupposes intellectual honesty'.

Objectivity is particularly important to an auditor, whose role it is to provide an independent opinion on financial statements. ACCA's detailed guidance on the question of objectivity of auditors states that:

'A member's objectivity must be beyond question if he is to report as an auditor. That objectivity can only be assured if the member is and is seen to be independent'.

The ACCA then provides detailed guidance on how auditors should maintain their objectivity and independence. The guidance covers issues such as dependence on an audit client (fee-related issues), close relationships with the client, provision of other accountancy or other services to the client, and accepting goods and services.

The auditor must always strive to maintain his objectivity in all his dealings with the client.

(b)   **Audit engagement**

There are a number of matters to be considered in relation to accepting the audit of Rainbow.

Undue dependence

Accepting the work of Rainbow may lead to the firm having an undue dependence on the client. The audit fee discussed is substantial and, in connection with the tax work, may affect the objectivity of the firm. ACCA suggest that recurring fees from one client should not exceed 15% of gross practice income.

The recurring work outlined in the scenario amounts to $135,000 plus contingent element; this means that it does not meet the 15% guideline ($150,000).

However, consideration should be given to the regularity of special work undertaken by the firm on behalf of the client. It may be arguable that this work is in some sense 'recurring' and this would mean objectivity was impaired.

Contingency fee

This would be unacceptable. Linking the audit fee to the success of the client's business clearly affects objectivity. The firm should not accept these terms.

Unpaid fees

Overdue fees can be construed as a loan to the client, which would adversely affect objectivity. The auditor should consider whether the unpaid fees are overdue, or whether it is normal practice for the firm to have such outstanding fees.

Relationships

The audit partner is related to a member of the client's staff. This could affect objectivity. However, the staff member appears to be junior in the organization, and is an adult daughter and therefore not dependent on the auditor. This should not therefore adversely affect the auditor's objectivity.

Shareholding

As the daughter is not a dependant of the auditor, her shareholding should not affect his objectivity towards this audit.

Other services

Provision of other services to an audit client can affect objectivity of an audit. It appears that different staff would be involved in tax and audit work so (other than the fee issue above) this should not pose any issues in relation to objectivity.

Hospitality

Auditors should beware accepting excessive gifts which are given on terms other than normal commercial ones. The weekend in Tenerife appears to be excessive and should not be accepted. The auditor should consider whether the offer of the free holiday casts significant doubt on the integrity of the director, and whether this would affect his decision to accept the audit work.

ASSIGNMENTS

23   ROBSTER CO *Walk in the footsteps of a top tutor*

Key answer tips

This is a relatively straightforward matters/evidence question, albeit concerning two complex, technical accounting areas. It should be noted that the examiner has chosen two areas of financial reporting that she described as "likely to be examined in detail" in her article "The Importance of Financial Reporting Standards to Auditors."

Matters to consider at the review stage include: whether potential areas of contention are material; relevant accounting guidance; indications of potential errors; and impacts on the audit report. The audit procedures recommended in part a(ii) should link directly to your discussion of possible concerns in a(i).

The highlighted words are key phases that markers are looking for.

(a)   (i)   **Leases**

Matters to consider

Materiality

The amounts recognised in the statement of financial position in relation to the leases are material to the financial statements. The amount recognised in non-current assets amounts to 8% of total assets, and the total finance lease payable recognised amounts to 7.1% of total assets.

Accounting treatment

IAS 17 *Leases* contains detailed guidance on the classification and recognition of leased assets. There are several matters to consider:

- Whether the leases are correctly categorised as finance leases or operating leases. This depends on whether the risk and reward of ownership have passed to Robster Co (the lessee) from the lessor. The leases should only be recognised on the statement of financial position if Robster Co has the risk and reward of ownership.

- Indicators of risk and reward passing to Robster Co would include:
  - Robster Co is responsible for repairs and maintenance of the assets
  - A bargain purchase option exists
  - The lease period is for most of the expected useful life of the assets
  - The present value of the minimum lease payments is substantially all of the fair value of the asset.
- Whether the amounts capitalised are solely in respect of the buildings element of the leases. IAS 17 prohibits the recognition of leases of land as finance leases, all land leases must be classified and accounted for as operating leases. Leases of land and buildings should therefore be 'unbundled' and the two elements accounted for separately.
- The impact of the leases on the income statement must be considered. A finance charge should be calculated and expensed each accounting period, using the actuarial method of calculation (or the sum of digits method as an approximation). In addition, leased assets should be depreciated over the shorter of the lease term and the economic useful life of the asset.

Presentation and disclosure

The finance lease payable recognised of $3.2 million should be split between current and non-current liabilities in the statement of financial position.

IAS 17 requires extensive disclosure relating to leases in the notes to the financial statements, including an analysis showing the amounts outstanding under the lease, and the timing of the cash outflows.

Audit evidence

- A review of the lease contract (using a copy of the lease obtained from the lessor) including consideration of the major clauses of the lease which indicate whether risk and reward has passed to Robster Co.
- A calculation of the present value of minimum lease payments and comparison with the fair value of the assets at the inception of the lease (the fair value should be obtained from the lease contract).
- A recalculation of the finance charge expensed during the accounting period, and agreement of the interest rate used in the lease contract.
- Agreement to the cash book of amounts paid to the lessor i.e. deposit and instalments paid before the year end.
- A recalculation of the depreciation charged, and agreement that the period used in the calculation is the shorter of the lease term and the useful life of the assets.
- Confirmation using the lease contract that the amounts capitalised relate only to the buildings element of the lease.
- For the land elements which should be treated as operating leases, a recalculation of the lease expense recognised in the income statement (this should be calculated on a straight-line basis over the lease term).
- A recalculation and confirmation of the split of the total finance lease payable between current and non-current liabilities.

- A confirmation of the adequacy of the disclosure made in the notes to the financial statements, and agreement of the future payments disclosed to the lease contract.

(ii) **Financial assets**

Matters to consider

Materiality

The financial assets are material to the statement of financial position as the amount recognised in non-current assets amounts to 2.8% of total assets. The gain recognised is material to the income statement, representing 10.9% of profit before tax, and 3.3% of revenue.

Accounting treatment

IAS 39 *Financial Instruments: Recognition and Measurement* states that financial assets must be classified into one of four categories. Robster Co has classified financial assets into the category 'financial assets at fair value through profit or loss' as they are considered to be 'held for trading' investments. In order for this to be an acceptable classification of the investments, they must be:

- acquired or incurred principally for the purpose of selling or repurchasing it in the near term, and

- part of a portfolio of identified financial instruments that are managed together and for which there is evidence of a recent pattern of short-term profit-taking.

Investments classified in this way must be measured at fair value each year end, with gains and losses taken into the statement of comprehensive income as part of net profit for the year.

Disclosure

IFRS 7 *Financial Instruments: Disclosures* contains extensive disclosure requirements in relation to financial assets, including for example, a narrative description of how the risks in relation to the investments are managed and monitored, and quantitative disclosures including sensitivity analysis relating to the market risk associated with the valuation of investments.

Audit evidence

- A schedule showing all the investments held in the category, their purchase price and their year-end valuation.

- Agreement of the purchase prices of investments to supporting documentation, e.g. stockbrokers' statements.

- Agreement of the year end valuation for each investment to external sources of information, e.g. stock exchange website, financial press.

- Recalculation, and confirmation of the gain recognised in the income statement.

- A review of the internal function which has been set up to manage the investments, to confirm that investments are generally short-term in nature, that the investments are managed as a portfolio, and that there is evidence of frequent transactions.

- Confirmation that the other information published with the financial statements, e.g. the operating and financial review, describes Robster

Co's investment activities in line with the classification of investments as held for trading, and refers to the valuation and gain made during the year.

- A review of the proposed note to the financial statements confirming adherence to the disclosure requirements of IFRS 7, and recalculations of numerical disclosures.

(b) Guidance on reviews of interim financial statements is provided in ISRE 2410 *Review of Interim Financial Information Performed by the Independent Auditor of the Entity*. The standard states that the auditor should plan their work to gather evidence using analytical procedures and enquiry.

The auditor should perform analytical procedures in order to discover unusual trends and relationships, or individual figures in the interim financial information, which may indicate a material misstatement. Procedures should include the following:

- Comparing the interim financial information with anticipated results, budgets and targets as set by the management of the company.

- Comparing the interim financial information with:
  - comparable information for the immediately preceding interim period,
  - the corresponding interim period in the previous year, and
  - the most recent audited financial statements.

- Comparing ratios and indicators for the current interim period with those of entities in the same industry.

- Considering relationships among financial and non-financial information. The auditor also may wish to consider information developed and used by the entity, for example, information in monthly financial reports provided to the senior management or press releases issued by the company relevant to the interim financial information.

- Comparing recorded amounts or ratios developed from recorded amounts, to expectations developed by the auditor. The auditor develops such expectations by identifying and using plausible relationships that are reasonably expected to exist based on the accountant's understanding of the entity and the industry in which the entity operates.

- Comparing disaggregated data, for example, comparing revenue reported by month and by product line or operating segment during the current interim period with that of comparable prior periods.

As with analytical procedures performed in an audit, any unusual relationships, trends or individual amounts discovered which may indicate a material misstatement should be discussed with management. However, unlike an audit, further corroboration using substantive procedures is not necessary in a review engagement.

Examiner's comments

The first part of this question was a standard audit evidence question of the type seen in numerous previous examinations. Nearly all candidates correctly calculated and concluded on the materiality of both items, and considered the financial reporting implications of the information provided.

In terms of the finance leases, most candidates indentified the correct financial reporting standard, and discussed the classification of the lease as finance or operating lease. Some candidates could provide nothing further, but better answers continued on to describe the factors that should be considered in lease classification, referring not just to 'substance over form', but to the specific indicators that risk and reward had passed to the lessee. Only a small minority of candidates discussed whether the lease should be unbundled into the separate land and buildings elements.

The evidence points tended to be quite brief for this requirement, usually limited to 'check the lease document', 'check lease approved by management' and the inevitable 'get management representation that it is a finance lease'. Such comments are much too vague, and better answers provided more specific pieces of evidence that should be sought, such as a recalculation of minimum lease payments, and a review of the clauses of the lease in terms of responsibility for insurance and repairs to the assets.

(aii) was generally unsatisfactorily answered, and the information given in the question was often misinterpreted. Candidates tended to know the number of the relevant financial reporting standard for financial assets, but not the technical content of that standard. Despite the question clearly stating that the assets are all investments in listed companies, a significant proportion of candidates chose to base their answer around investment properties, and others seemed to think the assets were some kind of inventory, to be valued at the lower of cost and net realisable value. Even those candidates who appreciated that the assets were investments were confused by terminology, frequently stating that 'fair value through profit and loss' and 'held for trading' are contradictory, which is not the case. Most candidates thought that the revaluation gain should not be recognised in profit for the year, which again is not the case.

The evidence points were also inadequate for this requirement. Even a candidate lacking knowledge of the financial reporting issues for investments in listed companies should be able to suggest confirming the year end share price to an external source of information on share prices, such as the financial times, but unfortunately few candidates could even provide this as a piece of evidence.

Requirement (b) was unsatisfactorily answered by almost all candidates. This asked for the principal analytical procedures that should be used to gather evidence in a review of interim financial information. Candidates are repeatedly reminded that non-audit engagements are part of the syllabus, and likely to feature regularly in the examination. However, few candidates seemed to know the purpose of a review of interim financial information, which meant that their answers lacked clarity. Most answers could only suggest a comparison with the prior period, and hardly any answers mentioned the disaggregation of data, or comparison with budget. Only a handful of candidates seemed aware of the existence of ISRE 2410, *Review of Interim Financial Information Performed by the Independent Auditor of the entity,* on which the requirement is based.

Some candidates confused a 'review of interim financial information' with an 'interim audit', despite the short scenario describing a review of interim financial information for the avoidance of any such confusion.

		Marking scheme	
(a)		**(i) Leases**	*Marks*
		Generally 1 mark per matter/evidence point:	
		Matters: - Correct calculation and assessment of materiality - Classification of lease - IAS 17 indicators of finance lease - Split between land and buildings - Finance charge - Depreciation - Disclosure Evidence - Lease clauses re risk and reward - Recalculate PV of MLP v FV - Recalculate depn and finance charge - Cash book for payments - Review of disclosures - Split current/non-current payable ½ mark ref IAS 17	
		Maximum marks	**8**
		(ii) Financial Assets	
		Generally 1 mark per matter/evidence point:	
		Matters: - Correct calculation and assessment of materiality - Classification as held for trading - Assets shown at fair value – could be subjective - Disclosure Evidence - Agree purchase price - Agree fair value - Recalculate gain - Review of disclosures in notes - Review of disclosures in OFR/other information published with financial statements ½ mark ref IAS 39 and IFRS 7	
		Maximum marks	**5**
(b)		**Interim Financial Information**	
		Generally 1 mark per procedure:	
		- Comparisons with past data e.g. to preceding period, to corresponding interim last year, to last audited accounts - Comparisons to anticipated results - Comparisons to non financial data/ratios - Comparisons to similar entities - Disaggregation of data ½ ref ISRE 2410	
		Maximum marks	**4**
		Total	**17**

24   POPPY CO (A) *Walk in the footsteps of a top tutor*

Key answer tips

Question 3 begins with a discussion of audit risk and fair values. The first thing to note is that much of this is basic common sense: why do estimates increase audit risk? Secondly, the question asks you to *discuss* the statement. You must therefore produce a balanced argument, i.e. discuss why fair value accounting may also lead to a reduction of audit risk. The marking guide does cap one-sided arguments below the maximum attainable marks.

Part b(i) requires a discussion of how auditors assess the reliability and objectivity of external valuers and part b(ii) requires little more than a basic knowledge of how to audit the value of property, which should have been covered at F8 level.

The highlighted words are key phases that markers are looking for.

(a)   Balances held at fair value are frequently recognised as material items in the statement of financial position. Sometimes it is required by the financial reporting framework that the measurement of an asset or liability is at fair value, e.g. certain categories of financial instruments, whereas it is sometimes the entity's choice to measure an item using a fair value model rather than a cost model, e.g. properties. It is certainly the case that many of these balances will be material, meaning that the auditor must obtain sufficient appropriate evidence that the fair value measurement is in accordance with the requirements of financial reporting standards. ISA 540 *Auditing Accounting Estimates Including Fair Value Accounting Estimates and Related Disclosures* contains guidance in this area.

As part of the understanding of the entity and its environment, the auditor should gain an insight into balances that are stated at fair value, and then assess the impact of this on the audit strategy. This will include an evaluation of the risk associated with the balance(s) recognised at fair value.

Audit risk comprises three elements; each is discussed below in the context of whether material balances shown at fair value will lead to increased risk for the auditor.

Inherent Risk

Many measurements based on estimates, including fair value measurements, are inherently imprecise and subjective in nature. The fair value assessment is likely to involve significant judgments, e.g. regarding market conditions, the timing of cash flows, or the future intentions of the entity. In addition, there may be a deliberate attempt by management to manipulate the fair value to achieve a desired aim within the financial statements, in other words to attempt some kind of window dressing.

Many fair value estimation models are complicated, e.g. discounted cash flow techniques, or the actuarial calculations used to determine the value of a pension fund. Any complicated calculations are relatively high risk, as difficult valuation techniques are simply more likely to contain errors than simple valuation techniques. However, there will be some items shown at fair value which have a low inherent risk, because the measurement of fair value may be relatively straightforward, e.g.

assets that are regularly bought and sold on open markets that provide readily available and reliable information on the market prices at which actual exchanges occur.

In addition to the complexities discussed above, some fair value measurement techniques will contain significant assumptions, e.g. the most appropriate discount factor to use, or judgments over the future use of an asset. Management may not always have sufficient experience and knowledge in making these judgments.

Thus the auditor should approach some balances recognised at fair value as having a relatively high inherent risk, as their subjective and complex nature means that the balance is prone to contain an error. However, the auditor should not just assume that all fair value items contain high inherent risk – each balance recognised at fair value should be assessed for its individual level of risk.

Control risk

The risk that the entity's internal monitoring system fails to prevent and detect valuation errors needs to be assessed as part of overall audit risk assessment. One problem is that the fair value assessment is likely to be performed once a year, outside the normal accounting and management systems, especially where the valuation is performed by an external specialist. Therefore, as a non-routine event, the assessment of fair value is likely not to have the same level of monitoring or controls as a day-to-day business transaction.

However, due to the material impact of fair values on the statement of financial position, and in some circumstances on profit, management may have made great effort to ensure that the assessment is highly monitored and controlled. It therefore could be the case that there is extremely low control risk associated with the recognition of fair values.

Detection risk

The auditor should minimise detection risk via thorough planning and execution of audit procedures. The audit team may lack experience in dealing with the fair value in question, and so would be unlikely to detect errors in the valuation techniques used. Over-reliance on an external specialist could also lead to errors not being found.

Conclusion

It is true that the increasing recognition of items measured at fair value will in many cases cause the auditor to assess the audit risk associated with the balance as high. However, it should not be assumed that every fair value item will be likely to contain a material misstatement. The auditor must be careful to identify and respond to the level of risk for fair value items on an individual basis to ensure that sufficient and appropriate evidence is gathered, thus reducing the audit risk to an acceptable level.

(b) (i) **Enquiries in respect of the external valuer**

Enquiries would need to be made for two main reasons, firstly to determine the competence, and secondly the objectivity of the valuer. ISA 620 *Using the Work of an Auditor's Expert* contains guidance in this area.

Competence

Enquiries could include:

- Is the valuer a member of a recognised professional body, for example a nationally or internationally recognised institute of registered surveyors?

- Does the valuer possess any necessary licence to carry out valuations for companies?

- How long has the valuer been a member of the recognised body, or how long has the valuer been licensed under that body?

- How much experience does the valuer have in providing valuations of the particular type of investment properties held by Poppy Co?

- Does the valuer have specific experience of evaluating properties for the purpose of including their fair value within the financial statements?

- Is there any evidence of the reputation of the valuer, e.g. professional references, recommendations from other companies for which a valuation service has been provided?

- How much experience, if any, does the valuer have with Poppy Co?

Using the above enquiries, the auditor is trying to form an opinion as the relevance and reliability of the valuation provided. ISA 500 *Audit Evidence* requires that the auditor gathers evidence that is both sufficient and appropriate. The auditor needs to ensure that the fair values provided by the valuer for inclusion in the financial statements have been arrived at using appropriate knowledge and skill which should be evidenced by the valuer being a member of a professional body, and, if necessary, holding a licence under that body.

It is important that the fair values have been arrived at using methods allowed under IAS 40 *Investment Property*. If any other valuation method has been used then the value recognised in the statement of financial position may not be in accordance with financial reporting standards. Thus it is important to understand whether the valuer has experience specifically in providing valuations that comply with IAS 40, and how many times the valuer has appraised properties similar to those owned by Poppy Co.

In gauging the reliability of the fair value, the auditor may wish to consider how Poppy Co decided in appointing this particular valuer, e.g. on the basis of a recommendation or after receiving references from companies for which valuations had previously been provided.

It will also be important to consider how familiar the valuer is with Poppy Co's business and environment, as a way to assess the reliability and appropriateness of any assumptions used in the valuation technique.

Objectivity

Enquiries could include:

- Does the valuer have any financial interest in Poppy Co, e.g. shares held directly or indirectly in the company?

- Does the valuer have any personal relationship with any director or employee of Poppy Co?

– Is the fee paid for the valuation service reasonable and a fair, market based price?

With these enquiries, the auditor is gaining assurance that the valuer will perform the valuation from an independent point of view. If the valuer had a financial interest in Poppy Co, there would be incentive to manipulate the valuation in a way best suited to the financial statements of the company. Equally if the valuer had a personal relationship with a senior member of staff at Poppy Co, they may feel pressured to give a favourable opinion on the valuation of the properties.

The level of fee paid is important. It should be commensurate with the market rate paid for this type of valuation. If the valuer was paid in excess of what might be considered a normal fee, it could indicate that the valuer was encouraged, or even bribed, to provide a favourable valuation.

(ii) **Additional audit procedures**

Audit procedures should focus on the appraisal of the work of the expert valuer. Procedures could include the following:

– Inspection of the written instructions provided by Poppy Co to the valuer, which should include matters such as the objective and scope of the valuer's work, the extent of the valuer's access to relevant records and files, and clarification of the intended use by the auditor of their work.

– Evaluation, using the valuation report, that any assumptions used by the valuer are in line with the auditor's knowledge and understanding of Poppy Co. Any documentation supporting assumptions used by the valuer should be reviewed for consistency with the auditor's business understanding, and also for consistency with any other audit evidence.

– Assessment of the methodology used to arrive at the fair value and confirmation that the method is consistent with that required by IAS 40.

– The auditor should confirm, using the valuation report, that a consistent method has been used to value each property.

– It should also be confirmed that the date of the valuation report is reasonably close to the year-end of Poppy Co.

– Physical inspection of the investment properties to determine the physical condition of the properties supports the valuation.

– Inspect the purchase documentation of each investment property to ascertain the cost of each building. As the properties were acquired during this accounting period, it would be reasonable to expect that the fair value at the year end is not substantially different to the purchase price. Any significant increase or decrease in value should alert the auditor to possible misstatement, and lead to further audit procedures.

– Subsequent events should be monitored for any additional evidence provided on the valuation of the properties. For example, the sale of an investment property shortly after the year end many provide additional evidence relating to the fair value measurement.

– Obtain a management representation regarding the reasonableness of any significant assumptions, where relevant, to fair value measurements or disclosures.

Examiner's comments

This was the least popular of the optional questions, though it was attempted by approximately half of the candidates. The question dealt with a high profile topical issue – the recognition of items in financial statements at fair value, and the auditing implications of this.

Requirement (a) was a discussion as to whether having items recognised at fair value would lead to an increase in audit risk. A small minority of answers were sound, referring to the current trend in financial reporting for fair value accounting, and linking this to the various elements of audit risk. Some answers used examples to illustrate their comments, and some referred to the current economic climate and inactive markets which make determining a fair value difficult. Such answers display not only technical knowledge, but also commercial awareness of an important issue.

However, many answers to (a) focussed incorrectly on materiality, and while many were strong on the financial reporting issues, this was not often successfully linked to audit risk implications. The recent examiner's article on financial reporting issues for the auditor had clearly not been read by many candidates.

Requirement (b) provided a brief scenario setting the scene of an audit client which has revalued several investment properties. **Requirement (bi)** asked for a recommendation and explanation of enquiries that should be made before relying on the work of an external valuer. Most candidates successfully recommended enquiries, but a number then failed to explain the reason for the enquiries. Candidates should take care to follow the question requirement carefully, as failing to provide an explanation when one is asked for will severely restrict the marks that can be awarded.

Requirement (bii) asked the candidate to 'identify and explain principal audit procedures to be performed on the valuation of the investment properties'. Answers here were unsatisfactory. This requirement was the most mis-read of all on the paper. Many answers repeated the points made in (bi). Most ignored the fact that procedures relevant to valuation had been asked for, and instead provided a list of general procedures covering other assertions, in particular existence, and rights and obligations. Some scripts provided a heading for every single assertion and one procedure for each assertion. Candidates must follow the instructions given in the requirement, in order to give a focussed answer. Unfortunately many candidates wasted a lot of time here on writing completely irrelevant answers.

	Marking scheme	
(a)	**Fair values and audit risk**	**Marks**
	Generally 1 mark per point:	
	– Introduction referring to need to recognise fair values	
	– Example of item recognised at fair value	
	– Discussion of inherent risk – subjectivity	
	– Discussion of inherent risk – deliberate manipulation	
	– Discussion of inherent risk – complexity	
	– Discussion of control risk – non routine transactions	
	– BUT may lead to increased level of monitoring	
	– Discussion of detection risk	
	– Conclusion	
	Allow 1 mark for definition of fair value	
	½ mark for reference to ISA 545/ISA 540	
	Cap marks at 5 if no attempt is made to produce a rounded discussion (i.e. should not assume that fair value automatically increases audit risk)	
	Maximum marks	**7**
(b)	**(i) Enquiries of valuer**	
	Generally ½ mark per enquiry and 1 mark per point of explanation from ideas list:	
	– Membership of professional body	
	– Whether a license is held	
	– Reputation – references, etc	
	– Experience with Poppy Co's type of property	
	– Experience with preparing valuations under IAS 40	
	– Financial interest	
	– Personal interest	
	Up to 4 marks for assessment of reliability, up to 2 marks for assessment of objectivity.	
	Maximum marks	**7**
(b)	**(ii) Audit procedures**	
	Generally 1 mark per procedure from ideas list:	
	– Review written instructions	
	– Evaluate assumptions	
	– Check consistent method used	
	– Check date of report close to year end	
	– Method to follow IAS 40 fair value framework	
	– Physical inspection	
	– Review of purchase documentation	
	– Subsequent events	
	– Management representation	
	Maximum marks	**6**
	Total	**20**

25 PULP CO *Walk in the footsteps of a top tutor*

Key answer tips

The question requires knowledge of accounting for and auditing related party transactions. The examiner has indicated her intention to examine complex areas of accounting that are the subject of their own International Standard of Auditing, such as ISA's 540 to 570. You must therefore be able to discuss both the accounting requirements of IAS 24 and the auditing applications of ISA 550.

> Matters to consider at the review stage include: whether potential areas of contention are material; relevant accounting guidance; indications of potential errors; and impacts on the audit report. The audit procedures recommended in part b(ii) should link directly to your discussion of possible concerns in b(i).

(a)   **Identification of related parties**

Related parties and associated transactions are often difficult to identify, as it can be hard to establish exactly who, or what, are the related parties of an entity. IAS 24 *Related Party Disclosures* contains definitions which in theory serve to provide a framework for identifying related parties, but deciding whether a definition is met can be complex and subjective. For example, related party status can be obtained via significant interest, but in reality it can be difficult to establish the extent of influence that potential related parties can actually exert over a company.

The directors may be reluctant to disclose to the auditors the existence of related parties or transactions. This is an area of the financial statements where knowledge is largely confined to management, and the auditors often have little choice but to rely on full disclosure by management in order to identify related parties. This is especially the case for a close family member of those in control or having influence over the entity, whose identity can only be revealed by management.

Identification of material related party transactions

Related party transactions may not be easy to identify from the accounting systems. Where accounting systems are not capable of separately identifying related party transactions, management need to carry out additional analysis, which if not done makes the transactions extremely difficult for auditors to find. For example sales made to a related party will not necessarily be differentiated from 'normal' sales in the accounting systems.

Related party transactions may be concealed in whole, or in part, from auditors for fraudulent purposes. A transaction may not be motivated by normal business considerations, for example, a transaction may be recognised in order to improve the appearance of the financial statements by 'window dressing'. Clearly if the management is deliberately concealing the true nature of these items it will be extremely difficult for the auditor to discover the rationale behind the transaction and to consider the impact on the financial statements.

Finally, materiality is a difficult concept to apply to related party transactions. Once a transaction has been identified, the auditor must consider whether it is material. However, materiality has a particular application in this situation. ISA 550 *Related Parties* states that the auditor should consider the effect of a related party transaction on the financial statements. The problem is that a transaction could occur at an abnormally small, even nil, value. Determining materiality based on monetary value is therefore irrelevant, and the auditor should instead be alert to the unusual nature of the transaction making it material.

(b)   (i)   **Matters to consider**

Materiality

The receivable represents only 0.2% (25,000/12 million × 100) of total assets so is immaterial in monetary terms. However, the details of the transaction could make it material by nature.

The amount is outstanding from a company under the control of Pulp Co's chairman. Readers of the financial statements would be interested to know the details of this transaction, which currently is not disclosed. Elements of the transaction could be subject to bias, specifically the repayment terms, which appear to be beyond normal commercial credit terms. Paul Sheffield may have used his influence over the two companies to 'engineer' the transaction. Disclosure is necessary due to the nature of the transaction, the monetary value is irrelevant.

A further matter to consider is whether this is a one-off transaction, or indicative of further transactions between the two companies.

Relevant accounting standard

The definitions in IAS 24 must be carefully considered to establish whether this actually constitutes a related party transaction. The standard specifically states that two entities are not necessarily related parties just because they have a director or other member of key management in common. The audit senior states that Jarvis Co is controlled by Peter Sheffield, who is also the chairman of Pulp Co. It seems that Peter Sheffield is in a position of control/significant influence over the two companies (though this would have to be clarified through further audit procedures), and thus the two companies are likely to be perceived as related.

IAS 24 requires full disclosure of the following in respect of related party transactions:

–   the nature of the related party relationship,

–   the amount of the transaction,

–   the amount of any balances outstanding including terms and conditions, details of security offered, and the nature of consideration to be provided in settlement,

–   any allowances for receivables and associated expense.

There is currently a breach of IAS 24 as no disclosure has been made in the notes to the financial statements. If not amended, the audit opinion on the financial statements should be qualified with an 'except for' disagreement. In addition, if practicable, the auditor's report should include the information that would have been included in the financial statements had the requirements of IAS 24 been adhered to.

Valuation and classification of the receivable

A receivable should only be recognised if it will give rise to future economic benefit, i.e. a future cash inflow. It appears that the receivable is long outstanding – if the amount is unlikely to be recovered then it should be written off as a bad debt and the associated expense recognised. It is possible that assets and profits are overstated.

Although a representation has been received indicating that the amount will be paid to Pulp Co, the auditor should be sceptical of this claim given that the same representation was given last year, and the amount was not subsequently recovered. The $25,000 could be recoverable in the long term, in which case the receivable should be reclassified as a non-current asset. The amount advanced to Jarvis Co could effectively be an investment rather than a short term receivable. Correct classification on the statement of financial position (balance sheet) is crucial for the financial statements to properly show the liquidity position of the company at the year end.

Tutorial note

Digressions into management imposing a limitation in scope by withholding evidence are irrelevant in this case, as the scenario states that the only evidence that the auditors have asked for is a management representation. There is no indication in the scenario that the auditors have asked for, and been refused any evidence.

(ii)   **Further audit procedures:**

Request from Peter Sheffield a written representation detailing:

–   the exact nature of his control over Jarvis Co, i.e. if he is a shareholder then state his percentage shareholding, if he is a member of senior management then state his exact position within the entity,

–   a comment on whether in his opinion the balance is recoverable,

–   a specific date by which the amount should be expected to be repaid, and

–   a confirmation that there are no further balances outstanding from Jarvis Co, or any further transactions between Jarvis Co and Pulp Co.

Tutorial note

Reference to the Exposure Draft ISA 550 Related Parties (Revised and Redrafted) requirement for both general and specific management representations will be awarded credit.

Review the terms of any written confirmation of the amount, such as a signed agreement or invoice, checking whether any interest is due to Pulp Co. The terms should be reviewed for details of any security offered, and the nature of the consideration to be provided in settlement.

From discussion with Peter Sheffield, develop an understanding of the business purpose of the transaction, particularly to understand whether the balance is a trade receivable or an investment.

Review the board minutes for evidence of any discussion of the transaction and the recoverability of the balance outstanding.

Obtain the most recent audited financial statements of Jarvis Co and:

–   ascertain whether Peter Sheffield is disclosed as the ultimate controlling party or disclosed as a member of key management personnel,

–   scrutinise the disclosure notes to find any disclosure of the transaction, where it should be described as a related party liability, and

– perform a liquidity analysis to establish whether the amount can be repaid from liquid assets.

(c) **Quality control issues raised from the senior's comments**

There are several issues raised, all of which indicate that quality control procedures have not functioned adequately. The planned audit procedures appear to be inadequate, further tests should have been performed to confirm the completeness, existence and valuation of the balance.

In last year's audit, the management representation was accepted as sufficient evidence in relation to the receivable. Possibly the item was not identified as a related party transaction, or it was not considered to be material enough to warrant further investigation.

At the planning stage, it is standard procedure to identify key related parties of an entity, and to plan procedures specific to them. Inadequate planning may lead to a lack of prioritisation of this as an area of relatively high audit risk.

Work on receivables is often carried out by a relatively inexperienced member of the audit team. Audit juniors may not appreciate the potential breach of IAS 24, or the complexities regarding materiality assessment for this type of transaction.

Insufficient review by the audit manager has been performed on completed working papers, which then failed to spot the weakness of the management representation as a source of evidence. This year the audit senior has highlighted the matter, which can now be resolved through additional audit procedures.

Examiner's comments

Requirement (a) asked candidates to discuss the difficulties facing auditors in the identification of related parties and related party transactions. Some answers started with a definition of related parties and went on to discuss the various factors which create problems for the auditor, including the complex and sometimes subjective way of deciding whether a party is related to an entity, the specific issues with materiality not being based on a monetary amount, and the fact that knowledge may be confined to the highest level of management within an entity. Weaker answers simply stated that the directors will try to hide the existence of related party transactions, and often went on to stress that related party transactions are almost always fraudulent, masking illegal activities or creative accounting. Only a handful of candidates mentioned the existence of ISA 550, which provides guidance to auditors in this area.

In **requirement (b)** despite the clue given in requirement (a), a surprising number of candidates did not mention that the transaction described in the scenario appeared to be a related party transaction. Those that did pick up on this fact failed to develop or explain the point fully, and although there were many comments along the lines of 'the transaction should be disclosed', hardly any answers provided an indication of what exactly should be disclosed and why (losing relatively easy marks for not stating the various disclosure requirements of IAS 24 *Related party disclosures*), or that a lack of disclosure would result in qualification of the audit opinion by disagreement.

A large minority of candidates focussed on the fact that the receivable should be provided for, which is reasonable, but then went on to suggest that not providing for the balance would lead to a qualified opinion, despite the amount being clearly immaterial by reference to monetary amount. Many answers seemed not to understand that receivables are contained within current assets, with a worrying number of scripts stating that 'if the receivable is written off, the current assets should also be written off'.

On the whole the answers to (bi) were confused, resulting in inadequate answers to (bii), where audit procedures should have been recommended. Very few candidates suggested that the auditor should try to understand the nature of the transaction in question ('normal' trade receivable or loan), with procedures usually restricted to vague comments like 'inspect invoice' – but what it is being inspected for, and would there even be an invoice? Or 'speak to management' – but about what, and who would the discussion be with? Answers to audit procedure questions must be much more specific.

Requirement (c) was often not attempted; however, relatively easy marks were available for commenting on possible weaknesses in the auditor's quality control procedures which failed to spot the related party issue in the previous year, and the over-reliance on a management representation as a source of evidence. Some answers resulted from a mis-reading of the requirement, and commented on Pulp's poor credit control function. Some candidates seemed to want to punish this year's audit senior for the deficiencies in the audit which happened in the previous year, and which the audit senior had spotted, leading to the inevitable comments about 'punishing' the senior for his incompetence. Better answers discussed a need for the training of audit staff with respect to related parties, and the need for a thorough review of this relatively high risk section of the audit.

	Marking scheme	
(a)	Problems in identifying related parties and transactions	*Marks*
	1 mark per point:	
	Ideas list:	
	– Complex/subjective definition of related party	
	– Reluctance of management to disclose	
	– Hard to identify from accounting system	
	– Deliberate concealment for fraud/window dressing	
	– Materiality relatively complex to apply	
	– Reference IAS 24, ISA 500 (½ mark each)	
	Maximum marks	**5**
(b)	**(i) Matters to consider**	
	1 mark per comment from ideas list:	
	– Immaterial (only award mark if calculation provided)	
	– Material by nature	
	– Whether this is a one-off transaction	
	– IAS 24 – whether meets definition of related party	
	– IAS 24 – matters to be disclosed (1/2 mark per specific disclosure point required)	
	– IAS 24 – breach and impact on audit report – only give mark for specific reference to except for disagreement	
	– Recoverability of balance	
	– Possible misclassification	
	Maximum marks	**5**
	(ii) Further audit procedures	
	1 mark per comment from ideas list:	
	– Specific written representations from Peter Sheffield (½ mark per specific point requested)	
	– Terms of transaction from written documentation	
	– Develop understanding of nature of transaction	
	– Review of Jarvis Co financial statements (½ mark per specific item looked for in the review)	
	Maximum marks	**4**
(c)	**Quality control issues**	
	1 mark per comment	
	Ideas list:	
	– Not identified as high risk area	
	– Inexperienced member of team/poor training given	
	– Inadequate review of working papers	
	Maximum marks	**3**
	Total	**17**

26 MULLIGAN CO *Walk in the footsteps of a top tutor*

Key answer tips

The question is very similar in nature to reporting on PFI. As with all PFI engagements it is important to define who the ultimate user of the report is and what their needs are. In this instance there are two critical pieces of information: firstly, you have already agreed to perform the engagement; and, secondly, the bank needs assurance that the finance is 'adequate for the proposed business venture.' The first piece of information shapes the nature of the discussions you would have with the client. The latter piece of information requires not only a discussion of whether the estimates are appropriate but also whether the planned resources are sufficient to set up and sustain the business in the future.

(a) **Matters to be discussed would include the following:**

The exact content of the business plan which could include:

- description of past business performance and key products
- discussion of the new product
- evidence of the marketability of the new product
- cash flow projections
- capital expenditure forecasts
- key business assumptions.

The form of the assurance report that is required – in an assurance engagement the nature and wording of the expected opinion should be discussed. Webb & Co should clarify that an opinion of 'negative assurance' will be required, and whether this will meet the bank's lending criteria.

The intended recipient of the report – Webb & Co need to clarify the name and address of the recipient at LCT Bank. For the limitation of professional liability, it should be clarified that LCT Bank will be the only recipient, and that the assurance opinion is being used only as part of the bank's overall lending decision.

Limiting liability – Webb & Co may want to receive in writing a statement that the report is for information purposes only, and does not give rise to any responsibility, liability, duty or obligation from the firm to the lender.

Deadlines – it should be discussed when the bank need the report. This in turn will be influenced by when Mulligan Co needs the requested $3 million finance. The bank may need a considerable period of time to assess the request, review the report, and ensure that their lending criteria have been fully met prior to advancing the finance.

Availability of evidence – Mulligan Co should be made aware that in order to express an opinion on the finance request, they must be prepared to provide all the necessary paperwork to assist the assurance provider. Evidence is likely to include discussions with key management, and written representations of discussions may be required.

Professional regulation – Webb & Co should discuss the kind of procedures that will be undertaken, and confirm that they will be complying with relevant professional guidance, for example:

- ISAE 3000 *Assurance Engagements other than Audits or Reviews of Historical Financial Information*
- ISAE 3400 *The Examination of Prospective Financial Information*.

Engagement administration – any points not yet discussed in detail when deciding to take the assurance engagement should be finalised at the meeting. These points could include the following:

- **fees** – the total fee and billing arrangements must be agreed before any work is carried out
- **personnel** – Webb & Co should identify the key personnel who will be involved in the assignment
- **complaints procedures** – should be briefly outlined (the complaints procedures in an assurance engagement may differ from an audit assignment)
- **engagement letter** – if not already signed by both Webb & Co and Mulligan Co, the engagement letter should be discussed and signed at the meeting before any assignment work is conducted.

Tutorial note

The scenario states that Webb & Co have already decided to take the assurance assignment for their existing client, therefore the answer to this requirement should not focus on client or engagement acceptance procedures.

(b) It is important to appreciate that the finance request should cover not only the cost of the construction of the new facility, but also costs in order to get the business unit up and running, and enough cash to meet initial working capital requirements. Mulligan Co may have sufficient cash to cover such additional expenses, but the bank will want comfort that this is the case.

Enquiries would include the following:

Who has prepared the forecast? It is important to evaluate the experience and competence of the preparer. If management has previously prepared forecasts and capital expenditure budgets that were reliable and accurate, this adds a measure of confidence in the preparation of the new forecast and the underlying assumptions used.

To what extent is internal finance available to cover any shortfall in the finance requirement? If there is surplus cash within the organisation then the bank need not provide the full amount of finance necessary to start up the new business operation.

Has the cost of finance been included in the forecast? It appears that this cost is missing. Finance costs should be calculated based on the anticipated interest rate to be applied to the loan advanced, and included in the total finance requirement.

What is the forecast operating cycle of the new business unit? In particular how long is the work in progress period, and how much credit will be extended to customers? i.e. when will cash inflows specific to the new business unit be received? More finance might be required to fund initial working capital shortfalls during the period when work in progress is occurring, and before cash receipts from customers are received.

Will further raw materials be required? A request has been made for $250,000 for raw materials of timber. Other materials may need to be purchased, for example, non-timber raw materials, and inventory of other consumables such as nuts and bolts.

How long will the 'initial' inventory of raw material last? What is the planned work in progress time for the new product? More finance may be needed to avoid a stock out of raw materials.

Construction of the new factory – is there any documentation to support the capital expenditure? For example, architect's plans, surveyor's reports. This will support the accuracy of the finance requested and is an important source of evidence given the materiality of the premises to the total amount of finance requested.

How likely is it that costs may be subject to inflation before actually being incurred? This could increase the amount of finance required by several percentage points.

Have quotes been obtained for the new machinery to be purchased?

Purchase of new machinery – will any specific installation costs be incurred? These costs can be significant for large pieces of capital equipment. Also, enquiries should be made regarding any delivery costs.

The budget does not appear to contain any finance request for overheads such as use of electricity during the construction period, and hire of installation equipment. Have these overheads been included in the construction cost estimate?

Will staff need to be trained in using the new machinery? If so, any incremental costs should be included in the finance request.

Advertising and marketing of new product – enquire of Patrick Tiler the methods that will be used to market the new product. Some types of advertising are more of a cash drain due to their high expense e.g. television advertising is expensive and 'up front' compared to magazine advertising, which is cheap and spread out. As Patrick Tiler is new to Mulligan Co, his forecast is not based on past experience of this particular business.

LCT Bank will also consider the recoverability of the amount advanced by looking at the cash generating potential of the new business unit. Enquiries should therefore be made regarding the likely success of the new products, for example:

- Has any market research been carried out to support the commercial viability of the new products?
- Have any contracts with retailers to carry the new products been negotiated?
- How quickly have past products generated a cash inflow?
- Is there a contingency plan in place in case the new products fail to be successful?

(c) Forensic accounting is where an assurance provider investigates a specific issue, often with a legal consequence, such as a suspected fraud. Specifically it is the process of gathering, analysing and reporting on data for the purpose of finding facts and/or evidence in the context of financial/legal disputes and/or irregularities. The forensic accountant will also give preventative advice based on evidence gathered. This advice is based usually on recommendations to improve the internal control systems to prevent and detect fraud.

The relevance here is that Webb & Co are likely to be asked to provide a forensic accounting service to Mulligan Co.

The investigation will consider two issues – firstly whether the fraud actually happened, and secondly, if a fraud has taken place, the financial value of the fraud. The investigation should determine who has perpetrated the fraud, and collect evidence to help prosecute those involved in the deception.

In this case the suspicion that inventory is being stolen should be investigated, as there could be other reasons for the discrepancy found in the inventory records. For example, the discrepancy could be caused by:

- obsolete or damaged inventory thrown away but not eliminated from the inventory records
- despatches from the warehouse not recorded in the inventory management system
- incoming inventory being recorded incorrectly (e.g. recorded twice in the inventory management system)
- inventory being held at a separate location and therefore not included in the count.

If it is found that thefts have taken place, then the forensic accountant should gather evidence to:

- prove the identity of the persons involved
- quantify the value of inventory taken.

The evidence gathered could be used to start criminal proceedings against those found to have been involved in the fraud.

Examiner's comments

Requirement (a)

Answers were often blighted by two common factors. Firstly, many comments were vague, examples of common vague points being 'discuss terms with management', 'outline the scope of work' and 'agree a fee for the assignment'. These comments on their own do not answer the requirement which is to EXPLAIN the matters to be discussed. Candidates need to be much clearer in exactly what they mean – what does 'discussing terms' actually entail? How do you 'outline the scope of work'? Answers that are not even full sentences will rarely score well.

The second common problem comes back to the issue that candidates lack commercial sense. The vast majority of answers to requirement (a) stated that at the meeting they would discuss 'whether we are competent to take on the work'. Surely this is not something you would raise at a meeting with your client having just agreed to do the work. Similarly many candidates wanted to 'ask the management if they are competent to produce the figures'. I think that most clients would be quite insulted to be interrogated as to their competence in drafting some basic budgeted figures.

Finally many candidates wanted to discuss at the meeting matters such as 'do we have the experience to perform the work'. Again, I would think that the client would be surprised to learn that you may not be knowledgeable enough to conduct the assignment, especially considering that you are the auditor of their business. I would urge candidates to stop and think, and consider if the matters they are suggesting discussing at the meeting are tactful, commercial, professional, and fit in with the scenario provided.

Requirement (b)

The point here was the adequacy of the finance i.e. candidates should have been asking questions in relation to missing capital or revenue expenses. Many answers here were reasonable, and appreciated that the budget did not contain expenses for items such as finance costs, staff training, installation and delivery costs and a contingency fund for potential cost over-runs. Some answers also contained very specific information requests, such as quotes for the machinery, and planning permission for the construction of the factory. However some answers suffered from vagueness, and the inevitable request for a management representation. Some answers also confused requirements (a) and (b) with answers even sometimes combining the two requirements into one answer. It is important that candidates read all question requirements before starting to answer the first requirement, as this should clarify exactly what has been asked for in each requirement, and enable the candidate to separate their comments accordingly between the requirements. It is never appropriate to 'merge' answers for different requirements.

Requirement (c)

It was pleasing to see that the majority of candidates who attempted Question 3 had prepared for this topic, could provide a sound definition, and could apply their knowledge to the brief scenario provided. However, only a few candidates actually questioned that a fraud was taking place and discussed that the alleged loss of inventory could have been caused not by theft, but by errors in the inventory recording system.

	Marking scheme	
(a)	**Matters to be discussed at planning meeting**	*Marks*
	Generally 1 mark per matter specific to the scenario	
	Ideas list:	
	– Exact contents of business plan	
	– Recipient of report	
	– Confirmation report for information only	
	– Deadlines	
	– Liability issues	
	– Evidence availability	
	– Fees	
	– Professional regulations	
	– Personnel	
	– Complaints procedure	8
(b)	**Enquiries regarding adequacy of finance requested**	
	Generally 1 mark per specific enquiry stated	
	Ideas list:	
	– Who prepared?	
	– Availability of internal finance?	
	– Operating cycle?	
	– Raw materials required?	
	– WIP period?	
	– Documentation to support costs?	
	– Inflation effects?	
	– Training costs?	
	– Advertising costs?	
	– Finance costs?	7
(c)	**Forensic accounting**	
	Definition – 1 mark	
	1 mark for each comment relevant to scenario:	
	– Investigate whether theft has actually occurred	
	– Example of factor other than theft that could have caused discrepancy	
	– Evidence to prove financial consequence of theft	
	– Evidence to prove identity	5
	Total	20

27 CUSITER

Key answer tips

A challenging question, linking prospective financial information to practice management and liability. In part (c) try to talk about each of the specific numbers in the forecast and how you would check it, in order to get more marks.

(a) **'Prospective financial information' (PFI)**

PFI is financial information based on:

- assumptions about events that may occur in the future; and
- possible actions by an entity.

Prospective financial information can be in the form of a forecast, a projection or a combination of both.

A forecast is PFI prepared on the basis of assumptions about future events that management *expects* to take place and the actions management *expects* to take at the time the information is prepared (best-estimate assumptions).

A projection is prepared on the basis of:

- hypothetical assumptions about future events and management actions which are not necessarily expected to take place (e.g. when entities are starting up or restructuring); or
- a mixture of best-estimate and hypothetical assumptions.

(b) **Matters to be considered**

Tutorial note

Candidates at this level must appreciate that the matters to be considered when planning the nature and scope of the examination are not the same matters to be considered when deciding whether or not to accept an engagement. The scenario clearly indicates that the assignment is being undertaken by the current auditor rendering any 'pre-engagement'/'professional etiquette' considerations irrelevant to answering this question.

This PFI has been prepared to show an external user, the bank, the financial consequences of Cusiter's plans to help the bank in making an investment decision. If Cusiter is successful in its loan application the PFI provides a management tool against which the results of investing in the plant and equipment can be measured.

The PFI is unpublished rather than published. That is, it is prepared at the specific request of a third party, the bank. It will not be published to users of financial information in general.

The auditor's report on the PFI will provide only negative assurance as to whether the assumptions provide a reasonable basis for the PFI and an opinion whether the PFI is:

- properly prepared on the basis of the assumptions; and
- presented in accordance with the relevant financial reporting framework.

The nature of the engagement is an examination to obtain evidence concerning:

- the reasonableness and consistency of assumptions made;
- proper preparation (on the basis of stated assumptions); and
- consistent presentation (with historical financial statements, using appropriate accounting principles).

Such an examination is likely to take the form of enquiry, analytical procedures and corroboration.

The period of time covered by the prospective financial information is two years. The assumptions for 2008 are likely to be more speculative than for 2007, particularly in relation to the impact on earnings, etc of the investment in new plant and equipment.

The forecast for the year to 31 December 2007 includes an element of historical financial information (because only part of this period is in the future) hence actual evidence should be available to verify the first three months of the forecast (possibly more since another three-month period will expire at the end of the month).

Cusiter management's previous experience in preparing PFI will be relevant. For example, in making accounting estimates (e.g. for provisions, impairment losses, etc) or preparing cash flow forecasts (e.g. in support of the going concern assertion).

The basis of preparation of the forecast. For example, the extent to which it comprises:

- proforma financial information (i.e. historical financial information adjusted for the effects of the planned loan and capital expenditure transaction);
- new information and assumptions about future performance (e.g. the operating capacity of the new equipment, sales generated, etc).

The nature and scope of any standards/guidelines under which the PFI has been prepared is likely to assist the auditor in discharging their responsibilities to report on it. Also, ISAE 3400 *The Examination of Prospective Financial Information*, establishes standards and provides guidance on engagements to examine and report on PFI including examination procedures.

The planned nature and scope of the examination is likely to take into account the time and fee budgets for the assignments as adjusted for any 'overlap' with audit work. For example, the examination of the PFI is likely to draw on the auditor's knowledge of the business obtained in auditing the financial statements to 31 December 2006. Analytical procedures carried out in respect of the PFI may provide evidence relevant to the 31 December 2007 audit.

(c)   **Examination procedures**

- The arithmetic accuracy of the PFI should be confirmed, i.e. subtotals and totals should be recast and agreed.
- The actual information for the year to 31 December 2006 that is shown as comparative information should be agreed to the audited financial statements for that year to ensure consistency.
- Balances and transaction totals for the quarter to 31 March 2007 should be agreed to general ledger account balances at that date. The net book value of property, plant and equipment should be agreed to the non-current asset register; accounts receivable/payable to control accounts and cash at bank to a bank reconciliation statement.

- Tenders for the new equipment should be inspected to confirm the additional cost included in property, plant and equipment included in the forecast for the year to 31 December 2008 and that it can be purchased with the funds being lent by the bank.

- The reasonableness of all new assumptions should be considered. For example, the expected useful life of the new equipment, the capacity at which it will be operating, the volume of new product that can be sold, and at what price.

- The forecast statement of comprehensive income should be reviewed for completeness of costs associated with the expansion. For example, operating expenses should include salaries of additional equipment operatives or supervisors.

- The consistency of accounting practices reflected in the forecast with International Financial Reporting Standards (IFRS) should be considered. For example, the intangible asset might be expected to be less than $10,000 at 31 December 2008 as it should be carried at amortized cost.

- The cost of property, plant and equipment at 31 December 2008 is $280,000 more than as at 31 December 2007. Consideration should be given to the adequacy of borrowing $250,000 if the actual investment is $30,000 more.

- The terms of existing borrowings (both non-current and short-term) should be reviewed to ensure that the forecast takes full account of existing repayment schedules. For example, to confirm that only $23,000 of term borrowings will become current by the end of 2007.

- Trends should be reviewed and fluctuations explained, for example:

- Revenue for the first quarter of 2007 is only 22% of revenue for 2006 and so may appear to be understated. However, revenue may not be understated if sales are seasonal and the first quarter is traditionally 'quieter'.

- Forecast revenue for 2007 is 18% up on 2006. However, forecast revenue for 2008 is only 19% up on 2007. As the growth in 2007 is before the investment in new plant and equipment it does not look as though the new investment will be contributing significantly to increased growth in the first year.

- The gross profit % is maintained at around 29% for the three years. However, the earnings before interest and tax (EBIT) % is forecast to fall by 2% for 2008. Earnings after interest might be worrying to the potential lender as this is forecast to rise from 12.2% in 2006 to 13.7% in 2007 but then fall to 7.6% in 2008.

The reasonableness of relationships between statement of comprehensive income and statement of financial position items should be considered. For example:

- The average collection period at each of the statement of financial position dates presented is 66, 69, 66 and 66 days respectively (e.g. 71/394 × 365 = 66 days). Although it may be realistic to assume that the current average collection period may be maintained in future it is possible that it could deteriorate if, for example, new customers taken on to launch the new product are not as credit worthy as the existing customer base.

- The number of days sales in inventory at each statement of financial position date is 66, 88, 66 and 65 days respectively (e.g. 50/278 × 365 = 66 days). The reason for the increase to 88 at the end of the first quarter must be established and management's assertion that 66 days will be re-established as the 'norm' corroborated.

- As the $42,000 movement on retained earnings from 2007 to 2008 is the earnings before income tax for 2008 it may be that there is no tax in 2008 or that tax effects have not been forecast. (However, some deferred tax effect might be expected if the investment in new plant and equipment is likely to attract accelerated capital allowances.)

(d) **Professional accountant's liability**

Liability for reporting on PFI

Independent accountants may be required to report on PFI for many reasons (e.g. to help secure a bank loan). Such forecasts and projections are inherently unreliable. If the forecast or projection does not materialize, and the client or lenders (or investors) consequently sustain financial loss, the accountant may face lawsuits claiming financial loss. Courts in different jurisdictions use various criteria to define the group of persons to whom independent accountants may be held liable for providing a report on an inaccurate forecast or projection. The most common of these are that an accountant is liable to persons with whom there is proximity:

(i)   only (i.e. the client who engaged the independent accountant);

(ii)   or whose relationship with the accountant sufficiently approaches privity;

(iii)   and to persons or members of a limited group of persons for whose benefit and guidance the accountant supplied the information or knew that the recipient of the information intended to supply it;

(iv)   and to persons who reasonably can be foreseen to rely on the information.

Measures to reduce liability

As significant assumptions will be essential to a reader's understanding of a financial forecast, the independent accountant should ensure that they are adequately disclosed and clearly stated to be the management's responsibility. Hypothetical assumptions should be clearly distinguished from best estimates.

The introduction to any forecast (and/or report thereon) should include a caveat that the prospective results may not be attained. Specific and extensive warnings ('the actual results ... will vary') and disclaimers ('we do not express an opinion') may be effective in protecting an independent accountant sued for inaccuracies in forecasts or projections that they have reported on.

Any report to a third party should state:

- for whom it is prepared, who is entitled to rely on it (if anyone) and for what purpose;
- that the engagement was undertaken in accordance with the engagement terms;
- the work performed and the findings.

An independent accountant's report should avoid inappropriate and open-ended wording, for example, 'we certify ...' and 'we obtained all the explanations we considered necessary'.

Engagement terms to report on PFI should include an appropriate liability cap that is reasonable given the specific circumstances of the engagement.

The independent accountant may be able to obtain indemnity from a client in respect of claims from third parties. Such 'hold harmless' clauses obligate the client to indemnify the independent accountant from third party claims.

28 SEYMOUR

Key answer tips

(i)   'Matters' will often encompass considerations of risk, materiality, accounting treatment, responsibilities and audit reporting implications.

(ii) 'Evidence' (ISA 500) -> consider sufficiency and appropriateness for the three issues:

–   The financial statement assertions to be tested

–   Source and nature: written/oral; internal/external; auditor generated

–   Audit testing techniques to be used (Inspection, enquiry, etc.)

You will need to consider the relevant accounting standards/principles to deal with the three issues properly.

(a)   **Costs of Tournose**

(i)   **Matters**

• Development costs at 30 September 2005 have a carrying value of $3 million (i.e. $4 million less 5 years' amortization at 5% p.a.) that represents 7.4% of total assets at that date (5.6% of total assets at 30 September 2006) and are therefore material.

• Straight line annual amortization based on 20 year estimate of useful life ($200,000) represents 1.5% of 2006 profit before tax (PBT) and is not material. The patent cost, $11,600 is very immaterial.

• Management must review the useful life of the development costs at 30 September 2006 (IAS 38 *Intangible Assets*).

• The competitor's announcement during the current year (to 30 September 2006) may provide evidence that:

–   the useful life of the development costs is substantially less than the remaining period covered by the patent;

–   there has been a change in the expected pattern of consumption of future economic benefits;

–   development costs are impaired (i.e. recoverable amount is less than carrying value).

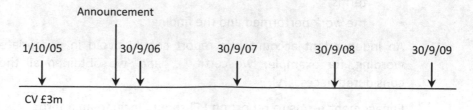

- A change in the estimated useful life should be accounted for as a change in accounting estimate in accordance with IAS 8 *Accounting Policies, Changes in Accounting Estimates and Errors*. For example, if the development costs have little, if any, useful life after the introduction of the alternative drug ('worst case' scenario), the carrying value ($3 million) should be written off over the current and remaining years, i.e. $1 million p.a. The increase in amortization/decrease in carrying value ($800,000) is material to PBT (6%) and total assets (1.5%).

- Similarly a change in the expected pattern of consumption of the future economic benefits should be accounted for as a change in accounting estimate (IAS 8). For example, it may be that the useful life is still to 2020 but that the economic benefits may reduce significantly in two years time.

- After adjusting the carrying amount to take account of the change in accounting estimate(s) management should have tested it for impairment and any impairment loss recognized in profit or loss.

(ii) **Audit evidence**

- $3 million carrying amount of development costs brought forward agreed to prior year working papers and financial statements.

- A copy of the press release announcing the competitor's alternative drug.

- Management's projections of future cashflows from Tournose-related sales as evidence of the useful life of the development costs and pattern of consumption

- Reperformance of management's impairment test on the development costs: Recalculation of management's calculation of the carrying amount after revising estimates of useful life and/or consumption of benefits compared with management's calculation of value in use.

- Sensitivity analysis on management's key assumptions (e.g. estimates of useful life, discount rate).

- Written management representation on the key assumptions concerning the future that have a significant risk of causing material adjustment to the carrying amount of the development costs. (These assumptions should be disclosed in accordance with IAS 1 *Presentation of Financial Statements*.)

(b) **Goodwill**

(i) **Matters**

- Cost of goodwill, $1.8 million, represents 3.4% consolidated total assets and is therefore material.

- It is correct that the goodwill is not being amortized (IFRS 3 *Business Combinations*). However, it should be tested at least annually for impairment, by management.

- Aragon has incurred losses amounting to $1.1 million since it was acquired (two years ago). The write-off of this amount against goodwill in the consolidated financial statements would be material (being 61% cost of goodwill, 8.3% PBT and 2.1% total assets).

- The cost of the investment ($4.5 million) in Seymour's separate financial statements will also be material and should be tested for impairment.

- The fair value of net assets acquired was only $2.7 million ($4.5 million less $1.8 million). Therefore the fair value less costs to sell of Aragon on other than a going concern basis will be less than the carrying amount of the investment (i.e. the investment is impaired by at least the amount of goodwill recognized on acquisition).

- In assessing recoverable amount, value in use (rather than fair value less costs to sell) is only relevant if the going concern assumption is appropriate for Aragon.

- Supporting Aragon financially may result in Seymour being exposed to actual and/or contingent liabilities that should be provided for/disclosed in Seymour's financial statements in accordance with IAS 37 *Provisions, Contingent Liabilities and Contingent Assets*.

(ii) Audit evidence

- Carrying values of cost of investment and goodwill arising on acquisition to prior year audit working papers and financial statements.

- A copy of Aragon's draft financial statements for the year ended 30 September 2006 showing loss for year.

- Management's impairment test of Seymour's investment in Aragon and of the goodwill arising on consolidation at 30 September 2006. That is a comparison of the present value of the future cash flows expected to be generated by Aragon (a cash-generating unit) compared with the cost of the investment (in Seymour's separate financial statements).

- Results of any impairment tests on Aragon's assets extracted from Aragon's working paper files.

- Analytical procedures on future cash flows to confirm their reasonableness (e.g. by comparison with cash flows for the last two years).

- Bank report for audit purposes for any guarantees supporting Aragon's loan facilities.

- A copy of Seymour's 'comfort letter' confirming continuing financial support of Aragon for the foreseeable future.

(c) Discontinued operation

(i) Matters

- Petcare product revenue represents 12% consolidated revenue and is therefore very material. Consolidated PBT would be 10% higher if the loss on the petcare products was excluded – so also material in relation to Seymour's results.

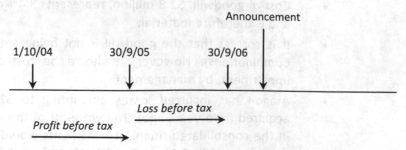

- Under IFRS 5 the 'petcare' operation should only be treated as a discontinued operation if either it was discontinued before the year end or is held for sale as at the year end, neither of which seem to be the case here.

- It should not, therefore, be treated as discontinued in the current year's financial statements.
- However the discontinuation of the product line after the statement of financial position date provides additional evidence that, as at the statement of financial position date, it was of poor quality. Therefore, as at the statement of financial position date:
    - an allowance ('provision') may be required for credit notes for returns of products after the year end that were sold before the year-end;
    - goods returned to inventory should be written down to net realisable value (may be nil);
    - any plant and equipment used exclusively in the production of the petcare range of products should be tested for impairment;
    - any material contingent liabilities arising from legal claims should be disclosed.

(ii) **Audit evidence**

- A copy of Seymour's announcement (external 'press release' and any internal memorandum).
- Credit notes raised/refunds paid after the year end for faulty products returned.
- Condition of products returned as inspected during physical attendance of inventory count.
- Correspondence from customers claiming reimbursement/compensation for poor quality.
- Direct confirmation from legal adviser (solicitor) regarding any claims for customers including estimates of possible payouts.

29 RBG

Key answer tips

This question should be fairly straightforward with the possible exception of Part (b) which links into practice management and requires a bit more thought.

(a) **Potential advantages and disadvantages to RBG of outsourcing internal audit services**

Advantages

- Affordability as there should be a cost benefit (budget savings) of replacing fixed cost full-time employees with a variable cost service.
- Further, if reliance on internal audit by the external auditors is substantially increased, the external audit fee may be reduced.
- Even if there are some changes in staff within the audit firm providing the internal audit services, there should be greater continuity than currently (as RBG has high employee turnover in this department).
- A wider range of industry-related expertise might be available to RBG from contracted-in auditors that would be too expensive to maintain internally. This may be particularly beneficial for ad hoc needs such as due diligence reviews for acquisitions or business continuity plans in the event of fire or flood.

- Experienced internal auditors will be available as and when needed (as typically the audit firm's staff will be experienced) whereas RBG is currently losing its experienced employees to other departments. Outsourcing also offers flexibility to provide more staff at busy times.

- Outsourcing to an audit firm can provide geographic coverage and more advanced technology.

- Independent evaluation (e.g. of organizational risk) by the audit firm may provide new ideas for improvements (e.g. enhancing risk management).

- Better recommendations for improvements as the audit firm can suggest practical, tried and tested solutions and not just theoretical ones.

- Greater assistance to management in the evaluation of the performance of the external auditors (because the outsourced internal audit firm should be more experienced to make this assessment).

- Earlier assessment of the impact of changes in financial reporting requirements (because the outsourced internal audit firm should be technically up-to-date).

- Better utilization of core competencies, for example, management will have more time to focus on strategic objectives.

- The audit firm may provide a customer-focused service that could be lacking in an in-house department.

Disadvantages

- Over time the audit firm may command a greater premium for internal audit services as RBG becomes dependent on the audit firm's knowledge of the group (i.e. cost savings may be only short term).

- An out-sourced department may not be as effective as an in-house department if, for example, the audit firm's staff assigned to RBG are changed regularly.

- The audit firm's staff may not understand RBG's business as well as employed staff if, for example, they work only part-time on the RBG assignment. Employed staff are more likely to have a broader perspective of the group from having worked in other parts of it.

- The internal audit staff's principle allegiance will be to the audit firm, not RBG. If the services provided by the audit firm are not seen to be an integral part of management, the company may not buy-in to their suggestions.

- If the audit firm plans to schedule internal audit services to RBG in its 'quiet periods', they may not always be available when needed.

- RBG will lose a valuable management training ground that provides a source of future managers. The internal audit department's current loss of high performing employees to other departments is a gain to the other departments.

(b) **Principal matters to be included in submission to provide internal audit services**

- Introduction/background – details about York including its organization (of functions), offices (locations) and number of internal auditors working within each office. The office that would be responsible for managing the contract should be stated.

- A description of York's services most relevant to RBG's needs (e.g. in the areas of risk management, IT audits, value for money (VFM) and corporate governance).

- Client-specific issues identified. For example, revenue audits will be required routinely for control purposes and to substantiate the contingent rents due. Other areas of expertise that RBG may be interested in taking advantage of, for example, special projects such as acquisitions and mergers.

- York's approach to assessing audit needs including the key stages and who will be involved. For example:

  (1) Preliminary – review of business, industry and the entity's operating characteristics

  (2) Planning – including needs analysis and co-ordination with external audit plan

  (3) Post-Audit – assurance that activities were effectively and efficiently executed

  (4) Review – of services provided, reports issued and management's responses.

- A description of internal audit tools used and methodologies/approach to audit fieldwork including use of embedded audit software and programs developed by York.

- A description of York's systems-based audit, the IT issues to be addressed and the technological support that can be provided.

- Any training that will be offered to RBG's managers and staff, for example, in a risk management approach.

- A description and quantity of resources, in particular the number of full-time staff, to be deployed in providing services to RBG. An outline of RBG's track record in human resource retention and development.

- Relevant experience – e.g. in internal and external audit in the retail industry. The relative qualifications and skills of each grade of audit staff and the contract manager in particular.

- Insurance certifications covering, for example, public liability and professional indemnity insurance.

- Work ethic policies relating to health and safety, equal opportunities' and race relations.

- How York ensures quality throughout the internal audit process including standards to be followed (e.g. Institute of Internal Auditors' standards).

- Sample report templates – e.g. for reporting the results of risk analysis, audit plans and quarterly reporting of findings to the Audit and Risk Management Committee.

- Current clients to whom internal audit services are provided from whom RBG will be able to take up references, by arrangement, if York is short-listed.

- Any work currently carried out/competed for that could cause a conflict of interest (and the measures to avoid such conflicts).

- Fees (daily rates) for each grade of staff and travel and other expenses to be reimbursed. An indication of price increases, if any, over the three-year contract period. Invoicing terms (e.g. on presentation of reports) and payment terms (e.g. the end of the month following receipt of the invoice).

- Performance targets to be met such as deadlines for completing work and submitting and issuing reports.

(c)   **Impact on the audit of the financial statements**

Tutorial note

The answer to this part should reflect that it is not the external auditor who is providing the internal audit services. Thus comments regarding objectivity impairment are not relevant.

- As Grey & Co is likely to be placing some reliance on RBG's internal audit department in accordance with ISA 610 *Using the Work of Internal Auditors* the degree of reliance should be reassessed.

- The appointment will include an evaluation of organizational risk. The results of this will provide Grey with evidence, for example:

   –   supporting the appropriateness of the going concern assumption;

   –   of indicators of obsolescence of goods or impairment of other assets.

- As the quality of internal audit services should be higher than previously, providing a stronger control environment, the extent to which Grey may rely on internal audit work could be increased. This would increase the efficiency of the external audit of the financial statements as the need for substantive procedures should be reduced.

- However, if internal audit services are performed on a part-time basis (e.g. fitting into the provider's less busy months) Grey must evaluate the impact of this on the prevention, detection and control of fraud and error.

- The internal auditors will provide a body of expertise within RBG with whom Grey can consult on contentious matters.

30   KEFFLER CO

Key answer tips

(i)   'Matters' will often encompass considerations of risk, materiality, accounting treatment, responsibilities and audit reporting implications

(ii)   'Evidence' (ISA 500) – consider sufficiency and appropriateness for the three issues:

   –   The financial statement assertions to be tested

   –   Source and nature: written/oral; internal/external; auditor generated

   –   Audit testing techniques to be used (Inspection, enquiry, etc.)

You will need to consider the relevant accounting standards/principles to deal with the three issues properly:

Issue (a) – IAS 38 and IAS 37

Issue (b) – IAS 16, IAS 1, IAS 24, IAS 10, IAS 8 and IAS 36

Issue (a) – IAS 37 and IAS 10

(a)   **Landfill site**

(i)   **Matters**

- $1.1m cost of the right represents 3.3% of total assets and is therefore material.

- The right should be amortized over its useful life, that is just 10 years, rather than the 15-year period for which the right has been granted.

- The amortization charge represents 1% of profit before tax (PBT) and is not material.

- The amortization method used should reflect the pattern in which the future economic benefits of the right are expected to be consumed by Keffler. If that pattern cannot be determined reliably, the straight-line method must be used (IAS 38 *Intangible Assets*).

- Using an increasing sum-of-digits will 'end-load' the amortization charge (i.e. least charge in the first year, highest charge in the last year). However, according to IAS 38 there is rarely, if ever, persuasive evidence to support an amortization method that results in accumulated amortization lower than that under the straight-line method.

- On a straight line basis the annual amortization charge would be $0.11m, an increase of $90,000. Although this difference is just below materiality (4.5% PBT) the cumulative effect (of undercharging amortization) will become material.

- Also, when account is taken of the understatement of cost (see below), the undercharging of amortization will be material.

- The sum-of-digits method might be suitable as an approximation to the unit-of-production method if Keffler has evidence to show that use of the landfill site will increase annually.

- However, in the absence of such evidence, the audit opinion should be qualified 'except for' disagreement with the amortization method (resulting in intangible asset overstatement/amortization expense understatement).

- The annual restoration provision represents 5% of PBT and 0.3% of total assets. Although this is only borderline material (in terms of profit), there will be a cumulative impact.

- Annual provisioning is contrary to IAS 37 *Provisions, Contingent Liabilities and Contingent Assets*.

- The estimate of the future restoration cost is (presumably) $1.5m (i.e. $0.1 × 15). The present value of this amount should have been provided in full in the current year and included in the cost of the right.

- Thus the amortization being charged on the cost of the right (including the restoration cost) is currently understated (on any basis).

    Total amount expensed ($120k) is less than what should have been expensed (say $146k amortization + $36k unwinding of discount). However, this is not material.

- Whether Keffler will wait until the right is about to expire before restoring the land or might restore earlier (if the site is completely filled in 10 years).

(ii)   **Audit evidence**

- Written agreement for purchase of right and contractual terms therein (e.g. to make restoration in 15 years' time).
- Cash book/bank statement entries in April 2005 for $1.1m payment.
- Physical inspection of the landfill site to confirm Keffler's use of it.
- Annual dump budget/projection over next 10 years and comparison with sum-of-digits proportions.
- Amount actually dumped in the year (per dump records) compared with budget and as a percentage/proportion of the total available.
- Recalculation of current year's amortization based on sum-of-digits. That is, $1.1m ÷ 55 = $20,000.
- The basis of the calculation of the estimated restoration costs and principal assumptions made.
- If estimated by a quantity surveyor/other expert then a copy of the expert's report.
- Written management representation confirming the planned timing of the restoration in 15 years (or sooner).

(b)   **Sale of industrial equipment**

(i)   **Matters**

- The industrial equipment was in use for nine years (from April 1996) and would have had a carrying value of $660,000 at 31 March 2005 ($\frac{11}{20} \times$ $1.2m – assuming nil residual value and a full year's depreciation charge in the year of acquisition and none in the year of disposal). Disposal proceeds were therefore $360,000.
- The $0.3m loss represents 15% of PBT (for the year to 31 March 2006) and is therefore material. The equipment was material to the statement of financial position at 31 March 2005 representing 2.6% of total assets ($\frac{\$0.66}{\$25.7} \times 100$).
- Separate disclosure, of a material loss on disposal, on the face of the statement of comprehensive income is in accordance with IAS 16 *Property, Plant and Equipment*. However, in accordance with IAS 1 *Presentation of Financial Statements*, it should not be captioned in any way that might suggest that it is not part of normal operating activities (i.e. not 'extraordinary', 'exceptional', etc).
- The reason for the sale. For example, whether the equipment was:
  - surplus to operating requirements (i.e. not being replaced); or
  - being replaced with newer equipment (thereby contributing to the $8.1m increase (33.8 – 25.7) in total assets).
- The reason for the loss on sale. For example, whether:
  - the sale was at an under-value (e.g. to a related party);
  - the equipment had a bad maintenance history (or was otherwise impaired);
  - the useful life of the equipment is less than 20 years;
  - there is any deferred consideration not yet recorded;

 – any non-cash disposal proceeds have been overlooked (e.g. if another asset was acquired in a part-exchange).

- If the useful life was less than 20 years, tangible non-current assets may be materially overstated in respect of other items of equipment that are still in use and being depreciated on the same basis.

- If the sale was to a related party then additional disclosure should be required in a note to the financial statements for the year to 31 March 2006 (IAS 24 *Related Party Disclosures*).

- Whether the sale was identified in the prior year audit's post statement of financial position event review. If so:

 – the disclosure made in the prior year's financial statements (IAS 10 *Events After the Statement of financial position Date*);

 – whether an impairment loss was recognized at 31 March 2005.

- If not, and the equipment was impaired at 31 March 2005, a prior period error should be accounted for (IAS 8 *Accounting Policies, Changes in Accounting Estimates and Errors*). An impairment loss of $0.3m would have been material to prior year profit (12.5%).

- Failure to account for a prior period error (if any) would result in modification of the audit opinion 'except for' non-compliance with IAS 8 (in the current year) and IAS 36 (in the prior period).

(ii) **Audit evidence**

- Carrying amount ($0.66m as above) agreed to the non-current asset register balances at 31 March 2005 and recalculation of the loss on disposal.

- Cost and accumulated depreciation removed from the asset register in the year to 31 March 2006.

- Receipt of proceeds per cash book agreed to bank statement.

- Sales invoice transferring title to Deakin.

- A review of maintenance expenses and records (e.g. to confirm reason for loss on sale).

- Post statement of financial position event review on prior year audit working papers file.

- Management representation confirming that Deakin is not a related party (provided that there is no evidence to suggest otherwise).

(c) **Ban on emptying waste water**

(i) **Matters**

- $0.9m provision for upgrading the process represents 45% PBT and is very material. This provision is also material to the statement of financial position (2.7% of total assets).

- The provision for penalties is immaterial (2.2% PBT and 0.1% total assets).

- The ban is an adjusting post statement of financial position event in respect of the penalties (IAS 10). It provides evidence that at the statement of financial position date Keffler was in contravention of local government standards. Therefore it is correct (in accordance with IAS 37) that a provision has been made for the penalties. As the matter is not material inclusion in 'other provisions' is appropriate.

- However, even if Keffler has a legal obligation to meet minimum standards, there is no obligation for upgrading the purifying process at 31 March 2006 and the $0.9m provision should be written back.

- If the provision for upgrading is not written back the audit opinion should be qualified 'except for' (disagreement).

- Keffler does not even have a contingent liability for upgrading the process because there is no present obligation to do so. The obligation is to stop emptying unclean water into the river. Nor is there a possible obligation whose existence will be confirmed by an uncertain future event not wholly within Keffler's control.

- The need for a technological upgrade may be an indicator of impairment. Management should have carried out an impairment test on the carrying value of the water purifying process and recognized any impairment loss in the profit for the year to 31 March 2006.

- Management's intention to upgrade the process is more appropriate to an environmental responsibility report (if any).

- Whether there is any other information in documents containing financial statements.

(ii) Audit evidence

- Penalty notices of fines received to confirm amounts and period/dates covered.

- After-date payment of fines agreed to the cash book.

- A copy of the ban and any supporting report on the local government's findings.

- Minutes of board meetings at which the ban was discussed confirming management's intentions (e.g. to upgrade the process)

- Any tenders received/costings for upgrading.

- Physical inspection of the emptying point at the river to confirm that Keffler is not still emptying waste water into it (unless the upgrading has taken place).

31 PRESCOTT CO

Key answer tips

Part (a): As well as generally applicable points when agreeing terms of engagements consider the specific circumstances of the scenario that will need to be clearly acknowledged and acceptable to the parties concerned. Consider if any relevant professional guidance exists.

Part (b): Clearly, there is not sufficient time for extensive detailed testing. Consider with whom does the company have legal agreements and contractual arrangements. What past and projected financial information is available? Legal matters? Operational matters? Etc. Remember to justify the use of this further information!

Part (c): Consider the accounting requirements under IAS 11; the adequacy of the contractual arrangements; and the current and future performance of the contracts.

(a)   **Terms of engagement – matters to be clarified**

- Objective of the review: for example, to find and report facts relevant to Prescott's decision whether to acquire Robson. The terms should confirm whether Prescott's interest is in acquiring the company (i.e. the share capital) or its trading assets (say), as this will affect the nature and scope of the review.

- Prescott's management will be solely responsible for any decision made (e.g. any offer price made to purchase Robson).

- The nature and scope of the review and any standards/guidelines in accordance with which it will be conducted. That investigation will consist of enquiry (e.g. of the directors and the quantity surveyor) and analytical procedures (e.g. on budgeted information and prior period financial statements).

- The level of assurance will be 'negative'. That is, that the material subject to review is free of material misstatement. It should be stated that an audit is not being performed and that an audit opinion will not be expressed.

- The timeframe for conducting the investigation (two days next week) and the deadline for reporting the findings.

- The records, documentation and other information to which access will be unrestricted. This will be the subject of agreement between Prescott and Robson.

- A responsibility/liability disclaimer that the engagement cannot be relied upon to disclose errors, illegal acts or other irregularities (e.g. fraudulent financial reporting or misappropriations of Robson's assets).

(b)   **Principal additional information**

- Any service contracts with the directors or other members of the management team (e.g. the quantity surveyor). These may contain 'exit' or other settlement terms in the event that their services are no longer required after a takeover/buyout.

- Prior period financial statements (to 30 June 2005) disclosing significant accounting policies and the key assumptions concerning the future (and other key sources of estimation uncertainty) that have a significant risk of causing a material adjustment to the carrying amounts of assets and liabilities in the year to 30 June 2006.

   For example, concerning:

   – the outcome on the Sarwar dispute;

   – estimates for guarantees/claims for rectification;

   – assumptions made in estimating costs to completion (e.g. for increases in costs of materials or labour).

- The most recent management accounts and cash flow forecasts to assess the quality of management information being used for decision-making and control. In particular, in providing Robson with the means of keeping its cash flows within its overdraft limit.

- A copy of the signed bank agreement for the overdraft facility (and any other agreements with finance providers). Any breaches in debt covenants might result in penalties of contingent liabilities that Prescott would have to bear if it acquired Robson.

- The standard terms of contracts with customers for construction works. In particular, for:

    - guarantees given (e.g. for rectification under warranty);

    - penalty clauses (e.g. in the event of overruns or non-completion);

    - disclaimers (including conditions for invoking force majeure).

    Prescott will want to make some allowance for settlement of liabilities arising on contracts already completed/in-progress when offering a price for Robson.

- Legal/correspondence files dealing with matters such as the claims of the residents of the housing development and Robson's claim against Sarwar Services Co. Also, fee notes rendered by Robson's legal advisers showing the costs incurred on matters referred to them.

- Robson's insurer's 'cover note' to determine Robson's exposure to claims for rectification work, damages, injuries to employees, etc.

- The quantity surveyor's working papers for the last quarterly count (presumably at 31 March 2006) and the latest available rolling budgets. Particular attention should be given to loss-making contracts and contracts that have not been started. (Prescott might seek to settle rather than fulfil them.) The pattern of taking profits on contracts will be of interest, for example, to determine the accuracy of the quantity surveyor's estimates.

- Type and frequency of constructions undertaken. Prescott is interested in the building and refurbishment of hotels and leisure facilities. Robson's experience in this area may not be extensive.

- Non-current asset register showing location of plant and equipment so that some test checking on physical existence might be undertaken (if an agreed-upon-procedure).

(c) **Specific enquiries – accounting for construction contracts**

- Are any constructions being undertaken without signed contracts?

- Is full provision made for future losses foreseen on loss-making contracts?

- Which contracts started during the year are likely to be/have been identified as loss-making (for which no provision has yet been made)?

- What are management's assumptions and judgments on the likely future outcome on the Sarwar contract (and other actual and contingent liabilities)?

- What claims history has Robson experienced? (What proportion of contracts have been subject to claims? What proportion of claims brought have been successful? How have they been settled? Under insurance? Out-of-court settlement?) How effective are the penalty clauses? (Is Robson having to pay penalties for overrunning on contracts?)

- What are the actual useful lives of assets used in construction? What level of losses are made on disposal?

- What is the cause of losses on contracts? For example, if due to theft of building supplies Robson's management is not exercising sufficient control over the company's assets.

32 ALBREDA

Key answer tips

'Matters' will often encompass considerations of 'risk', 'materiality' and 'accounting treatment' (i.e. the omission of recognition and/ or disclosure as well as treatment under GAAP). A good working knowledge of various accounting standards is essential to the production of a good answer as well as a clear understanding of the relevant financial statement assertions and audit testing techniques as regards the audit evidence.

(a) **Cessation of 'home delivery' service**

(i) *Matters*

$0.6 million represents 1.4% of reported revenue (prior year 1.9%) and is therefore material.

The home delivery service is not a component of Albreda and its cessation does not classify as a discontinued operation (IFRS 5 *Non-current Assets Held for Sale and Discontinued Operations*).

It is not a cash-generating unit because home delivery revenues are not independent of other revenues generated by the restaurant kitchens.

1.4% of revenue is not a 'major line of business'.

Home delivery does not cover a separate geographical area (but many areas around the numerous restaurants).

The redundancy provision of $0.2 million represents 11.1% of profit before tax (10% before allowing for the provision) and is therefore material. However, it represents only 0.6% of total assets and is therefore immaterial to the statement of financial position.

As the provision is a liability it should have been tested primarily for understatement (completeness).

The delivery vehicles should be classified as held for sale if their carrying amount will be recovered principally through a sale transaction rather than through continuing use. For this to be the case the following IFRS 5 criteria must be met:

– the vehicles must be available for immediate sale in their present condition; and

– their sale must be highly probable.

However, even if the classification as held for sale is appropriate the measurement basis is incorrect.

Non-current assets classified as held for sale should be carried at the lower of carrying amount and fair value less costs to sell.

It is incorrect that the vehicles are being measured at fair value less costs to sell which is $0.3 million in excess of the carrying amount. This amounts to a revaluation. Wherever the credit entry is (equity or statement of comprehensive income) it should be reversed. $0.3 million represents just less than 1% of assets (16.7% of profit if the credit is to the statement of comprehensive income).

Comparison of fair value less costs to sell against carrying amount should have been made on an item by item basis (and not on their totals).

(ii) *Audit evidence*

- Copy of board minute documenting management's decision to cease home deliveries (and any press releases/internal memoranda to staff).

- An analysis of revenue (e.g. extracted from management accounts) showing the amount attributed to home delivery sales.

- Redundancy terms for drivers as set out in their contracts of employment.

- A 'proof in total' for the reasonableness/completeness of the redundancy provision (e.g. number of drivers × sum of years employed × payment per year of service).

- A schedule of depreciated cost of delivery vehicles extracted from the non-current asset register.

- Checking of fair values on a sample basis to second hand market prices (as published/advertised in used vehicle guides).

- After-date net sale proceeds from sale of vehicles and comparison of proceeds against estimated fair values.

- Physical inspection of condition of unsold vehicles.

- Separate disclosure of the held for sale assets on the face of the statement of financial position or in the notes.

- Assets classified as held for sale (and other disposals) shown in the reconciliation of carrying amount at the beginning and end of the period.

- Additional descriptions in the notes of:
  - the non-current assets; and

  - the facts and circumstances leading to the sale/disposal (i.e. cessation of home delivery service).

(b) Revaluation of owned premises

(i) Matters

The revaluations are clearly material as $1.7 million, $5.4 million and $7.1 million represent 5.5%, 17.6% and 23.1% of total assets, respectively.

The change in accounting policy, from a cost model to a revaluation model, should be accounted for in accordance with IAS 16 *Property, Plant and Equipment* (i.e. as a revaluation).

The basis on which the valuations have been carried out, for example, market-based fair value (IAS 16).

Independence, qualifications and expertise of valuer(s).

IAS 16 does not permit the selective revaluation of assets thus the whole class of premises should have been revalued.

The valuations of properties after the year end are adjusting events (i.e. providing additional evidence of conditions existing at the year end) per IAS 10 *Events after the Statement of Financial Position Date.*

If $5.4 million is a net amount of surpluses and deficits it should be grossed up so that the credit to equity reflects the sum of the surpluses with any deficits being expensed through profit and loss (IAS 36 *Impairment of Assets*).

The revaluation exercise is incomplete. If the revaluations on the remaining three properties are expected to be material and cannot be reasonably estimated for inclusion in the financial statements for the year ended 30 September 2005 perhaps the change in policy should be deferred for a year.

Depreciation for the year should have been calculated on cost as usual to establish carrying amount before revaluation.

Any premises held under finance leases should be similarly revalued.

(ii) *Audit evidence*

- A schedule of depreciated cost of owned premises extracted from the non-current asset register.
- Calculation of difference between valuation and depreciated cost by property. Separate summation of surpluses and deficits.
- Copy of valuation certificate for each property.
- Physical inspection of properties with largest surpluses (including the two valued before the year end) to confirm condition.
- Extracts from local property guides/magazines indicating a range of values of similarly styled/sized properties.
- Separate presentation of the revaluation surpluses (gross) in:
  - the statement of changes in equity; and
  - reconciliation of carrying amount at the beginning and end of the period.
- IAS 16 disclosures in the notes to the financial statements including:
  - the effective date of revaluation;
  - whether an independent valuer was involved;
  - the methods and significant assumptions applied in estimating fair values; and
  - the carrying amount that would have been recognized under the cost model.

(c) **Fines and penalties**

(i) *Matters*

$0.1 million represents 5.6% of profit before tax and is therefore material. However, profit has fallen, and compared with prior year profit it is less than 5%. So 'borderline' material in quantitative terms.

Prior year amount was three times as much and represented 13.6% of profit before tax.

Even though the payments may be regarded as material 'by nature' separate disclosure may not be necessary if, for example, there are no external shareholders.

Treatment (inclusion in cost of sales) should be consistent with prior year ('The Framework'/IAS 1 *Presentation of Financial Statements*).

The reason for the fall in expense. For example, whether due to an improvement in meeting health and safety regulations and/or incomplete recording of liabilities (understatement).

The reason(s) for the breaches. For example, Albreda may have had difficulty implementing new guidelines in response to stricter regulations.

Whether expenditure has been adjusted for in the income tax computation (as disallowed for tax purposes).

Management's attitude to health and safety issues (e.g. if it regards breaches as an acceptable operational practice or cheaper than compliance).

Any references to health and safety issues in other information in documents containing audited financial statements that might conflict with Albreda incurring these costs.

Any cost savings resulting from breaches of health and safety regulations would result in Albreda possessing proceeds of its own crime which may be a money laundering offence.

(ii) *Audit evidence*

- A schedule of amounts paid totalling $0.1 million with larger amounts being agreed to the cash book/bank statements.

- Review/comparison of current year schedule against prior year for any apparent omissions.

- Review of after-date cash book payments and correspondence with relevant health and safety regulators (e.g. local authorities) for liabilities incurred before 30 September 2005.

- Notes in the prior year financial statements confirming consistency, or otherwise, of the lack of separate disclosure.

- A 'signed off' review of 'other information' (i.e. directors' report, chairman's statement, etc).

- Written management representation that there are no fines/penalties other than those which have been reflected in the financial statements.

33   VOLCAN

Key answer tips

'Matters' will often encompass considerations of 'risk', 'materiality' and 'accounting treatment' (i.e. the omission of recognition and/ or disclosure as well as treatment under GAAP). A good working knowledge of various accounting standards is essential to the production of a good answer as well as a clear understanding of the relevant financial statement assertions and audit testing techniques as regards the audit evidence.

(a) **Store impairment**

   (i) *Matters*

   Materiality

   The cost of goodwill represents 3.1% of total assets and is therefore material.

   However, after three years the carrying amount of goodwill ($2.2m) represents only 1.2% of total assets –and is therefore immaterial in the context of the statement of financial position.

   The impact of writing off the whole of the carrying amount would be material to PBT (23%).

   The announcement is after the statement of financial position date and is therefore a non-adjusting event (IAS 10 *Events After the Statement of financial position Date*) insofar as no provision for restructuring (for example) can be made.

   However, the event provides evidence of a possible impairment of the cash-generating unit which is this store and, in particular, the value of goodwill assigned to it.

   If the carrying amount of goodwill ($2.2m) can be allocated on a reasonable and consistent basis to this and the other two stores (purchased at the same time) Volcan's management should have applied a 'bottom-up' test to determine whether or not there is an impairment loss.

   If more than 22% of goodwill is attributable to the City Metro store – then its write-off would be material to PBT (22% × $2.2m ÷ $9.5m = 5%).

   If the carrying amount of goodwill cannot be so allocated; a 'top-down' test should have been applied also.

   Management should have considered whether the other four stores in Urvina (and elsewhere) are similarly impaired.

   Going concern is unlikely to be an issue unless all the supermarkets are located in cities facing a downward trend in demand.

   (ii) *Audit evidence*

   - Board minutes approving the store's 'facelift' and documenting the need to address the fall in demand for it as a supermarket.
   - Recomputation of the carrying amount of goodwill ($\frac{2}{5}$ × $5.5m = $2.2m).
   - A schedule identifying all the assets that relate to the store under review and the carrying amounts thereof agreed to the underlying accounting records (e.g. non-current asset register).
   - Recalculation of value in use and/or net selling price of the cash-generating unit (that is to become the City Metro) as at 31 March 2005.
   - Agreement of cash flow projections (e.g. to approved budgets/forecast revenues and costs for a maximum of five years, unless a longer period can be justified).
   - Written management representation relating to the assumptions used in the preparation of financial budgets.

- Agreement that the pre-tax discount rate used reflects current market assessments of the time value of money (and the risks specific to the store) and is reasonable. For example, by comparison with Volcan's weighted average cost of capital.

- Inspection of the store (if this month it should be closed for refurbishment).

- Revenue budgets and cash flow projections for:
  - the two stores purchased at the same time;
  - the other stores in Urvina; and
  - the stores elsewhere.

  Also actual after-date sales by store compared with budget.

(b) **Reward scheme**

(i) *Matters*

If the entire year's revenue ($303m) attracted store points then the cost of the reward scheme in the year is at most $3.03m. This represents 1% of revenue, which is material to the statement of comprehensive income and very material (31.9%) to profit before tax (PBT).

The proportion of customers who register for loyalty cards and the percentage of revenue (and profit) which they represent (which may vary from store to store depending on customer profile).

In accordance with the assumption of accruals, which underlies the preparation and presentation of financial statements (The Framework/IAS 1 *Presentation of Financial Statements*), the expense and liability should be recognized as revenue is earned. (It is of the nature of a discount.)

Any restrictions on the terms for converting points (e.g. whether they expire if not used within a specified time).

To the extent that points have been awarded but not redeemed at 31 March 2005, Volcan will have a liability at the statement of financial position date.

Agree the total balance due to customers at the year end under the reward scheme to the sum of the points on individual customer reward cards.

The proportion of reward points awarded which are not expected to be claimed (e.g. the 'take up' of points awarded may be only 80%, say).

Whether reward points are valued at selling price or cost. For example, if the average gross profit margin is 20%, one point is equivalent to 0.8 cents of goods at cost.

(ii) *Audit evidence*

- New/updated systems documentation explaining how:
  - loyalty cards (and numbers) are issued to customers;
  - points earned are recorded at the point of sale; and
  - points are later redeemed on subsequent purchases.
- Walk-through tests (e.g. on registering customer applications and issuing loyalty cards, awarding of points on special offer items).
- Tests of controls supporting the extent to which audit reliance is placed on the accounting and internal control system. In particular, how points are extracted from the electronic tills (cash registers) and summarized

into the weekly/monthly financial data for each store which underlies the financial statements.

- Analytical procedures on the value of points awarded by store per month with explanations of variations ('variation analysis'). For example, similar proportions (not exceeding 1% of revenue) of points in each month might be expected by store – possibly increasing following any promotion of the 'loyalty' scheme.

- Tests of detail on a sample of transactions with customers undertaken at store visits. For example, for a sample of copy till receipts:

    - check the arithmetic accuracy of points awarded (1 per $1 spent + special offers);

    - agree points awarded for special offers to that week's special offers;

    - for cash discounts taken confirm the conversion of points is against the opening balance of points awarded (not against purchases just made).

(c)   **Site restoration**

(i)   *Matters*

The provision for site restoration represents nearly 2.5% of total assets and is therefore material if it is not warranted.

The estimated cost of restoring the site is a cost directly attributable to the initial measurement of the tangible fixed asset to the extent that it is recognized as a provision under IAS 37 *Provisions, Contingent Liabilities and Contingent Assets* (IAS 16 *Property, Plant and Equipment*).

A provision should not be recognized for site restoration unless it meets the definition of a liability, i.e:

    - a present obligation;

    - arising from past events;

    - the settlement of which is expected to result in an outflow of resources embodying economic benefits.

The provision is overstated by nearly $0.34m since Volcan is not obliged to relocate the trees and de facto has only an obligation of $60,000 as at 31 March 2005 (being the penalty for having felled them). When considered in isolation, this overstatement is immaterial (representing only 0.2% of total assets and 3.6% of PBT).

It seems that even if there are local government regulations calling for site restoration there is no obligation unless the penalties for non-compliance are prohibitive (unlike the fines for the trees).

It is unlikely that commencement of site development has given rise to a constructive obligation, since past actions (disregarding the preservation of the trees) must dispel any expectation that Volcan will honour any pledge to restore the valley.

Whether commencing development of the site, and destroying the trees, conflicts with any statement of socio-environmental responsibility in the annual report.

(ii)   *Audit evidence*

- A copy of the planning application and permission granted setting out the penalties for non-compliance.

- Payment of $60,000 to local government in May 2005 agreed to the bank statement.

- The present value calculation of the future cash expenditure making up the $4.0m provision.

- Agreement that the pre-tax discount rate used reflects current market assessments of the time value of money (as for (a)).

- Asset inspection at the site as at 31 March 2005.

- Any contracts entered into which might confirm or dispute management's intentions to restore the site. For example, whether plant hire (bulldozers, etc) covers only the period over which the warehouse will be constructed – or whether it extends to the period in which the valley would be 'made good'.

COMPLETION AND REPORTING

34   PLUTO CO (A) *Walk in the footsteps of a top tutor*

Key answer tips

Part (a) of the question follows on from two fraud based articles written by both the F8 and the P7 exam team. Therefore prior to answering this question it would be worth reviewing these on the ACCA website.

The bulk of the question asks you to consider the wording of an audit report. In order to answer these questions think of the following structure:

- is there any relevant guidance? (i.e. standards)

- what should have been done and what has been done?

- does it lead to a misstatement or a lack of sufficient appropriate evidence?

- is it material or pervasive?

- in the circumstances what audit report should be issued?

The highlighted words are key phases that markers are looking for.

(a)   Fraudulent financial reporting is a type of fraud that causes a material misstatement in the financial statements.

The term is defined in ISA 240 *The Auditor's Responsibilities Relating to Fraud in an Audit of Financial Statements*. Fraudulent financial reporting is a deliberate act, i.e. an intentional misstatement, and can include omissions. The aim of the activity is to deceive the users of the financial statements. Fraudulent financial reporting tends to fall into three categories, described below:

Manipulation, falsification (including forgery), or alteration of accounting records or supporting documentation from which the financial statements are prepared. An example would be where the management deliberately change the trial balance which is then used as the basis of preparation of the financial statements. Fictitious journal entries could be used to 'window dress' the year-end figures.

Misrepresentation in, or deliberate omission from, the financial statements of events, transactions or other significant information. An example would be where management knowingly fail to account for a transaction, so that the financial statements are incomplete. Revenue or costs could be omitted or delayed until the next accounting period. Failure to provide information about going concern problems is a deliberate omission of significant information.

Intentional misapplication of accounting principles relating to amounts, classification, presentation or disclosure within the financial statements. An example would be the deliberate breach of a financial reporting standard. This could mean that balances are recognised inappropriately, necessary disclosures are not made, or the presentation is not correct.

Such actions are often carried out to manage earnings in order to influence the perceptions of the company's performance. This is commonly referred to as 'earnings management' and is prone to occur due to pressure on management to achieve a certain performance target. Alternatively, the statement of financial position of the company could be manipulated with the aim of securing finance.

(b) **Adverse opinion paragraph**

The title of the opinion paragraph clearly states that it is an adverse opinion. For the sake of clarity it may be better just to state that the opinion is adverse rather than go into the reason for the opinion in the title, i.e. remove wording 'arising from disagreement about application of IAS 37'.

Normally the reason for any modification to the audit report affecting the opinion is explained in a separate paragraph immediately preceding the opinion paragraph. Here the reason for the modification is explained within the opinion paragraph which could be confusing for the readers.

ISA 705 *Modifications to the Opinion in the Independent Auditor's Report* states that a clear description of all of the substantive reasons for any modification to the opinion should be included in the report, including, where practicable, an estimate of the financial effect. The proposed audit report partially explains the material misstatement but does not go into sufficient detail. Specifically no estimate of the financial effect has been provided. Quantification of the amount of the omitted provision must be available. Other detail of the provision should also be provided, such as the timing of the probable cash outflow.

To aid the readers' understanding of the breach of financial reporting standards that has occurred, it would be useful to fully state the title of IAS 37 Provisions, Contingent Liabilities and Contingent Assets.

The paragraph refers to a note to the financial statements where 'the matter is more fully explained'. This is ambiguous. Does the note explain the reason why the directors feel unable to quantify the value of the provision? Does the note describe the situation in terms of a contingent liability (which appears to be how the directors are treating the item)? The paragraph should be more precise in referring to what the note actually contains. A page reference should also be given to help the readers to find the note.

The paragraph ends with an observation that profits are overstated as a result of the non-recognition of the provision. There should also be a comment on the impact on the statement of financial position, in which liabilities are understated. The effect should be quantified, as discussed above.

Finally, and most importantly, whether this issue should give rise to an adverse opinion is debatable. An adverse opinion should be given when the effect of a disagreement is so material and pervasive that the financial statements are rendered meaningless. Without any figures being provided it is not possible to comment on materiality, however, the provision would have to be extremely significant for its omission to make the financial statements meaningless.

The report itself could appear to be contradictory, as it states that the omission has caused a 'material misstatement', implying a material but not a pervasive impact on the financial statements. It is likely in this case that an 'except for' qualification would be sufficient.

Emphasis of matter paragraph

The paragraph appears to be describing a breach of financial reporting standards. IAS 33 *Earnings per Share* requires that listed companies must disclose basic and diluted earnings per share figures, including comparatives, on the face of the financial statements. The fact that the directors have decided not to disclose is a clear misapplication of the standard. Earnings per share is material by nature, so its omission represents a material misstatement in the financial statements.

The audit opinion should be qualified 'except for' due to a material misstatement. Therefore a paragraph discussing the misstatement should be inserted above the opinion paragraph, including an estimate of the financial effect, and a reference to a note to the financial statements if this has been provided.

The emphasis of matter paragraph does not state whether the prior year's earnings per share figure has been disclosed or not. A comparative is required by IAS 33.

The emphasis of matter paragraph should not be used to highlight situations where the directors have decided not to include a matter in the financial statements. The paragraph is reserved for use to explain significant uncertainties or going concern issues, and its use in this situation is entirely inappropriate.

(c) ISQC 1 *Quality Control for Firms that Perform Audits and Reviews of Historical Financial Information, and Other Assurance and Related Services Engagements* outlines how a firm decides on the eligibility of a person to perform an engagement review.

Firstly, the reviewer must have a high standard of technical knowledge, encompassing a thorough understanding of auditing and financial reporting standards, as well as any specific regulatory issues (such as stock exchange listing rules) which may be relevant to the client.

In addition, the reviewer should be an experienced auditor, preferably with specific practical experience of auditing companies operating in a similar industry or business sector as the client.

The reviewer should possess a level of authority within the firm. This will allow the reviewer to challenge the decisions made by other members of the firm, including senior managers and partners. It is important that the reviewer is not intimidated by the senior members of the audit team who could feel criticised by any negative comments that the reviewer may have on their work and decisions. ISQC 1 recommends that a reviewer of listed client's audits should normally be at partner level within the firm.

Finally, the reviewer must be independent of the audit team. This allows a totally objective review to take place. The engagement partner therefore should not be involved in deciding who should review the audit. Consultations between the engagement partner and the reviewer can take place during the audit, but care should be taken to preserve the reviewer's objectivity.

Examiner's comments

Requirement (a)

Answers on the whole were reasonable, and in terms of illustration, a range of examples were usually provided.

Requirement (b)

Answers were on the whole unsatisfactory. As noted in previous examiners' reports, candidates seem not to understand the concepts underpinning the qualification of an audit report, and have even less comprehension of the use of an emphasis of matter paragraph.

Looking initially at the adverse opinion, most candidates correctly suggested that a disagreement had indeed occurred, and that an adverse opinion may be too harsh, meaning that an except for qualification would be more suitable. Fewer went on to criticise the audit report for its lack of quantification of the amount of the material misstatement.

Most candidates did not appraise the wording of the extract, but there were easy marks to be gained here, for example, for suggesting that the title of the financial reporting standard should be written in full, and the lack of reference to note or page numbers where more information about the redundancy costs could be found in the financial statements. Few candidates suggested that the description of the disagreement was inadequate, though it was deliberately so. The best answers rightly criticised the use of the word 'feel' in an audit report, as well as it being inappropriate to put forward the views of the directors in the report.

Regarding the emphasis of matter paragraph, a significant proportion of candidates did not attempt this part of the requirement. Those that did gained credit for briefly explaining the correct use of such a paragraph, but fewer went on to say why its use in this situation was inappropriate. Many candidates did not appreciate that the company in the question was listed, so disclosure of the earnings per share figure would be required.

Finally, many candidates were extremely concerned about the audit report containing both an adverse opinion and an emphasis of matter paragraph, missing the point that the opinion and the emphasis of matter paragraph dealt with two completely separate issues.

Requirement (c)

Answers tended to be very brief, often in a bullet point format. The majority of answers mentioned that it should be a partner with experience who should perform the review. Though most candidates could suggest that the reviewer should be independent of both the audit team, and the audit client, few could suggest why.

	Marking scheme	Marks
(a)	**Fraudulent financial reporting**	
	Generally 1 mark per comment/example:	
	- Material misstatement	
	- Deliberate/intentional	
	- Manipulation of underlying accounting records	
	- Misrepresentation/omission in financial statements	
	- Misapplication of IFRS	
	- Earnings management	
	- Ref ISA 240 ½ mark	
	Maximum marks	**4**
(b)	**Critical appraisal of audit report**	
	Up to 1½ marks per issue explained:	
	- Adverse opinion	
	- Inadequate explanation of disagreement	
	- No financial impact given	
	- Clearer title needed	
	- Better to refer to IAS 37 in full	
	- Clearer reference to note needed	
	- Explanation of disagreement should be in separate paragraph	
	- Except for rather than adverse?	
	- Emphasis of matter	
	- EOM not used for this situation	
	- Ref ISA 701 ½ mark	
	- Ref IAS 33 ½ mark	
	Maximum marks	**9**
(c)	**Eligibility to perform an engagement quality control**	
	Generally 1 mark per comment:	
	- Technical expertise	
	- Experience	
	- Authority	
	- Independence from audit team	
	Ref ISQC 1 ¼ mark	
	Maximum marks	**4**
	Total	**17**

35 DEXTER CO (A) *Walk in the footsteps of a top tutor*

Key answer tips

This question focuses on going concern. Students are required to discuss who is responsible for assessing the going concern status of a business and how disclosures relating to going concern (or a lack of them) affect the audit opinion.

Part (a) requires a little basic knowledge regarding who prepares the accounts and IAS 1. It also requires students to suggest specific procedures used to support going concern assessments.

Part (b) requires some common sense regarding why directors may not want to publish accounts that indicate going concern problems.

Part (c) requires students to consider whether the lack of disclosure contravenes any financial reporting standards and the consequent affect on the opinion. It is important that students use the language of audit reports, i.e. qualified/unqualified, disagreement/ limitation of scope, except for/adverse/disclaimer. It should also be noted that the scenario states *"working papers conclude that the going concern assumption is appropriate."* Therefore the going concern status is not under dispute, merely the lack of disclosure regarding a material uncertainty.

The highlighted words are key phases that markers are looking for.

(a) **Responsibilities of management and auditors**

Basic responsibilities

ISA 570 *Going Concern* provides a clear framework for the assessment of the going concern status of an entity, and differentiates between the responsibilities of management and of auditors. Management should assess going concern in order to decide on the most appropriate basis for the preparation of the financial statements. IAS 1 *Presentation of Financial Statements (revised)* requires that where there is significant doubt over an entity's ability to continue as a going concern, the uncertainties should be disclosed in a note to the financial statements. Where the directors intend to cease trading, or have no realistic alternative but to do so, the financial statements should be prepared on a 'break up' basis.

Thus the main focus of the management's assessment of going concern is to ensure that relevant disclosures are made where necessary, and that the correct basis of preparation is used.

The auditor's responsibility is to consider the appropriateness of the management's use of the going concern assumption in the preparation of the financial statements and to consider whether there are material uncertainties about the entity's ability to continue as a going concern that need to be disclosed in a note.

The auditor should also consider the length of the time period that management have looked at in their assessment of going concern.

The auditor will therefore need to come to an opinion as to the going concern status of an entity but the focus of the auditor's evaluation of going concern is to see whether they agree with the assessment made by the management. Therefore whether they agree with the basis of preparation of the financial statements, or the inclusion in a note to the financial statements, as required by IAS 1, of any material uncertainty.

Evaluation techniques

In carrying out the going concern assessment, management will evaluate a wide variety of indicators, including operational and financial. An entity employing good principles of corporate governance should be carrying out such an assessment as part of the on-going management of the business.

Auditors will use a similar assessment technique in order to come to their own opinion as to the going concern status of an entity. They will carry out an operational review of the business in order to confirm business understanding, and will conduct a financial review as part of analytical procedures. Thus both management and auditors will use similar business risk assessment techniques to discover any threats to the going concern status of the business.

Auditors should not see going concern as a 'completion issue', but be alert to issues affecting going concern throughout the audit. In the same way that management should continually be managing risk (therefore minimising going concern risk), auditors should be continually be alert to going concern problems throughout the duration of the audit.

However, one difference is that when going concern problems are discovered, the auditor is required by IAS 570 to carry out additional procedures. Examples of such procedures would include:

– Analysing and discussing cash flow, profit and other relevant forecasts with management

– Analysing and discussing the entity's latest available interim financial statements

– Reviewing events after the period end to identify those that either mitigate or otherwise affect the entity's ability to continue as a going concern, and

– Reading minutes of meetings of shareholders, those charged with governance and relevant committees for reference to financing difficulties.

Management are not explicitly required to gather specific evidence about going concern, but as part of good governance would be likely to investigate and react to problems discovered.

(b) **Directors reluctance to disclose**

The directors are likely to have several reasons behind their reluctance to disclose the note as recommended by the audit manager. The first is that the disclosure of Dexter Co's poor cash flow position and perilous going concern status may reflect badly on the directors themselves. The company's shareholders and other stakeholders will be displeased to see the company in such a poor position, and the directors will be held accountable for the problems. Of course it may not be the case that the directors have exercised poor management of the company – the problems could be caused by external influences outside the control of the directors. However, it is natural that the directors will not want to highlight the situation in order to protect their own position.

Secondly, the note could itself trigger further financial distress for the company. Dexter Co is trying to raise finance, and it is probable that the availability of further finance will be detrimentally affected by the disclosure of the company's financial problems. In particular, if the cash flow difficulties are highlighted, providers of finance will consider the company too risky an investment, and are not likely to make funds available for fear of non-repayment. Existing lenders may seek repayment of their funds in fear that the company may be unable in the future to meet repayments.

In addition, the disclosures could cause operational problems, for example, suppliers may curtail trading relationships as they become concerned that they will not be paid, or customers may be deterred from purchasing from the company if they feel that there is no long-term future for the business. Unfortunately the mere disclosure of financial problems can be self-fulfilling, and cause such further problems for the company that it is pushed into non-going concern status.

The directors may also be concerned that if staff were to hear of this they may worry about the future of the company and seek alternative employment, which could lead in turn to the loss of key members of staff. This would be detrimental to the business and trigger further operational problems.

Finally, the reluctance to disclose may be caused by an entirely different reason. The directors genuinely feel that the cash flow and operational problems faced by the company do not constitute factors affecting the going concern status. They may be confident that although a final decision has not been made regarding financing, the finance is likely to be forthcoming, and therefore there is no long-term material uncertainty over the future of the company. However audit working papers conclude that there is a significant level of doubt over the going concern status of Dexter Co, and therefore it seems that the directors may be over optimistic if they feel that there is no significant doubt to be disclosed in the financial statements.

(c) (i) **Audit report implications**

Audit procedures have shown that there is a significant level of doubt over Dexter Co's going concern status. IAS 1 requires that disclosure is made in the financial statements regarding material uncertainties, which may cast significant doubt on the ability of the entity to continue as a going concern. If the directors refuse to disclose the note to the financial statements, there is a clear breach of financial reporting standards.

In this case the significant uncertainty is caused by not knowing the extent of the future availability of finance needed to fund operating activities. If the note describing this uncertainty is not provided, the financial statements are not fairly presented.

The audit report should contain a qualified or an adverse opinion due to the material misstatement. The auditors need to make a decision as to the significance of the non-disclosure. If it is decided that without the note the financial statements are not fairly presented, and could be considered misleading, an adverse opinion should be expressed. However, it could be decided that the lack of the note is material, but not pervasive to the financial statements, then a qualified 'except for' opinion should be expressed.

ISA 570 *Going Concern* and ISA 705 *Modifications to the Opinion in the Independent Auditor's Report* provides guidance on the presentation of the audit report in the case of a modification. The audit report should include a paragraph which contains specific reference to the fact that there is a material uncertainty that may cast significant doubt about the entity's ability to continue as a going concern. The paragraph should include a clear description of the uncertainties and would normally be presented immediately before the opinion paragraph.

(ii) If the directors agree to disclose the note, it should be reviewed by the auditors to ensure that it is sufficiently detailed. In evaluating the adequacy of the disclosure in the note, the auditor should consider whether the disclosure explicitly draws the reader's attention to the possibility that the entity may not be able to continue as a going concern in the foreseeable future. The note should include a description of conditions giving rise to significant doubt, and the directors' plans to deal with the conditions. If the note provided contains adequate information then there is no breach of financial reporting standards, and so no misstatement in the financial statements.

If the disclosure is considered adequate, then the opinion should not be modified. The auditors should consider a modification by adding an emphasis of matter paragraph to highlight the existence of the material uncertainties, and to draw attention to the note to the financial statements. The matter of emphasis paragraph should firstly contain a brief description of the uncertainties, and also refer explicitly to the note to the financial statements where the situation has been fully described. The emphasis of matter paragraph should re-iterate that the audit opinion is not qualified.

However, it could be the case that a note has been given in the financial statements, but that the details are inadequate and do not fully explain the significant uncertainties affecting the going concern status of the company. In this situation the auditors should express a qualified opinion due to a material misstatement in the financial statements, as the disclosure requirements of IAS 1 have not been followed.

Examiner's comments

Requirement (a)

The main deficiency in answers to this requirement was the lack of any kind of comparison of the responsibilities of management and auditors, despite the fact that the requirement began with 'compare and contrast'. The other problem was that many candidates did not restrict their answer, as requested, to the assessment of going concern, but digressed into issues such as corporate governance and maintaining shareholder value.

Requirement (b)

Many answers were provided here. However, some candidates failed to provide more than a couple of reasons, which is not enough for the mark allocation.

Requirement (c)

This question was rarely well answered, and many candidates obviously do not understand the different types of modifications to audit reports at all, let alone the implication for the audit report of non-disclosure of going concern issues. There was a tendency in (ci) to go straight for an adverse opinion, without any discussion of the level of significance of the non-disclosure. There was also confusion over the use of an adverse opinion and a disclaimer of opinion. Some candidates put down all possible types of audit opinion as their answer in the hope that one of them would be correct.

In (cii) very few candidates suggested that the auditor should consider the adequacy of the note if the directors agree to provide one. For (cii) most candidates did mention the emphasis of matter paragraph, but seemed unclear as to whether the inclusion of the paragraph in an audit report resulted in a qualification or a modification. Some candidates confused an emphasis of matter paragraph with an 'except for' opinion, and seemed to provide the same answer for (ci) and (cii).

In this advanced audit paper it is inexcusable that students do not know these basic facts about the audit report. It is strange that most candidates elected to answer this question on audit reports when clearly they did not have the technical knowledge to answer such a question. Candidates should also remember that writing one or two sentences is unlikely to be sufficient to answer an eight mark question requirement.

	Marking scheme		Marks
(a)	Compare and contrast management and auditors' responsibilities regarding going concern		*Marks*
	Management	**Auditors**	
	Focus is to follow IAS 1 requirements regarding disclosure of going concern problems or to prepare on break up basis.	Focus is to form independent opinion on going concern status and to see if IAS 1 requirements adhered to.	
	Range of indicators assessed	Range of indicators assessed	
	No requirement to perform specific procedures	ISA 570 requires specific procedures and assessment of period reviewed by management	
	Should be part of on going management of the business	Going concern should be considered throughout the audit	
	½ mark ref IAS 1, ½ mark ref ISA 570 Generally 1 mark per explained point. **Maximum 3 marks for procedures.** Maximum capped at 4 if no attempt to explain similarities or differences. Allow ½ mark for definition of going concern.		
	Maximum marks		7
(b)	**Reluctance to disclose note**		
	Generally 1 mark per comment:		
	– Directors fear they will be held accountable for problems		
	– Trigger further financial distress as necessary finance is withheld		
	– Trigger operational distress due to reactions of suppliers and customers		
	– Trigger operational problems if key members of staff leave		
	– Directors may feel the problems do not impact on going concern status		
	Maximum marks		5
(c)	**(i) Audit report – note not provided**		
	Generally 1 mark per comment:		
	– Breach of IAS 1 leading to disagreement		
	– Opinion could be qualified or adverse		
	– Judgement needed		
	– Report to refer to material uncertainty		
	Maximum marks		4
	(ii) Audit report – note provided		
	Generally 1 mark per comment and ½ mark ref ISA 701		
	– Review adequacy of disclosure		
	– If note is sufficient – unqualified opinion		
	– Emphasis of matter paragraph to highlight uncertainties		
	– If note inadequate – qualify 'except for' disagreement		
	Maximum marks		4
	Total		20

36   BLOD CO (A) *Walk in the footsteps of a top tutor*

Key answer tips

This question requires a broader consideration of reporting issues, other than just 'what audit opinion would you make?' Instead the question requires consideration of the other main product of the audit: the management letter (of weaknesses). Auditors communicate with directors, primarily via an audit committee, about issues such as: weaknesses in internal controls; areas where accounting standards have not been followed; errors identified in the draft accounts; updates to or newly introduced standards; potential qualifications, to name a few.

> The question followed an article entitled 'auditors reports to those charged with governance' published in April 2008. It may be useful to review this article prior to reading the model answer.
>
> The highlighted words are key phases that markers are looking for.

(a) (i) A report to those charged with governance is produced to communicate matters relating to the external audit to those who are ultimately responsible for the financial statements. ISA 260 *Communication with Those Charged With Governance* and ISA 265 *Communicating Deficiencies in Internal Control to Those Charged with Governance* require the auditor to communicate many matters, including independence and other ethical issues, the audit approach and scope, the details of management representations, and the findings of the audit. The findings of the audit are commonly referred to as management letter points. By communicating these matters, the auditor is confident that there is written documentation outlining all significant matters raised during the audit process, and that such matters have been formally notified to the highest level of management of the client. For the management, the report should ensure that they fully understand the scope and results of the audit service which has been provided, and is likely to provide constructive comments to help them to fulfil their duties in relation to the financial statements and accounting systems and controls more effectively. The report should also include, where relevant, any actions that management has indicated they will take in relation to recommendations made by the auditors.

(ii) **Control weakness**

ISA 265 contains guidance on the type of issues that should be communicated. One of the matters identified is a control weakness in the capital expenditure transaction cycle. The assets for which no authorisation was obtained amount to 0.3% of total assets (225,000/78 million × 100%), which is clearly immaterial. However, regardless of materiality, the auditor should ensure that the weakness is brought to the attention of the management, with a clear indication of the implication of the weakness, and recommendations as to how the control weakness should be eliminated.

The auditor is providing information to help those charged with governance improve the internal systems and controls and ultimately reduce business risk. In this case there is a high risk of fraud, as the lack of authorisation for purchase of office equipment could allow expenditure on assets not used for bona fide business purposes.

Material Misstatement of Intangible Brand Assets

Audit procedures have revealed a breach of IAS 38 *Intangible Assets*, in which internally generated brand names are specifically prohibited from being recognised. Blod Co has recognised an internally generated brand name which is material to the statement of financial position (balance sheet) as it represents 12.8% of total assets (10/78 × 100%). The statement of financial position (balance sheet) therefore contains a material misstatement.

The report to those charged with governance should clearly explain the rules on recognition of internally generated brand names, to ensure that the management has all relevant technical facts available. In the report the auditors should request that the financial statements be corrected, and clarify that if the brand is not derecognised, then the audit opinion will be modified on the grounds of a material misstatement – an 'except for' qualification would be provided. Once the breach of IAS 38 is made clear to the management in the report, they then have the opportunity to discuss the matter and decide whether to amend the financial statements, thereby avoiding a qualified audit opinion.

Audit inefficiencies

Documentation relating to inventories was not always made readily available to the auditors. This seems to be due to poor administration by the client rather than a deliberate attempt to conceal information. The report should contain a brief description of the problems encountered by the audit team. The management should be made aware that significant delay to the receipt of necessary paperwork can cause inefficiencies in the audit process. This may seem a relatively trivial issue, but it could lead to an increase in audit fee. Management should react to these comments by ensuring as far as possible that all requested documentation is made available to the auditors in a timely fashion.

(b)   It is not uncommon for audit firms to word process and typeset the financial statements of their clients, especially where the client is a relatively small entity, which may lack the resources and skills to perform this task. It is not prohibited by ethical standards.

However, there could be a perceived threat to independence, with risk magnified in the case of Blod Co, which is a listed company. The auditors could be perceived to be involved with the preparation of the financial statements of a listed client company, which is prohibited by ethical standards. IFAC's *Code of Ethics for Professional Accountants* states that for a listed client, the audit firm should not be involved with the preparation of financial statements, which would create a self-review threat so severe that safeguards could not reduce the threat to an acceptable level. Although the typing of financial statements itself is not prohibited by ethical guidance, the risk is that providing such a service could be perceived to be an element of the preparation of the financial statements.

It is possible that during the process of typing the financial statements, decisions and judgments would be made. This could be perceived as making management decisions in relation to the financial statements, a clear breach of independence.

Therefore to eliminate any risk exposure, the prudent decision would be not to type the financial statements, ensuring that Blod Co appreciates the ethical problems that this would cause.

Tutorial note

This is an area not specifically covered by ethical guides, where different audit firms may have different views on whether it is acceptable to provide a typing service for the financial statements of their clients. Credit will be awarded for sensible discussion of the issues raised bearing in mind other options for the audit firm, for example, it could be argued that it is acceptable to offer the typing service provided that it is performed by people independent of the audit team, and that the matter has been discussed with the audit committee/those charged with governance.

(c) It has become increasingly common for audit firms to include a disclaimer paragraph within the audit report. However, it is not a requirement of auditing standards and individual audit firms need to assess the advantages and disadvantages of the use of a disclaimer paragraph.

The wording is used to state the fact that the auditor's report is intended solely for the use of the company's members as a body, and that no responsibility is accepted or assumed to anyone other than the company and the company's members as a body.

The main perceived advantage is that the disclaimer should help to reduce the exposure of the audit firm to liability claims from anyone other than the company or the company's body of shareholders. The disclaimer makes it clear that the audit firm reports only to those who appointed the firm, i.e. the members of the company, and this may make it more difficult for the audit firm to be sued by a third party.

It is also argued that the use of a disclaimer could help to bridge the 'expectation gap' by providing a clearer indication of the responsibility of the auditor.

In this way the audit firm can manage its risk exposure in an increasingly litigious environment. Recent high profile legal cases against audit firms, such as the Bannerman case in Scotland, illustrate that an audit firm's duty of care can extend beyond the company and its shareholders, and that audit firms should consider how to protect themselves against liability claims.

Tutorial note

It is appropriate here to quote recent cases such as the Bannerman case to illustrate the reason why audit firms face increased potential exposure to claims from third parties. However, knowledge of specific legal cases is not required to gain full marks for this requirement.

However, it can be argued that a disclaimer does not necessarily work to protect an audit firm. Each legal case has individual circumstances, and while a disclaimer might protect the audit firm in one situation, equally it may not offer any protection where the facts of the case are different.

In addition, it is often argued that if an audit firm conducts an audit using full due care and diligence, there is no need for a disclaimer, as a high quality audit would be very unlikely to lead to any claims against the audit firm. Consequently, it could be argued that the use of disclaimers as a means to limit liability could permit low quality audits to be performed, the auditors being confident that legal cases against them are restricted due to the presence of a disclaimer within the audit report.

Examiner's comments

Candidates should be aware that the syllabus section on 'Reporting' is not confined to the audit report, but includes other outputs from the audit, as well as reports given for non-audit engagements. Therefore it should not be assumed that every P7 exam will include a question specifically on audit reports.

Requirement (a): Some candidates simply repeated facts from the scenario and provided very little comment of their own as to why the matters they identified should be included. There were very few references to the existence of ISA 260 or 265.

The first matter dealt with in the scenario involved a deterioration of internal controls with regard to capital expenditure. Most candidates calculated the materiality of the breakdown in controls in question, but an alarming minority calculated this incorrectly, which led them to believe that the control weakness had led to a material mis-statement in the financial statements, which was technically incorrect, especially as the scenario stated that there were no material errors found during audit procedures on property, plant and equipment. The second matter, a material breach of financial reporting standards was generally well dealt with, although again there were a surprisingly large number of mistakes in the calculation of materiality.

It was the final matter in the scenario, which dealt with inefficient responses by the client to requests for information from the audit firm, which prompted the weakest answers to requirement (a). The most common mistake made by candidates was to assume that the client had caused a limitation in the scope of the audit, leading to speculation that the client was 'trying to hide something' or that a fraud was being perpetrated, and developed into a call for a disclaimer of audit opinion. Only a handful of candidates appreciated the importance of co-operation between internal and external auditors, and that failure to provide information to the external audit team not only delays the audit process, but also casts doubt on the efficiency and effectiveness of the internal audit team, and could potentially result in an increased audit fee. This is a crucial matter to raise with those charged with governance, who ultimately are responsible for the actions of the internal auditors who report to them.

Requirement (b): This requirement asked candidates to comment on a request made by the client, a listed company, for the audit firm to type the financial statements. This is not specifically prohibited by ethical guidelines, and the point of the requirement was to test the candidates' ability to think on their feet about a relatively common request. The issue is that the auditor could be perceived to be involved with the preparation of the financial statements or to be taking management decisions; however, with appropriate safeguards a typing service could be provided. As the client in this case was a listed company, some candidates suggested that even with safeguards, it may be a safer decision to explain to the client the threats and decline to provide the service.

Requirement (c): Auditor's liability is a topical issue and it was disappointing to see that roughly half of the candidates who chose to attempt this question had no comprehension of the concept of the liability disclaimer. Most of these answers instead discussed an opinion modified due to limitation in scope, while others made much of a paragraph which explains the responsibilities of auditors compared to managers. Those candidates who correctly identified the liability disclaimer (a paragraph used to clarify that the auditor's report is intended to be used by the shareholders of the company as a whole, and thus the auditors accept no responsibility towards third parties) tended to do very well, with clear arguments for and against the use of such paragraphs discussed. Many strong answers referred to the Bannerman case which prompted the widespread use of these paragraphs, and some even mentioned ACCA's views on the use of the paragraph (though this was not necessary to score full marks).

	Marking scheme	
(a)	**(i) Purpose of including audit findings in a report to those charged with governance**	*Marks*
	1 mark per comment:	
	– Formal communication of key audit matters	
	– Recommendations made to management	
	– Reference ISA 260 – ½ mark	
	Maximum marks	2
	(ii) Identification and explanation of matters	
	½ mark for identification, up to 2 marks for explanation:	
	Identification *Reason for inclusion*	
	Control weakness – Not material to financial statements	
	– But indicates serious weakness which could allow fraud to occur	
	– Recommendations to help management reduce business risk	
	Standards breach – Financial statements materially misstated	
	– Give technical detail to non-financial directors	
	– Report to state opinion will be modified unless brand derecognised	
	– Management have full facts and can decide whether to amend	
	Delay in receiving paperwork – Audit inefficiencies and possible increased audit fee	
	– Management to realise problems caused and react	
	Maximum marks	7
(b)	**Provision of typing service**	
	1 mark per comment from ideas list:	
	– Typing service not prohibited	
	– Could be seen as preparation of financial statements	
	– For listed client risk is increased	
	– Safest option to refuse/service	
	– Could be provided if significant safeguards in place	
	Maximum marks	3
(c)	**Disclaimer content and advantages and disadvantages**	
	1 mark per point:	
	Content of disclaimer:	
	– Report intended for use by company's members as a whole	
	– No responsibility accepted to third parties	
	– Commonly used but not required by standards	
	Advantages:	
	– Potential to limit liability exposure	
	– Clarifies extent of auditor's responsibility	
	– Reduces expectation gap	
	– Manages audit firm's risk exposure	
	Disadvantages:	
	– Each legal case assessed individually – no evidence that a disclaimer would offer protection in all cases	
	– May lead to reduction in audit quality	
	Maximum marks	5
Total		17

37 BERTIE & CO (A) *Walk in the footsteps of a top tutor*

Key answer tips

This is a more traditional reporting question whereby the candidate must review a scenario and decide what the appropriate audit opinion should be. When trying to tackle questions of this nature it is important to: identify relevant areas of accounting regulation; discuss the appropriate accounting treatment and whether the client has made an error; identify whether the topic is 'material' or 'material and pervasive'; and finally discuss the wording of the opinion. It is important to note that the difference between 'material' and 'material and pervasive' is not simply the scale of the error. It is more concerned with whether the error is isolated or whether it permeates all of the accounts, thus making them unreliable as a whole.

The highlighted words are key phases that markers are looking for.

(a) (i) **Alpha Co**

The factory closures constitute a discontinued operation per IFRS 5 *Non-Current Assets Held for Sale and Discontinued Operations*, due to the discontinuance of a separate major component of the business. It is a major component due to the 10% contribution to revenue in the year to 30 September 2007 and 23% contribution in 2006. It is a separate business component of the company due to the factories having made only one item, indicating a separate income generating unit.

Under IFRS 5 there must be separate disclosure on the face of the statement of comprehensive income of the post tax results of the discontinued operation, and of any profit or loss resulting from the closures. The revenue and costs of the discontinued operation should be separately disclosed either on the face of the statement of comprehensive income or in the notes to the financial statements. Cash flows relating to the discontinued operation should also be separately disclosed per IAS 7 *Cash Flow Statements*.

In addition, as Alpha Co is a listed company, IFRS 8 *Operating Segments* requires separate segmental disclosure of discontinued operations.

Failure to disclose the above information in the financial statements is a material breach of International Accounting Standards. The audit opinion should therefore be modified on the grounds of a material misstatement. The matter is material, but not pervasive, and therefore an 'except for' qualification should be issued.

The opinion paragraph should clearly state the reason for the misstatement, and an indication of the financial significance of the matter.

The audit opinion relates only to the financial statements which have been audited, and the contents of the other information (chairman's statement and Directors' Report) are irrelevant when deciding if the financial statements show a true and fair view, or are fairly presented.

Tutorial note

There is no indication in the question scenario that Alpha Co is in financial or operational difficulty therefore no marks are awarded for irrelevant discussion of going concern issues and the resultant impact on the audit opinion.

(ii) **Deema Co**

The claim is an event after the reporting date. If the accident occurred prior to the year end of 30 September 2007, the claim gives additional evidence of a year-end condition, and thus meets the definition of an adjusting post reporting period event. In this case the matter appears to have been properly disclosed in the notes to the financial statements per IAS 10 *Events After the Reporting Period* and IAS 37 *Provisions, Contingent Liabilities and Contingent Assets*. A provision would only be necessary if the claim was probable to succeed and there is sufficient appropriate evidence that this is not the case. There is therefore no misstatement and sufficient appropriate evidence has been obtained.

Therefore the senior is correct to propose an unmodified opinion.

However, it is not necessary for the audit report to contain an emphasis of matter paragraph.

ISA 706 *Emphasis of Matter Paragraphs and Other Matter Paragraphs in the Independent Auditor's Report* states that an emphasis of matter paragraph should be used to highlight a matter where there is significant uncertainty.

Uncertainties are normally only regarded as significant if they involve a level of concern about the going concern status of the company or would have an unusually great effect on the financial statements. This is not the case here as there is enough cash to pay the damages in the unlikely event that the claim goes against Deema Co. This appears to be a one-off situation with a low risk of the estimate being subject to change and thus there is no significant uncertainty.

(b) There are several benefits for Hugh Co in choosing a voluntary financial statement audit.

An annual audit will ensure that any material mistakes made by the part-qualified accountant in preparing the year end financial statements will be detected. This is important as the directors will be using the year end accounts to review their progress in the first year of trading and will need reliable figures to assess performance. An audit will give the directors comfort that the financial statements are a sound basis for making business decisions.

Accurate first year figures will also enable more effective budgeting and forecasting, which will be crucial if rapid growth is to be achieved.

The auditors are likely to use the quarterly management accounts as part of normal audit procedures. The auditors will be able to advise Monty Parkes of any improvements that could be made to the management accounts, for example, increased level of detail, more frequent reporting. Better quality management accounts will help the day-to-day running of the business and enable a speedier response to any problems arising during the year.

As a by-product of the audit, a management letter (report to those charged with governance) will be produced, identifying weaknesses and making recommendations on areas such as systems and controls which will improve the smooth running of the business.

It is likely that Hugh Co will require more bank funding in order to expand, and it is likely that the bank would like to see audited figures for review, before deciding on further finance. It will be easier and potentially cheaper to raise finance from other providers with an audited set of financial statements.

As the business deals in cash sales, and retails small, luxury items there is a high risk of theft of assets. The external audit can act as both a deterrent and a detective control, thus reducing the risk of fraud and resultant detrimental impact on the financial statements.

Accurate financial statements will be the best basis for tax assessment and tax planning. An audit opinion will enhance the credibility of the figures.

If the business grows rapidly, then it is likely that at some point in the future, the audit exemption limit will be exceeded and thus an audit will become mandatory.

Choosing to have an audit from the first year of incorporation will reduce potential errors carried down to subsequent periods and thus avoid qualifications of opening balances.

(c) The objective of a review engagement is to enable the auditor to obtain moderate assurance as to whether the financial statements have been prepared in accordance with an identified financial reporting framework. This is defined in ISRE 2400 *Engagements to Review Financial Statements*.

In order to obtain this assurance, it is necessary to gather evidence using analytical procedures and enquiries with management. Detailed substantive procedures will not be performed unless the auditor has reason to believe that the information may be materially misstated.

The auditor should approach the engagement with a high degree of professional scepticism, looking for circumstances that may cause the financial statements to be misstated. For example, in Hugh Co, the fact that the preparer of the financial statements is part-qualified may lead the auditor to believe that there is a high inherent risk that the figures are misstated.

As a result of procedures performed, the auditor's objective is to provide a clear written expression of negative assurance on the financial statements. In a review engagement the auditor would state that 'we are not aware of any material modifications that should be made to the financial statements....'

This is normally referred to as an opinion of 'negative assurance'.

Negative assurance means that the auditor has performed limited procedures and has concluded that the financial statements appear reasonable. The user of the financial statements gains some comfort that the figures have been subject to review, but only a moderate level of assurance is provided. The user may need to carry out additional procedures of their own if they want to rely on the financial statements. For example, if Hugh Co were to use the financial statements as a means to raise further bank finance, the bank would presumably perform, or require Hugh

Co to perform, additional procedures to provide a higher level of assurance as to the validity of the figures contained in the financial statements.

In comparison, in an audit, a high level of assurance is provided. The auditors provide an opinion of positive, but not absolute assurance. The user is assured that the figures are free from material misstatement and that the auditor has based the opinion on detailed procedures.

Examiner's comments

This question tested knowledge of audit reports, and also the differences between an audit and a review of historical information.

Requirement (a) produced very mixed results. Some answers displayed a sound knowledge of audit reports, could differentiate between 'material' and 'pervasive' in the context of audit reports, and knew the purpose of an emphasis of matter paragraph. On the whole, however, answers to requirement (a) were inadequate. Common problems in requirement (a) included:

- A total lack of understanding about the use and purpose of an emphasis of matter paragraph – candidates appear to think that an emphasis of matter paragraph can be used by the auditor whenever there is an issue that they want to bring to the attention of the readers of the audit report, when in reality the paragraph is very limited in its use.

- An inability to comment on the appropriateness of the report suggested by the audit senior in the question – candidates must be able to reach an opinion of their own and to say if they agree or disagree with the view of someone else.

- A fixation with creating a provision where this would be the incorrect accounting treatment – candidates must be guided by the information in the scenario and not interpret the information in such a way to fit the answer that they would like to write.

- A fixation with the going concern concept – the discontinuation of a business segment does not mean that the entire company is going to cease to trade.

Requirements (b) and (c) were better. Most candidates could provide benefits for a small company in choosing to have a financial statement audit. One weakness here was a reluctance to make the answer specific to the question. The scenario gave lots of information specific to Hugh Co that could have been used in the answer, but many candidates chose to ignore the scenario and instead provide a list of benefits that could be equally relevant to any small company. A second weakness with reference to requirement (c) was a lack of points made specifically contrasting the level of assurance, as directed in the question requirement. However, on the whole these weaknesses did not detract heavily from the quality of answers provided to the final requirements of the examination.

Marking scheme		Marks
(a)	**(i) Comment on audit report – Alpha Co** Generally 1 mark per comment: – Discontinued operation – Cash flow disclosure (max ½ mark) – Segmental disclosure (max ½ mark) – Disagree with senior's proposal – Material – except for – Disagreement – reason must be explained in audit report – Audit opinion does not cover other information **(ii) Comment on audit report – Deema Co** Generally 1 mark per comment: – Accounting treatment of contingency (up to 2 marks for detailed discussion) – Unqualified opinion appears correct – Report does not need to be modified by EofM paragraph – Explanation why emphasis of matter not needed	*Marks* 10
(b)	**Benefits to Hugh Co in choosing to have financial statement audit** Generally 1 mark per comment NB COMMENTS MUST BE SPECIFIC TO HUGH CO – Improves reliability of figures – Improve quality of management accounts – Detective and preventative control – Increased assurance for external users – Reduces accumulation of errors carried down – Advice provided in letter to management – May need audit in future years	 4
(c)	**Objective of review engagement and assurance provided** Definition/objective – 2 marks maximum 2 marks for each comment on level of assurance NB NEEDS TO BE CONTRASTED WITH AUDIT – Limited procedures – Negative assurance – Only moderate level of assurance	 6
	Total	**20**

38   CLEEVES (A)

(a)   Reporting non-compliance

Non-compliance refers to acts of omission or commission by the entity being audited, either intentional or unintentional, that are contrary to the prevailing laws or regulations.

To management

Regarding non-compliance that comes to the auditor's attention the auditor should, as soon as practicable, either:

- communicate with those charged with governance; or

- obtain audit evidence that they are appropriately informed.

However, the auditor need not do so for matters that are clearly inconsequential or trivial and may reach agreement[1] in advance on the nature of such matters to be communicated.

If in the auditor's judgment the non-compliance is believed to be intentional and material, the auditor should communicate the finding without delay.

If the auditor suspects that members of senior management are involved in non-compliance, the auditor should report the matter to the next higher level of authority at the entity, if it exists (e.g. an audit committee or a supervisory board). Where no higher authority exists, or if the auditor believes that the report may not be acted upon or is unsure as to the person to whom to report, the auditor would consider seeking legal advice.

To the users of the auditor's report on the financial statements

If the auditor concludes that the non-compliance has a material effect on the financial statements, and has not been properly reflected in the financial statements, the auditor expresses a qualified (i.e. 'except for') or an adverse opinion.

If the auditor is precluded by the entity from obtaining sufficient appropriate audit evidence to evaluate whether or not non-compliance that may be material to the financial statements has (or is likely to have) occurred, the auditor should express an 'except for' qualified opinion or a disclaimer of opinion on the financial statements due to being unable to obtain sufficient appropriate evidence.

If the auditor is unable to determine whether non-compliance has occurred because of limitations imposed by circumstances rather than by the entity, the auditor should consider the effect on the auditor's report.

[1]   ISA 250 does not specify with whom agreement should be reached but presumably with those charged with corporate governance (e.g. audit committee or other supervisory board).

To regulatory and enforcement authorities

The auditor's duty of confidentiality ordinarily precludes reporting non-compliance to a third party. However, in certain circumstances, that duty of confidentiality is overridden by statute, law or by courts of law (e.g. in some countries the auditor is required to report non-compliance by financial institutions to the supervisory authorities). The auditor may need to seek legal advice in such circumstances, giving due consideration to the auditor's responsibility to the public interest.

(b)   (i)   **Appropriateness of audit opinion given**

Tutorial note

The answer points suggested by the marking scheme are listed in roughly the order in which they might be extracted from the information presented in the question. The suggested answer groups together some of these points under headings to give the analysis of the situation a possible structure.

Heading

- The opinion paragraph is not properly headed. It does not state the form of the opinion that has been given nor the grounds for modification.

- The opinion 'the financial statements do not give a true and fair view' is an 'adverse' opinion.

- That 'provision should be made', but has not, should be clearly stated as non-compliance with IAS 36. The title of IAS 36 *Impairment of Assets* should be given in full.

- The opinion should be headed 'Adverse Opinion'.

Content

- It is appropriate that the opinion paragraph should refer to the note(s) in the financial statements where the matter giving rise to the modification is more fully explained. However, this is not an excuse for the audit opinion being 'light' on detail. For example, the reason for impairment could be summarized in the auditor's report.

- The effects have not been quantified, but they *should* be quantifiable. The maximum possible loss would be the carrying amount of the non-current assets identified as impaired.

- It is not clear why the directors have been 'unable to quantify the amounts'. Since impairments should be quantifiable any 'inability' suggest an inability to gather sufficient appropriate evidence, in which case the opinion should be disclaimed (or 'except for') on grounds of lack of evidence rather than material misstatement.

- The wording is confusing. There must be sufficient evidence to support a claim of material misstatement. Although the directors cannot quantify the amounts it seems the auditors must have been able to (estimate at least) in order to form an opinion that the amounts involved are sufficiently material to warrant a modification.

- The first paragraph refers to 'non-current assets'. The second paragraph specifies 'tangible and intangible assets'. There is no explanation why or how both tangible and intangible assets are impaired.

- The first paragraph refers to 'profit or loss' and the second and third paragraphs to 'loss'. It may be clearer if the first paragraph were to refer to recognition in the statement of comprehensive income.

- It is not clear why the failure to recognize impairment warrants an adverse opinion rather than 'except for'. The effects of non-compliance with IAS 36 are to overstate the carrying amount(s) of non-current assets (that can be specified) and to understate the loss. The matter does not appear to be pervasive and so an adverse opinion looks unsuitable as the financial statements as a whole are not incomplete or misleading. A loss is already being reported so it is not that a reported profit would be turned into a loss (which is sometimes judged to be 'pervasive').

Prior year

- As the 2005 auditor's report, as previously issued, included an adverse opinion and the matter that gave rise to the modification:

  - is unresolved; and

  - results in a modification of the 2006 auditor's report,

the 2006 auditor's report should also be modified regarding the corresponding figures (ISA 710 *Comparative Information – Corresponding Figures and Comparative Financial Statements*).

- The 2006 auditor's report does not refer to the prior period modification nor highlight that the matter resulting in the current period modification is not new. For example, the report could say 'As previously reported and as more fully explained in notes ....' and state 'increase the loss by $x (2005 – $y)'.

(ii) **Implications for audit opinion on consolidated financial statements of Cleeves**

- If the potential adjustments to non-current asset carrying amounts and loss are not material to the consolidated financial statements there will be no implication. However, as Howard is material to Cleeves and the modification appears to be 'so material' (giving rise to adverse opinion) this seems unlikely.

- As Howard is wholly-owned the management of Cleeves must be able to request that Howard's financial statements are adjusted to reflect the impairment of the assets. The auditor's report on Cleeves will then be unmodified (assuming that any impairment of the investment in Howard is properly accounted for in the separate financial statements of Cleeves).

- If the impairment losses are not recognized in Howard's financial statements they can nevertheless be adjusted on consolidation of Cleeves and its subsidiaries (by writing down assets to recoverable amounts). The audit opinion on Cleeves should then be unmodified in this respect.

- If there is no adjustment of Howard's asset values (either in Howard's financial statements or on consolidation) it is most likely that the audit opinion on Cleeves's consolidated financial statements would be 'except for'. (It should not be adverse as it is doubtful whether even the opinion on Howard's financial statements should be adverse.)

39 JOHNSTON CO (A)

Key answer tips

This question obviously requires a working knowledge of the auditing standard referred to (ISA 510) without which students will struggle.

For part (a) as a new auditor consider the impact on this year's audit of: qualifications on the previous year's financial statements; accounting policy changes, accuracy of balances brought forward, etc.

For part (b) consider the materiality of the items concerned and the appropriate accounting treatment by reference to relevant accounting standards and principles:

For item (i) IAS 2 and IAS 8 and for item (ii) IAS 37, IAS 10 and IFRS 3 are relevant. In reaching your conclusions (and having regard to an appropriate range of potential outcomes) you must justify the wording of the audit opinions in accordance with ISAs 700-706.

(a)   **Reporting responsibilities specific to initial engagements**

For initial audit engagements, the auditor should obtain sufficient appropriate audit evidence that:

- the opening balances do not contain misstatements that materially affect the current period's financial statements;

- the prior period's closing balances have been correctly brought forward to the current period (or, where appropriate, have been restated); and

- appropriate accounting policies are consistently applied or changes in accounting policies have been properly accounted for (and adequately presented and disclosed).

If the auditor is unable to obtain sufficient appropriate audit evidence concerning opening balances they may need to modify the audit opinion. The auditor's report should include:

- a qualified ('except for') opinion;

- a disclaimer of opinion; or

- in those jurisdictions where it is permitted, an opinion which is:
  - qualified (or disclaimed) regarding the results of operations (i.e. on the statement of comprehensive income); and
  - unqualified regarding financial position (i.e. on the statement of financial position).

If the effect of a misstatement in the opening balances is not properly accounted for and adequately presented and disclosed, the auditor should express a qualified ('except for') opinion or an adverse opinion due to a misstatement, as appropriate.

If the current period's accounting policies have not been consistently applied in relation to opening balances and if the change has not been properly accounted for and adequately presented and disclosed, the auditor should similarly modify the opinion due to a misstatement ('except for' or adverse opinion as appropriate).

However, if a modification regarding the prior period's financial statements remains relevant and material to the current period's financial statements, the auditor should modify the current auditor's report accordingly.

(b)   **Tiltman Co**

Tiltman's total assets at 31 March 2006 represent 29% (16.1/55.2 × 100) of Johnston's total assets. The subsidiary is therefore material to Johnston's consolidated financial statements.

Tutorial note

Tiltman's profit for the year is not relevant as the acquisition took place just before the year end and will therefore have no impact on the consolidated statement of comprehensive income. Calculations of the effect on consolidated profit before taxation are therefore inappropriate and will not be awarded marks.

(i)   **Inventory overvaluation**

This should have been written off to the statement of comprehensive income in the year to 31 March 2005 and not spread over three years (contrary to IAS 2 *Inventories*).

At 31 March 2006 inventory is overvalued by $0.9m. This represents all Tiltmans's profit for the year and 5.6% of total assets and is material. At 31 March 2005 inventory was materially overvalued by $1.8m ($1.7m reported profit should have been a $0.1m loss).

That the prior period's auditor's report was unmodified means that the previous auditor concurred with an incorrect accounting treatment (or otherwise gave an inappropriate audit opinion).

As the matter is material a prior period adjustment is required (IAS 8 *Accounting Policies, Changes in Accounting Estimates and Errors*). $1.8m should be written off against opening reserves (i.e. restated as at 1 April 2005).

(ii) **Restructuring provision**

$2.3m expense has been charged to Tiltman's profit and loss in arriving at a draft profit of $0.7m. This is very material. (The provision represents 14.3% of Tiltman's total assets and is material to the statement of financial position date also.)

The provision for redundancies and onerous contracts should not have been made for the year ended 31 March 2006 unless there was a constructive obligation at the statement of financial position date (IAS 37 *Provisions, Contingent Liabilities and Contingent Assets*). So, unless the main features of the restructuring plan had been announced to those affected (i.e. redundancy notifications issued to employees), the provision should be reversed. However, it should then be disclosed as a non-adjusting post statement of financial position event (IAS 10 *Events After the Statement of financial position Date*).

Given the short time (less than one month) between acquisition and the statement of financial position it is very possible that a constructive obligation does not arise at the statement of financial position date. The relocation in May was only part of a restructuring (and could be the first evidence that Johnston's management has started to implement a restructuring plan).

There is a risk that goodwill on consolidation of Tiltman may be overstated in Johnston's consolidated financial statements. To avoid the $2.3m expense having a significant effect on post-acquisition profit (which may be negligible due to the short time between acquisition and year end), Johnston may have recognized it as a liability in the determination of goodwill on acquisition.

However, the execution of Tiltman's restructuring plan, though made for the year ended 31 March 2006, was conditional upon its acquisition by Johnston. It does not therefore represent, immediately before the business combination, a present obligation of Johnston. Nor is it a contingent liability of Johnston immediately before the combination. Therefore Johnston cannot recognize a liability for Tiltman's restructuring plans as part of allocating the cost of the combination (IFRS 3 *Business Combinations*).

Tiltman's auditor's report

The following adjustments are required to the financial statements:

- restructuring provision, $2.3m, eliminated;
- adequate disclosure of relocation as a non-adjusting post statement of financial position event;
- current period inventory written down by $0.9m;
- prior period inventory (and reserves) written down by $1.8m.

Profit for the year to 31 March 2006 should be $3.9m ($0.7 + $0.9 + $2.3).

If all these adjustments are made the auditor's report should be unmodified. Otherwise, the auditor's report should be modified 'except for' due to material misstatement. If none of the adjustments are made, the modification should still be 'except for' as the matters are not pervasive.

Johnston's auditor's report

If Tiltman's auditor's report is unmodified (because the required adjustments are made) the auditor's report of Johnston should be similarly unmodified. As Tiltman is wholly-owned by Johnston there should be no problem getting the adjustments made.

If no adjustments were made in Tiltman's financial statements, adjustments could be made on consolidation, if necessary, to avoid modification of the auditor's report on Johnston's financial statements.

The effect of these adjustments on Tiltman's net assets is an increase of $1.4m. Goodwill arising on consolidation (if any) would be reduced by $1.4m. The reduction in consolidated total assets required ($0.9m + $1.4m) is therefore the same as the reduction in consolidated total liabilities (i.e. $2.3m). $2.3m is material (4.2% consolidated total assets). If Tiltman's financial statements are not adjusted and no adjustments are made on consolidation, the consolidated financial position (statement of financial position) should be modified 'except for'. The results of operations (i.e. profit for the period) should be unmodified (if permitted in the jurisdiction in which Johnston reports).

Adjustment in respect of the inventory valuation may not be required as Johnston should have consolidated inventory at fair value on acquisition. In this case, consolidated total liabilities should be reduced by $2.3m and goodwill arising on consolidation (if any) reduced by $2.3m.

Tutorial note

The effect of any possible goodwill impairment has been ignored as the subsidiary has only just been acquired and the statement of financial position date is very close to the date of acquisition.

---

40 BEIGE INTERIORS (A)

Key answer tips

In part (a) a definition of materiality is not called for whereas an appreciation of its relevance and context at the different stages of an audit is.

In part (b) requires an understanding of the appropriate wording in different circumstances.

(a) **Materiality**

Planning stage

- An audit is planned (and performed) to provide reasonable assurance that the financial statements are free from material misstatement (and give a true and fair view).

- Assessing materiality is a matter of professional judgment, made in light of the surrounding circumstances. This is affected by both the size and/or the nature of the misstatement.

- The auditor's determination of materiality is affected by their perception of the financial information needs of the users of the financial statements.

- The assessment of materiality at the planning stage provides a basis for determining the nature, timing and extent of risk assessment procedures; identifying and assessing the risk of material misstatement; and determining the nature, timing and extent of further audit procedures.

- When establishing audit strategy the auditor shall determine materiality for the financial statements as a whole. However the auditor also needs to consider 'performance materiality.' This is an amount set at below the materiality level for the financial statements as a whole that reduces, to an acceptable level, the probability that the aggregate of uncorrected/undetected misstatements exceeds materiality for the financial statements as a whole.

- If the entity has more than one class of transaction or account balance for which misstatements lower than materiality could influence the decisions of users then the auditor shall determine materiality to be applied to those classes of transactions and balances.

Overall review stage

- If the financial statements are perceived to contain any material misstatement (whether due to a misstatement that breaches the materiality level set for the accounts as a whole; or the total of individually immaterial misstatements that in aggregate breach materiality; or for a particular balance/class of transaction assessed in relation to its own materiality limit) the audit report would require modification.

- At this stage qualitative factors may render monetary (quantifiable) materiality irrelevant. For example, where matters are required to be disclosed in accordance with the financial reporting framework (e.g. related party transactions).

(b) **Suitability of Jade's draft**

- Jade has drafted a 'disclaimer' of opinion, which is appropriate if the effect of being unable to obtain sufficient appropriate evidence is considered pervasive.

Principal matters relevant to forming an appropriate opinion

- Conduct of the audit in compliance with International Standards on Auditing (ISAs) is affected if the auditor is unable to gather sufficient appropriate audit evidence. The fact that some accounting records were not available means that the scope of the audit has been limited. Although Jade has stated this, users of the financial statements will not know which accounting records were missing, or why, or the accounting period covered.

- An audit includes an assessment of significant estimates and judgments made by management. Management will have had to make estimates and judgments with regard to the reconstruction of financial information. Evidence about transactions in the first four months of the financial year may not be sufficient to form an unmodified opinion. Factors to be taken into account include the extent to which financial records have been reconstructed (e.g. from prior year closing balances, bank statements, invoices, etc). The adequacy of management's disclosure in the notes to the financial statements about the effects of reconstruction on classes of transactions and account balances will affect how much disclosure needs to be made in the auditor's report. If there is none, as in Jade's draft, there should be a cross-reference to the notes.

- An unmodified opinion provides reasonable assurance that the financial statements are free of misstatement caused by fraud or error. Even if the amount of reconstruction was extensive the auditor would most likely modify their opinion 'to be on the safe side'. Error is generally quantifiable. The former CEO's actions (and timing) may suggest fraudulent reporting which may not be quantifiable (in the absence of accounting records). Jade has not referred to 'fraud' or the CEO. This is appropriate as there can only be suspicion of fraud (until it is proven in law) and it would not be reported on.

- Depending on the amount of reconstruction undertaken the potential misstatement, though material, may not be pervasive. Jade has supposed the matter to be pervasive in disclaiming an opinion on the financial statements as a whole. However, the loss of accounting records is unlikely to affect the carrying amounts of non-current assets, inventory, trade receivables, cash at bank etc as at 30 September 2004. Disclaiming an opinion on the statement of comprehensive income can be achieved with 'except for'.

- The prior year audit opinion (unmodified) may not have been appropriate. The accounting records that were taken would have provided evidence about balances at 30 September 2003. The auditor should reconsider the extent to which the CEO contributed to sufficient evidence in forming the prior period opinion. The fact that the prior year's opinion was unmodified does not preclude a disclaimer of opinion on the comparative information. Since reference to comparatives is not standard wording Jade has not considered this.

41 JINACK (A)

Key answer tips

Part (a) requires a knowledge of IAS 10 and the auditor's responsibilities at the different phases of the audit as described in ISA 560 *Subsequent events.*

Part (b) requires application of these principles and an understanding of the consequential effects on the wording of the audit report in a given set of circumstances.

(a) **Auditor's responsibilities for subsequent events**

- Auditors must consider the effect of subsequent events on:
    - the financial statements;
    - the auditor's report.
- Subsequent events are *all* events occurring after a period end (i.e. reporting date) i.e.:
    - events after the statement of financial position date (as defined in IAS 10); and
    - events after the financial statements have been authorised for issue.

Events occurring up to date of auditor's report

- The auditor is responsible for carrying out procedures designed to obtain sufficient appropriate audit evidence that all events up to the date of the auditor's report that may require adjustment of, or disclosure in, the financial statements have been identified.
- These procedures are in addition to those applied to specific transactions occurring after the period end that provide audit evidence of period-end account balances (e.g. inventory cut-off and receipts from trade receivables). Such procedures should ordinarily include:
    - reviewing minutes of board/audit committee meetings;
    - scrutinising latest interim financial statements/budgets/cash flows, etc;
    - making/extending inquiries to legal advisors on litigation matters;
    - inquiring of management whether any subsequent events have occurred that might affect the financial statements (e.g. commitments entered into).
- When the auditor becomes aware of events that materially affect the financial statements, the auditor must consider whether they have been properly accounted for and adequately disclosed in the financial statements.

Facts discovered after the date of the auditor's report but before financial statements are issued

- If the auditor becomes aware of such facts which may materially affect the financial statements, the auditor:
    - considers whether the financial statements need amendment;
    - discusses the matter with management; and
    - takes appropriate action (e.g. audit any amendments to the financial statements and issue a new auditor's report).

- If management does not amend the financial statements (where the auditor believes they need to be amended) and the auditor's report has not been released to the entity, the auditor should express a qualified opinion or an adverse opinion (as appropriate).

- If the auditor's report has been released to the entity, the auditor must notify those charged with governance not to issue the financial statements (and the auditor's report thereon) to third parties.

Facts discovered after the financial statements have been issued

- The auditor has no obligation to make any enquiry regarding financial statements that have been issued.

- However, if the auditor becomes aware of a fact which existed at the date of the auditor's report and which, if known at that date, may have caused the auditor's report to be modified, the auditor should:

   – consider whether the financial statements need revision;

   – discuss the matter with management; and

   – take appropriate action (e.g. issuing a new report on revised financial statements).

(b) **Implications for the auditor's report**

(i) *Corruption of perpetual inventory records*

- The loss of data (of physical inventory quantities at the statement of financial position date) means the auditor may not be able to obtain sufficient appropriate evidence.

- The systems failure in October 2005 is clearly a non-adjusting event after the reporting period (IAS 10). If it is material (such that non-disclosure could influence the economic decisions of users) Jinack should disclose:

   – the nature of the event (i.e. systems failure); and

   – an estimate of its financial effect (i.e. the cost of disruption and reconstruction of data to the extent that it is not covered by insurance).

- If material this disclosure could be made in the context of explaining how inventory has been estimated at 30 September 2005 (see later). If such disclosure, that the auditor considers to be necessary, is not made, the audit opinion should be modified 'except for' due to a material misstatement (i.e. lack of disclosure).

- The inability to obtain sufficient appropriate evidence has been imposed by circumstances. Jinack's accounting records (for inventory) are inadequate (non-existent) for the auditor to perform tests on them.

- An alternative procedure to obtain sufficient appropriate audit evidence of inventory quantities at a year-end is subsequent count and 'rollback'. However, the extent of 'roll back' testing is limited as records are still under reconstruction.

- The auditor may be able to obtain sufficient evidence that there is no material misstatement through a combination of procedures:

   – testing management's controls over counting inventory after the statement of financial position date and recording inventory movements (e.g. sales and goods received);

   – reperforming the reconstruction for significant items on a sample basis;

- analytical procedures, such as a review of profit margins by inventory category.

- 'An extensive range of inventory' is clearly material. The matter (i.e. systems failure) is not however pervasive, as only inventory is affected.

- Unless the reconstruction is substantially completed (i.e. inventory items not accounted for are insignificant) the auditor cannot determine what adjustment, if any, might be determined necessary. The auditor's report should then be modified, 'except for.'

- However, if sufficient evidence is obtained the auditor's report should be unmodified.

- An 'emphasis of matter' paragraph would not be appropriate because this matter is not one of significant uncertainty.

2006

- If the 2005 auditor's report is modified 'except for' due to a lack of sufficient appropriate evidence there are two possibilities for the inventory figure as at 30 September 2005 determined on completion of the reconstruction exercise:

    (1) it is not materially different from the inventory figure reported; or

    (2) it is materially different.

- In (1), with the lack of evidence now removed, the need for modification is removed and the 2006 auditor's report would be unmodified (in respect of this matter).

- In (2) the opening position should be restated and the comparatives adjusted in accordance with IAS 8 *Accounting Policies, Changes in Accounting Estimates and Errors*. The 2006 auditor's report would again be unmodified.

(ii) *Wholly-owned foreign subsidiary*

- The cash transfer is a non-adjusting post statement of financial position event. It indicates that Batik was trading after the statement of financial position date. However, that does not preclude Batik having commenced trading before the year end.

- The finance director's oral representation is wholly insufficient evidence with regard to the existence (or otherwise) of Batik at 30 September 2005. If it existed at the statement of financial position date its financial statements should have been consolidated (unless immaterial).

- The evidence that might reasonably be expected to be available includes legal papers, registration payments, etc.

- If such evidence has been sought but not obtained then the auditor may have to modify their opinion on the basis of not being able to obtain sufficient appropriate evidence.

- Whilst the transaction itself may not be material, the information concerning the existence of Batik may be material to users and should therefore be disclosed (as a non-adjusting event). The absence of such disclosure, if the auditor considered necessary, would result in a qualified 'except for', opinion.

- If Batik existed at the statement of financial position date and had material assets and liabilities then its non-consolidation would have a pervasive effect. This would warrant an adverse opinion.

- Also, the nature of the lack of evidence could have a pervasive effect if the auditor is suspicious that other audit evidence has been withheld. In this case the auditor should disclaim an opinion

42 HEGAS (A)

Key answer tips

To answer this question effectively students must be able to clearly distinguish between their reporting responsibilities for the financial statements themselves (and their composition), the directors' report and, other information (for example the chairman's report). A working knowledge of ISAs 700-706 and 720 is therefore a pre-requisite. Materiality levels should always be considered where information in the question permits as well as relevant accounting/disclosure requirements.

(a) **Auditor's responsibilities for 'other information'**

- The auditor has a professional responsibility to read other information to identify material inconsistencies with the audited financial statements (ISA 720 *The Auditor's Responsibilities Relating to Other Information in Documents Containing Audited Financial Statements*).

- A 'material inconsistency' arises when other information contradicts that which is contained in the audited financial statements. It may give rise to doubts about:
  - the auditor's conclusions drawn from audit evidence; and
  - the basis for the auditor's opinion on the financial statements.

- In certain circumstances, the auditor may have a statutory obligation (under national legislation) to report on other information (e.g. Management Report).

- Even where there is no such obligation (e.g. chairman's statement), the auditor should consider it, as the credibility of the financial statements may be undermined by any inconsistency.

- The auditor must arrange to have access to the other information on a timely basis prior to dating the auditor's report.

Material inconsistency

- If a material inconsistency is identified, the auditor should determine whether it is the audited financial statements or the other information which needs amending.

- If an amendment to the audited financial statements is required but not made, there will be misstatement, which may result in the expression of a qualified or adverse opinion. (Such a situation would be extremely rare.)

- Where an amendment to other information is necessary, but refused, the auditor's report may include an Other Matter paragraph (since the audit opinion cannot be other than unmodified with respect to this matter).

Material misstatement of fact

- A material misstatement of fact in other information exists when information which is not related to matters appearing in the audited financial statements is incorrectly stated or presented in a misleading manner.

- If management do not act on advice to correct a material misstatement the auditors should document their concerns to those charged with corporate governance and obtain legal advice.

(b) **Implications for the auditor's report**

(i) *Management Report*

- $4.5 million represents 3.75% of total assets, 1.7% of revenue and 48.9% profit before tax. As this is material by any criteria (exceeding all of 2% of total assets, $^1/_2$% revenue and 5% PBT), the specific disclosure requirements of IASs need to be met (IAS 1 *Presentation of Financial Statements*).

- The Management Report discloses the amount and the reason for a material change in equity whereas the financial statements do not show the reason for the change and suggest that it is immaterial. As the increase in equity attributable to this adjustment is nearly half as much as that attributable to PBT there is a material inconsistency between the Management Report and the audited financial statements.

- Amendment to the Management Report is not required.

- Amendment to the financial statements is required because the disclosure is:

  – incorrect – as, on first adoption of IAS 40, the fair value adjustment should be against the opening balance of retained earnings; and

  – inadequate – because it is being 'supplemented' by additional disclosure in a document which is not within the scope of the audit of financial statements.

- Whilst it is true that the adoption of IAS 40 did not have a significant impact on results of operations, Hegas's financial position has increased by nearly 4% in respect of the revaluation (to fair value) of just one asset category (investment properties). As this is significant, the statement in the notes should be redrafted.

- If the financial statements are not amended, the auditor's report should be modified 'except for' on grounds of misstatement (non-compliance with IAS 40) as the matter is material but not pervasive. Additional disclosure should also be given (e.g. that the 'other difference' is a fair value adjustment).

- However, it is likely that when faced with the prospect of a modified auditor's report Hegas' management will rectify the financial statements so that an unmodified auditor's report can be issued.

(ii) *Chairman's statement*

- The assertion in the chairman's statement, which does not fall within the scope of the audit of the financial statements, claims two things, namely that the company:

  (1) is 'one of the world's largest generators of hydro-electricity'; and

  (2) has 'a dedicated commitment to accountable ethical professionalism'.

- To the extent that this information does not relate to matters disclosed in the financial statements it may give rise to a material misstatement of fact. In particular, the first statement presents a misleading impression of the company's size. In misleading a user of the financial statements with this statement, the second statement is not true (as it is not ethical or professional to mislead the reader and potentially undermine the credibility of the financial statements).

- The first statement is a material misstatement of fact because, for example:

  - the company is privately-owned, and publicly-owned international/multi-nationals are larger;

  - the company's main activity is civil engineering not electricity generation (only 14% of revenue is derived from HEP);

  - as the company ranks at best eighth against African companies alone it ranks much lower globally.

- Hegas should be asked to reconsider the wording of the chairman's statement (i.e. removing these assertions) and consult, as necessary, the company's legal advisor.

- If the statement is not changed there will be no grounds for modification of the opinion on the audited financial statements. The audit firm should therefore take legal advice on how the matter should be reported.

- However, an Other Matter paragraph may be used to report on matters other than those affecting the audited financial statements. For example, to explain the misstatement of fact if management refuses to make the amendment.

Tutorial note

Marks will also be awarded for relevant comments about the chairman's statement being perceived by many readers to be subject to audit and therefore that the unfounded statement might undermine the credibility of the financial statements. Shareholders tend to rely on the chairman's statement, even though it is not regulated or audited, because modern financial statements are so complex.

43 KITE ASSOCIATES (A)

Key answer tips

As well as an understanding of what 'quality' is, *Part (a)* requires a practical solution to the problem of achieving quality control in a small firm environment. Its rather like the problem that small companies have in establishing effective internal control – the difficulties of having small numbers of people. *Part (b)* requires a working knowledge of ISAs 700-706 and the nature and wording of modifications.

(a)   **Quality control in a smaller audit firm**

Why difficult to implement

Audit quality depends, inter alia, on the quality of the people. Smaller firms may lack resources and specialist (audit) expertise. In particular, small firms may not be able to offer the same reward structures to attract and retain staff as larger firms.

Also, whereas larger firms can afford to recruit staff in sufficient numbers to allow for subsequent leavers and provide for their training needs, smaller firms may not be able to offer the same training opportunities. Prospective trainees may perceive a smaller firm's client base to be less attractive than that of a larger firm (e.g. in terms of the on-the-job training which it offers).

Smaller practices may have less scope to provide staff with internal and on-the-job training and costs of external training may be costly in comparison and also fail to provide the 'hands-on' experience necessary for professional development.

The cost of access to external specialists may be prohibitive for smaller firms.

Audit committees play an oversight role which contributes to quality control in larger firms (e.g. on matters of client acceptance/retention, independence issues, etc). When the client base is largely of owner-managed businesses, as for many smaller audit firms, there are no non-executive directors to support the auditor when difficult issues arise.

Quality control requires leadership within the firm. In a larger firm one senior partner may have responsibility for establishing quality control policies and procedures and another, responsibility for monitoring work performed. Splitting these roles may not be practical for a smaller firm (and impossible for sole practitioners).

Small firms operate in a highly competitive environment for audit work and are often busy with non-audit work and under-resourced. Technical updating on audit matters may not be as regular as desirable and audit practice may become inefficient.

How overcome

Where in a larger firm quality control procedures might be the responsibility of a central technical team, in a smaller firm those same responsibilities might be distributed between the reporting partners.

Smaller firms may draw, judiciously, on the expertise of suitably qualified external consultants (e.g. on technical matters).

Small firms and sole practitioners have the same access to a wide range of technical and ethical advisory services provided by ACCA (and other professional bodies) and should take advantage of these.

Small firms may work together as a consortium to share training opportunities and sometimes staff. For example, an association of small firms may adopt the same methodology and meet annually (say) for technical updates.

(b)   **Lammergeier Group – auditor's report**

- The report is confused. It is clearly headed 'Qualified opinion arising from material misstatement ...' yet the reasons for departure (from IAS 7) are 'sound and acceptable'. The heading is a statement of disagreement with the application of a standard, the latter a statement of concurrence. If the auditor concurs with a departure the opinion should not be modified.

- What is 'IAS 7'? This should be stated in full, i.e. 'International Accounting Standard 7 Cash Flow Statements'.

- It might be simpler/clearer to head the opinion paragraph 'Qualified opinion arising from omission of statement of cashflows'.

- The auditors should not be expressing an opinion of Lammergeier's management in their report. Management's 'justification' should be set out in a note to the financial statements (e.g. in the accounting policies section). The auditor's report should clearly state that there is non-compliance with IAS 7. For example, 'As explained in note ... the financial statements do not contain a statement of cashflows as required by IAS 7 [written out in full]'.

- It cannot be true that the departure 'does not impact on the truth and fairness ...'. The requirement to prepare a statement of cashflows (and its associated notes) stems from the need to provide users of financial statements with information about changes in financial resources. If this information is omitted the financial statements cannot show a true and fair view.

- 'Except for [the non-preparation of the group statements of cashflows and associated notes] ....' is a modified audit opinion. This contradicts Rook & Co's assertion that the matter 'does not impact on the truth and fairness ...'.

- If the departure from IAS 7 were justified it would assist the user of the financial statements to know precisely where the 'adequate disclosure has been made'. If the auditor wished to draw attention to the matter, without modifying the audit opinion, an Other Matter paragraph should refer to the specific note where the departure is explained.

- The grounds for non-compliance is 'the complexity involved'. This does not seem likely. IAS 7 offers no exemption on these (or any other) grounds.

- The fact that the audit opinion was similarly modified in the prior year shows that the matter has not been resolved even after a year.

- It is possible that, having modified on the prior year, it was an 'easy option' to do so again in the same terms rather than draft a more appropriate opinion for the consecutive year.

- The 2003 opinion makes no reference to the fact that the matter is 'not new' and that the opinion was similarly modified in the prior year.

Section 5

PILOT PAPER EXAM QUESTIONS

SECTION A – <u>BOTH</u> QUESTIONS ARE COMPULSORY AND <u>MUST</u> BE ATTEMPTED

1 BEESKI CO

You are an audit manager in Ribi & Co, a firm of Chartered Certified Accountants. One of your audit clients Beeski Co provides satellite broadcasting services in a rapidly growing market.

In November 2005 Beeski purchased Xstatic Co, a competitor group of companies. Significant revenue, cost and capital expenditure synergies are expected as the operations of Beeski and Xstatic are being combined into one group of companies.

The following financial and operating information consolidates the results of the enlarged Beeski group:

	Year end 30 September	
	2006 (Estimated)	**2005 (Actual)**
	$m	**$m**
Revenue	6,827	4,404
Cost of sales	(3,109)	(1,991)
Distribution costs and administrative expenses	(2,866)	(1,700)
Research and development costs	(25)	(22)
Depreciation and amortization	(927)	(661)
Interest expense	(266)	(202)
Loss before taxation	(366)	(172)
Customers	14.9m	7.6m
Average revenue per customer (ARPC)	$437	$556

In August 2006 Beeski purchased MTbox Co, a large cable communications provider in India, where your firm has no representation. The financial statements of MTbox for the year ending 30 September 2006 will continue to be audited by a local firm of Chartered Certified Accountants. MTbox's activities have not been reflected in the above estimated results of the group. Beeski is committed to introducing its corporate image into India.

In order to sustain growth, significant costs are expected to be incurred as operations are expanded, networks upgraded and new products and services introduced.

Required:

(a) Identify and describe the principal business risks for the Beeski group. **(9 marks)**

(b) Explain what effect the acquisitions will have on the planning of Ribi & Co's audit of the consolidated financial statements of Beeski Co for the year ending 30 September 2006. **(10 marks)**

(c) Explain the role of 'support letters' (also called 'comfort letters') as evidence in the audit of financial statements. **(6 marks)**

(d) Discuss how 'horizontal groups' (i.e. non-consolidated entities under common control) affect the scope of an audit and the audit work undertaken. **(5 marks)**

(Total: 30 marks)

2 EFEX ENGINEERING CO

You have been asked to carry out an investigation by the management of Xzibit Co. One of the company's subsidiaries, Efex Engineering Co, has been making losses for the past year. Xzibit's management is concerned about the accuracy of Efex Engineering's most recent quarter's management accounts.

The summarized statements of comprehensive income for the last three quarters are as follows:

Quarter to	30 June 2006	31 March 2006	31 December 2005
	$000	$000	$000
Revenue	429	334	343
	——	——	——
Opening inventory	180	163	203
Materials	318	251	200
Direct wages	62	54	74
	——	——	——
	560	468	477
	——	——	——
Less: Closing inventory	(162)	(180)	(163)
	——	——	——
Cost of goods sold	398	288	314
	——	——	——
Gross profit	31	46	29
Less: Overheads	(63)	(75)	(82)
	——	——	——
Net loss	(32)	(29)	(53)
	——	——	——
Gross profit (%)	7.2%	13.8%	8.5%
Materials (% of revenue)	78.3%	70.0%	70.0%
Labour (% of revenue)	14.5%	16.2%	21.6%

Xzibit's management board believes that the high material consumption as a percentage of revenue for the quarter to 30 June 2006 is due to one or more of the following factors:

(1)   under-counting or under-valuation of closing inventory;

(2)   excessive consumption or wastage of materials;

(3)   material being stolen by employees or other individuals.

Efex Engineering has a small number of large customers and manufactures its products to each customer's specification. The selling price of the product is determined by:

(1)   estimating the cost of materials;

(2)   estimating the labour cost;

(3)   adding a mark-up to cover overheads and provide a normal profit.

The estimated costs are not compared with actual costs. Although it is possible to analyse purchase invoices for materials between customers' orders this analysis has not been done.

A physical inventory count is carried out at the end of each quarter. Items of inventory are entered on stocksheets and valued manually. The company does not maintain perpetual inventory records and a full physical count is to be carried out at the financial year end, 30 September 2006.

The direct labour cost included in the inventory valuation is small and should be assumed to be constant at the end of each quarter. Historically, the cost of materials consumed has been about 70% of revenue.

The management accounts to 31 March 2006 are to be assumed to be correct.

Required:

(a)   **Define 'forensic auditing' and describe its application to fraud investigations.**
(5 marks)

(b)   **Identify and describe the matters that you should consider and the procedures you should carry out in order to plan an investigation of Efex Engineering Co's losses.**
(10 marks)

(c)   (i)   **Explain the matters you should consider to determine whether closing inventory at 30 June 2006 is undervalued; and**

(ii)   **Describe the tests you should plan to perform to quantify the amount of any undervaluation.**   **(8 marks)**

(d)   (i)   **Identify and explain the possible reasons for the apparent high materials consumption in the quarter ended 30 June 2006; and**

(ii)   **Describe the tests you should plan to perform to determine whether materials consumption, as shown in the management accounts, is correct.**
(7 marks)

(Total: 30 marks)

SECTION B – TWO QUESTIONS ONLY TO BE ATTEMPTED

3   INGOT & CO

You are a manager in Ingot & Co, a firm of Chartered Certified Accountants, with specific responsibility for the quality of audits. Ingot was appointed auditor of Argenta Co, a provider of waste management services, in July 2006. You have just visited the audit team at Argenta's head office. The audit team comprises an accountant in charge (AIC), an audit senior and two trainees.

Argenta's draft accounts for the year ended 30 June 2006 show revenue of $11.6 million (2005 – $8.1 million) and total assets of $3.6 million (2005 – $2.5 million). During your visit, a review of the audit working papers revealed the following:

(a)   On the audit planning checklist, the audit senior has crossed through the analytical procedures section and written 'not applicable – new client'. The audit planning checklist has not been signed off as having been reviewed.   (4 marks)

(b)   The AIC last visited Argenta's office when the final audit commenced two weeks ago on 1 August. The senior has since completed the audit of tangible non-current assets (including property and service equipment) which amount to $0.6 million as at 30 June 2006 (2005 – $0.6 million). The AIC spends most of his time working from Ingot's office and is currently allocated to three other assignments as well as Argenta's audit.   (4 marks)

(c)   At 30 June 2006 trade receivables amounted to $2.1 million (2005 – $0.9 million). One of the trainees has just finished sending out first requests for direct confirmation of customers' balances as at the statement of financial position date.   (4 marks)

(d)   The other trainee has been assigned to the audit of the consumable supplies that comprise inventory amounting to $88,000 (2005 – $53,000). The trainee has carried out tests of controls over the perpetual inventory records and confirmed the 'roll-back' of a sample of current quantities to book quantities as at the year end.   (3 marks)

(e)   The AIC has noted the following matter for your attention. The financial statements to 30 June 2005 disclosed, as unquantifiable, a contingent liability for pending litigation. However, the AIC has seen a letter confirming that the matter was settled out of court for $0.45 million on 14 September 2005. The auditor's report on the financial statements for the year ended 30 June 2005 was unmodified and signed on 19 September 2005. The AIC believes that Argenta's management is not aware of the error and has not brought it to their attention.   (5 marks)

Required:

Identify and comment on the implications of these findings for Ingot & Co's quality control policies and procedures.

Note: The mark allocation is shown against each of the five issues.   (Total: 20 marks)

4   AXIS & CO

You are the manager responsible for four audit clients of Axis & Co, a firm of Chartered Certified Accountants. The year end in each case is 30 June 2006.

You are currently reviewing the audit working paper files and the audit seniors' recommendations for the auditors' reports. Details are as follows:

(a)   **Mantis Co is a subsidiary of Cube Co. Serious going concern problems have been noted during this year's audit. Mantis will be unable to trade for the foreseeable future unless it continues to receive financial support from the parent company. Mantis has received a letter of support ('comfort letter') from Cube Co.**

The audit senior has suggested that, due to the seriousness of the situation, the audit opinion must at least be qualified 'except for'.   **(5 marks)**

(b)   **Lorenze Co has changed its accounting policy for goodwill during the year from amortization over its estimated useful life to annual impairment testing. No disclosure of this change has been given in the financial statements. The carrying amount of goodwill in the statement of financial position as at 30 June 2006 is the same as at 30 June 2005 as management's impairment test show that it is not impaired.**

The audit senior has concluded that a qualification is not required but suggests that attention can be drawn to the change by way of an emphasis of matter paragraph.
(6 marks)

(c)   The directors' report of Abrupt Co states that investment property rental forms a major part of revenue. However, a note to the financial statements shows that property rental represents only 1.6% of total revenue for the year. The audit senior is satisfied that the revenue figures are correct.

The audit senior has noted that an unqualified opinion should be given as the audit opinion does not extend to the directors' report.   **(4 marks)**

(d)   **Audit work on the after-date bank transactions of Jingle Co has identified a transfer of cash from Bell Co. The audit senior assigned to the audit of Jingle has documented that Jingle's finance director explained that Bell commenced trading on 7 July 2006, after being set up as a wholly-owned foreign subsidiary of Jingle.**

The audit senior has noted that although no other evidence has been obtained an unmodified opinion is appropriate because the matter does not impact on the current year's financial statements.   **(5 marks)**

Required:

For each situation, comment on the suitability or otherwise of the audit senior's proposals for the auditors' reports. Where you disagree, indicate what audit modification (if any) should be given instead.

Note: **The mark allocation is shown against each of the four issues.**   **(Total: 20 marks)**

5 DEDZA & CO

(a) Comment on the need for ethical guidance for accountants on money laundering.

(5 marks)

(b) You are senior manager in Dedza & Co, a firm of Chartered Certified Accountants. Recently, you have been assigned specific responsibility for undertaking annual reviews of existing clients. The following situations have arisen in connection with three clients:

(i) Dedza was appointed auditor and tax advisor to Kora Co last year and has recently issued an unmodified opinion on the financial statements for the year ended 31 March 2006. To your surprise, the tax authority has just launched an investigation into the affairs of Kora on suspicion of underdeclaring income. (7 marks)

(ii) The chief executive of Xalam Co, an exporter of specialist equipment, has asked for advice on the accounting treatment and disclosure of payments being made for security consultancy services. The payments, which aim to ensure that consignments are not impounded in the destination country of a major customer, may be material to the financial statements for the year ending 31 December 2006. Xalam does not treat these payments as tax deductible. (4 marks)

(iii) Your firm has provided financial advice to the Pholey family for many years and this has sometimes involved your firm in carrying out transactions on their behalf. The eldest son, Esau, is to take up a position as a senior government official to a foreign country next month. (4 marks)

Required:

Identify and comment on the ethical and other professional issues raised by each of these matters and state what action, if any, Dedza & Co should now take.

Note: The mark allocation is shown against each of the three situations.

(Total: 20 marks)

Section 6

ANSWERS TO PILOT PAPER EXAM QUESTIONS

1 BEESKI CO

(a) Principal business risks

Communications industry

- Rapid and new technological developments in the industry, providing faster data transmission and increasingly interactive capabilities, will render certain existing products and services obsolete.

- Beeski cannot predict how emerging and future technologies (e.g. 'Bluetooth') will affect demand for its services.

Competition

- Although Beeski may have reduced competition in the short-term (by having acquired a competitor), the communications market is still expanding. Increasing competition from other existing and new competitors offering new technologies could:
    - affect Beeski's ability to attract and retain customers
    - reduce Beeski's share of new and existing customers
    - force Beeski to reduce prices.

- The cost (and revenue-generating capabilities) of new technologies tends to fall significantly and relatively quickly (e.g. mobile phone technology is available in disposable form).

Integration

- Combining two groups which have previously operated independently (and competitively against each other) is likely to result in disruption.

- Potential difficulties may be encountered in seeking to retain customers and key personnel.

- The anticipated 'significant synergies' (in revenue, cost and capital expenditure) may have been optimistic. If they do not materialize to the extent predicted, Beeski's operational activities, financial condition and future prospects are likely to be adversely affected.

- Beeski may have difficulty in adapting its corporate image to the culture of the Indian network.

Operating losses

- Loss before taxation has more than doubled (increased by 113%). If Xstatic was making significant losses before it was acquired by Beeski those losses may have been expected to continue in the short-term. Although the groups operations are being combined and synergies are expected, recurring losses will clearly threaten the new group's operational existence as a going concern.

Falling ARPC

- ARPC, a key performance indicator, has fallen by more than 20% ((437-556/556 = 21.4%). This is likely to reflect falling tariffs in a competitive market.

- Although the number of customers has nearly doubled (increased by 96%), revenue has increased by only 55%. It seems unlikely that such a growth in customer base can be maintained, therefore the reduction in tariffs could result in falling revenues.

- Some (if not all) of the growth, is due to the acquisition of Xstatic. The fall in ARPC may indicate that Xstatic's ARPC (now absorbed into the enlarged Beeski group) is substantially less than that of Beeski. If Xstatic's tariffs were lower than Beeski's because it was offering a lower level of service it may be difficult for Beeski to increase them albeit for an enhanced service.

Sustaining growth

- Growth may not be sustainable as further expansion will incur significant costs and investment which must be financed.

- The significant costs expected to be incurred in upgrading networks may not be recouped if additional revenues are insufficient. Failure to maintain existing networks is likely to result in a loss of customers and market share.

- If Beeski's financial resources are insufficient to meet the operating losses it may need to issue equity and/or increase its debt. Possible adverse consequences of increasing indebtedness include:

    - high debt-service costs;

    - operating and financial restrictions being imposed by lenders;

    - difficulty in obtaining further finance in the future;

    - being unable to take advantage of business opportunities;

    - reduction in credit ratings.

Tutorial note

Although there are relatively explicit pointers to the above business risks in the scenario, marks will also be awarded for other risks which are perhaps more implicit (as illustrated below).

Countries of operation

- Operations have been expanded from European countries to India. Beeski's inexperience of economic and legal developments in India may impair the investment in MTbox.

Foreign exchange rates

- Beeski transacts business in several countries and foreign exchange rate fluctuations could have a material adverse affect on operating results.

Highly regulated market

- Network operations could be adversely affected by changes in the laws, regulations or government policies which regulate the industry.

- Difficulties in obtaining approvals for the erection and operation of transmitters could have an adverse effect on the extent, quality and capacity of Beeski's network coverage.

- Allegations of health risks (e.g. associated with radio waves from transmitter masts and mobile handsets) could reduce customer demand and increase exposure to potential litigation.

Tutorial note

Candidates are not expected to have knowledge of industry-related complexities (e.g. of licensing, subsidies and network recharging) – however, appropriate marks would be awarded for comments on such business risks arising.

(b) **Impact of acquisition on planning**

Group structure

The new group structure must be ascertained to identify the entities that should be consolidated into the group financial statements of Beeski for the year ending 30 September 2006.

Materiality assessment

Preliminary materiality will be much higher, in monetary terms, than in the prior year. For example, if a % of revenue is a determinant of preliminary materiality, it will increase by 55% (based on estimate).

The materiality of each subsidiary should be assessed, in terms of the enlarged group as at the planning stage. For example, any subsidiary contributing more than 10% of the group's assets and revenue (but not result) is material and less than 5% (say) is not. This will identify, for example:

- those entities requiring an audit visit by the principal auditor; and

- those for which analytical procedures may suffice.

If MTbox is particularly material to the group, Ribi may plan (provisionally) to visit MTbox's auditors to discuss any problems shown to arise in their audit work summary (see group instructions below).

Goodwill arising

The audit plan should draw attention to the need to audit the amount of goodwill arising on the acquisitions and management's impairment test at the statement of financial position date.

The assets and liabilities of Xstatic and MTbox, at fair value to the group, will be combined on a line-by-line basis and any goodwill arising recognized.

The calculation of the amount attributed to goodwill must be agreed to be the excess of the cost of the acquisition over the fair value of the identifiable assets and liabilities existing at the date of acquisition (Xstatic – November 2005, MTbox – August 2006).

Significant non-current assets such as properties are likely to have been independently valued prior to the acquisition. It may be appropriate to plan to place reliance on the work of quantity surveyors or other property valuers.

Group (related party) transactions and balances

A list of all the companies in the group (including any associated companies) should be included in group audit instructions to ensure that intra-group transactions and balances (and any unrealized profits and losses on transactions with associated companies) are identified for elimination on consolidation.

It should be confirmed at the planning stage that inter-company transactions are identified as such in the accounting systems of all Beeski companies and that inter-company balances are regularly reconciled. (Problems are likely to arise if new intercompany balances are not identified/reconciled. In particular, exchange differences are to be expected.)

On analytical procedures

Having brought in the operations of a group of companies (Xstatic) with similar activities may extend the scope of analytical procedures available. This could have the effect of increasing audit efficiency.

MTbox – on statement of comprehensive income

The effective date of the acquisition of MTbox may be so late in the financial year (only four to eight weeks, say, before the year end) that it is possible that its post-acquisition results are not material to the consolidated statement of comprehensive income.

Other auditors

Other auditors will include:

–   any affiliates of Ribi in any of the countries in which Beeski (as combined with Xstatic) operates; and

–   unrelated auditors (including those of MTbox).

Ribi will plan to use the work of MTbox's auditors who are Chartered Certified Accountants. Their competence and independence should be assessed (e.g. through information obtained from a questionnaire and evidence of their work).

A letter of introduction should be sent to the unrelated auditors, with Beeski's permission, as soon as possible (if not already done) requesting their co-operation in providing specified information within a given timescale.

Group instructions will need to be sent to affiliated and unrelated auditors containing:

–   proforma statements;

–   a list of group and associated companies;

–   a statement of group accounting policies (see below);

–   the timetable for the preparation of the group accounts (see below);

–   a request for copies of management letters;

–   an audit work summary questionnaire or checklist;

–   contact details (of senior members of Ribi's audit team).

Accounting policies (Xstatic & MTbox)

Whilst it is likely that Xstatic has the same accounting policies as Beeski (because, as a competitor, it operates in the same jurisdictions) MTbox may have material accounting policies which do not comply with the rest of the group. Ribi may request that MTbox's auditors calculate the effect of any non-compliance with a group accounting policy for adjustment on consolidation.

Timetable

The timetable for the preparation of Beeski's consolidated financial statements should be agreed with management as soon as possible. Key dates should be planned for:

–   agreement of inter-company balances and transactions;

–   submission of proforma statements to Ribi;

–   completion of the consolidation package;

–   tax review of group accounts;

–   completion of audit fieldwork by other auditors;

–   subsequent events review;

–   final clearance on accounts of subsidiaries;

–   Ribi's final clearance of consolidated financial statements.

(c)   **'Support letters'**

Tutorial note

Although there are different types and uses of such letters (e.g. for registering a prospectus), the only reference to them in the P7 Syllabus and Study Guide is in the context of group audits.

Consolidated financial statements are prepared on a going concern basis when a group, as a single entity, is considered to be a going concern. However, the going concern basis may only be appropriate for certain separate legal entities (e.g. subsidiaries) because the parent undertaking (or a fellow subsidiary) is able and willing to provide support. Many banks routinely require a letter of reassurance from a parent company stating that the parent would financially or otherwise support a subsidiary with cashflow or other operational problems.

As audit evidence:

•   Formal confirmation of the support will be sought in the form of a letter of support or 'comfort letter' confirming the parent company's intention to keep the subsidiary in operational existence (or otherwise meet its obligations as they fall due).

•   The letter of support should normally be approved by a board minute of the parent company (or by an individual with authority granted by a board minute).

•   The ability of the parent to support the company should also be confirmed, for example, by examining the group's cash flow forecast.

- The period of support may be limited (e.g. to one year from the date of the letter or until the date of disposal of the subsidiary). Sufficient other evidence concerning the appropriateness of the going concern assumption must therefore be obtained where a later repayment of material debts is foreseen.

- The fact of support and the period to which it is restricted should be noted in the financial statements of the subsidiary.

(d) **'Horizontal groups'**

In general, the scope of a statutory audit should be as necessary to form an audit opinion (i.e. unlimited) and the nature, timing and extent of audit procedures (i.e. the audit work undertaken) should be as necessary to implement the overall audit plan.

Horizontal groups of entities under common control were a significant feature of the Enron and Parmalat business empires. Such business empires increase audit risk as fraud is often disguised through labyrinthine group structures. Hence auditors need to understand and confirm the economic purpose of entities within business empires (as well as special purpose entities (SPEs) and non-trading entities).

Horizontal groups fall outside the requirement for the preparation of group accounts so it is not only finance that is off-statement of financial position when controlled entities are excluded from consolidated financial statements.

In the absence of consolidated financial statements, users of accounts of entities in horizontal groups have to rely on the disclosure of related party transactions and control relationships for information about transactions and arrangements with other group entities. Difficulties faced by auditors include:

- failing to detect related party transactions and control relationships;

- not understanding the substance of transactions with entities under common control;

- excessively creative tax planning;

- the implications of transfer pricing (e.g. failure to identify profits unrealized at the business empire level);

- a lack of access to relevant confidential information held by others;

- relying on representations made in good faith by those whom the auditors believe manage the company when control rests elsewhere.

Audit work is inevitably increased if an auditor is put upon inquiry to investigate dubious transactions and arrangements. However, the complexity of business empires across multiple jurisdictions with different auditors may deter auditors from liaising with other auditors (especially where legal or professional confidentiality considerations prevent this).

	Marking scheme	
(a)	Principal business risks	*Marks*
	Generally ½ *mark* each risk identified and up to 1½ *marks* for a (good) description	
	Ideas	
	• technological obsolescence (communications industry)	
	• competition	
	• Integration (operations, cultures)	
	• operating losses	
	• falling ARPC (key performance indicator)	
	• sustaining growth	
	• exchange rate fluctuations	
	• market regulation	**max 9**
(b)	Impact on planning of audit	
	Generally *1 mark* each point contributing to an explanation to a maximum 3 marks each impact	
	Impact ideas	
	• group structure	
	• materiality assessment (NOT on profit)	
	• goodwill arising (amount/amortization)	
	• group (related party) transactions and balances	
	• on analytical procedures	
	• MTbox on statement of comprehensive income	
	• other auditors	
	– ACCA/competent/independent	
	– introductory/co-operation letter	
	• group instructions	
	• accounting policies (Xstatic & MTbox)	
	• timetable	
	Note: Two professional marks are included	**max 10**
(c)	'Support letters'	
	Generally *1 mark* each point contributing to an explanation of their role as audit evidence	
	Ideas	
	• Consolidated FS vs entity FS	
	• Bank requirement/routine	
	• Going concern basis	
	• Support by whom?	
	• For how long?	
	• Formal confirmation of *intent*	
	• Approved by board	
	• Need for evidence of *ability*	**max 6**
(d)	'Horizontal groups'	
	Generally *1 mark* each point contributing to a discussion	
	Ideas	
	• 'business empires'	
	• development (as off-statement of financial position vehicles)	
	• increased audit risk – related party/confidentiality issues	
	• complex fraud risk factor	
	• reliance on management representation	**max 5**
	Total	**30**

2 EFEX ENGINEERING CO

(a) 'Forensic auditing'

Definition

The process of gathering, analysing and reporting on data, in a pre-defined context, for the purpose of finding facts and/or evidence in the context of financial/legal disputes and/or irregularities and giving preventative advice in this area.

Tutorial note

Credit will be awarded for any definition that covers the key components: An 'audit' is an examination (e.g. of financial statements) and 'forensic' means used in connection with courts of law. Forensic auditing may be defined as 'applying auditing skills to situations that have legal consequences'.

Application to fraud investigation

As a fraud is an example of an irregularity, a fraud investigation is just one of many applications of forensic auditing, where evidence about a suspected fraud is gathered that could be presented in a court of law. The pre-defined objective of a fraud audit is:

– to prove or disprove the suspicions;

and, if proven,

– to identify the persons involved;

– to provide evidence for appropriate action, possibly criminal proceedings.

As well as being 'reactive', forensic auditing can be 'proactive' by being preventative. That is, the techniques of forensic auditing can be used to identify risks of fraud with a view to managing those risks to an acceptable level.

(b) Prior to commencement of the investigation

Tutorial note

The phrase 'matters … and … procedures' is used to encourage candidates to think more widely than just 'considerations' or just 'actions. A possible structure for this answer could be under two separate headings: 'matters' and 'procedures'. However, many matters could be phrased as procedures (and vice versa). For example, a matter would be 'the terms of reference' and the procedure 'to obtain and clarify the TOR'. Candidates should note that a tabular/columnar answer is NOT appropriate as any attempt to match matters and procedures is likely to result in repetition of the same point (differently phrased).

- Discuss the assignment with Xzibit's management to determine the purpose, nature and scope of the investigation. In particular, discuss whether any irregularity (theft/fraud) is suspected and, if so, whether evidence gathered will be used:
  - in criminal proceedings;
  - in support of an insurance claim.

- Obtain clarification of terms of reference (TOR) in writing from Xzibit's management.

- The TOR should give the investigating team full access to any aspect of Efex Engineering's operations relevant to their investigation.

- Investigation will involve consideration of:
  - possible understatement of inventory value at 30 June 2006;
  - high material consumption for the quarter ended 30 June 2006.

- Determine the level of experience of staff required for the investigation and the number of staff of each grade.

- The availability of suitable staff may affect the proposed start of the investigation. Alternatively, the timing of other assignments may have to be rescheduled to allow this investigation to be started immediately.

- Xzibit's management will presumably want the investigation completed before the next inventory count (at 30 September 2006) to know if the findings have any implications for the conduct of the count and the determination of year-end inventory.

- The investigation may have been commissioned to give credence to the period-end's accounts. The investigation may therefore be of the nature of a limited audit.

- Produce a budget of expected hours, grades of staff and costs. Agree the anticipated investigative fee with Xzibit's management.

- The depth of the investigation will depend on matters such as:
  - the extent of reliance expected to be placed on the investigation report;
  - whether the report is for Xzibit's internal use only or is it likely to be circulated to bankers and/or shareholders.

- The type of assurance (e.g. 'negative', reasonable) is likely to have a bearing on:
  - any caveats in the report;
  - the level of risk/potential liability for any errors in conclusions given in the final report;
  - the level of necessary detailed testing required (even if an audit is not requested).

- An engagement letter must be drafted and Xzibit's management must agree to its terms in writing before any investigative work can begin. The letter of engagement should include:
  - details of work to be carried out;
  - likely timescale;
  - basis of determining fee;
  - the reliance that can be placed on the final report and results of the investigation;
  - the extent of responsibilities agreed;
  - any indemnity agreed;

– the information to be supplied as a basis for the investigation; and

– any areas specifically excluded.

- Assess the appropriateness of an exclusion clause; for example: 'CONFIDENTIAL – this report has been prepared for the private use of Xzibit only and on condition that it must not be disclosed to any other person without the written consent of the preparing accountant'.

(c) (i) **Inventory undervaluation – matters to consider**

Physical inventory count

- Inventory will be undervalued at 30 June 2006 if all inventory is not counted. The investigation should consider the adequacy of quarterly physical count procedures. For example, whether or not:

  – all items are marked when counted;

  – management carries out test checks;

  – stocksheets are pre-numbered and prepared in ink;

  – a complete set of stocksheets is available covering all categories of inventory;

  – Efex Engineering's management uses the stocksheets to produce the inventory value.

Tutorial note

Inventory will not be undervalued if it does not exist (e.g. because it has been stolen). Theft would be reflected in higher than normal materials consumption (see (d)).

Cutoff

- Inventory will be undervalued at 30 June 2006 if:

  – any goods set aside for sale in July were excluded from the count;

  – a liability was recognized at 30 June 2006 for goods that were excluded from inventory (e.g. in transit from the supplier);

  – production did not cease during the physical count and raw materials being transferred between warehouse and production were omitted from inventory.

Scrap materials

- Inventory will be undervalued if any scrap from materials used in production that has a value (e.g. because it can be recycled) is excluded. Inventory may be undervalued compared with the previous quarter if there is any change in Efex's scrap/wastage policy (e.g. if previously it was valued in inventory but now it is excluded).

- If production problems increased wastage in the last period this would account for the lower value of inventory and higher materials consumption.

(ii)   **Tests to quantify the amount of any undervaluation**

Tutorial note

Any tests directed at quantifying an overstatement and/or instead of understatement will not be awarded credit.

Physical count

- Inspect the warehouse/factory areas to identify high value inventory items and confirm their inclusion on the stocksheets at 30 June 2006 (or otherwise vouch to a delivery note raised after that date).

- Recast all additions and recalculate all extensions on the stocksheets to confirm that there have been no omissions, transposition errors or other computational discrepancies that would account for an undervaluation.

Cutoff

- Ascertain the last delivery notes and despatch notes recorded prior to counting and trace to purchase/sales invoices to confirm that an accurate cutoff has been applied in determining the results for the quarter to 30 June 2006 and the inventory balance at that date.

- Trace any large value purchases in June to the 30 June stocksheets. If not on the stocksheets inquire of management whether they are included in production (or sold). Verify by tracing to production records, goods despatch notes, etc.

Analytical procedures

- Compare large volume/high value items on stocksheets at 31 March with those at 30 June to identify any that might have been omitted (or substantially decreased). Inquire of management if any items so identified have been completely used in production (but not replaced), scrapped or excluded from the count (e.g. if obsolete). Any inventory excluded should be counted and quantified.

- Compare inventory categories for 30 June against previous quarters. Inventory value at 30 June is 10% less than at 31 March, though revenue is 28% higher. An increase in inventory might have been expected to support increased revenue if there is a general increase in trading activity. (Alternatively, a decrease in inventory may reflect difficulties in obtaining supplies/maintaining inventory levels if demand has increased).

Scrap materials

- Make inquiries of Efex Engineering's warehouse and production officials regarding the company's scrap/wastage policy and any records that are kept.

- Review production records on a month-on-month basis and discuss with the factory manager whether any production problems have increased wastage in the quarter to 30 June 2006.

Pricing test

- Raw materials – select a sample of high value items from the 31 March 2006 inventory valuation and confirm that any unit price reductions as shown by the 30 June 2006 valuation are appropriate (e.g. vouch lower unit price to recent purchase invoices or write down to net realisable value).

- WIP and finished goods – agree a sample of unit prices to costing records (e.g. batch costings). Recalculate unit prices on a sample basis and vouch make-up to invoices/payroll records, etc.

(d)   (i)   **High materials consumption – matters to consider**

Tutorial note

Materials consumption has increased from 70% of revenue to 78%. There could be valid business reasons for this (e.g. there could be an abnormally high level of wastage) or accounting errors that result in overstatement of materials.

Cutoff

- Raw material purchases: Materials consumption will be overstated if goods delivered after the quarter-end have been included (incorrectly) in purchases to 30 June 2006 although excluded (correctly) from the June count.

- Revenue: Materials consumption will be overstated as a percentage of revenue if revenue is understated (e.g. if goods sold before 30 June 2006 are recorded in the next quarter).

Losses

- Materials consumption will be higher than normal if there is an abnormally high level of raw materials scrapped or wasted during the production process. This could be due to inferior quality raw materials or technical problems with the manufacturing process.

- Materials consumption will also be overstated if raw materials recorded as being used in production are stolen.

Obsolete or redundant inventory

- Materials consumption will appear higher if inventory at 30 June 2006 is lower. For example, if slow-moving, damaged or obsolete inventory identified at the count was excluded or written-down (although included in the previous quarter's inventory valuation).

Individual contracts

- Materials consumption will be higher if the increase in revenue is attributable to a small number of large contracts for which substantial discounts have been negotiated.

- Materials consumption will be higher if the cost of materials on customers' specifications has been underestimated in the determination of selling prices.

Purchasing

- Materials consumed will increase if Efex Engineering has changed to a more expensive supplier in the quarter to 30 June 2006.

(ii) **High materials consumption – tests**

Cutoff

- Purchases: Select a sample of invoices included in purchases to 30 June 2006 and match to goods received notes to confirm receipt at 30 June 2006 and hence inclusion in inventory at that date.
- Revenue: Inspect despatch notes raised on or shortly before 30 June 2006 and trace goods sold to invoices raised on or before 30 June 2006.

Scrap

- Inquire of production/factory and warehouse officials the reasons for scrap and wastage and how normal levels are determined.
- Inspect records of materials wastage and confirm the authorization for scrapping materials and/or reissuing replacement materials to the production process.
- Physically inspect scrap, if any, to confirm that its condition renders it unsuitable for manufacture (and hence confirm its exclusion from inventory at 30 June 2006).
- Review credit notes received after 30 June 2006 to identify materials returned (e.g. of inferior quality).

Obsolete or redundant inventory

- Inspect the stocksheets at 30 June 2006 for goods identified as obsolete, damaged, etc and compare with the level (and value) of the same items identified at the previous quarter's count.

Individual contracts

- Compare discounts given on new contracts with normal discount levels and confirm the authority of the person approving discounts.
- Calculate actual material cost as a percentage of revenue on individual major contracts and compare with the 70% benchmark.

Tests of controls

- Purchases: Inspect goods received notes to confirm that raw materials are being checked for quality and quantity upon receipt. Inspect invoices recorded to confirm that goods have been received (as evidenced by a goods received note).
  - Review goods returns recorded on pre-numbered goods return notes and confirm matched to subsequent credit notes received.
  - Observe gate controls and other physical security over inventory and review the segregation of duties that seek to prevent or detect theft of inventory.
- Sales: Review goods despatch notes and confirm matching to sales invoices that have been raised promptly and recorded on a timely basis.
- Sales returns: Review credit notes for authorization and matching to goods returns notes.

Marking scheme		
(a)	'Forensic auditing Generally *1 – ½ mark* each point Ideas Definition • e.g. of Institut des Fraud Auditeurs de Fraude (IFA-IAF) • audit (examination) + forensic (legal) Application to fraud investigation • irregular nature of fraud • objective(s) • reactive vs proactive (preventative)	*Marks* **max 5**

(b)	Prior to commencing investigation
	Generally *1 mark* each matter/procedure
	Ideas
	Matters
	• Terms of reference (obtaining is a procedure)
	• Purpose/scope of investigation
	     – possible understatement of inventory at 30/6
	     – high material consumption in quarter to 30/6
	     – give credence to y/e amount (next quarter to 30/9)
	• Access to records/restrictions/Information to be supplied
	• Staffing – experience/availability/other client commitments
	• Reliance placed on report and by whom? – insurer?
	• Timeframe – before next (= annual) physical count
	• Form of report required – Any caveats?
	Procedures
	• Discuss assignment with directors – responsibilities etc
	• obtain engagement letter (terms are a matter)
	• Agree investigative fee
	Note: two professional marks are included
		
		max 10

(c)	Inventory undervaluation Generally up to *1½ marks* each matter explained *1 mark* each test Ideas (i) matters • omission from count • cut-off • scrap/waste etc (ii) tests • physical inspection • arithmetic checks • cut-off tests • analytical procedures • tests on production records/pricing	 **max 8**
(d)	High materials consumption Generally up to *1½ marks* each matter explained *1 mark* each test Ideas (i) matters • cut-off • losses • absolescence etc • major contracts • change of supplier (ii) tests • physical inspection • arithmetic checks • cut-off tests • tests of control	 **max 7**
	Total	**30**

3   INGOT & CO

(a)   Analytical procedures

Applying analytical procedures at the planning stage, to assist in understanding the business and in identifying areas of potential risk, is an auditing standard and therefore mandatory. Analytical procedures should have been performed (e.g. comparing the draft accounts to 30 June 2006 with prior year financial statements).

The audit senior may have insufficient knowledge of the waste management service industry to assess potential risks. In particular, Argenta may be exposed to risks resulting in unrecorded liabilities (both actual and contingent) if claims are made against the company in respect of breaches of health and safety legislation or its licence to operate.

The audit has been inadequately planned and audit work has commenced before the audit plan has been reviewed by the AIC. The audit may not be carried out effectively and efficiently.

Tutorial note

An alternative stance might be that the audit senior did in fact perform the analytical procedures but was careless in completion of the audit planning checklist. This would have quality control implications in that the checklists cannot be relied on by the reviewer.

(b)   AIC's assignments

The senior has performed work on tangible non-current assets which is a less material (17% of total assets) audit area than trade receivables (58% of total assets) which has been assigned to an audit trainee. Non-current assets also appear to be a lower risk audit area than trade receivables because the carrying amount of non-current assets is comparable with the prior year ($0.6m at both year ends), whereas trade receivables have more than doubled (from $0.9m to $2.1m). This corroborates the implications of (a).

The audit is being inadequately supervised as work has been delegated inappropriately. It appears that Ingot & Co does not have sufficient audit staff with relevant competencies to meet its supervisory needs.

(c)   Direct confirmation

It is usual for direct confirmation of customers' balances to be obtained where trade receivables are material and it is reasonable to expect customers to respond. However, it is already six weeks after the statement of financial position date and, although trade receivables are clearly material (58% of total assets), an alternative approach may be more efficient (and cost effective). For example, monitoring of after-date cash will provide evidence about the collectibility of receivables (as well as corroborate their existence).

This may be a further consequence of the audit having been inadequately planned.

Alternatively, supervision and monitoring of the audit may be inadequate. For example, if the audit trainee did not understand the alternative approach but mechanically followed circularization procedures.

(d)   **Inventory**

Inventory is relatively immaterial from an auditing perspective, being less than 2.4% of total assets (2005 – 2.1%). Although it therefore seems appropriate that a trainee should be auditing it, the audit approach appears highly inefficient. Such in depth testing (of controls and details) on an immaterial area provides further evidence that the audit has been inadequately planned.

Again, it may be due to a lack of monitoring of a mechanical approach being adopted by a trainee.

This also demonstrates a lack of knowledge and understanding about Argenta's business – the company has no stock-in-trade, only consumables used in the supply of services.

(e)   **Prior period error**

It appears that the subsequent events review was inadequate in that an adjusting event (the out-of-court settlement) was not taken account of. This resulted in material error in the financial statements to 30 June 2005 as the provision for $0.45 million which should have been made represented 12.5% of total assets at that date.

The AIC has not taken any account of the implications of this evidence for the conduct of the audit as the overall audit strategy and audit plan should have been reconsidered. For example:

–   the oversight in the subsequent events review may not have been isolated and there could be other errors in opening balances (e.g. if an impairment was not recognized);

–   there may be doubts about the reliability of managements' representations if it confirmed the litigation to be pending and/or asserted that there were no events after the reporting period to be taken account of.

The error has implications for the quality of the prior period's audit that may now require that additional work be carried out on opening balances and comparatives.

As the matter is material it warrants a prior period adjustment (IAS 8 *Accounting Policies, Changes in Accounting Estimates and Errors*). If this is not made Argenta's financial statements for the year ended 30 June 2006 will be materially misstated with respect to the current year and comparatives – because the expense of the out-of-court settlement should be attributed to the prior period and not to the current year's net profit or loss.

The need for additional work may have a consequential effect on the current year's time/fee/staff budgets.

The error should have been brought to the attention of Argenta's management when it was discovered, so that a prior year adjustment could be made. If the AIC did not feel competent to raise the matter with the client he should have discussed it immediately with the audit manager and not merely left it as a file note.

QC policies procedures at audit firm level/Conclusions

That the audit is not being conducted in accordance with ISAs (e.g. 300 *Planning an Audit of Financial Statements*, 315 *Identifying and Assessing the Risks of Material Misstatement Through Understanding the Entity and Its Environment* and 520 *Analytical Procedures*) means that Ingot's quality control policies and procedures are not established and/or are not being communicated to personnel.

That audit work is being assigned to personnel with insufficient technical training and proficiency indicates weaknesses in procedures for hiring and/or training of personnel.

That there is insufficient direction, supervision and review of work at all levels to provide reasonable assurance that audit work is of an acceptable standard suggests a lack of resources.

Procedures for the acceptance of clients appear to be inadequate as the audit is being conducted so inefficiently (i.e. audit work is inappropriate and/or not cost-effective). In deciding whether or not to accept the audit of Argenta, Ingot should have considered whether it had the ability to serve the client properly. The partner responsible for accepting the engagement does not appear to have evaluated the firm's (lack of) knowledge of the industry.

The staffing of the audit of Argenta should be reviewed and a more experienced person assigned to its completion and overall review.

Marking scheme	
Implications of findings	*Marks*
Generally up to *1½ marks* each (good) implication	
Specific finding ideas	
• relevant ISAs	
(a) APs mandatory at planning stage (520)	
(e) subsequent events (560)	
• materiality (ISA 320)	
(b) non-current assets 17%	
(c) receivables 58%	
(d) inventory 2.4%	
(e) prior period error 12.5%	
• inappropriate procedures?	
• inventory 'roll back' (immaterial)	
• inappropriate timing	
• external confirmations (ISA 505) – too late?	
• QC at audit firm level ideas/Conclusions	
- professional behaviour	
- skills and competence	
- assignment/delegation	
- consultation	
- acceptance of clients	
- monitoring	
(a)	max 4
(b)	max 4
(c)	max 4
(d)	max 3
(e)	max 5
Total	**Max 20**

4   AXIS & CO

(a)   **Mantis Co**

If a letter of support had not been received, then a modified opinion due to material misstatement (re. the appropriateness of the going concern presumption) would be required. As the matter is likely to be pervasive an adverse opinion would be appropriate (ISA 570 *Going Concern*).

However, the company has received a letter of support from its parent company to the effect that it will enable Mantis to continue trading. If this evidence (together with other evidence such as management's representations) is considered to be sufficient to support the appropriateness of the going concern presumption, a modified opinion will not be necessary provided that the support is adequately disclosed in a note to the financial statements. If the evidence is sufficient, but the disclosure inadequate, an 'except for' opinion would be required.

If the letter of support does not provide sufficient evidence (e.g. if there are doubts about Cube's ability to provide the required finance), the significant uncertainty arising should be disclosed in an Emphasis of Matter paragraph in the auditor's report. This would not result in a modified opinion (unless the disclosure relating to it were considered inadequate).

Conclusion

The audit senior's proposal is unsuitable. The auditor's report should be unmodified (assuming that disclosures are adequate).

(b)   **Lorenze Co**

In order to show fair presentation, in all material respects, the financial statements of an entity should contain not only accurate figures, but also sufficient disclosure in relation to those figures in order to allow the user to understand them. As required by IAS 1 *Presentation of Financial Statements*, items should be treated on a consistent basis from year to year. If this is not the case, then any change, together with the financial impact of this change, will need to be disclosed in a note to the financial statements.

Failure to disclose the reasons for change in policy (i.e. to comply with IFRS 3 *Business Combinations*) and its effects (e.g. the lack of annual amortization) means that the financial statements do not comply with IAS 8 *Accounting Policies, Changes in Accounting Estimates and Errors*. A modified opinion is therefore required on the grounds of material misstatement. Assuming the matter to be material (but clearly not pervasive), an 'except for' opinion should be expressed.

The main purpose of an Emphasis of Matter paragraph is to describe a matter of significant uncertainty which has been taken into account in forming the audit opinion – it does not modify that opinion. Such a paragraph highlights a note in the financial statements that more extensively discusses the matter. An Emphasis of Matter paragraph cannot therefore be used to 'make good' a lack of disclosure.

IFRS 3 also requires disclosure of a reconciliation of the carrying amount of goodwill at the beginning and end of the year. This should show no movement for the year ended 30 June 2006.

Conclusion

The audit senior's proposal is unsuitable. Unless all aspects of the change (including reason and effect) are adequately disclosed an 'except for' qualification will be required due to material misstatement.

(c)   **Abrupt Co**

The audit opinion states whether the financial statements:

- –   are presented fairly, in all material respects (or give a true and fair view) in accordance with the financial reporting framework; and

- –   comply with statutory requirements (where appropriate).

The directors' report is not a part of financial statements prepared under International Financial Reporting Standards (IFRS). However, auditors have a professional responsibility to read other information in documents containing audited financial statements (e.g. the directors' report in an annual report) to identify material inconsistencies with the audited financial statements (or material misstatements of fact).

A material inconsistency exists when other information contradicts information contained in the audited financial statements. Clearly, 'major' is inconsistent with 1.6%.

If the inconsistency is resolved (e.g. because the directors' report is corrected to state '... major part of other income...') an unmodified auditor's report will be given.

If the inconsistency is not resolved, the audit opinion on the financial statements cannot be modified (because the inconsistency is in the directors' report). In this case, an Other Matter paragraph may be used to report on this matter that does not affect the financial statements (ISA 706 *Emphasis of Matter Paragraphs and Other Matter Paragraphs in the Independent Auditor's Report* and ISA 720 *the Auditor's Responsibilities Relating to Other Information in Documents Containing Audited Financial Statements*).

Conclusion

An unmodified opinion on the financial statements is appropriate. If, however, the inconsistency is not resolved, it should be reported in a separate Other Matter paragraph, after the opinion paragraph.

(d)   **Jingle Co**

The cash transfer is a non-adjusting events after the reporting period. It indicates that Bell was trading after the statement of financial position date. However, that does not preclude Bell having commenced trading before the year end.

The finance director's oral representation is wholly insufficient evidence with regard to the existence (or otherwise) of Bell at 30 June 2006. If it existed at the statement of financial position date its financial statements should have been consolidated (unless immaterial).

The evidence that might reasonably be expected to be available includes. legal papers, registration payments. If such evidence has been sought but not obtained then the auditor will have to modify their report on the grounds of being unable to obtain sufficient appropriate evidence.

Whilst the transaction itself may be immaterial, the information concerning the existence of Bell may be material to users and should therefore be disclosed (as a non-adjusting event). The absence of such disclosure, if the auditor considered necessary, would result in a modified 'except for', opinion.

Tutorial note

Any matter that is considered sufficiently material to be worthy of disclosure as a non-adjusting event must result in such a modified opinion if the disclosure is not made.

If Bell existed at the statement of financial position date and had material assets and liabilities then its non-consolidation would have a pervasive effect. This would warrant an adverse opinion.

Also, the nature of the lack of evidence (being imposed by the entity) could have a pervasive effect if the auditor is suspicious that other audit evidence has been withheld. In this case the auditor should disclaim an opinion.

Conclusion

Additional evidence is required to support an unodified opinion. If this were not forthcoming a disclaimer may be appropriate.

Marking scheme	
Auditors' reports proposals	*Marks*
Generally *1 mark* each comment on suitability and *1 mark* each conclusion (alternative, if any)	
Ideas	
(a) Going concern (ISA 570 reporting implications)	
(b) Change in accounting policy – inadequate disclosure	
(c) 'Other Information' (ISA 720)	
(d) Subsequent event (ISA 560)	
• Disagreement vs limitation	
• Material vs pervasive	
• Statutory/professional requirements	
• Relevant IFRSs (IASs 1, 8, 36, IFRS 3)	
• Disclosure (adequate?) ==> disagreement	
• Evidence (sufficient?) ==> limitation	
• Validity of senior's argument/justification	
• Alternative proposal ==> Conclusion	
(a)	max 5
(b)	max 6
(c)	max 4
(d)	max 5
Total	**20**

5   DEDZA & CO

(a)   Need for ethical guidance

- Accountants (firms and individuals) working in a country that criminalizes money laundering are required to comply with anti-money laundering legislation and failure to do so can lead to severe penalties. Guidance is needed because:

    –   legal requirements are onerous;

    –   money laundering is widely defined; and

    –   accountants may otherwise be used, unwittingly, to launder criminal funds.

- Accountants need ethical guidance on matters where there is conflict between legal responsibilities and professional responsibilities. In particular, professional accountants are bound by a duty of confidentiality to their clients. Guidance is needed to explain:

    –   how statutory provisions give protection against criminal action for members in respect of their confidentiality requirements;

    –   when client confidentiality over-ride provisions are available.

- Further guidance is needed to explain the interaction between accountants responsibilities to report money laundering offences and other reporting responsibilities, for example:

    –   reporting to regulators;

    –   auditor's reports on financial statements (ISA 700/705/706);

    –   reports to those charged with governance (ISA 260/265);

    –   reporting misconduct by members of the same body.

- Professional accountants are required to communicate with each other when there is a change in professional appointment (i.e. 'professional etiquette'). Additional ethical guidance is needed on how to respond to a 'clearance' letter where a report of suspicion has been made (or is being contemplated) in respect of the client in question.

Tutorial note

Although the term 'professional clearance' is widely used, remember that there is no 'clearance' that the incumbent accountant can give or withhold.

- Ethical guidance is needed to make accountants working in countries that do not criminalize money laundering aware of how anti-money laundering legislation may nevertheless affect them. Such accountants may commit an offence if, for example, they conduct limited assignments or have meetings in a country having anti-money laundering legislation (e.g. UK, Ireland, Singapore, Australia and the United States).

(b)   **Annual reviews of existing clients**

(i)   **Tax investigation**

- Kora is a relatively new client. Before accepting the assignment(s) Dedza should have carried out customer due diligence (CDD). Dedza should therefore have a sufficient knowledge and understanding of Kora to be aware of any suspicions that the tax authority might have.

- As the investigation has come as a surprise it is possible that, for example:

  – the tax authorities suspicions are unfounded;

  – Dedza has failed to recognize suspicious circumstances.

- Dedza should review any communication from the predecessor auditor obtained in response to its 'professional inquiry' (for any professional reasons why the appointment should not be accepted).

- A quality control for new audits is that the audit opinion should be subject to a second partner review before it is issued. It should be considered now whether or not such a review took place. If it did, then it should be sufficiently well documented to evidence that the review was thorough and not a mere formality.

- Criminal property includes the proceeds of tax evasion. If Kora is found to be guilty of under-declaring income that is a money laundering offence.

- Dedza's reputational risk will be increased if implicated because it knew (or ought to have known) about Kora's activities. (Dedza may also be liable if found to have been negligent in failing to detect any material misstatement arising in the 31 March 2006 financial statements.)

- Kora's audit working paper files and tax returns should be reviewed for any suspicion of fraud being committed by Kora or error overlooked by Dedza. Tax advisory work should have been undertaken and/or reviewed by a manager/partner not involved in the audit work.

- As tax advisor, Dedza could soon be making disclosures of misstatements to the tax authorities on behalf of Kora. Dedza should encourage Kora to make necessary disclosure voluntarily.

- If Dedza finds reasonable grounds to know or suspect that potential disclosures to the tax authorities relate to criminal conduct, then a suspicious transaction report (STR) should be made to the financial intelligence unit (FIU) also.

Tutorial note

Though not the main issue credit will be awarded for other ethical issues such as the potential self-interest/ self-review threat arising from the provision of other services.

(ii)   **Advice on payments**

- As compared with (i) there is no obvious tax issue. Xalam is not overstating expenditure for tax purposes.

- Dedza should consider its knowledge of import duties, etc in the destination country before recommending a course of action to Xalam.

- The payments being made for security consultancy services may amount to a bribe. Corruption and bribery (and extortion) are designated categories of money laundering offence under The Forty Recommendations of the Financial Action Task Force on Money Laundering (FATF).

If this is a bribe:

- Xalam clearly benefits from the payments as it receives income from the contract with the major customer. This is criminal property and possession of it is a money laundering offence

- Dedza should consider the seriousness of the disclosure made by the chief executive in the context of domestic law.

- Dedza may be guilty of a money laundering offence if the matter is not reported. If a report to the FIU is considered necessary Dedza should encourage Xalam to make voluntary disclosure. If Xalam does not, Dedza will not be in breach of client confidentiality for reporting knowledge of a suspicious transaction.

(iii)   **Financial advisor**

- Customer due diligence (CDD) and record-keeping measures apply to designated non-financial businesses and professions (such as Dedza) who prepare for or carry out certain transactions on behalf of their clients.

- Esau is a 'politically exposed person' ('PEP' i.e. an individual who is to be entrusted with prominent public functions in a foreign country).

- Dedza's business relationships with Pholey therefore involve reputational risks similar to those with Esau. In addition to performing normal due diligence measures Dedza should:

    – have risk management systems to have determined that Esau is a PEP;

    – obtain senior partner approval for maintaining business relationships with such customers;

    – take reasonable measures to establish the source of wealth and source of funds;

    – conduct enhanced ongoing monitoring of the business relationship.

- Dedza can choose to decline to act for Pholey and/or Esau (if asked).

- If the business relationship is to be continued senior partner approval should be obtained for any transactions carried out on Pholey's behalf in future.

Tutorial note

The Pholey family is not described as an audit client therefore no familiarity threat arises in relation to an audit (the family may not have any involvement in entities requiring an audit).

	Marking scheme	
(a)	Need for ethical guidance for accountants	*Marks*
	Generally *1 mark* a point up to	
	Ideas (illustrative)	
	• Legal responsibilities	
	• Risk of offence	
	• Confidentiality	
	• Other reporting responsibilities	
	• Professional etiquette	
	• Accountants working in other jurisdictions	**max 5**
(b)	Ethical and other professional issues	
	Generally *½ mark* each issue identified + *1 mark* each comment/action	
	Ideas	
	(i) Tax investigation	
	• new client (relatively) – CDD	
	• 'professional etiquette' – change in professional appointment	
	• quality control e.g. second review	
	• criminal property includes proceeds of tax evasion	
	• money laundering offence?	
	• suspicion of fraud (intent) vs error in incorrect tax returns	
	• disclosure by Dedza vs voluntary (confidentiality)	
	• need for STR	**max 7**
	(ii) Advice on payments	
	• not a tax issue	
	• corruption and bribery/extortion – designated categories of offence	
	• clear intent	
	• seriousness in context of domestic laws	
	• need to report to FIU?	**max 4**
	(iii) Financial advisor	
	• designated non-financial profession	
	• customer due diligence/record keeping	
	• politically exposed person (PEP)	
	• reputational risk	
	• additional measures	
	• refusal to act	**max 4**
	Total	**20**